Careers in Writing & Editing

Careers in Writing & Editing

SALEM PRESS

A Division of EBSCO Information Services, Inc.

Ipswich, Massachusetts

GREY HOUSE PUBLISHING

Publisher's Cataloging-In-Publication Data
(Prepared by The Donohue Group, Inc.)

Title: Careers in writing & editing.
Other Titles: Careers in writing and editing | Careers in--
Description: [First edition]. | Ipswich, Massachusetts : Salem Press, a division of EBSCO
          Information Services, Inc. ; Amenia, NY : Grey House Publishing, [2020] |
          Includes bibliographical references and index.
Identifiers: ISBN 9781642653953 (hardcover)
Subjects: LCSH: Authorship--Vocational guidance--United States. | Editing--Vocational
          guidance--United States. | Computer programming--Vocational guidance--
          United States.
Classification: LCC PN151 .C37 2020 | DDC 808.02023--dc23

First Printing

PRINTED IN THE UNITED STATES OF AMERICA

CONTENTS

PUBLISHER'S NOTE

Careers in Writing & Editing contains a thorough introduction to the career opportunities available to those with an interest in writing and editing. Today's jobseekers are almost all in need of excellent writing and editing skills. Business communications from tweets to blogs to podcasts depends at its heart on the skillful use of the written word, which puts writing and editing skills at the forefront for jobs in industries as diverse at technology and dance. The types of careers available today still include such traditional positions as newspaper or magazine editor, copywriter, and writer. In this book, the scope of writing and editing includes some non-literary forms of writing and editing as well: choreography, graphic design, software coding, music composition, and film editing.

This volume begins with an overview of the "gig economy," followed by thirteen industry overviews that explore the options available in a range of environments and industries including Advertising and Marketing; Higher Education; Internet and Cyber Communications; Legal Services and Law Firms; Libraries and Archives; Motion Picture and Television; Museums and Cultural Institutions; Music; Philanthropic, Charitable, Religious, Civic, and Grant-Making; Public Elementary and Secondary Education; Publishing and Information; Theater and Performing Arts; Video, Computer, and Virtual Reality Games.

The next section of the book presents twenty-seven occupational profiles including Advertising, Promotions, and Marketing Managers; Archivists, Curators, and Museum Workers; Clergy; Copywriters; Court Reporters; Dancers and Choreographers; Editors; Film and Video Editors and Camera Operators; Grant Writers; Graphic Designers; Historians; Interpreters and Translators; Journalists; Judges and Hearing Officers; Lawyers; Librarians; Multimedia Artists and Animators; Music Directors and Composers; Paralegal and Legal Assistants; Postsecondary Teachers; Producers and Directors; Public Relations Specialists; Radio and Television Broadcasters; Social Media Specialists; Software Developers; Technical Writers; Writers and Editors. These career profiles offer details about a particular career path by providing:

Snapshot details including the most current data about
- Median Pay
- Typical Entry-Level Education
- On-the-job Training
- Number of Jobs
- Job Outlook
- Employment Change

Career Overview includes a description of the career in terms of its
- Duties
- Examples of titles for positions in that specific career
- Work environment
- Work schedules

Each profile provides details about **How to become**… that explain how to begin and grow a career within a specific career profile by describing
• Important qualities
• Education
• Licenses, certifications, and registrations that may be required
• Advancement opportunities

Profiles also include the most current details about pay compared to other career clusters as well as a look at pay by industry as well as a description of **Similar Occupations** that lists specific jobs that are related in some way to the protective service career being profiled.

Job Outlook and **Job Prospects** describe current and anticipated rate of growth for a specific career, and compares the rate to other jobs in areas in the same career cluster, as well as to career growth taken as a whole.

Each profile concludes with **More Information** to direct readers to additional resources such as specific associations or certifying bodies for further details.

Merging scholarship with occupational development, this single comprehensive guidebook provides students passionate about finding a career in writing and editing with the necessary insight into the wide array of options available in this evolving and important field. The book offers guidance regarding what job seekers can expect in terms of training, advancement, earnings, job prospects, working conditions, relevant associations, and more. *Careers in Writing & Editing* is specifically designed for a high school and undergraduate audience and is edited to align with secondary or high school curriculum standards.

Scope of Coverage

Understanding the wide scope of jobs, settings for providing care, and industries where nurses typically work is important for anyone preparing for a career in protective services, from government to nonprofits, to private industry.

Careers in Writing & Editing is enhanced with numerous charts and tables, including projections from the U.S. Bureau of Labor Statistics, and median annual salaries or wages for those occupations profiled. Enhancements, like Fun Facts, Famous Firsts, and dozens of photos, add depth to the discussion. Additional highlights in the book include twenty-two interviews—**Conversation With…**—featuring a professional working in a related job who can offer insight into specific areas of practice as administrator of a psychiatric unit in a hospital; the head of a human resources agency; a school superintendent; a psychiatric nurse working for the Veteran's Administration; or a probation office. The respondents share their personal career paths, detail potential for career advancement, offer advice for students, and include a "try this" for those interested in embarking on a career in their profession.

Special Features

Several features continue to distinguish this reference series from other career-oriented reference works. The back matter includes:

Appendix A: Guide to Holland Code. This discusses John Holland's theory that people and work environments can be classified into six different groups: Realistic; Investigative; Artistic; Social; Enterprising; and Conventional. See if the job you want is right for you!

Appendix B: General Bibliography. This is a collection of suggested readings suitable for further reading about a career in writing and editing.

Appendix C: Web Resources. Online resources for education, certification, professional development, and networking can be found in this appendix.

Index: Includes people, concepts, technologies, terms, principles, and all specific occupations discussed in the occupational profile chapters.

Acknowledgments

Thanks are due to Allison Blake, who took the lead in developing "Conversations With," with help from Cynthia Hibbert, as well as to the professionals who communicated their work experience through interview questionnaires. Their frank and honest responses provide immeasurable value to *Careers in Writing & Editing*. The contributions of all are gratefully acknowledged.

INTRODUCTION

It's no stretch to say writing was invented to earn money. Ancient Sumerians created cuneiform, the earliest-known script, to make accounts and written contracts. By pressing a stylus into soft clay, the resulting pictographs told a story and, later, evolved into word concepts that more closely resemble what we understand a word to be today. And, in a neat parallel to modern life, archaeologists call slabs of cuneiform "tablets."

Today, writing remains a money-maker for those who consider it a career, art form, and tool. Writers and editors find success across a variety of pursuits in communications and media. Technical writers edit complex material so that it's easily understood by the layperson. Public relations specialists and marketing experts know how to use their writing skills to target an audience of consumers. Editors who can make a time-pressed executive's annual report read smoothly and clearly are often well-compensated.

Consider this volume a guide to career opportunities in editing and writing, while understanding that videography, film, photography and voice—such as podcasting—have become as critical to telling a story as the written word.

The tectonic shift from print to digital is well underway and impacting the profession. The changing landscape is pushing change in traditional jobs such as newspaper reporting and creating new opportunities in content-driven media. This extends across media including TV, radio, and old-school print publications, as well as business-focused fields such as advertising, marketing and public relations. The name of the game is storytelling, and smart writers and editors know it's necessary to perfect the multimedia skills required to communicate on a twenty-first-century tablet. These skills are executed across any number of platforms, whether websites, specialized apps, or social media.

Making a successful career means making strategic decisions as you learn your craft and adapting to market and technology changes. Many journalists, for instance, make the leap to public relations and marketing after several years because earnings are higher and opportunities are more abundant. From there, many fan out across the gig economy, adding business development skills so they can sell their writing skills to clients.

And while there are many practical ways to earn money by writing, creative and literary writers who aspire to be novelists still populate Master of Fine Arts programs. It's true that the literary life is well-known to be a tough road. Plan on rejection—from publishers, editors and fellow participants in writing workshops—and blaze your own trail. Academia is a well-trod, if challenging, path to literary success.

Here are career options to consider:

Advertising, including social media

Clients pay advertising firms to promote their brands and products. Advertisers create messages to influence behavior change in an audience in order to boost those brands and sell those products. Plenty of avenues exist to do so: print advertising, radio and TV commercials, online pop-ups, and search-engine and social-media ads, among others. Words and pictures in various formats, deployed under well-formed marketing strategies, deliver the message. The job growth among advertising, promotions, and marketing managers is faster than average, at 8 percent, through 2028, according to the U.S. Bureau of Labor Statistics.

Education, including testing & assessment and curriculum development

Writing as an educator includes writing curriculum; job growth for the people who do this work—called instructional coordinators—is keeping pace with the average of all occupations, according to the BLS. You could also teach writing, like former high school English teacher William Golding. He went on to write *Lord of the Flies*.

Arts & entertainment, including video and photography

Arts and entertainment jobs cover a wide range of possibilities and may take you to unexpected places. Consider a museum or historical site, for instance, that needs its story told using words and pictures. You may do this as a consultant hired to update a website, or you might do it as a member of the venue's public relations or marketing staff. Or, you may focus on being a film and video editor who organizes raw footage, sound and graphics to tell a story for a publication/platform, business, or motion picture. Film and video editors are seeing 11 percent job growth, much faster than average, according to the BLS.

Journalism, including correspondents and reporters

Journalism is fast-paced, exciting—and a terrific training ground if you want to write concisely and quickly. Unfortunately, newspapers have been consolidating and layoffs have become the norm in recent years, so keep your eye on successful digital platforms and move on as quickly as you can. Or head for TV and radio, armed with multi-platform reporting skills. Employment is expected to rise 2.4 percent among reporters and correspondents, with the best-paying jobs clustered in big cities and the Northeast corridor including Washington, D.C., metropolitan New York City, and metropolitan Boston, Massachusetts, according to the BLS.

Government, including grant writing, legal writing, and court reporting

Writing for or within government ranges across many jobs.

Grant writing is a highly valued and specific skill in which the writer targets an organization in need to an appropriate funding source and ensures the funding source's application and awards guidelines are met. Focusing an organization's story, including its needs and budget, and showing how the money will be spent are all part of a grant proposal. While grants are issued by any number of foundations and businesses, governments at the state, local and federal levels are well-known sources of grant opportunities.

Attorneys and, sometimes, paralegals, write for the courts. Attorneys, who write legal briefs, use persuasive language based on law and precedent to convince judges to accept their position. Paralegals are more likely to write pleadings, which are procedural in nature. Court reporters and captioners are hired to record, verbatim, the words spoken in a court room or other legal arena, including a conference room in an attorney's office where depositions are taken. Jobs as a lawyer are growing at the national average—6 percent—while court reporters and captioners can expect 7 percent job growth through 2028.

Science, including technical and academic writing

Science writing can take different forms. Technical writers specialize in making complicated or difficult technical information accessible by writing instruction manuals or articles for the general public and often work in tech or computer industries. Typically, scientific or medical writers might hold a graduate degree (MS, MD, or PhD) and often work for biotech or pharmaceutical companies to write literature on medications and products. These positions also are available in academic or nonprofit institutions writing about research, whether for an internal newsletter or a general audience. Scientific manuscripts are typically written by scientists who are principal investigators or post-doctoral researchers. However, some journalists specialize in writing about science for a general audience, turning the work into articles and books or, possibly, a public relations consulting opportunity. Job growth among technical writers is outpacing the national average and stands at 8 percent, according to the BLS.

Business, including finance and analysis

Businesses and corporations need clear-eyed and creative communicators, and many public relations (PR), marketing and advertising professionals work in-house for a particular company. In addition, many communications consulting firms contract to do PR, marketing or advertising work for businesses. Finally, independent PR consultants who can take a field's specialized writing and transform it into words easily understood by the general public often find work writing press releases, articles, and social media posts.

Publishing, including editors, authors, poets, and novelists

Fiction or non-fiction, publishing employs writers to execute articles, novels, poetry, books and even scripts. An editor acts as a sort of project manager, brainstorming ideas with writers, establishing production schedules, and editing work so it grammatically conforms to a style, is properly organized for readability, and retains a writer's style. This is not a growth industry; the BLS predicts flat growth for writers and authors and a decline in positions as editors. Many people who work in this field freelance, which means taking jobs on a project-by-project basis and often moving between traditional publishing clients and business clients.

—Allison Blake

WORKING IN A GIG ECONOMY

There is no official definition of the "gig economy"—or, for that matter, a gig. For purposes of this article, a gig describes a single project or task for which a worker is hired, often through a digital marketplace, to work on demand. Some gigs are a type of short-term job, and some workers pursue gigs as a self-employment option; those concepts aren't new. However, companies connecting workers with these jobs through websites or mobile applications (more commonly known as apps) is a more recent development.

The gig workforce

Gig workers are spread among diverse occupation groups and are not easily identified in surveys of employment and earnings. But they are similar in the way they earn money. These workers often get individual gigs using a website or mobile app that helps to match them with customers. Some gigs may be very brief, such as answering a 5-minute survey. Others are much longer but still of limited duration, such as an 18-month database management project. When one gig is over, workers who earn a steady income this way must find another. And sometimes, that means juggling multiple jobs at once.

Counting gig workers

You may have heard a lot of buzz about growth in the gig economy. But government data sources have difficulty counting how many gig workers there are. Among the sources that may shed light on this topic are data from the U.S. Bureau of Labor Statistics (BLS) and the U.S. Census Bureau.

Gig workers could be in contingent or alternative employment arrangements, or both, as measured by BLS. Contingent workers are those who don't have an implicit or explicit contract for long-term employment. Alternative employment arrangements include independent contractors (also called freelancers or independent consultants), on-call workers, and workers provided by temporary help agencies or contract firms.

The data BLS has for these types of workers are about a decade old. In 2005, contingent workers accounted for roughly 2 to 4 percent of all workers. About 7 percent of workers were independent contractors, the most common alternative employment arrangement, in that year.

Other, more recent, data from BLS likely reflect a lot of gig work, but these workers are not broken out separately. For example, gig workers may be included in counts of workers who are part-time, self-employed, or hold multiple jobs. But these counts also include workers who are not part of the gig workforce.

Nonemployer statistics data, created by the Census Bureau from tax data provided by the Internal Revenue Service (IRS), offer another possible look at what has been happening in the gig economy. Many gig workers fit the Census definition of a nonemployer: in most cases, a self-employed individual operating a very small, unincorporated business with no paid employees.

Between 2003 and 2013, all industry sectors experienced growth in nonemployer businesses. The "other services" sector gained nearly 1 million nonemployer businesses during that time, the most of any sector. Many of the occupations in this sector involve on-demand services, such as petsitting and appliance repair, making them well suited to gig employment.

Occupations for gig employment

Gigs are more likely in some occupations than in others. Work that involves a single task, such as writing a business plan, lends itself well to this type of arrangement. Any occupation in which workers may be hired for on-demand jobs has the potential for gig employment.

The BLS Occupational Outlook Handbook (OOH) covers about 83 percent of the jobs in the U.S. economy. Its 329 detailed profiles of occupations are sorted by group. This section highlights some of those groups in which gig work may be increasingly relevant, giving examples of occupations in each.

Arts and design. Many occupations in this group, including musicians, graphic designers, and craft and fine artists, offer specific one-time services or customized products, which makes them good candidates for gig work.

Computer and information technology. Web developers, software developers, and computer programmers are among the occupations in this group in which workers might be hired to complete a single job, such as to create a small-business website or a new type of software.

Media and communications. The services of technical writers, interpreters and translators, photographers, and others in this group are often project-based and easy to deliver electronically, fueling a market for gig workers.

Pros and cons of gig work

Gig workers may do varied tasks, but they have similar things they enjoy—and don't—about their arrangements. Freedom to work as they please is what many people like, but with autonomy comes responsibility. For example, it can be stressful for gig workers to ensure that they have consistent income.

Pros

Gig workers say that they like being in control. They can choose projects they enjoy and schedule their work around their lives. Some workers take gigs that allow them to encourage others in a field they enjoy.

Flexibility. People who want to work without having set hours may look for gigs to fit their schedules. Like other types of flexible employment arrangements, gigs may offer workers an option for adaptability.

Variety. Gigs may provide workers with a chance to try several types of jobs. As a result, they present variety and career exploration to both new and experienced workers. And if you're a "people person," gig work may offer interaction with a diverse clientele.

Passion. You might want to select gigs the same way you would traditional employment: by finding work in which you pursue your interests. And depending on how you schedule your gigs, you might be able to choose among many passions.

Cons

There's a lot of uncertainty associated with gig work. For example, you'll need to have a steady stream of gigs to get consistent pay. Even then, the amount you earn may not offset some of the costs you'll be responsible for outside of a traditional employment relationship, such as benefits.

Inconsistency. Landing enough work to provide a stable income from gigs alone isn't always easy, or even possible. As a result, many gig workers find gigs adequate for part-time work but not a full-time career. Workers may struggle with looking for jobs, not knowing what—if anything—will come next. And even after you complete a gig, you may face periods of no income if there are delays in getting paid.

Scheduling. Not having set hours or an employer who provides direction for the day is challenging for some gig workers. And depending on the gig, you may need to work nonstandard days or times to finish a job. If you get a gig requiring hours on the weekend, for example, you might not be able to spend time with friends who have traditional 9-to-5 workweeks.

Lack of benefits. Gig workers don't usually get employer-paid benefits, such as premiums on health insurance and contributions to retirement plans. You'll need to research these topics and pay for the products yourself. Other benefits that gig workers often miss out on are annual leave and sick leave. Like any employees who don't get paid time off, no work means no pay.

Getting gigs

There are different ways to get started in the gig economy. Identify what you do well and what you might enjoy doing. Then, search for opportunities while keeping in mind some practical matters.

Create your niche

Think about the types of services you might be able to offer. What skills, experience, or other assets do you have that you can share? Consider that some gigs are for general tasks and others require a specific skillset.

Learn from others. When you have an idea of the type of work you'd like to do, talk to people who are already doing it. Or browse blogs or other resources to learn from the experiences of others. Scoping out the market for your services will help you determine how much to charge—or even whether you should pursue your plan.

Stand out. Figure out ways to differentiate yourself from other workers, such as by offering a service that is unique or in high demand. You might want to consider becoming self-employed as a way to fill that niche.

As mentioned previously, gig workers may be counted among workers who are self-employed. Some industries are projected to have more growth than others in the number of self-employed jobs over the 2018–28 decade.

Find opportunities

Many gig workers use a platform (usually a third-party company that has a website or an app) to help connect them with jobs. But others find work off platform (such as through networking). Still others get gigs from both sources.

Sign up. Applying to work with a gig platform may involve providing information about yourself and your services. If you create a profile, be sure it's professional and complete. But, consider taking gigs on the side until you're sure you like working this way.

Consider off-platform work. With some types of work, you may be able to find jobs without the help of an intermediary. Many gig platforms take a cut of the money paid for services, so your work may be more profitable if you find jobs yourself. To get gigs off platform, you might advertise your services by distributing flyers or posting on a website. You might also try to drum up business by connecting

Famous First

In 1995, Craig Newmark began Craigslist as an email distribution list to friends, featuring local events in the San Francisco Bay Area. It became a web-based service in 1996 and expanded into other classified categories. The service has now expanded to cover seventy countries. In March 2008, Spanish, French, Italian, German, and Portuguese became the first non-English languages Craigslist supported. (Source: PeopleReady.com)

through community associations or your local chamber of commerce.

Build your base. Regardless of how you get gigs, referrals and positive feedback from clients are key. If you build a reputation for quality work, people may be more likely to seek you out for future gigs. In fact, successful gig workers often say that many of their jobs are from repeat business.

Be realistic. Deciding to take a gig approach to earning money requires patience, budgeting, and adaptability.

Give it time. Expect that it will take time to learn what works, and what doesn't, when pursuing gigs. It may take a few tries before you figure out which keywords to use when searching for jobs, for example. And even then, it could take months to get gigs regularly.

Manage money. Even if you're patient about making money, you should have a backup plan: figure out what you'll do for income if you don't get enough gig work to pay the bills. You might want to work a more traditional job, in addition to doing gigs, at least at first. Managing finances is an important part of making gig arrangements viable. As a gig worker, you'll need to keep track of the money you earn. You should also set aside some of your income for other purposes, such as an emergency fund for unplanned expenses.

Be adaptable. Not every gig is a good fit, and it's okay to trust your instincts. Gig workers also advise changing tactics when what you're doing isn't going well.

To stay competitive in the gig economy, be prepared to keep learning. For example, take advantage of free graphic design tutorials whenever they're offered, to keep your skills current to grow your design business over time.

Elka Torpey and Andrew Hogan
U.S. Bureau of Labor Statistics,

INDUSTRY PROFILES

ADVERTISING AND MARKETING INDUSTRY

Snapshot

General Industry: Communications

Career Clusters: Arts, A/V Technology, and Communication; Marketing, Sales, and Service

Subcategory Industries: Advertising Agencies; Advertising Material Distribution Services; Direct Mail Advertising; Display Advertising; Marketing Analysis Services; Marketing Consulting Services; Marketing Research Services; Media Buying Agencies; Media Representatives

Related Industries: Broadcast Industry; Food Retail Industry; internet and Cyber Communications Industry; Motion Picture and Television Industry; Publishing and Information Industry; Retail Trade and Service Industry

Summary

The advertising and marketing industry analyzes and influences consumer behavior and expectations through intentional communication campaigns. The industry systematically researches effective communications strategies. It then crafts messaging campaigns based on its research to create or increase demand for products and services and thereby to maximize profits for the companies that sell them. Advertising messages are usually distributed through print or broadcast media, public displays, direct mail, or the internet and related technologies.

History of the Industry

Marketing and advertising have existed in some form since the beginning of human commerce. Hawkers announcing the availability of products were a constant feature of public life in ancient Greece. In ancient Pompeii, archaeologists have uncovered printed materials promoting wares from, Carthage, and Rome. Advertising posters featuring alluring drawings of products for sale were common throughout medieval Europe.

The modern era of advertising may be traced back to the beginning of newspapers in seventeenth century Europe. By the beginning of the eighteenth century, newspaper advertising was common throughout Europe and the United States. In the middle of that century, magazines began to be published on a regular basis, providing another forum for print advertising.

Initially, newspaper and magazine advertising was created by the vendors of the goods and services being sold. In the middle of the nineteenth century, advertising agencies came into existence to take over marketing functions for business clients. The first American advertising agency is generally considered to have been founded in 1843 by Volney Palmer in Philadelphia, Pennsylvania. In the decades that followed its founding, many more firms emerged. The first major American advertising trade conference was held in New York in 1873. By then, the advertising and marketing industry had become well established in larger cities.

Many scholars contend that the industry's rapid growth resulted from the historical context in which it developed. In the latter half of the nineteenth century, the United States was transforming from a rural to an urban society. As people migrated to cities, they lost the ability to make their own essential goods, which created major opportunities for manufacturers and retailers. The resulting rapid increase in commercial activity produced an ideal environment for the new advertising and marketing industry.

Another social trend also hastened the growth of the advertising industry. In 1867, the United States created the Department of Education. Children of every economic and social class began to attend school, resulting in a dramatic increase in literacy by the end of the nineteenth century. As a result, newspaper and magazine circulation increased nearly tenfold. Advertising agencies began to purchase space in publications and resell it to their clients.

Two factors led to even further growth of the advertising industry in the first half of the twentieth century. One was the U.S. automotive industry, which began in the last decades of the nineteenth century and experienced unprecedented commercial success in the early twentieth century. The industry relied heavily on advertising to sell cars, pushing the advertising industry to new levels of economic success.

At the same time, radio was evolving into a form of popular mass media. By the 1930s, radios were common in American and European households. Radio networks produced news and entertainment programming and generated revenue through commercial sponsorship. In the middle of the twentieth century, television joined radio as a widely accessible broadcast medium. The impact of television on American culture was profound. As radio audiences migrated to television, advertising clients followed them. Once again, advertising firms were well positioned to take advantage of the change in information technology.

The Industry Today

Although it enjoyed overwhelming success a generation ago, the advertising and marketing industry faces significant challenges in the twenty-first century. One of the biggest factors in the industry's decline has been a steady decline in U.S. newspaper circulation that began in 1987. The estimated total U.S. daily newspaper circulation (print and digital combined) in 2018 was 28.6 million for weekday and 30.8 million for Sunday, down 8 percent and 9 percent, respectively, from the previous year.

The emergence of cable television has also affected advertising. Hundreds of new channels came onto the television scene, significantly weakening the traditional broadcast networks.

Perhaps the most significant factor influencing contemporary media consumption has been the emergence of the internet. According to the Pew Research Center, internet use increased from 14 percent of the American population in 1995 to more than 41 percent in 1998. By 2019, it was found that just 10 percent of U.S. adults said that they do not use the internet. Forty-three percent of surveyed adults said that they used the internet *several times a day* as of February 2018, compared to just eight percent who said they accessed the internet *about once a day*. A Pew Research Center report released in 2018 shows that social media sites have surpassed print newspapers as a news source for Americans with one-in-five U.S. adults stating that they often get news via social media, slightly higher than the share who often do so from print newspapers (16 percent) for the first time since Pew Research Center began asking these questions.

Internet advertising has resulted in a decline in employment at traditional advertising agencies. Social media advertising has changed the landscape and now, more brands and companies are creating their own in-house advertising departments to craft content and advertising messages that are distributed through social media outlets like Facebook, YouTube, Instagram, and Twitter.

Small Businesses
Small businesses are often specialized boutique agencies that focus on a single niche advertising activity and coordinate with other agencies to develop full marketing campaigns for client companies.

Pros of Working for a Small Advertising or Marketing Firm. Smaller firms tend to encourage closer and more personal interaction with clients, allowing account managers to develop lasting relationships with decision makers at the businesses they serve. Smaller advertising firms are also more likely to be niche-oriented boutique agencies. Employees at such boutiques have the opportunity to develop specialized skills and aptitudes.

Cons of Working for a Small Advertising or Marketing Firm. The primary drawback of working for a small firm is that such agencies tend to lack the capital base to survive major economic downturns. Smaller firms may also have difficulty attracting large national brands, somewhat limiting employee exposure to higher-level business contacts.

Midsize Businesses

Midsize businesses in the advertising and marketing industry typically have annual revenues between $2 million and $20 million and employ between fifty and five hundred people. In addition, midsize advertising agencies may have multiple locations, often in the same geographic area of operation. They tend to be more integrated than their smaller counterparts, handling all aspects of the advertising process for clients.

Pros of Working for a Midsize Advertising or Marketing Firm.
Midsize advertising companies tend to have stronger cash reserves than their smaller counterparts, allowing them to weather economic downturns. They usually handle all aspects of the advertising process for client businesses, allowing workers a chance to experience various aspects of the industry. Since they serve both small and large clients, employees have the chance to develop personal relationships with small-business owners, as well as to make contacts at larger corporations.

Cons of Working for a Midsize Advertising or Marketing Firm.
Workers at midsize companies may not be able to exert as much influence over company strategy as workers at small firms. They also do not have as many opportunities to make high-level client contacts as employees at the larger companies in the industry.

Large Businesses

The advertising and marketing industry has traditionally been dominated by very large businesses. Large advertising agencies usually have a number of different offices, often in multiple countries. Each branch is typically staffed with integrated teams of advertising professionals, able to handle every aspect of the marketing process for clients.

Pros of Working for a Large Advertising or Marketing Firm.
Working for a large company in the advertising industry affords employees many opportunities to influence well-known brands and network with executives at multinational corporations. Large advertising firms typically have massive cash reserves and may be publicly traded, meaning that they are better positioned to weather economic downturns than are their smaller counterparts. The size

of the company may also offer greater opportunities for career advancement.

Cons of Working for a Large Advertising or Marketing Firm.
At large (and sometimes publicly traded) companies, most individual employees have very little control over company governance or their own jobs. Some departmental staff, especially account managers, may be tied to specific clients. If those clients decide to leave the firm, associated account managers may lose their jobs. This can create a type of job insecurity that some professionals find unacceptable.

Organizational Structure and Job Roles

Advertising and marketing companies of all sizes require similar business activities. Smaller agencies tend to be more specialized and provide a narrower range of services. Larger firms are normally more integrated and handle a wider range of advertising services. At these larger firms, activities are conducted by complementary divisions that are often located on different floors or in separate buildings.

The following umbrella categories apply to the organizational structure of businesses in the advertising and marketing industry:
- Business Management
- Office Management
- Market Research
- Account Management
- Media Services
- Creative Services
- Interactive Services

Creative Services

The creative services department is responsible for creating advertisements. Creative services personnel work closely with account management and media services departments to develop ads, often to exacting client specifications.

Perhaps the most important part of the creative process is copywriting. Copywriters create the text of print ads and write scripts for broadcast commercials. Copywriters must thoroughly understand the message and tone that a client wants to convey to the public, then use limited word space to convey this information in a compelling manner.

The design elements of advertisements are developed by other creative services personnel. Design staff members, who usually have formal artistic training, produce the nonverbal elements of print ads and broadcast commercials. In the case of print ads, this entails selecting or creating art to go along with copy. For broadcast commercials, the design staff manages backgrounds, costumes, framing, accompanying music, and other stylistic details.

Producing ads for any kind of media is a very time-consuming and complicated process. Because clients must ultimately be pleased with every detail of the ad, it is typical for creative service departments to develop drafts, known as mock-ups or comps. Account management staff then show these drafts to clients, who provide feedback about desired changes.

Creative services occupations may include the following:
- Art Director
- Producer
- Editor
- Senior Copywriter
- Associate Producer
- Graphic Designer
- Junior Copywriter

Outlook

The long-term outlook for this industry shows it to be stable or in modest decline. The advertising and marketing industries have been radically transformed by changes in technology. For example, while much market research has traditionally relied on talking to consumers to find out about their purchasing habits, many companies now amass vast databases that track every purchase a customer makes in their stores. Future market research is likely to increase its utilization of such databases and to develop as many methods as possible of tracking consumer behavior as it happens, such as using Global Positioning Satellite (GPS) systems to locate consumers and track their movements and buying patterns.

The U.S. Department of Labor projects that the advertising and marketing industry will experience an 8 percent rate of job growth through 2028, faster than average compared to total employment. However, other analysts are cautious about such positive predictions, noting that rapidly shifting media-consumption habits are likely to change the industry in unpredictable ways.

Famous First

Widely credited for coining the phrase, "There's a sucker born every minute," P.T. Barnum will always be remembered for promoting celebrated hoaxes and founding the Barnum & Bailey Circus. Barnum became known as the "Shakespeare of Advertising" due to his innovative and impressive ideas. Some say that he was a scam artist; others say he simply made the truth more appealing. However you want to look at it, he was a genius marketer and creative businessperson.
(Source: https://blog.cloudpeeps.com/)

Advertising has been a part of human culture since ancient times, and it is certainly going to remain an important element of the global economic system. Individuals with an interest in understanding and influencing patterns of commercial behavior would be well served to pursue a career in advertising. In the long term, the industry is experiencing radical changes that are largely due to the migration of audiences from analog to digital media. Although these changes will most likely disrupt traditional business models, they will also result in new opportunities for advertising professionals, although they are less and less likely to find jobs with traditional advertising agencies.

As the media landscape is increasingly transformed by the development of digital communication technologies, firms will be seeking innovative thinkers to pioneer new forms of advertising. In that sense, this is an ideal time for forward-thinking individuals to enter the advertising industry, as they will be called on to develop new and better approaches to influencing customer behavior.

Adam Berger/Editor

HIGHER EDUCATION INDUSTRY

Snapshot

General Industry: Education and Training

Career Clusters: Education and Training

Subcategory Industries: Business Schools; Colleges; Junior and Community Colleges; Music Conservatories; Professional Schools; Theological Seminaries; Universities

Related Industries: Private Education Industry; Public Elementary and Secondary Education Industry

Summary

The higher education industry serves students seeking postsecondary education—that is, education beyond the high school level. It includes colleges and universities with programs leading to undergraduate degrees such as associate's and bachelor's degrees, graduate degrees such as master's and doctoral degrees, and professional degrees such as medical or legal degrees. Higher education institutions may also offer other specialized degree programs, including a variety of academic and professional certificate programs. While the most obvious position within this industry is perhaps that of a professor, the industry also comprises numerous supporting roles across a variety of fields, including administration, management, marketing, and finance, all of which are essential to the operations of a postsecondary educational institution of any size.

History of the Industry

Higher education in the United States dates back to the seventeenth century, when its primary objective was to educate future members of the clergy. At that time, most higher education curricula were dominated by liberal arts subjects, particularly languages, literature, and religious studies. Faculties were small, and courses of study were often broad and designed on an individual basis depending on the interests of the student.

The nineteenth century saw significant change in the purpose of higher education, beginning with the Morrill Land-Grant Act of 1862. Signed by President Abraham Lincoln, the act included grants of land to states and territories to establish colleges devoted to agriculture, science, and engineering. This law sparked the growth of public colleges and universities, and it was an important step toward the explosive growth that would be experienced by the higher education industry during the twentieth century.

The most obvious position within the higher education industry is perhaps that of a professor like this one; however, the industry also offers many positions in a variety of fields, including administration, management, marketing, and finance.

Demand for higher education programs in the early twentieth century was frequently driven by the needs of the Industrial Revolution. During this time, many schools expanded their engineering and science offerings, particularly in the fields of chemistry and physics, and specialization became more common. Programs that assisted in the manufacture of steel, rubber, chemicals, sugar, drugs, petroleum, and electricity generation grew in popularity. As specialization increased, faculty size grew, and the higher education industry experienced a fundamental change in both the way students were taught and the way departments were organized.

Following World War II, increased federal funding to public colleges, along with the GI Bill (officially, the Servicemen's Readjustment Act of 1944), made higher education affordable for a wider range of students. As a result, more young people started to attend college than ever before. This growth in scholarship was in large part directed toward public colleges and universities, as the tuition at such institutions was generally more affordable and the large number of students at public schools resulted in larger departments offering a wider variety of programs.

In the latter part of the twentieth century, programs such as affirmative action encouraged ethnic diversity within student bodies, and increased federal funding in the form of government-sponsored student loans and grants provided more individuals with the opportunity to attend college. All these changes led to a more expansive and enriching experience in higher education, as well as an increased need for infrastructure and staff.

The Industry Today

Higher education in the twenty-first century has grown to include a vast number of academic and vocational disciplines and a wide variety of delivery systems. Many schools now offer certification programs, as well as programs designed to help working adults enhance their existing careers. Additionally, many programs have begun to offer part-time and night programs, distance learning, online courses, and academic credit for employment experience.

Many schools are moving away from hiring full-time tenured professors and toward hiring part-time adjunct instructors in order to save money on salaries and benefits. This may have an unexpected up-side, however, in that these part-time instructors are often working professionals. As a result, they may be better able to relate to working adults returning to school and can help students of all ages integrate their academic experiences into the workplace upon graduation. On the other hand, adjunct instructors do not have the institutional service requirements that full-time faculty have. They are not required to serve on committees and are usually not asked to serve as advisers to students. As schools hire more adjuncts, then, the fewer remaining tenured and tenure-track faculty must pick up the slack, and each professor's workload outside the classroom increases significantly.

In response to their changing environment, many schools are also branching out with respect to their private industry associations. Historically, many schools (particularly large ones with science and medical programs) have affiliated themselves with hospitals and other research institutions to exchange facilities, equipment, expertise, and revenue. Schools are also increasingly seeking funding sources from private industries to finance everything from research labs to programs that provide computers and other equipment directly to students. These affiliations can be of great benefit, as the schools may be able to obtain resources that they could not otherwise afford. However, such affiliations raise ethical questions about potential conflicts of interest if private industry becomes too closely associated with teaching methods within a school.

Small Schools

Many small schools in the higher education industry are community colleges offering two-year associate degree programs, possibly along with some additional certification programs. However, there are some small schools that offer four-year bachelor degree programs and even some graduate-level programs. Small schools generally have fewer degree options than their larger counterparts, and their offerings are likely to be influenced by the types of jobs that are in high demand in the geographic area where the school is located. Smaller schools tend to attract local students, as well as older students who are returning to school after time spent in the workforce. Small schools generally have less than two thousand students and may have as few as twenty or thirty.

Pros of Working for a Small School. Small schools generally employ fewer people within each department, and with fewer fellow employees as competition, it may be easier to distinguish oneself professionally, as well as to develop personal relationships with colleagues and supervisors. There may be greater opportunities to take on leadership roles or to expand the scope of an employment position to include new responsibilities. There may also be less bureaucracy within smaller colleges, as there are fewer employees and fewer layers of management. Smaller schools also usually provide more opportunity for interacting with students, regardless of position, and instructors in particular may find that their smaller class sizes allow for more meaningful relationships with students.

Cons of Working for a Small School. Many smaller schools operate with a smaller staff, so any individual job description may expand beyond its expected scope. Even those occupying positions such as professor, dean, or upper-level management may occasionally need to perform their own administrative support tasks. With a smaller infrastructure, there may be less opportunity for advancement and fewer opportunities to develop new programs or courses. Smaller schools may also operate on smaller budgets, which could entail lower salaries than those paid for comparable positions at larger schools.

Midsize Schools

A midsize school in the higher education industry generally offers four-year bachelor's degree programs, along with some graduate-level programs and possibly a variety of certificate programs. Midsize schools will usually offer more degree options than their smaller counterparts but not the same variety as are available at large schools. A midsize institution may specialize in a particular area, offering a variety of degree programs within a single category (for example, liberal arts or science and engineering) and a limited number of programs in the other categories. Midsize schools have approximately two thousand to six thousand students across their various programs.

Pros of Working for a Midsize School. Midsize schools are in many ways a happy medium between the smallest and largest schools. Each department is generally moderate in size, not only providing employees the opportunity for personal relationships but also allowing them to benefit from a more hierarchical management structure than at small schools. This structure may allow for upward mobility within the organization. There may be opportunities to take on leadership roles on certain projects or to expand the scope of a particular job to include new responsibilities. Midsize schools are likely to enjoy more funding than smaller schools and thus more opportunities to create or expand programs to better serve students.

Cons of Working for a Midsize School. Since midsize schools employ more people, their hierarchical management structure creates more bureaucracy than at a typical smaller school. More departments compete with one another for funds and students, and more people within each department compete for their particular resources and operations. Competition for full-time faculty positions is very intense in midsize schools, and such positions often come with a requirement to conduct research and contribute to academic and scholarly publications to attract outside funding to the school.

Large Schools

Large colleges and universities offer a wide variety of degree programs across many disciplines, including associate's and bachelor's degree programs, graduate programs that offer master's and doctoral degrees, and possibly professional programs that offer medical, law, or business degrees, among others. These schools (which are often classified as universities) usually offer research facilities for a variety of fields. Large schools have more than six thousand students.

Pros of Working for a Large School. Large schools have far more amenities and a far greater amount of funding than their smaller counterparts. Because each department is larger, there are greater opportunities for advancement within the hierarchical management system. Because of the increased funding and increased availability of support staff, there are often more opportunities to create or expand programs to better serve students. For academics, research facilities at large schools encourage professional growth by providing equipment and funding for advanced study of highly specialized subjects. The greater number of faculty and graduate students provides a support system to better distribute basic tasks such as teaching lower-level courses and grading papers, which allows professors more time to conduct research. Additionally, supervising graduate students can be a rewarding experience, as it provides additional teaching opportunities and helps prepare the next generation of academics for careers in teaching and research.

Cons of Working for a Large School. Since large schools employ more people, the more hierarchical management structure creates more bureaucracy. More departments compete for funds and students. Competition for full-time faculty positions can be extremely competitive, and such positions often come with a requirement to conduct research and contribute to scholarly publications in order to attract outside funding to the school. While there is significant variation among schools, the research orientation of many large schools makes them poor fits for professors who see themselves primarily as teachers. Indeed, there may be fewer opportunities for people in all positions within a large school to work directly with students, and those interactions may not be as meaningful as they might be in a smaller setting.

Organizational Structure and Job Roles

Any size school within the higher education industry needs to account for activities in the areas listed below. In smaller schools, one person may hold several roles within several groups, and several of these functions may be combined into a single department. In larger schools, specialists often fulfill unique requirements in specific groups. Regardless of size and scope, the functions must be fulfilled.

The following umbrella categories apply to the organizational structure of institutions of higher education:
- Business Management
- Customer Services
- Sales and Marketing
- Facilities and Security
- Technology, Research, Design, and Development
- Production and Operations
- Human Resources

Sales and Marketing

Within any given school, there are several different departments that can be categorized as sales and marketing. These include the admissions office, which recruits new students; the development office, which brings in funds and manages the school's image both professionally and within the community; and the alumni relations office, which raises funds to support the school's endowment through alumni donations and works to maintain an active community of graduates.

Schools of all sizes need to bring in new students each year to maintain their business. Although this function is often called admissions or recruitment, the reality is that the school is marketing itself to prospective students. The admissions office has two objectives: First, it seeks to recruit students to enroll in the school. Responsibilities in this area include developing marketing materials in print and online, as well as visiting high schools and hosting prospective students on campus. Employees who serve these functions in the admissions office usually have four-year degrees in public relations or communication, sometimes with a concentration in education or academic administration.

Second, the admissions office is responsible for selecting which students to admit to the school. This task requires reviewing application materials and possibly conducting interviews with individual students. Employees who serve this function in the admissions department generally have degrees in academic administration for higher education and often have experience working with postsecondary students either as an instructor or as an administrator.

For privately funded schools, the development office is responsible for seeking out funding sources in the form of contracts for research activities and donations. In larger schools, the development or alumni relations office may also be responsible for attracting investments from outside organizations and school alumni. They solicit contributions to capital and endowment campaigns that fund research and academic facilities, as well as scholarships and faculty chairs. Fulfilling these responsibilities requires employees to develop marketing materials that showcase a school's current facilities and potential for innovation in a particular field, as well as to cultivate relationships with business leaders and alumni. A typical employee in these areas has a four-year degree in a field such as public relations or communication, sometimes with a focus on academic administration or education.

Sales and marketing occupations may include the following:
- Admissions Director
- Gift Planning Director
- Development Director
- Treasurer
- Director of Foundation Relations
- Vice President of External Relations
- Public Relations Director
- Marketing Director
- Graphic Designer
- Copywriter
- Photographer

Production and operations

Increasingly, colleges are relying on adjunct professors rather than hiring (and providing full tenure and benefits to) full-time professors. Adjunct professors typically teach only one or two courses per term, are not required to conduct research or publish papers, and receive few or no employment benefits beyond their salary. Adjuncts often teach basic first- and second-year courses, reserving the major-specific courses for full-time professors. Many adjuncts have doctorates, but some schools will hire adjuncts with master's degrees in the appropriate subject.

Some of the largest schools employ individuals solely to conduct research or run research labs at the institution, usually within scientific fields. This is not especially common; more often, researchers are also professors, and they are required to teach at least an occasional class or supervise students conducting graduate-level research. Researchers have doctoral degrees in their specific fields and may have outside experience managing research laboratories.

Librarians and library staff also play a very important role in the academic experience at a college. Librarians are in charge of selecting materials for the library, maintaining an organized facility, and assisting students in finding the materials they need for their research and projects. Full librarians have master's degrees in library science, while other library support staff may hold bachelor's degrees in related fields.

Production and operations occupations may include the following:
- Professor
- Associate Professor
- Assistant Professor
- Adjunct Professor or Instructor
- Researcher
- Teaching Assistant
- Librarian
- Library Support Staff

Outlook

The BLS projects significant growth for the higher education industry, particularly in the private and for-profit segments. Much of this growth can be attributed to continued education, as many adults are returning to school to further their education or change careers. This new segment growth will be in addition to an expected increase in the number of students who pursue higher education immediately following high school.

As student enrollment increases, there will be an increased demand for individuals working in higher education across all occupations within the industry. Demand for course instructors will grow as colleges fill their classrooms and seek to expand their course offerings, although many institutions are choosing to meet this increased demand by hiring more part-time adjuncts, rather than creating additional full-time tenured professor positions.

Importantly, many of the new opportunities will come in less traditional forms, as many colleges and universities expand specifically to cater to working adults who might otherwise not pursue higher education. This expansion may include night and part-time programs, online and distance-learning programs, and programs that provide academic credit for on-the-job experience. Schools will need administrators, managers, and facilities directors with training and experience that are different from those traditionally expected in the field in order to adapt to these new educational models. There will be many opportunities, particularly for individuals with strong backgrounds in computers and technology, to play important roles in the development of these schools and their programs.

Most people choose to work in the higher education industry because they enjoy and gain satisfaction from working with young people and returning adult students. This field can be incredibly rewarding, as

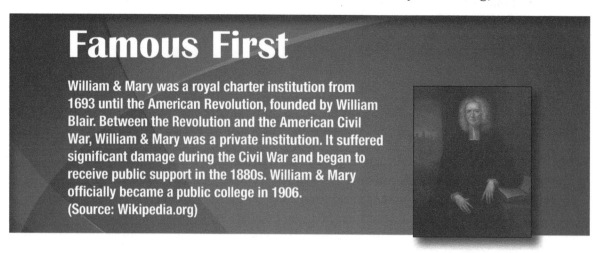

Famous First

William & Mary was a royal charter institution from 1693 until the American Revolution, founded by William Blair. Between the Revolution and the American Civil War, William & Mary was a private institution. It suffered significant damage during the Civil War and began to receive public support in the 1880s. William & Mary officially became a public college in 1906.
(Source: Wikipedia.org)

there are many opportunities to help individuals make a difference in their own lives through education. Individuals who enjoy working with people and who are willing to provide a high level of personalized service will succeed in this industry and will find they are able to make satisfying and lasting interpersonal connections with the students whose lives they influence in a positive way. For those individuals working in research areas within colleges and universities, much depends on the availability of funds to support that research. When university coffers are well stocked, the role of a researcher can be fulfilling and challenging. Even those who choose to work within the industry in support positions that require minimal direct contact with students often find the work to be satisfying because their efforts to maintain the required infrastructure ultimately support the goal of helping students of all ages meet their goals.

Tracey M. DiLascio/Editor

INTERNET AND CYBER COMMUNICATIONS INDUSTRY

Snapshot

General Industry: Information Technology

Career Clusters: Arts, A/V Technology, and Communication; Information Technology

Subcategory Industries: Application Hosting; Custom Web Page Design Services; internet Entertainment Sites; internet Publishers; internet Service Providers; Social Networking Sites; Video and Audio Streaming Services; Web Hosting; Web Search Portals

Related Industries: Advertising and Marketing Industry; Broadcast Industry; Computer Hardware and Peripherals Industry; Computer Software Industry; Computer Systems Industry; Publishing and Information Industry; Telecommunications Equipment Industry; Telecommunications Infrastructure Industry

Summary

From businesses and schools to individuals and governments, the rise of Web sites, e-commerce, e-mail, and social media has changed how humankind interacts and communicates. The internet offers businesses and individuals instant access to digital information. Employees and entrepreneurs working in this industry create the content that, as of 2019, attracted 3.2 billion people worldwide according to International Telecommunication Union. The number will only rise as developing countries continue to gain an

increasing online presence. Internet advertising, paid online services, and online database publishing represent the important revenue streams for the internet industry.

History of the Industry

The evolution of the internet represented an incredible leap forward in human interconnectivity. When programmers took their first tentative steps toward the information network that would become the internet, there were only ten thousand computers in the entire world. In 1962, J. C. R. Licklider, head of the new military computer research program at the Advanced Research Projects Agency (ARPA), first envisioned an "intergalactic network" that would give people instant access to digital information. He began collaborating with scientists and researchers across the country to investigate the possibility of forming new communication networks.

The National Aeronautics and Space Administration (NASA) had launched its first communications satellite by 1963. The development of communications satellites, first proposed by science-fiction author Arthur C. Clarke, played an important role in the development of the internet. Meanwhile, scientists at the Massachusetts Institute of Technology (MIT), the RAND Corporation, and the National Physical Laboratory began researching ways to allow computers to exchange information in small units known as packets. This technology was called packet switching, and it remains the basis for most modern internet communications.

By 1965, ARPA researchers were able to connect a computer in Massachusetts to a computer in California using a telephone line. This connection constituted the world's first wide-area network. This network became ARPANET, the first real precursor to the modern internet.

The burgeoning growth of the earliest modern personal computers, led by Apple and International Business Machines (IBM), led to a revolution in computer technology. Governments, companies, universities, organizations, and individuals soon recognized the usefulness of connecting computers through a stable network, and the International Organization for Standards (ISO) created a universal standard for exchanging information over the internet in 1982.

Universal standard domains such as .com, .org, .gov, .edu, and .net were adopted by 1984. However, it was not until internet pioneer Tim Berners-Lee developed hypertext in 1989 that computers running different operating systems were able to connect easily via the World Wide Web. Working alongside collaborator Robert Cailliau, Berners-Lee created the world's first browser and developed the Hyper Text Markup Language (HTML), which is still used by millions of Web sites around the world.

The Industry Today

Throughout the 1990s and into the early twenty-first century, the rapid rise of the internet economy created a massive speculative bubble. The skyrocketing growth of internet users led to a rush of new dot-com companies hoping to attract customers, with venture capitalists investing an estimated $106 billion in start-up internet firms by 2000. By 2001, the bubble burst, as investors and shareholders rushed to abandon tech companies, many of which had never realized a profit. The collapse of the dot-com bubble left many thousands of people unemployed and many investors with significant—often devastating—losses.

Despite these challenges, some companies founded during the 1990s survived. These included eBay, Amazon, and Yahoo!. In addition, the internet infrastructure set up during the dot-com bubble opened up Web access on a global scale, making it possible for the next generation of internet companies to prosper.

Web sites such as Amazon and eBay have grown into thriving e-commerce companies with tens of thousands of employees. Meanwhile, hosting companies such as GoDaddy, HostGator, and DreamHost offer customers easy, inexpensive ways to publish their Web sites online. In addition, there are many Web-based companies that focus exclusively on the business and financial needs of their customers, offering job postings, stock trading, accounting, or database services. In fact, most businesses, large or small, have their own Web sites and social networking accounts. Many outsource their internet needs to Web designers and consulting firms, while others hire part-time or full-time employees to handle their online presence.

A new development in the internet and cyber communications industry is the growth of cloud computing. Companies such as IBM,

Amazon, Apple, Microsoft, and Google all offer robust cloud computing services that allow businesses and individuals to access programs and documents from a decentralized system of servers. By dispersing data off-site, users can securely back up their data and easily collaborate across long distances. Businesses can also cut costs by outsourcing expensive server operations.

Small Businesses

Since start-up costs for online business have fallen considerably, many new entrepreneurs are attracted to launching internet businesses. Freelance consultants and Web designers also conduct much of their business through the internet. In addition, community leaders with proven track records of founding successful internet businesses often continue to launch small new start-ups or invest in promising new companies. Many entrepreneurs, freelancers, and small businesses in this industry attract visitors to their own Web sites, while others focus on providing Web advertising, Web design, Web hosting, database management, search engine optimization (SEO), or social networking services for other businesses and individuals.

Since most internet-based businesses do not require physical warehouse space and server needs can easily be outsourced, even extremely high profile companies may have very small staffs of fewer than one hundred employees. Web-based businesses at this stage normally focus on providing new, often experimental features and attracting new visitors and clients.

Pros of Working for a Small Internet Company. Freelance Web designers, consultants, and entrepreneurs running their own Web sites have the freedom to pick which projects to work on and which clients to accept. They can also determine how much to charge for their services and set their own advertising rates, and they often make their own schedules. Employees for small firms may also enjoy greater creative input, since they can usually take their ideas directly to the owner or manager. internet start-ups, in particular, offer a relaxed, laid back communal atmosphere with many new challenges and opportunities as the business grows. They may also enjoy generous stock options or other opportunities to invest in their companies, and early employees may reap great financial rewards if a company goes public or is bought up by a larger firm.

Cons of Working for a Small Internet Company. Since freelance Web designers, consultants, and entrepreneurs work for themselves, they are completely responsible for attracting new clients and Web site visitors. This can take a certain amount of luck, as well as tireless efforts and many long hours. They may hold down day jobs in unrelated fields for years before they attract enough clients or advertisers to make a living through their Web-based businesses. Income can also vary widely year-to-year, or even month-to-month, since online trends can change rapidly.

Employees at small start-ups may also face job insecurity, since many start-ups may take years to earn a profit and investors can abandon a company at any time. At small, established firms, employees are often expected to work long hours, with programming sessions that can last late into the night. At the same time, unexpected crashes may result from hacking attacks, server malfunctions, or simply too many people trying to log on at the same time. Employees at these companies are expected to continue working until the issue is resolved, no matter how long it takes.

Midsize Businesses

Most midsize businesses in the internet and cyber communications industry are well established, with hundreds of thousands of regular visitors, significant investors, and profitable revenue streams. They usually maintain their own on-site servers and may have multiple offices. Since successful midsize internet-based companies already enjoy large followings, employees must focus on introducing innovative new features, preventing outages, and ensuring visitors enjoy an extremely reliable level of service.

Pros of Working for a Midsize Internet Company. Most midsize internet companies are stable and well established. They often have multiple offices and may have international headquarters, which can give employees added mobility. They are also small enough that the companies can retain a sense of close camaraderie that may be lost in larger companies. Midsize companies may also offer employees more opportunities to experiment with new designs and features. Compared with smaller companies and Web-based start-ups, midsize firms may offer more job security and can often provide more generous salaries and benefits.

Cons of Working for a Midsize Internet Company. Midsize companies can be relatively stressful places to work. Employees may occasionally work late into the night in the case of outages or when rolling out new features. Midsize firms are also more likely to be purchased by larger companies, which can often result in layoffs as parent companies streamline operations after an acquisition. In addition, employees at midsize firms may not be able to obtain the generous stock options and investment opportunities offered to employees at small start-up companies.

Large Businesses

By the time an internet company has grown into a large, established business, it normally receives millions of visitors every day, generating large advertising and sales revenues. Several of the world's most popular Web sites, social networking sites, search engines, and e-commerce companies are large enough to fit into this category, including Amazon, eBay, Google, and Yahoo!.

Pros of Working for a Large Internet Company. Employees at large internet companies often enjoy many benefits, including high salaries, increased job security, many opportunities for advancement, and the ability to transfer to other locations. Employees often have the chance to work on multiple projects and experiment with new ideas. They benefit from having a large, creative team of coworkers, representing the best and the brightest in the industry. Working for large, well-known firms is very prestigious and may make it easier to find work in the future. Employees may also utilize the knowledge and business connections they gain at large, successful firms to later launch their own start-up companies.

Cons of Working for a Large Internet Company. Finding work at a large internet company can be extremely challenging. Competition for open positions is fierce. Candidates need to have significant experience in the field and often have degrees from top universities such as Stanford, Massachusetts Institute of Technology, and Harvard. While employees have more opportunities to advance than they might have at smaller companies, they face significant competition, both internally and externally. The workloads at these companies can be extremely stressful and demanding, and with so many employees, the sense of camaraderie often experienced at smaller firms and internet start-ups can be lost. In addition, since most of these companies already have established business models and a devoted following, it may be difficult to propose radical changes, although that may depend on the atmosphere of the individual company.

Organizational Structure and Job Roles

Companies in the internet and cyber communications industry share similar organizational structures, although in smaller firms a single person may handle many tasks that are overseen by several different departments in larger firms. In the case of a single freelancer or an entrepreneur launching his or her own site, one person may handle nearly every single aspect of the business while, outsourcing Web hosting and data storage needs to other firms.

The following umbrella categories apply to the organizational structure of businesses in the internet and cyber communications industry:

- Executive Management
- Web Design and Development
- Software Development
- Sales and Marketing
- Information Technology
- Human Resources
- Technical Support
- Administrative Staff

Web Design and Development

Web developers usually focus on testing and implementing new Web-site features and layout designs. They may engage in beta testing and usually work closely with software engineers, project managers, technical support specialists, and public relations personnel to ensure that new innovations match user expectations. They also focus on the day-to-day operations required to keep Web sites up and running.

Web design and development occupations may include the following:

- Web Designer
- Webmaster
- Graphic Designer
- User Interface Engineer
- Product Tester

Software Development

As opposed to Web developers, who focus on layout designs and user features, software engineers design the underlying architecture that allows Web sites to function on a more basic level. This usually involves writing the code to create the tools that Web developers and advertisers use to update content or implement layout changes or new features, as well as the programs and applications that individual users may utilize online or download to their computers. Web sites such as Facebook, for example, offer downloadable applications that help users more easily share photos or information, allowing programs such as iPhoto to upload photos directly from users' computers to their online profiles. Software engineers also play a major role at companies specializing in Web hosting, since they create the programs that allow users easily to upload their Web sites and make them available for online viewing.

Software development occupations may include the following:
- Computer Applications Software Engineer
- Computer Systems Software Engineer
- Sales Engineer
- Data Analyst
- Database Administrator

Sales and Marketing

Employees in the sales and marketing departments of internet companies are normally responsible for attracting new visitors, forming internet advertising partnerships, and helping spread awareness about their companies. Public relations employees, meanwhile, usually interact with journalists and keep users informed about new developments. This may include launching viral marketing campaigns, buying and selling Web banner ads, collecting user comments on upcoming changes, and increasing e-commerce sales.

Sales and marketing occupations may include the following:
- Marketing Manager
- Sales Executive
- Sales Manager
- Marketing Strategist
- Public Relations Specialist

Information Technology

The information technology (IT) staff at companies in the internet and cyber communications industry are responsible for maintaining the extensive computer networks and data-storage hardware facilities needed to ensure visitors have access to Web sites. Normally, they also provide technical support for employees. They are usually responsible for cyber security needs within an organization, which may include preventing hackers from accessing sensitive user information, protecting against viruses, fighting back against denial-of-service attacks, and securing both external and internal computer networks. They are usually highly trained, most commonly earning bachelor's or master's degrees at a minimum.

IT occupations may include the following:
- Network Specialist
- Computer Systems Analyst
- Information Technology Director
- Information Technology Support Specialist
- Computer Security Specialist

Outlook

Since the first researchers successfully connected two computers through a simple phone line in 1965, the internet has grown into a constantly evolving communications medium that continues rapidly to integrate countless aspects of society. As increasing numbers of people use the internet as their primary source for information, older forms of media, including television, films, newspapers, and radio, are rushing to get their products online. This trend will only continue as the number of people with internet access skyrockets on a global scale.

By 2019, the total number of internet users worldwide reached more than 3.2 billion, with 87 million users located in the least developed nations of the world. Services that allow users to access the internet in their native languages include the ability to create domain names featuring non-Latin characters, in such languages as Arabic and Japanese.

The growth in the number of wireless access points at businesses, homes, schools, libraries, government facilities, and even entire cities and neighborhoods has made high-speed broadband freely available to more people than ever before. The growth of cloud computing allows businesses and individual users to archive digital information such as pictures, documents, music, and programs online, often for backup purposes but also to gain access to these files from multiple computers or other devices capable of accessing the internet.

Criminal activity on the internet has also grown. According to Security Watch, criminal activity online had become a $600 billion industry by 2019.

Famous First

The first text message was transmitted December 3, 1992. Engineer Neil Papworth typed "Merry Christmas" on a computer and sent the first SMS message to the cellphone of Vodafone director Richard Jarvis.
(Source: npr.org)

As the internet continues to become more fully integrated into daily life, it will continue to evolve and expand. The tremendous expected growth of the internet and cyber communications industry will give future entrepreneurs many opportunities to launch new businesses and will also allow many established internet firms to continue to attract new customers and advertising partners.

Elizabeth Fernandez/Editor

LEGAL SERVICES AND LAW FIRMS

Snapshot

General Industry: Law, Public Safety, and Security

Career Clusters: Law, Public Safety, and Security

Subcategory Industries: Corporate Law Offices; Criminal Law Offices; Estate and Tax Law Offices; Family Law Offices; Intellectual Property Law Offices; Labor Law Offices; Law Firms; Legal Aid Services; Notary Offices; Paralegal Services; Process Servers; Public Interest Law Offices; Title Abstract and Settlement Offices

Related Industries: Civil Services: Public Safety; Criminal Justice and Prison Industry; Environmental Engineering and Consultation Services; Federal Public Administration; Local Public Administration; Political Advocacy Industry; Public Health Services

Summary

The law firm and legal services industry provides legal advice, assistance and representation to individuals, groups, and corporations. By engaging in legal research, preparing and filing legal documents, drafting contracts, giving advice, petitioning courts, attempting to persuade opposing parties, litigating, and appealing adverse judgments, lawyers use many diverse tools to help their clients. Law firms predominantly employ attorneys, paralegals, and administrative assistants and range in

size from multinational corporations employing thousands globally, to solo practitioners doing business in small towns. Lawyers in private law firms usually charge clients for the legal services they provide, although some types of lawyers are paid only by opposing parties when they win judgements at trial that include legal fees, and many lawyers represent select clients for free (pro bono). A law firm's success is largely dependent on its financial stability. In this respect, it is very similar to any other private business.

The legal services industry is substantially similar in function to law firms. Hundreds of legal service organizations exist in the United States alone. They range from small, local offices in rural areas to large international organizations with offices globally. Much like law firms, these organizations provide legal services for clients, but their fee structure and business goals are drastically different. Legal service organizations seek to assist individuals who otherwise may not be able to afford legal representation and, accordingly, legal service providers generally charge reduced fees. They may also provide pro bono legal representation. Instead of focusing on profits, many of these organizations are nonprofit; they solicit and accept donations from the public, the government, and business owners in order to cover their overhead costs.

History of the Industry

The legal industry has existed, in some form, for thousands of years. In ancient times, many countries and religions developed their own sets of rules, which were essentially common laws: laws that are not written out in books but that are implicitly adopted by society over generations of legal practice. In ancient Greece, common citizens argued legal matters on behalf of other citizens, notwithstanding the absence of formal training. They were not allowed, officially, to accept fees for their representation. Ancient Rome developed a much more comprehensive legal system under which attorneys practiced law as a vocation and could accept fees for their representation. This system was the genesis of the modern practice of law. Notably, however, neither Roman lawyers nor the judges they practiced before had formal legal educations.

The practice of law became more regulated in the first few centuries of the Byzantine Empire (330–1453). By the sixth century, a course of study was required in order to be admitted to the practice of law. By the thirteenth century, many other countries had followed suit, requiring some formal education and an oath of admission in order to practice. The United States developed many of its laws, as well as the traditions and customs surrounding the practice of law, based on the English model. By the time the United States had declared its independence from Great Britain, English legal scholars had drafted important treatises concerning, among other things, principles of property law, civil law, and criminal law. These treatises helped form both U.S. common law and, later, the country's statutory body of laws.

The first dedicated law school in the United States was the Litchfield Law School, established in 1784 in Litchfield, Connecticut, by American lawyer Tapping Reeve. At that time, no official law degree was required in order to practice law; to the contrary, individuals became lawyers by apprenticing with practicing attorneys. This form of apprenticeship existed into the 1890s, when the newly formed American Bar Association (ABA) strongly encouraged states to begin requiring potential lawyers to receive formal education in order to be considered attorneys. The first American law firms employing multiple attorneys appeared just prior to the Civil War (1861-1865). In 1906, the Association of American Law Schools (AALS) adopted a rule that law students must receive three years of study to earn their degrees. By 2020, there were approximately 205 ABA-accredited law schools.

In order to attend law school, most state laws require applicants to have completed undergraduate degrees, to have achieved satisfactory grade point averages (GPAs), and to have successfully completed the Law School Admissions Test (LSAT). In order to be admitted as an attorney, an applicant must satisfactorily complete law school, must fill out a comprehensive application (including a complete job history and criminal background check), and must successfully pass the state's bar examination, which is traditionally administered twice each year.

A large proportion of newly admitted attorneys—approximately half—enter into private practice at law firms. Law firms may employ anywhere from one to thousands of attorneys and staff, located in one small office or spread throughout dozens of offices in major cities around the world. A small percentage of attorneys chooses to practice at legal service organizations, such as local legal aid offices or nongovernmental organizations (NGOs) such as Amnesty International. Much like law firms, these organizations run the gamut from operating as small businesses to, in the case of Amnesty International, functioning as national or multinational organizations with significant influence and lobbying power.

There are many other areas in which an attorney can seek employment. For example, attorneys are employed at nearly every corporation as in-house counsel. Similarly, federal, state, and local governments employ attorneys as prosecutors and judges. Furthermore, most every governmental agency employs staff attorneys who work on general legal matters within the agencies' spheres of influence, and legislatures employ legal counsel to aid in investigations and to produce the legal language from which new laws are crafted.

The Industry Today

A law firm is composed of a group of attorneys—anywhere from one individual to thousands globally—who combine skills, resources, and revenue and who work under a shared name. Some law firms practice in only certain areas of law in which the attorneys have particular expertise. For instance, it is very common to find small personal injury litigation firms, or small plaintiffs firms, which are law firms that represent victims of car crashes, slip-and-falls, and other personal injury claims. The attorneys in this type of firm have particular expertise in plaintiffs' injury litigation, and they often provide very efficient and effective representation in this area of the law.

In contrast, many larger firms advertise themselves as full-service firms. This designation suggests that the firms are capable of handling any legal question or issue with which a client is concerned. Traditionally, individual attorneys at large firms retain expertise in one or two areas of the law, meaning that each attorney is not a general practitioner. When the attorneys and their diverse fields of expertise combine forces at a large firm, however, the firm is able to handle most legal issues. In general, particular legal practice areas include civil personal injury litigation, criminal cases, contract negotiation, property and real estate law and transactions, estate and probate law, intellectual property, patents and trademarks, mergers and acquisitions, administrative law, and appellate law.

At law firms, newly admitted attorneys are commonly referred to as first-year associate attorneys. Depending on the particular firm, they may carry that title for as little as one year or as many as eight years. After an associate's required service, the partners (part-owners) of the law firm vote to decide whether an associate will become a partner. The partners evaluate, among other things, associates' performance, work habits, and the amount of business they bring to the firm. Not only is the receipt of a partnership both a promotion and a recognition that an associate has performed well for the firm, but it is also financially rewarding. As a part-owner, the partner earns a share of the firm's annual revenue, rather than just a set salary with the potential for a bonus—simply stated, when the firm succeeds financially, so do the partners. Partners' shares at the largest American law firms can be several hundred thousand dollars per year. It is also important to note, however, that if the firm loses money, partners also share in the losses. In order to gain their part shares, moreover, the partners must buy into the partnership, so the promotion requires an outlay of capital on the part of the employee. In addition to partners and associates, law firms employ paralegals, administrative assistants, and a host of other employees to assist the firm.

Hundreds of legal service organizations exist in the United States alone. Although these organizations may receive some state or federal funding, many are private organizations. They seek to provide legal services for those who cannot ordinarily afford to hire an attorney. Commonly, legal service providers provide assistance in the following areas: civil and criminal law, property law (especially landlord-renter disputes and foreclosure cases), immigration law, administrative proceedings, and constitutional issues involving civil rights and liberties. An example of the latter might be assisting a high school student who wrote a controversial school newspaper article and was subsequently disciplined by school administrators in a freedom of speech case.

Some legal service providers are able to provide services free of charge for clients who satisfy certain financial eligibility rules. Others provide services and representation at rates that, when compared to comparable fees at private law firms, are drastically reduced. Traditionally, many legal service providers receive assistance from the federal or state government and seek donations from individuals and corporations to help cover overhead costs. Additionally, the operating costs of a legal service provider are significantly lower than those of a law firm, because the salaries paid to employees are often lower. Most legal service providers are local or operate within one particular state. Other legal service providers, such as the American Civil Liberties Union (ACLU) and the National Right to Work Legal Defense Foundation, operate on the national level.

Small Law Firms and Legal Service Providers

Small firms generally employ between one and ten attorneys. They usually handle relatively few cases at a time, although some branches of legal practice require a heavier caseload in order to earn sufficient income. In addition, sole practitioners may be "of counsel" to firms, meaning that they are neither associates nor partners but they are contracted by the firms to help with specific cases as necessary.

Pros of Working for a Small Firm. Small-firm owners are their own bosses, and they may not be expected to work the grueling hours that so-called big law attorneys are expected to work. Accordingly, many nights and weekends are free, and for some the job resembles a traditional forty-hour-per-week occupation, thus allowing attorneys to have lives outside of work. Additionally, for those who view client contact as particularly important, operating a small firm may be a great fit, as clients who can easily communicate with their lawyers are likely to feel that they are receiving better representation. Finally, small firms can be very successful financially. Like any small business, a small firm is built on trust and reputation; after establishing the trust of a community, life in a small firm can be emotionally and financially satisfying. Similarly, attorneys running small legal service organizations generally find the work to be both important and rewarding—both professionally and financially.

Cons of Working for a Small Firm. Although there are many benefits associated with running a small firm, there are also opportunity costs. First and foremost, the opportunity for financial success can be limited. Because the owner of a firm is responsible for paying salaries, rent, utilities, and a host of other bills, if the firm has a slow month, there may not be enough money left for the owner to pay her- or himself. Additionally, owners of small firms and legal service providers may find themselves working several hours per week on nonlegal matters, such as building maintenance or personnel issues, thus detracting from their ability to represent clients and build the business of their firms. Finally, the owners of small firms must decide what benefit packages to provide to their employees. Providing health care and a retirement plan can be very costly and can significantly detract from profit margins. Though an attractive benefit package can entice qualified employees into accepting offers of employment, the cost of providing benefits can be difficult for small businesses to afford. In legal service organizations, the benefits are generally very good, but often the attorneys in charge of these organizations sacrifice the potential for high salaries. Although they may love their work, they are often compensated at lower rates than those in the private sector.

Midsize Law Firms and Legal Service Providers

Midsize law firms generally employ between ten and fifty people. They are usually local or regional in nature, serving clients predominantly in one general locale. Midsize firms almost always have associates in addition to partners, whereas small firms may consist solely of partners.

Pros of Working for a Midsize Firm. With a sufficient number of attorneys, a midsize firm may truly be a full-service organization, effectively representing clients in nearly every type of legal dispute. Whereas sole practitioners and small firms often concentrate on one or two areas in the law, a midsize firm can practice in all areas, thus increasing both its clientele and its revenue. Additionally, because the firm is larger, each partner may carry fewer nonlegal burdens than they do at small firms. Midsize firms should generate more revenue and, consequently, have fewer cash-flow problems. Because their cash flow is generally higher, the opportunity for increased compensation should also exist. As with small firms, many midsize firms offer a good quality of life to their employees. Their benefit packages may be very competitive, but attorneys may not be required to work as many hours in order to succeed as are their counterparts at large firms or multinational corporations.

Cons of Working for a Midsize Firm. Although midsize firms and legal service organizations often provide excellent benefits and allow the attorneys to have a life outside the office, the potential earnings of managing partners pale in comparison to those of managing partners at large firms. Additionally, the owner or managing partner of a midsize firm often faces the same concerns as the owner of a small firm. Depending on the success of the firm, there could be cash-flow issues, employee termination issues, and issues affecting the firm's reputation in the community. Though these are important concerns, they are just as important as client responsibilities and the traditional day-to-day practice of the law necessary to generate revenue. Finally, as with small firms, the cost of providing benefits for employees and their dependents is difficult for many midsize firm owners. It is usually necessary to offer benefits (sometimes including paying the new associate's bar examination and study course fees) in order to attract top talent, but the return on investment for the firm may not be seen for some time.

Moreover, while attorneys at midsize firm may work fewer hours than those at major corporations, they still must work far more than forty hours per week. Because benefits and support staff represent significant expenses, many firms hire one new attorney instead of two, paying the attorney a high salary and expecting at least eighty hours of work per week in exchange. The firm thereby saves money by paying for only one benefits package and one secretary, even if the salary itself is equivalent to the combined salaries of two lawyers who are expected to work forty-hour weeks.

Large Law Firms and Legal Service Providers

Large law firms employ more than fifty attorneys, sometimes far more. The largest are multinational for-profit entities and nonprofit NGOs that practice on multiple continents and represent the interests of their clients across national borders.

Pros of Working for a Large Firm. Those in charge of large firms are among the most well compensated attorneys in the world. They are partners and, accordingly, get a share of the success of an extremely large business. In the largest firms, most partners earn over $1 million annually, including bonuses. Partners are treated very well within the firm, as they have several associate attorneys working on their files and reporting to them; they have wealthy and successful clients; and they enjoy a high standard of living. For other attorneys, and even administrative employees, compensation at these firms is very competitive, as are the benefit packages. Though the work may be difficult and the hours long, employees are compensated for these sacrifices. In fact, large firms pay bonuses to associates and will even assist with bar exam fees, relocation expenses, and other professional fees associated with the practice of law.

Cons of Working for a Large Firm. The life of a partner in a large firm is not without sacrifice. The hours spent at the office can be grueling. As a general rule, attorneys at large firms are required to bill a minimum of eighteen hundred hours per year. The term "billing" does not refer to all time spent at work, however. Rather, this term describes only time that can legitimately be billed to clients; that is, time actually spent on files, including such activities as researching, writing, deposing a witness, or attending court. Furthermore, there are often limits for certain projects. As a result, while an attorney may spend ten hours working on a particular project, he or she may only be able to bill five or six of those hours toward his or her annual billable goal.

After vacation and holidays, a typical billable requirement averages around forty billed hours per week. Since not all time spent at work is billable, big firms' attorneys are at work many more than forty hours per week (seventy-, eighty-, and even one-hundred-hour work weeks are not unheard of in big firms). This leaves little time for a social life or a family. Additionally, the environment is often stressful. Attorneys' work products are carefully scrutinized and, if not satisfactory to their superiors, must be perfected. Finally, attorneys must wait several years at large firms before learning whether they will become partners. In large firms, the wait is often at least seven years.

Organizational Structure and Job Roles

Any size law firm or legal services provider will need to account for activities in the following areas. In smaller companies and firms, one person often holds several roles within several groups. In larger companies, specialists generally fulfill unique requirements in specific groups. Regardless of size and scope, the functions must be fulfilled.

The following umbrella categories apply to the organizational structure of law firms and legal service providers:
- Legal Practice
- Business Management
- Customer Service
- Sales and Marketing

- Facilities and Security
- Human Resources

Legal Practice

Law firms and legal service providers exist primarily to practice law and to assist individuals or corporations in need of legal advice. At large firms, there may exist several categories of attorneys and administrative staff who do the work necessary to satisfy and retain clients and to earn revenue. Attorneys research the law, attend and argue at court hearings and trials, advise their clients, and draft documents, among other responsibilities. Administrative staff assist the attorneys in any number of ways, from helping keep files up to date to researching the law and drafting memoranda.

Legal occupations may include the following:
- Managing Partner
- Partner
- Senior Associate Attorney
- Associate Attorney
- First-Year Associate Attorney
- Staff Attorney
- Of Counsel Attorney
- Law Clerk
- Intern
- Paralegal
- Administrative Assistant
- Legal Secretary
- Receptionist
- Volunteer (at nonprofit legal service providers)

Customer Service

Unlike most industries, in which customers can call a 1-800 number to reach customer service, customer service at law firms is relatively individualized. There is not a dedicated team of employees fielding calls from across the world; rather, clients in need of service call the attorney or paralegal handling their matter directly.

Customer service occupations may include the following:
- Attorney
- Paralegal
- Administrative Assistant
- Secretary
- Receptionist

Outlook

Attorneys may always be terminated for poor performance. Industry-wide layoffs, however, are usually relatively rare. In 2009, though, some of the largest—and traditionally the most successful—law firms undertook unusual measures aimed at surviving the tough economy. Some firms laid off attorneys, while others instituted pay cuts or froze wages. Finally, some firms delayed the traditional fall hiring of the new class of first-year associates. Though new attorneys still gained positions with these firms, they had to wait six months, or even a year, before beginning their employment and earning a paycheck.

Famous First

Arabella Mansfield (May 23, 184–August 1, 1911), born Belle Aurelia Babb, became the first female lawyer in the United States in 1869. Despite an Iowa state law restricting the bar exam to males, Mansfield had taken it and earned high scores. Shortly after her court challenge, Iowa amended its licensing statute and became the first state to accept women and minorities into its bar. (Source: npr.org)

Positions at legal services providers may be more stable than positions in law firms during economic downturns. Because many of the former entities are nonprofits, their bottom line is not associated solely with finances. Additionally, the salaries of attorneys, paralegals, and administrative assistants employed by legal service providers are traditionally lower than the salaries of those same positions at large law firms.

Andrew Walter/Editor

LIBRARIES AND ARCHIVES INDUSTRY

Snapshot

General Industry: Government and Public Administration

Career Clusters: Government and Public Administration Occupations

Subcategory Industries: Archives; Bookmobiles; Centers for Documentation; Circulating Libraries; Film Archives; Lending Libraries; Libraries; Motion Picture Film Libraries and Archives; Music Archives; Reference Libraries

Related Industries: Local Public Administration; Publishing and Information Industry

Summary

An archive is a repository of original documents, such as diaries, manuscripts, photographs, and letters. Historians and other researchers use this "raw material" to write books and articles for magazines; the "finished products" are then housed in libraries. Both of these institutions exist for the primary purposes of collecting and preserving materials, making these available to interested parties, and using them to answer questions. In addition, libraries offer such services as public use of computers and the internet, borrowing privileges for a range of media (books, films, compact discs, and so on), and in-person classes, all of which are free of charge at public libraries.

History of the Industry

Archaeological evidence indicates that archives and libraries have existed since ancient times, with sites in what used to be the empires of Sumeria, Babylonia, and Assyria. The most important and well known of these early libraries was that of Alexandria in Egypt. Handwritten clay tablets and papyrus rolls, made from reeds, were typical of this era.

Literature arose with the Greek and Roman civilizations. Wealthy citizens amassed impressive private holdings of epics, poetry, and the like by such classical greats as Sophocles and Euripides, while temples to the various gods contained public records and official histories. Reading materials consisted of scrolls of parchment, made from the skins of sheep or goats, and vellum, a more durable substance created from unsplit lambskin, kidskin, or calfskin.

The end of the Roman Empire in 476 CE brought with it marauding bands of Vandals, Goths, Huns, and other barbarian tribes, who burned and pillaged cities and the libraries they harbored. This destruction was offset by other developments, principally the rise of monasteries throughout Europe and especially in Ireland. The monks of these bastions of faith scoured the countryside for ancient manuscripts and laboriously copied them by hand.

Paralleling this trend was the establishment of universities, which, like the monasteries, were under the purview of the church. In large cities such as Paris, Oxford, and Heidelberg, with stable social structures and economies, more people were encouraged to matriculate, so the demand for books increased, and college libraries were established. By this time, paper had been introduced via the trade routes from China, and a primitive form of the book, known as the codex, was displacing parchment and vellum.

The Renaissance saw the advent of printing with movable type, when Johann Gutenberg of Mainz, in what is now Germany, produced the now famous Bible of 1455. With mass production of books possible, their cost diminished considerably, giving rise to increased demand, which led to the establishment of private libraries. Members of royalty, not to be outdone, often donated their monumental collections to found public libraries. Influential individuals, such as Martin

Luther, became advocates for libraries and encouraged their founding and maintenance.

The Enlightenment in the eighteenth century was a further impetus to the growth of libraries and archives throughout Europe and the British colonies in the new world. It was also at this juncture that archives and libraries became separate institutions. Up to this time, documents, records, books, and periodicals had been housed in single repositories. With the turmoil of the French Revolution, the value of preserving national heritage through historic documents and public records was recognized. In 1789, the Archives Nationales were founded in France. Their underlying model, in which the state is responsible for collecting and preserving important papers, was soon copied by other governments around the world.

With the nineteenth century came the establishment of national repositories, such as the British Library and the Library of Congress in the United States. Library and archive administration also became professionalized during that century. In 1876, the American Library Association was founded, and Melvil Dewey created his decimal classification system, which is still in wide use today. This period also saw the creation of specialized schools for the training of librarians and archivists. By the twentieth century, library construction and maintenance in the United States was furthered by such philanthropists as steel magnate Andrew Carnegie and by governmental foresight. The Library Services and Construction Act of 1964, for example, helped ensure that just about any school or town of any size had a library that it could call its own.

The Industry Today

Archives and libraries have evolved considerably from what they were in the past, namely, warehouses for papers and books run largely by clerks. Today, they reflect not only advances in technology but also the wishes of the clientele they serve, and they are administered by highly trained professionals. In the United States, the majority of librarians possess undergraduate degrees in the liberal arts and master's degrees in library science from schools accredited by the American Library Association. Archivists must also possess master's degrees, and, while a few institutions of higher learning offer archival studies or archival science programs, it is much more common for archivists to hold master's degrees in history or library science, with course work in such areas as records management, materials preservation, and so on.

Over time, libraries and archives have increased greatly in number and in the process have become quite specialized. According to the American Library Association, there are 116,867 libraries of all kinds in the United States in 2019. Some of these are legal libraries at law firms, in which librarians must also be familiar with the law, oftentimes holding juris doctor degrees. Others are medical libraries at hospitals, where librarians need to understand medical terminology and procedures. Corporate libraries are located at the headquarters of Fortune 500 companies, and academic libraries exist on college campuses across the country. By far the most common type of library, however, is the public library, which can be found in the smallest towns and the largest metropolitan areas. Funded by appropriations from local governments, these institutions are often regarded as among the best uses of taxpayer dollars. The services they offer are many, varied, and generally free of charge.

Libraries today offer their visitors traditional services with a modern-day emphasis on convenience and expediency. A cornerstone of public librarianship, for example, has been reference service. Traditionally stationed at a reference desk or information desk, reference librarians receive customers, known in the profession as "patrons," or sometimes as "users" or "borrowers." Patrons may ask for information on any topic, from the telephone number of a local business to how plants harness the rays of the sun in the process known as photosynthesis.

While patrons may pose their queries in person or over the telephone as they have in the past, alternative time-saving options now abound. Virtual reference allows patrons to communicate with librarians over the internet via real-time chat software. This process allows patrons the luxury of receiving answers regardless of location or time of day, assuming that they have internet access. The rise of the internet itself and, more particularly, of freely available search engines such as Google, has been something of a double-edged sword for the profession, as many individuals now choose to do their own research, meaning that demand for this service has diminished somewhat. However, the questions posed, while fewer in number, have increased in complexity. For example, a patron may want to know if a book written in, say,

French, has ever been translated into English and, if so, when it was published, whether it is available for loan, and from which library.

Archives, too, have harnessed the internet to enhance service to their customers. Historically, those who wished to view public records or other documents had to do so in person. Many archives have digitized their holdings or are in the process of doing so, allowing researchers to view items of interest at any time of the day or night, without the expenditure of time and travel necessary to visit the archive in person.

Today, archivists work in a variety of locations. Many are employed by government, such as those at the National Archives and Records Administration (NARA). Academia represents another generator of archivist jobs, as many college and university departments are responsible for preserving one-of-a-kind documents and objects. Some archivists are employed by private firms, while still others may make a living at state and local historical societies.

Classes on a variety of topics are held at libraries. Newly arrived immigrants may take English as a second language (ESL), the unemployed may learn how to navigate the Web to search for jobs or polish their resumes, and senior citizens may learn new hobbies such as bird watching or quilting. Because there has always been a teaching element to this profession, these classes are generally taught by librarians themselves, especially if they happen to have personal knowledge of the subjects. At the same time, librarians can recommend to their students relevant books, magazines, and other materials that their libraries have in their collections.

Libraries have been affected by a continuing shift from print to electronic and digital resources. Many reference books are now being purchased as part of electronic databases, which may be accessed remotely via the internet. Novels have been available on compact disc for some time, and they are now becoming available as downloadable e-books, which can be read on personal computers; dedicated e-book readers, such as Amazon's Kindle and Barnes and Noble's Nook; or multipurpose mobile devices, such as tablet computers, handheld computers, and smart phones.

Small Institutions

Libraries typically reflect their surrounding geographic and physical locations. Therefore, a rural community may have a single room set aside in its city hall as its designated library, with a single employee, known as a "solo librarian." A small library is defined as a facility serving a population of from ten thousand to twenty-five thousand. Libraries in this category generally have a minimal selection of materials and only a handful of public-access computers for internet searching.

Pros of Working for a Small Library or Archive. Librarians and archivists derive a deep sense of satisfaction from being able to answer questions or solve problems for their patrons. Because of the more intimate working relationship, helping someone find just the right book or document goes beyond merely doing one's job; on the part of both the professional and the patron, it seems more personal than that, as if the former were doing the latter a favor. The fact that the staff of a small library or archive is limited to one or two people generally makes service more responsive to requests, since patrons need not go through various levels of management or be shunted from one department to another, as might be the case at larger institutions.

Cons of Working for a Small Library or Archive. The one or two employees of a small library or archive must handle all necessary tasks related to running their institution, from shelving books and documents to fielding questions from visitors to opening the daily mail. The job may therefore involve a good deal of stress, as the workday is a constant balancing act between providing personal attention to users and still performing all requisite daily tasks.

Because small libraries and archives are not as heavily used as are larger institutions, they are often open fewer hours each week. They are generally open for business only during weekdays, and even then probably less than the standard eight hours per day. The resulting short shifts translate into reduced earning potential for their employees.

Midsize Institutions

A midsize public library is defined as a facility serving a population of from 25,000 to just under 100,000. Midsize libraries typically are housed in buildings constructed for that specific purpose or are part of multifunction spaces, such as structures that also contain indoor parks, health and fitness centers, and community meeting rooms. These are often found in suburban areas.

Pros of Working for a Midsize Library or Archive. Employees of midsize institutions get to meet people from all walks of life. Dealing with such a diverse clientele helps them grow professionally, since the variety of questions and requests they receive almost invariably involves research and study. Thus librarians and archivists learn much in the course of their work. The fast-paced nature of the workday makes the time seem to go by quickly. Because there are more positions and job openings available at midsize facilities than at small facilities, there are greater opportunities for career advancement.

Cons of Working for a Midsize Library or Archive. The hectic pace of most days does not lend itself to forming lasting or meaningful relationships, such as may be formed at small libraries and archives. By the same token, there is usually little time to interact with coworkers. Library jobs can be hectic and stressful, involving people waiting in line at the reference desk, telephones ringing, and random interruptions such as photocopiers malfunctioning, all at once. Because facilities of this size are generally open evenings and weekends, librarians must expect to spend at least some of these hours away from home and family. Archivists may also work evening and weekend hours in order to accommodate students facing deadlines for term papers, reports, and other research projects.

Large Libraries and Archives

Large libraries and archives can be state or federal government entities, such as the Library of Congress or the National Archives, both of which are located in Washington, D.C. Other large libraries serve as central or main branches of multibranch systems in major metropolitan areas. Generally speaking, a large public library serves a population of from 100,000 to just under 500,000. National libraries serve the entire nation, albeit in a less direct fashion.

Ample square footage and hefty budgets ensure that the maximum amount of material will be available for patrons. Large libraries are destinations, in that patrons make special trips to these facilities, as it is well known that they have the best selections of books, films on

DVD, audio books, and the like. Large libraries also have the greatest number of public computer stations. Free internet access is a major driver of traffic at all libraries, but this is especially true of large facilities, as many people cannot afford to purchase access for their own homes.

Large libraries also offer many special features and comforts that are beyond the reach of smaller facilities with limited budgets. Overstuffed chairs for comfortable reading, fireplaces to create warm and cozy corners, meeting rooms available for community groups or quiet study, and coffee shops for refreshment are just some of the amenities available in this market segment. Special events, too, play a role in large libraries, as well-known authors make appearances there to read from their latest novels and sign books. Classes on various topics are held at regular intervals for the edification of interested parties on such topics as gardening in cold climates or how to navigate the electronic databases that the library offers.

Pros of Working for a Large Library or Archive. The relatively large workforce of this type of establishment affords greater opportunities for career advancement, since there is more turnover in personnel and more positions of responsibility. Also, the many operational areas of large institutions, such as reference work, cataloging, information technology, and so forth, present learning opportunities for ambitious librarians. Pay tends to be higher and fringe benefits more generous, owing to larger institutional budgets and the bargaining power of unions.

Cons of Working for a Large Library or Archive. Employees of large institutions tend to have narrower, more specialized sets of duties. Many of their tasks can therefore become repetitive and routine, leading to on-the-job burnout. Contact with coworkers and members of the public may be perfunctory and impersonal as a result of employees' hectic work schedules and compartmentalization.

Organizational Structure and Job Roles

Administratively, libraries fulfill their duties to the public by allocating labor into three broad categories: User services include reference, reader's advisory (which provides help and advice on what to read), circulation, and interlibrary loan. Technical services encompass information technology (IT), acquisitions, and cataloging staff. Administrative services comprise library directors, managers, and other supervisory personnel who solve problems, create policy, and generally run their establishments. At small libraries, a single person may fulfill all of these tasks. Archives, on the other hand, being generally much smaller both physically and in terms of staff, are much more flexible in regard to organization and job roles. A hypothetical state historical society, for example, might have such job titles as collections assistant, government records specialist, and state archivist.

The following umbrella categories apply to the organizational structure of institutions in the libraries and archives industry:
- Management
- Reference Services
- Reader's Advisory
- Interlibrary Loan
- Circulation
- Information Technology
- Acquisitions
- Serials
- Cataloging
- Administrative Support
- Children's Services
- Special Collections
- Government Documents
- Outreach Services

Management occupations may include the following:
- Library Director
- Deputy Director
- Library Manager
- Assistant Manager

Reference Services

Every library, regardless of size, offers reference service free of charge. Anyone may ask any question about almost any topic and expect to receive an answer. These services are provided by reference librarians, who by virtue of formal education and experience are familiar with all manner of reference books, internet searching, electronic databases, and other information sources. Ethically, a reference librarian would refuse a request on how to construct an atomic bomb or anything else that might be construed as dangerous or illegal. Typically, librarians conduct what are known as "reference interviews" with requestors, whether the transaction is in person, on the telephone, or via virtual reference. Often, requestors are not entirely certain of what they want to know, so a series of questions is asked of them in order to arrive at the heart of the matter. It is not uncommon, especially in academic libraries, for reference librarians to be experts in specific subjects by dint of holding additional master's degrees beyond the master of library science.

Reference services occupations may include the following:
- Head of Reference
- Supervising Reference Librarian
- Reference Librarian

Reader's Advisory

Known as RA for short within the profession, reader's advisory staff provide consultation services to help patrons find and enjoy books they might not find on their own. RA staff may suggest authors whose work is similar to authors a patron already likes, or they may simply answer questions about titles in a series of which a patron has read only part.

Interlibrary Loan

Interlibrary loan refers to the lending of books from one library to another for the benefit of patrons, so they need not travel about in search of the reading material they desire. Formerly taking up much time and paperwork, interlibrary loan has become largely automated with the advent of computers and the internet. Closely allied to interlibrary loan is document delivery, which refers to the acquisition of photocopied individual articles from within periodicals in other libraries. Because the delivered documents are photocopies (or other facsimiles), they need not be returned.

Circulation

Circulation is the library department responsible for handling the checking in and checking out of library materials, issuing library cards to patrons, levying fines for overdue or damaged materials, and ensuring that materials are returned to their proper place on the shelves. Many positions in this category are part-time, also known as full-time equivalent, or FTE, positions. For example, two people each working twenty hours per week are considered equivalent to one full-time (forty-hour) worker.

Circulation occupations may include the following:
- Head of Circulation
- Library Clerk
- Library Technician
- Library Page
- Shelver

Information Technology

Computers and the internet are integral parts of any library, regardless of size. Information technology, or IT, comprises computer acquisition, maintenance, and repair; firewall installation and maintenance; internet connectivity; software upgrades; and automated equipment, such as self-checkout machines and receipt printers.

IT occupations may include the following:
- Systems Technician
- Chief Information Officer (CIO)
- Database Administrator

Acquisitions

Acquisitions staff oversee the purchase and receipt of library materials. In addition to acquiring newly released materials, libraries must regularly replace popular titles, which experience significant wear and tear through constant circulation, as well as being lost and stolen outright. Libraries are high-volume purchasers, so they often receive discounts from vendors.

Acquisitions occupations may include the following:
- Head of Acquisitions
- Acquisitions Librarian

Serials

Also known as periodicals, serials are magazines, journals, quarterlies, and other print materials that are published at regular intervals. With the advent of the internet, many titles come with online versions bundled to physical subscriptions. Often, articles from back issues are also available online. Many libraries do not keep back issues for more than about two years because they take up so much shelf space and their content tends to become dated quickly. Others bind together each year's worth of a given periodical, providing those issues with hardcover protection.

Serials occupations may include the following:
- Serials Librarian
- Binding Technician

Cataloging

All incoming material must be classified, described, added to the library catalog, and processed, which entails applying protective material (such as a mylar cover over the dust jacket of a book), antitheft devices and stamps, and identification or shelf stickers. Catalogers typically work in staff-only work areas and normally do not have contact with the public. However, the results of their labors are immediately apparent to anyone who uses the Online Public Access Catalog (OPAC), the modern-day electronic version of physical card catalogs. Catalogers typically take specialized courses in this field, as their work is considered a specialty of librarianship, just as cardiology and gastroenterology are specialties of medicine.

Public Relations

Every library needs to engage its public. This engagement can take the form of author readings, classes, special events, used book sales, other fund-raisers, or any other modes of generating positive publicity. While flyers, banners, newspaper notices, and other traditional means are still used, the major forms of communication have become electronic. Libraries publish calendars of events on their Web sites, and they often send e-mail notifications or even full electronic newsletters to patrons who sign up to receive them.

Public relations occupations may include the following:
- Public Relations Librarian
- Webmaster

Children's Services

Most libraries have areas set aside just for children. These may include one corner of a small library or an entire wing of a larger facility. Children's areas are staffed by dedicated children's librarians, who are well versed in literature for young people. Special services include regularly scheduled story times, in which librarians read story books to children; show and tell sessions, in which various objects are presented for discussion; and furnishings built low to the floor for the comfort of youngsters. Very often, books are arranged by reading level, for ease of selection. It is also not uncommon for stuffed toys, puzzles, and other amusements to be available for those children who may have short attention spans.

Special Collections

Special collections is an all-encompassing category that can include material not easily stored on shelves, such as pamphlets housed in file cabinets, or material of a significant nature, such as local history books, photographs, or artifacts. In a sense, a special collection is an archive housed within a library.

Special collections occupations may include the following:
- Special Collections Director
- Special Collections Librarian

Government Documents

While publications are produced by many political subdivisions, such as city councils and county boards, the majority of such documents come from the federal government. So prolific a publisher is the federal government, in fact, that a separate classification system has been devised to organize its documents, the Superintendent of Documents, or SUDOCS. Large libraries in the United States are known as "depository libraries," and these institutions automatically receive every book, pamphlet, map, or document printed by the government in Washington, D.C. Because of the amount and complexity of this material, special areas of large libraries are set aside for government documents, and librarians in charge of these areas must have specialized training.

Outreach Services

Many people cannot physically come to the library, including disabled persons and incarcerated convicts. Libraries reach out to these persons in order to serve their needs. Most libraries, for example, have homebound services, in which couriers deliver library materials to disabled persons' residences. Bookmobiles, essentially libraries on wheels, make regular stops in the neighborhoods of large cities. Libraries also have programs dedicated to loaning books and other materials to prisoners.

Outlook

The outlook for this industry shows it to be stable. In 2019, the BLS's *Occupational Outlook Handbook*, shows that employment for librarians is predicted to rise by 6 percent between 2018 and 2028, or as fast as average for all employment.

Also affecting the industry outlook are younger librarians who are just entering the profession. The American Library Association runs an active recruitment campaign to entice college students to choose librarianship as a career. Anecdotal evidence suggests that many librarians made midcareer switches, having found that their bachelor's degrees in one of the humanities, such as English or history, led to less-than-satisfying career paths. While library careers may not be particularly remunerative, there are many positive factors that lead people to abandon their former occupations to become involved with books and people.

Entirely apart from the issue of incoming and outgoing individuals within the profession is the topic of funding. The vast majority of librarians work in public libraries and are therefore at the mercy of the political winds. During times of economic distress, elected officials look for easy targets to cut budgets, and libraries are usually at the top of the list of potential victims. The irony is that it is during these same periods that library usage spikes, as the unemployed flock to their neighborhood branches to use public internet stations to look for work and to take classes in resume writing and other job-related skills.

Librarians are nothing if not innovative, however, and many are entering nontraditional employment. The more entrepreneurial are going into business for themselves as consultants and information brokers. They charge hourly fees to search for information and hard-to-find documents or to, say, analyze the competition for a particular business or industry. Still others engage in teaching at library schools, or in writing books on topics of interest to other librarians.

Employment Advantages

Those who enjoy literature and learning are able to indulge their twin passions as librarians, since to a large degree the profession involves being familiar with works of the past and present, from

Famous First

The first totally tax-supported library was established in Peterborough, New Hampshire, in 1833. While there were many other libraries that met new public-oriented milestones—like the Darby Free Library in Pennsylvania, which has been in continuous service since 1793—the first large public library was the Boston Public Library, founded in 1848. By 1854, all Massachusetts residents could borrow from its collection, which began with 16,000 volumes.
(Source: https://dp.la/exhibitions)

classics to contemporary best-selling novels. Librarianship is a helping profession, and in that regard it shares much with teaching and nursing. Librarians may derive satisfaction from matching people with the books they wish to read and from helping them discover new authors and works.

The work of librarians is intellectual, rather than physical. Librarians typically work in comfortable surroundings and are stimulated both by their association with patrons asking questions and by their interactions with colleagues who share their love of learning.

Mike Bemis/Editor

MOTION PICTURE AND TELEVISION INDUSTRY

Snapshot

General Industry: Arts and Entertainment

Career Clusters: Arts, A/V Technology, and Communication

Subcategory Industries: Cable Broadcasting; Motion Picture and Video Distribution; Motion Picture and Video Exhibition; Motion Picture and Video Production; Postproduction Services; Satellite Television Broadcasting; Television Broadcasting Networks; Television Broadcasting Stations

Related Industries: Advertising and Marketing Industry; Apparel and Fashion Industry; Broadcast Industry; internet and Cyber Communications Industry; Music Industry; Publishing and Information Industry; Theater and Performing Arts Industry; Themed Entertainment Industry; Video, Computer, and Virtual Reality Games Industry

Summary

The motion picture and television industry creates and disseminates audiovisual entertainment, news, sports coverage, documentary material, and other film and video content to viewers worldwide. The industry comprises two major components: The film industry provides small-, medium-, and large-scale productions spanning a wide range of genres. The television industry provides similar entertainment products for broadcast

directly to viewers' homes. Each of these components has seen dramatic growth over the last several decades, and both have enjoyed relative stability.

Motion picture and television production constitute a multibillion-dollar industry with visibility in virtually every country in the world. Employing millions of workers across a broad spectrum of professional pursuits, the industry is perhaps best known for its high profile in Hollywood, New York, Canada, Great Britain, and India. However, it has seen consistent growth into other regions, maintaining a presence in every developed country and in most developing nations as well.

History of the Industry

The motion picture industry owes its roots to the eighteenth century, when moving projected images were first introduced by the magic lantern. This device, the first slide projector, projected images that had been drawn on glass slides. Some of these slide projectors incorporated levers and other devices to bring simple movements to the screen; for example, in a comic slide, a man's pants might fall down when the lever was pushed.

Magic lanterns remained popular through the mid-1800s. Even those that did not move helped form the foundation of the later cinema by creating a language for telling stories on a screen. Such cinematic conventions as the establishing shot and shot-reverse shot were invented by magic lantern devisers who used them to order the still images from which they formed their narratives.

The photographic camera was invented in 1826 and became popular beginning in 1839. In 1879, Eadweard Muybridge developed the zoopraxiscope, a device that created the illusion of motion by projecting a series of still images based on photographs he had taken of people and animals in motion. (Because of the way the device worked, it was necessary to project elongated drawings based on photographs to compensate for the zoopraxiscope's tendency to shorten images.) The zoopraxiscope was itself based on an earlier device, the phenakistoscope, which similarly created simple moving images that were viewed by individual spectators looking through a series of slits in the side of a spinning disc.

In 1888, Muybridge and American inventor Thomas Alva Edison met at Edison's West Orange, New Jersey, laboratory. The two collaborated on the development of the zoopraxiscope and Edison's groundbreaking phonograph. Edison, however, balked at the notion of full collaboration, looking instead to develop a motion picture system that could both capture and recreate motion directly. Edison introduced the kinetoscope, a peepshow device that was capable of recording and reproducing objects in motion, for which he received a patent in October 1888.

When Edison's product was unveiled a year later, the search began for a medium by which the new technology might record its images. After exploring several avenues, Edison and his colleagues settled on celluloid film purchased from Eastman. From that point forward, the technology attracted considerable attention. In 1891, kinetoscopes began to appear in the form of coin-operated machines in public parlors in New York and Europe. Edison resisted creating motion picture projectors based on the kinetoscope, however, for simple economic reasons. A coin parlor would purchase six or eight kinetoscopes, so it could serve six or eight customers at a time. A machine that projected an image onto a screen would serve many more customers, so Edison feared he would sell far fewer of them.

In 1895, the development of film technology took a great leap forward when the French brothers Auguste and Louis Lumière introduced their cinematograph, a single portable device that was a camera, film developer, and projector all in one. The Lumières began producing short films for public viewing. One of their most well-known films was *L'Arrivée d'un train à La Ciotat* (1896; *Arrival of a Train at La Ciotat*; better known as *Train Arriving at a Station*). Viewers unaccustomed to moving images reportedly thought the train was coming toward them and reacted with shock at the realism of the image. Over the course of the decade after the Lumière films gained prominence, film production became more standardized and marketed to audiences around the world.

With the increased popularity of films in the Lumière vein, known as "actualities," filmmakers concurrently sought new ways to develop their technology. In one of the first examples of special effects, for example, French magician Georges Méliès discovered that by stopping the camera mid-scene, rearranging the scene, and starting the camera again, he could cause characters and objects to appear and disappear in a variety of manners. The novelty and creativity that films fostered at the end of the nineteenth century helped lay the groundwork for the industry's explosive growth during the twentieth century. Films were produced by the hundreds in Europe and the United States, with new techniques being employed to develop characters and scenes. Over the decade from roughly 1907 to 1917, the language of classical cinema was developed and standardized. By the end of the 1910s, film was both an industry and a medium of standardized communication.

During the 1920s, the industry began to move and jell in Hollywood. Large studios were built that could produce countless films to meet audience demands. The so-called studio system in Hollywood lasted roughly from 1917 to 1960. During that time, it was common for creative talent—including actors, writers, directors, costumers, and so on—to work "on contract" at a given studio. These professionals received weekly salaries year-round, and they worked on whatever project their studio assigned them. After the end of the studio system, reliable salaries independent of a given production became a thing of the past. Instead, creative professionals were paid by each production on which they worked and had no source of income between jobs. Studios continued to employ executives, including some producers, but they no longer permanently employed actors, writers, directors, and other creators.

When World War II came to an end in 1945, another medium began to grow in popularity. Television had been introduced several years earlier at the 1939 World's Fair, but with the economic boom of the postwar period, television became both extremely popular and affordable for consumers. The number of television stations increased dramatically, as sales of television sets grew by 500 percent. Over the course of the next few decades, picture quality improved. The diversity of programs also grew, as comedies, game shows, mysteries, dramas, and other shows were broadcast, in addition to news programs and other scheduled items. Advances in television technology also made it easier to produce shows anywhere, increasing viewers' access, as well as the volume of entertainment options available. By the late twentieth century, television and film had become the most popular forms of entertainment, not just in the United States but also around the world.

The Industry Today

Motion picture and television production are lucrative, revenue-generating businesses. Their impact on local economies has led them to be sought after by economies seeking a strong boost, and local governments compete to bring productions to their areas by offering tax breaks and other incentives. In the United States, the industry accounts for 2.5 million jobs, paying over $41 billion in wages to its employees, as well as over $38 billion for external vendors and businesses. In 2008, it generated $13 billion in federal and state income and sales taxes.

The industry provides a wide range of entertainment opportunities for viewers and audiences around the world. There are more than a dozen film studios, as well as nearly a dozen television studios, in greater Los Angeles and Hollywood alone. Each of these studios generates a large volume of films and programs to suit a broad variety of audience tastes. Hollywood does not hold a monopoly on the industry, however. Greater New York boasts over two dozen television studios, and a growing number of major studios are appearing in such areas as western Canada. One of the fastest-growing venues for film studios is located in Mumbai (formerly Bombay), India, where the Bollywood style of filmmaking has gained increasing worldwide popularity. The world's largest broadcasting company is the British Broadcasting Company (BBC), with one of the planet's biggest studio campuses located just outside London.

The world's film and television studios have increased not only in number but also in diversity. In addition to large-scale studios such as Universal, the BBC, and Walt Disney, many small and midsize studios are in operation. Streaming services including Netflix, Amazon Prime, Hulu, and Disney+, along with premium cable channels like HBO and Showtime, are all producing new content in the form of movies and series.

The motion picture and television industry is an extremely complex business, comprising a wide range of networks and professions. The studio (which may be defined as both a facility in which productions and programs are filmed and a centralized business housing every component of film and television production) is a microcosm of the larger industry. Studio executives, writers, directors, actors, technical crews, and other business professionals all collaborate to create feature films, broadcast programming, and other films and television shows. It is an exciting field, offering its employees opportunities to help build films and programs that will be viewed by millions of people at a time. Much of the industry is also extremely competitive, with would-be actors and screenwriters flocking to film capitols such as Hollywood, New York, and Mumbai to join the industry.

The creation of a major motion picture or television show is not limited to the studios. In fact, the industry frequently relies on many outside companies to assist in special effects, graphics, set design, and other aspects of film production. Films and programs are often filmed on location (meaning anywhere outside of a controlled sound stage or other studio set). Many film and television locations, however, do not correspond to their settings. For example, Los Angeles may be represented on screen by Los Angeles, Vancouver, Cincinnati, a sound stage in London, or any combination thereof. Indeed, many film and television locations are pieced together by filming in a number of cities or areas that present the most aesthetic and cost-effective sites.

Small Studios and Production Companies

Small film and television businesses include small studios, as well as the minor production companies assembled to create individual properties. In television, such companies include Bad Robot, Mutant Enemy Productions, MTM Enterprises, and a host of other companies whose logos are flashed briefly at the end of television shows. Most small production companies establish relationships with major studios, and some are even housed entirely on the lots of those studios. Small studios, meanwhile, create or acquire independent films. Some produce films that are distributed by major studios. Others act primarily as arthouse distributors, finding and sometimes funding promising small-scale films and paying for their distribution to movie theaters in return for a percentage of their profits.

Pros of Working for a Small Studio or Production Company.

Some small studios have less-corporate, top-down atmospheres and structures than do large studios, so creative employees may experience or perceive less artistic intrusion by executives at smaller companies. These employees may be able to take on projects that they find more artistically satisfying, as well as to enjoy more artistic control over their projects. Many small studio features are created by one person, who may write, produce, direct, and star in the film. While small productions are not always financially rewarding, many workers appreciate the process of creating original and unique work.

Cons of Working for a Small Studio or Production Company. Small studios may afford creative employees no more artistic control than do large studios, and they may lack the financial resources of larger companies. Although many small films flourish despite low budgets, the norm is that films require financial backing. If small companies seek such backing from large distribution companies, for example, they give up some of their creative independence as a result. Pay for employees (including actors) on a given film is generally lower at small studios than it is at larger studios. Limited budgets may also preclude small studios from filming in a particular locale or acquiring a marketable star or stars to act in a film. If a small studio seeks to distribute a film itself, the scope of its distribution may be seriously curtailed, limiting its ability to reach audiences and maximize its revenue potential and cultural impact.

Midsize Studios
Midsize studios are generally significant corporations that are nonetheless smaller than the major studios. They may include the largest production companies, as well as the creative divisions of some television networks and the largest independent film studios.

Pros of Working for a Midsize Studio. Midsize studios offer those who work for them the opportunity to work not only on independent films but also on major productions. Because they are often part of, or closely connected to, much larger production companies, midsize studios tend to have more diverse productions, some of which target the arthouse crowd and some of which are more commercial, major productions. In light of this diversity, midsize studios may achieve greater influxes of producer money, enabling them to provide above-average salaries.

Cons of Working for a Midsize Studio. Many midsize film and television studios are subject to absorption into larger production companies. Thus, those who work for them may find their job stability somewhat unpredictable. Additionally, the increased potential for major productions may increase competition for jobs on those productions, making work more difficult to come by.

Major Studios

The major motion picture and television studios are the icons of the industry, located on studios whose back lots have hosted some of the most famous productions in history. Almost all major studios in the twenty-first century either are owned by or are portions of even larger multinational corporations with multiple entertainment and nonentertainment properties. For example, Disney owns the Walt Disney Studios, the Walt Disney Theme Parks, the American Broadcasting Corporation (ABC), ESPN, and several other television stations. NBC Universal, which owns both the National Broadcasting Company (NBC) and Universal Entertainment (the parent company of Universal Studios), is itself owned by Comcast since 2013. In addition to the divisions that give the company its name, it also owns the USA Network, Syfy (formerly the Sci Fi Channel), and many other television and internet properties. As these examples demonstrate, it is often very difficult to draw the line between a single major studio and the portfolio of properties of which it is a part and which it owns. As a result, though amorphous, the major studios are massive, multinational, multibillion-dollar corporations with many thousands of employees.

Pros of Working for a Major Studio. The notion of working at a major studio is attractive for many who would like to work with the biggest names on the biggest films. Indeed, a major studio is filled with many different projects, offering a high degree of diversity and energy that is rarely found in any other industry. Salaries at major studios tend to be higher on average than those offered at midsize or small studios, largely because the productions and programs have higher budgets.

Cons of Working for a Major Studio. One of the most challenging aspects of working at a major studio is the high level of competition for each position. Countless people actively pursue employment at major studios and, as a result, those who hold positions there are under heightened pressure to retain their jobs. In addition, actors and other members of the industry working for major studios on large-scale projects have high expectations. In light of these two factors, employees at major studios have very little margin for error during the course of their work.

Organizational Structure and Job Roles

The organizational structure of the motion picture and television industry comprises myriad jobs and responsibilities. Often, many of the facets of a film or television production's development span a plethora of professional trades and industries, in addition to occupations within the film and television industry. Each of these components works as part of an overall organization centered on the production or program being developed.

The following umbrella categories apply to the organizational structure of businesses within the motion picture and television industry:

- Executive Management
- Directing
- Casting
- Acting
- Set Design
- Hair/Makeup/Costume
- Writing
- Special Effects
- Technical Crew
- Postproduction
- Marketing and Advertising
- Representation

Writing

While directors are the ones who ensure that a film develops according to plan, it is the writers who develop the plot, dialogue, and other critical areas of a film or television program's production. Moreover, on many television shows, the show's creators and creative overseers are writers rather than directors. Television directors and writers generally work on some but not all episodes, whereas a show's creators and executive producers provide the overall vision for a series. These leaders are commonly the heads of a show's writing staff.

Writers are often called in on a contract basis when a given script is approved. They then help flesh out any aspects of the screenplay that previously appeared thin or shallow, as well as making any necessary modifications to the story line. Such changes in a film screenplay are generally requested and approved by directors or studio executives.

Writers create scripts that are designed to be filmed. Often, initial ideas for a film or television program lack a great deal of detail, so writers use the limited information available to create characters, dialogue, dramatic situations, and other aspects of the film.

Writers generally receive some form of training in the liberal arts that enables them to focus on creative writing. Some, however, combine theater with writing-centric undergraduate degrees (such as English) in order to focus professionally on script development. Screenwriting is an extremely competitive endeavor, as film and television studios receive countless scripts from writers but choose only a few for production.

Writing occupations may include the following:
- Teleplay Writer
- Senior Writer
- Screenplay Writer
- Script Supervisor
- Executive Story Editor
- Story Editor
- Staff Writer

Postproduction

Once the initial shooting of a film or television program is completed, the postproduction team reviews the resulting footage, pieces it together, and packages it. Postproduction staff are responsible for finalizing films and television programs and preparing them for distribution or broadcast.

Postproduction personnel must be very detail oriented, with a keen eye for ensuring that films are as perfectly shot and assembled as possible. Film editing, sound mixing, and other technical processes are managed by postproduction teams, who ensure that films are well constructed. Many postproduction professionals are college-educated in liberal arts programs.

Postproduction occupations may include the following:
- Story Post Producer
- Assistant Editor
- Editor
- Digital Media Technician
- Sound Mixer

Marketing and Advertising

The commercial success of a film or television program depends heavily on the efforts of marketing, advertising, and other public relations professionals. Marketing and advertising personnel spread the word about a film's impending release in order to generate interest among potential viewers. Marketing campaigns may involve trailers (short advertising programs promoting films), viral marketing (clips and advertisements distributed on the internet in such a fashion as to encourage people to spread the material to their friends via e-mail and social networking resources), and actor appearances in the media. Some marketing departments may also oversee distribution. In the case of the motion picture industry, that entails ensuring that films are shown in theaters with strong potential returns.

Marketing and advertising personnel tend to have undergraduate or advanced degrees in business and marketing. They must also have a strong understanding of the film industry and media outlets and how they operate. In addition to their work on behalf of individual productions, marketing personnel create campaigns to promote entire studios.

Marketing and advertising occupations may include the following:
* Marketing Director
* Marketing Manager
* Promotions Director
* Advertising Manager
* Distributor
* Intern

Outlook

The motion picture and television industry has undergone a dramatic evolution since its roots were laid near the end of the nineteenth century. The rate of change over the course of the twentieth century was driven by the strong desire of viewers and audiences for new experiences to entertain them. The Lumières' footage of an oncoming train thrilled audiences, as did the "magic" of special effects a few years later. In 1933, audiences were mesmerized at the giant gorilla brought to life and interacting with real-life characters in *King Kong*, and in 1956 special effects icon Ray Harryhausen created an army of skeletal warriors to battle humans in *Jason and the Argonauts* in a scene that took special effects to an entirely new level.

Special effects are not the only aspects of motion picture and television entertainment that have evolved over the course of the industry's history. Revolutionary storylines, plots, and characters have contributed to both areas' respective and rapid growth. Hollywood and other industry centers continue to see high volumes of incoming candidates offering screenplays and acting talent; still others arrive looking for any sort of work on a film or television production. The industry continues to produce a great deal of content, spanning all genres and budget parameters. It is expected that this ongoing operational growth will continue as video distribution channels and technologies multiply.

There are two issues, however, that will likely create a change within the industry. The first is the international development of the industry—no longer are places such as Hollywood the epicenter of the film and television world. Instead, studios are being constructed around the United States, a thriving Canadian studio industry continues to grow, and European and Asian industries are also seeing growth. This trend will most likely draw business away from traditional production centers such as Southern California and redistribute it (and its revenues) around the world. This trend will also probably increase inter-studio competition, as newer studios outside Hollywood are constructed in response to large tax incentives, enabling them to produce films with significantly lower budgets. The rapid growth of so-called independent films provides evidence of this trend, changing the landscape of the industry.

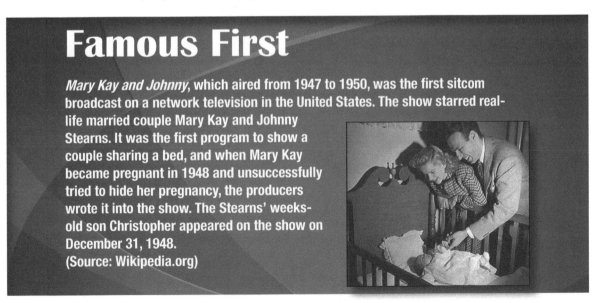

Famous First

Mary Kay and Johnny, which aired from 1947 to 1950, was the first sitcom broadcast on a network television in the United States. The show starred real-life married couple Mary Kay and Johnny Stearns. It was the first program to show a couple sharing a bed, and when Mary Kay became pregnant in 1948 and unsuccessfully tried to hide her pregnancy, the producers wrote it into the show. The Stearns' weeks-old son Christopher appeared on the show on December 31, 1948.
(Source: Wikipedia.org)

The second issue that continues to arise is piracy. Illegally obtained films and television programs are receiving increasing circulation (largely in less developed countries in Asia and the former Soviet Union). The revenues generated from the sale of these pirated recordings have a significant impact on the industry, costing jobs and future revenues.

New technologies for producing and distributing content have boosted the television, video, and film industry. Programming from outlets such as Amazon, Netflix, Apple, and Disney+ are increasing opportunities for all who work in the field.

Michael P. Auerbach/Editor

MUSEUMS AND CULTURAL INSTITUTIONS INDUSTRY

Snapshot

General Industry: Arts and Entertainment

Career Cluster: Arts, A/V Technology, and Communication

Subcategory Industries: Aquariums; Art Museums; Botanical Gardens; Halls of Fame; Historical Museums; Historical Ships; Historical Sites; Military Museums; Natural History Museums; Nature Parks; Nature Preserves; Nonretail Art Galleries; Observatories; Science and Technology Museums; Sculpture Gardens; Zoos

Related Industries: Libraries and Archives Industry; Outdoor Recreation Industry; Philanthropic, Charitable, Religious, Civic, and Grant-Making Industry; Themed Entertainment Industry; Travel and Tourism Industry

Summary

Historical, military, science, wax and art museums, galleries, and other cultural institutions are engaged in the preservation and exhibition of objects of historical, cultural and educational value. Many public museums make these items available for public viewing through exhibits that may be permanent or temporary. Museums have varying aims, ranging from serving researchers and specialists to serving the general public.

The American Association of Museums (AAM) defines a museum as

> an organized and permanent non-profit institution, essentially educational or aesthetic in purpose, with professional staff, which owns and utilizes tangible objects, cares for them, and exhibits them to the public on some regular schedule.

These definitions are also applicable to similar institutions, such as nonprofit art galleries, historical societies, zoos, and aquariums.

History of the Industry

The institution of the museum as a place of cultural significance finds its roots in the classical world. Ancient Greece and Rome constructed and valued various "musaeums" or "mouseions" (places of music or poetry)—the Museum at Alexandria being perhaps the most famous. Though these early cultural institutions were largely centers of philosophical thought rather than repositories of valuable objects, the ancient world still had public collections of objects that resembled the modern concept of a museum. Greek temples and Roman forums, for example, often displayed gold and silver offerings, sculptures, and paintings.

During the Middle Ages, churches and other religious institutions throughout Europe acted as cultural repositories, collecting vast numbers of religious artworks and manuscripts. During the fifteenth century, the more modern concept of museums came into fashion in Europe. Over the following few centuries, museums such as the Ashmolean Museum of Art and Archaeology, in Oxford, England; the Vatican museums; the British Museum in London; and the Louvre in Paris, France—considered the first art gallery—were founded. The first modern museums began as private collections of wealthy individuals who amassed extensive collections and then exhibited them to the public. These first museums were, however, rarely accessible to all members of the public, catering instead to the upper classes. In addition, though the ancient world is well known for its fantastic gardens, genuine botanical gardens began to appear at universities during the sixteenth and seventeenth centuries in the interest of scientific study.

Until the eighteenth century, museums were chiefly concerned with collecting the beautiful and the curious, and their collections were often motivated by personal interests. During the nineteenth and twentieth centuries, however, museums, cultural institutions, and public art galleries grew rapidly throughout Europe and the United States. It was during this intense period of proliferation that the concept of the museum as something more than just a storehouse for invaluable treasures was developed. Museums began to dedicate themselves to conservation, preservation, and, most important, research. Natural history, science, and art museums became scholarly centers of academic research and thought. Once museums and other cultural institutions became public, exhibition became a much more central concern. Prior museum goals, such as collection, conservation, and preservation, suddenly became the means to procure interesting and desirable exhibitions.

Museums developed slowly in the United States. American painter and naturalist Charles Wilson Peale founded a natural history museum in the late eighteenth century in Philadelphia. He is considered the first great American museum director. In 1846, James Smithson, a British scientist, made a bequest to the United States "for the increase and diffusion of knowledge" that led to the development of the Smithsonian Institution. In its formative years, however, the Smithsonian remained devoted to research; it was not until 1873 that it widened its scope to include all areas of the arts and humanities. The United States finally made its mark on the development of the modern museum in 1870, with the founding of the American Museum of Natural History (AMNH) and the Metropolitan Museum of Art in New York, as well as the Museum of Fine Arts in Boston.

The influence and spread of the automobile also led to museums, historical sites, and cultural institutions being located outside major cities. Historic homes, battlefields, and other such sites became more popular, and sites that were maintained and opened for the public became more widespread. Throughout the twentieth century, museums and other cultural institutions began to focus on education. American museums, especially, became devoted to public education. Many such organizations also transformed themselves into cultural centers with performing arts, music, and film presentations.

The Industry Today

An AAM survey identified four critical challenges that museums will face over the coming years: obtaining increased public funding rather than relying on private funds and benefactors; adapting to changes in technology, including new educational technologies, while still maintaining current museum practices and standards; developing new leaders, particularly among recent graduates and young professionals; and maintaining their relevance in the face of rapid social and cultural change. Though the industry is predicted to rise, it still faces considerable challenges in the face of the changing cultural landscape. Whereas museums were once regarded as warehouses of knowledge and shrines to specific aspects of history or culture, they have come under fire as outdated, stale buildings devoted to antiquated ways of thinking. In response, many cultural institutions have dedicated themselves to updating their exhibitions, expanding their collections and gift shops, and refining and publicizing their research. They have attempted to become more accessible through alternative approaches, such as mobile and online exhibits, as well as adopting educational programs for adults and children alike, including guided tours, demonstrations, lectures, and study groups.

Germain Bazin (1901-1990), former chief curator of the Louvre, once commented,

> Perhaps the most significant contribution America has made to the concept of the museum is in the field of education. It is common practice for a museum to offer lectures and concerts, show films, circulate exhibitions, publish important works of art. The museum has metamorphosed into a university for the general public—an institution of learning and enjoyment for all men. The concept has come full circle. The museum of the future will more and more resemble the academy of learning the "mouseion" connoted for the Greeks.

There are more than 35,000 museums in the United States; many offer free admission to the public. Rather than dusty storehouses of artifacts, these organizations have evolved into vital cultural institutions that strive to reach a wider population. They extend to classrooms, theaters, cinemas, performance halls, and the internet. As they continue to evolve and adapt to the changing interests and habits of their visitors, museums have never been more exciting.

Small Institutions
Museums may be classified as small if they have annual operating budgets of less than $250,000. Small institutions are commonly staffed

by volunteers and generally have only two or three full-time paid employees. Many small organizations target specific communities or neighborhoods, serve local interests, and represent local and regional cultures and communities. With the rise of the internet and digital access to collections and exhibitions, very small museums have been able to grow and reach a larger clientele that lives outside their immediate physical area.

An example of a small institution might be a historic home. The significance of such homes is intensely local; for example, one may have belonged to the founder of a small community, or it may have been the home or office of a local official who later went on to greater prominence. Staff might include only one or two full-time employees responsible for administration, maintenance, exhibitions, and visitor interaction. Curators or managers of small museums are generally experts in the relevant focus of the museum. They are in daily contact with visitors, becoming their institutions' primary educators. Volunteers may be involved in tours, interactive experiences, reenactments, and collections management.

Pros of Working for a Small Museum. Small institutions explore themes and topics of local relevance that are typically overlooked at larger institutions. This local relevance combined with a high level of staff-visitor interaction provides curators with the freedom to be more responsive to their communities' needs and interests. Collections and exhibitions at small institutions are usually immediately accessible, so visitors need not experience long waits. Such museums, then, can provide intimate visitor experiences unmatched at larger institutions. Volunteers at small museums tend to be committed and supportive, and both volunteers and staff enjoy relative freedom from bureaucracy.

Cons of Working for a Small Museum. The staff of a small museum or cultural institution often has a plethora of responsibilities, including collections management, conservation, exhibit design, administration, grounds maintenance, and facilities oversight. Budgets are usually small and tight, with no funds allocated for professional development or training. This means that staff members rarely have the opportunity to attend professional conferences or training sessions. Little time and few resources are spent on experimentation and collaboration. Small institutions tend to be undervalued in the wider industry, and board members tend to be unaware of protocols and procedures.

Midsize Institutions

Museums may be classified as midsize if they have annual operating budgets of between $250,000 and $1 million. Midsize institutions have many more people on staff than do small institutions, but they still rely heavily on volunteer support for various job responsibilities. Like small institutions, many midsize organizations target specific communities or neighborhoods, serve local interests, and represent local and regional cultures and communities. However, midsize museums and cultural institutions also serve wider audiences with broader interest bases. Many such organizations are able to compete with larger institutions for visitors, publicity, and funding.

An example of a midsize institution might be a state natural history museum. While such a museum's exhibitions and research focus on subjects of general interest and significance, they usually have a local or regional flavor. For example, the museum might mount an exhibit of North American mammals (general interest) found in the North Carolina Piedmont (regional interest). Staff would include a full roster of museum professionals, including administrators, maintenance crew, exhibition designers, and visitor-services staff. Many midsize institutions have reciprocal membership agreements with partner museums, so paying members of one museum enjoy membership privileges at the museum's partners as well. Such a partnering group may include institutions of similar size or focus located in different regions, or it may include a set of nearby cultural institutions within the same region.

Pros of Working for a Midsize Museum. Midsize institutions explore themes and topics of regional and national relevance that are typically glossed over at larger institutions. Staff members have the opportunity for more specialized positions, with the ability to focus on specific topics. The collections and exhibitions are also more accessible than at larger organizations. With larger budgets, larger membership, and wider publicity than small museums or cultural institutions, staff can afford more experimentation and collaboration in their work. There is also a greater possibility of career advancement; because of their larger budgets and wider renown, midsize institutions often have more qualified candidates for vacancies, and they are able to benefit from the skills, training, experience, and vision that such individuals bring to their work.

Cons of Working for a Midsize Museum. Some staff members at midsize institutions have a wide range of responsibilities, including collections management, registration, and conservation. Although budgets are significantly higher than at small institutions, they still remain tight in certain respects. While funds may be reserved for professional development, these are rarely sufficient to provide opportunities for all staff members. Many times, only those in supervisory roles receive training or attend conferences. Salaries and benefit packages also tend to be lower than they are at large institutions. While education and arts programs are offered, they tend to be individual events. Budgets are rarely large enough for the wide spectrum of rich programming found at large organizations.

Large Institutions

Museums may be classified as large if they have annual operating budgets of more than $1 million. Large institutions have many people on staff, and they typically offer volunteer positions for students interested in learning more about museum studies or about the particular focus of the institution. Large museums and cultural institutions serve extensive audiences with broad interest bases. They typically are founded on wide-reaching topics, such as natural history, American art, or African American culture. Many such organizations command significant visitorship, membership, publicity, and funding.

An example of a large institution might be an established zoo, such as the San Diego or Philadelphia zoos. Exhibitions and research at a municipal zoo target subjects of general interest and usually of national or international significance, such as wildlife conservation and the protection of natural habitats. The staff of any large institution includes a full roster of professionals, including such employees as administrators, maintenance crew, exhibition designers, conservation specialists, veterinarians, and visitor services staff. Visitors enjoy a wide range of opportunities, including permanent exhibitions, temporary exhibitions, education programs, arts programs, family events, travel opportunities, special holiday events, several museum shops, and several cafeterias or restaurants. Visitors may participate in robust membership programs that include many incentives.

Pros of Working for a Large Museum. Large institutions explore themes and topics of national and international relevance that simply cannot be covered in depth at smaller institutions. Staff members have the opportunity to occupy more specialized positions and focus on specific topics. Younger staff members also benefit from their proximity to senior professionals with significant knowledge and experience. With large budgets and membership, as well as wide publicity, staff can afford significant experimentation and collaboration in their work. Large institutional budgets also enhance program planning, exhibition design, and education programs.

Generally, large museums' budgets almost always have funds set aside for professional development and training. As a result of this funding, as well as of their larger and more hierarchically organized staffs, these institutions provide significant opportunities for career advancement. Because of their large budgets and wide renown, large institutions often receive applications from the most qualified candidates for vacancies, and they are able to benefit from the skills, training, experience, and vision that such individuals bring to their work. Salaries and benefit packages also tend to be among the most competitive available.

Cons of Working for a Large Museum. Because of their size and popularity, large institutions cannot offer the intimate, personal visitor experience that smaller institutions can. Exhibitions are typically conceived, planned, and implemented based on staff research interests, current events, or prevailing trends in the industry, rather than visitor feedback or the unique and specific interests of the local community. Many large institutions have such large collections that only a fraction can be displayed at any one time, thereby keeping a majority of the collection unknown to the general public. Staff members tend to become isolated within their departments, and interaction with other divisions (for example, between the collections and education departments) can be rare or limited.

Organizational Structure and Job Roles

Any size museum or cultural institution needs to account for activities in the following areas. In smaller institutions, one person generally holds several roles within several groups. In larger organizations, specialists fulfill unique requirements in specific groups. Regardless of size and scope, the functions must be fulfilled.

The following umbrella categories apply to the organizational structure of museums and cultural institutions:
- Business Management
- Education and Programming
- Collections and Registration
- Visitor Services
- Exhibitions
- Sales and Marketing
- Development
- Human Resources
- Libraries and Archives
- Facilities and Security

Education and Programming

Education and programming staff are responsible for the educational initiatives of an institution. They develop and teach classes for children and adults, organize outreach programs to local schools and community centers, program special events, and schedule and promote performing arts presentations, film screenings, and lectures. They are also responsible for recruiting and managing volunteers and docents.

Education and programming staff usually have advanced degrees in education or communications. They typically receive salaries that are on par with those of other nonadministrative staff at their institutions. In addition to programmatic responsibilities, individuals in education and programming roles coordinate relationships with local schools, community centers, parent groups, and special events vendors.

Education and programming occupations may include the following:
- Public Programming Director
- Special Events Director
- Education Curator
- Education Specialist
- Volunteer Coordinator

Collections and Registration

Collections and registration staff manage and preserve their institutions' collections and govern access to them. They ensure the proper care and handling of the objects in collections, including three-dimensional, multimedia, and document collections. These staff members store objects, register them in an institution's collections database, manage and track their documentation and provenance, package and ship them, and arrange access to them for researchers and scholars.

Collections staff usually have advanced degrees in art history or museum studies. They typically receive salaries that are on par with those of other nonadministrative staff at their institutions. Conservators have additional responsibilities to care for and conserve delicate or damaged objects. Many professional conservators tend to specialize—for example, in paper, textile, wood, art, or film conservation.

Collections and registration occupations may include the following:
- Collections Curator
- Collections Manager
- Registrar
- Conservator
- Museum Technician

Exhibitions

Exhibitions staff design and construct exhibits. They plan and design new exhibits, then construct and produce exhibit spaces, displays, and supporting materials. They must plan electric wiring and lighting for exhibits, as well as designing or commissioning the security devices and procedures necessary to protect fragile or valuable objects from damage or theft. They are also responsible for security and maintenance of existing and permanent exhibits.

Exhibitions staff members may or may not have advanced degrees, but they typically have either degrees or experience in design, architecture, or carpentry. They typically receive salaries on par with, or slightly lower than, those of other nonadministrative employees of their institutions. They often work with their hands, using power tools and construction equipment to engineer, design, and build unique exhibits. They must coordinate their activities with their collections and facilities departments, as well as with relevant external vendors.

Exhibitions occupations may include the following:
- Exhibitions Curator
- Exhibit Designer

- Electrician
- Lighting Technician

Sales and Marketing

Sales and marketing staff manage publicity for their institutions. They publicize and market temporary and permanent exhibits, special events, and institutions' broader social and cultural objectives. Their responsibilities include managing museum stores, conducting promotional campaigns to build membership and attendance, and publicizing their institutions' social, educational, and humanitarian efforts in order to build their brands and reputations. They must build relationships with news agencies, advertising agencies, and retail-store suppliers in the service of their organizations.

Sales and marketing staff members usually have advanced degrees in journalism, communications, or marketing. They typically earn salaries that are on par with those of other nonadministrative employees of their institutions.

Sales and marketing occupations may include the following:
- Retail Store Manager
- Retail Sales Associate
- Public Relations Director
- Marketing Manager
- Graphic Designer

Development

Development staff raise money for their institutions by cultivating and retaining members and by mounting fund-raising campaigns. They coordinate and implement initiatives to attract new members, organize membership benefit programs, identify potential donors, and organize and implement fund-raising efforts. They must coordinate relationships with charitable organizations and relevant foundations, as well as individual members. They may or may not have advanced degrees and typically earn salaries that are on par with those of other nonadministrative employees of their institutions.

Development occupations may include the following:
- Membership Coordinator
- Fund-Raising Coordinator
- Director of Planned Giving

Libraries and Archives

Librarians and archivists organize and manage their institutions'
public libraries and internal archives. They acquire new materials,
update and maintain internal databases, lend materials to researchers
and general patrons, and organize and maintain internal records
related to their archives. They coordinate relationships with libraries
and archives at similar institutions, as well as with publishers
and other staff members. They typically have advanced degrees in
library science and earn salaries that are on par with those of other
nonadministrative employees of their institutions.

Library and archive occupations may include the following:
- Librarian
- Archivist

Outlook

According to the BLS, faster-than-average growth is expected in
the museum industry, with employment expected to increase by
approximately 9 percent through 2028. In addition, the National
Employment Matrix projects employment for curators, archivists, and
museum technicians to increase from 35,000 positions nationwide in
2018 to 39,200 positions in 2026. Occupational employment statistics
indicate that the median hourly wages and annual salaries for these

Famous First

On August 10, 1846, the United States Congress passed legislation founding
the Smithsonian Institution as an establishment dedicated to the "increase
and diffusion of knowledge," and President James K. Polk signed it into law
the same day. This legislation was the culmination of over a decade of debate
within the Congress, and among the general public, over an unusual bequest.
When the English chemist and mineralogist, James Smithson, died in 1829, he
left a will stating that if his nephew and sole heir died without heirs, his estate
should go to the United States "to found
at Washington, under the name of the
Smithsonian Institution, an establishment
for the increase and diffusion of knowledge
among men."
(Source: https://siarchives.si.edu)

positions are also on the rise. A growing interest in establishing and maintaining museum collections, in preserving the growing volume of records and information, and in exhibiting various collections publicly are all contributing factors to this growth.

However, competition for museum positions is, and will continue to be, high. As more people choose to pursue museum studies as a career option, the number of qualified candidates will continue to outnumber vacancies. Students who establish themselves in a more competitive position tend to hold advanced degrees and have a keen ability to work in a digital environment. This is particularly true as cultural institutions are increasingly making their collections available online and offering education opportunities and exhibits on the internet and in other digital forms. (Digital media and skills are equally relevant and in demand in the for-profit art industry.)

Many museums and cultural institutions are highly dependent on outside funding to continue their operations. Budgets are largely based on fund-raising efforts, grant acquisition, and membership support, and museums generally generate revenue based on earned income, membership, and philanthropy. As a result, job security and institutional budgets can fluctuate with periods of strong and weak national economic growth. The number of visitors is also influenced by trends in the wider travel and tourism industries. When tourism is on the rise, museum visitorship and membership also increase. When tourism is on the decline, museums and other cultural institutions have fewer visitors, fewer members, and smaller funds from external sources.

Jamie Greene/Editor

MUSIC INDUSTRY

Snapshot

General Industry: Arts and Entertainment

Career Cluster: Arts, A/V Technology, and Communication

Subcategory Industries: Instrument Manufacturing and Repair Industry; Integrated Record Production/ Distribution; Music Arrangers; Music Directors; Music Publishers; Musical Groups and Artists; Musical Performance Organizers and Promoters; Sound Recording Industries

Related Industries: Broadcast Industry; Internet and Cyber Communications Industry; Motion Picture and Television Industry; Publishing and Information Industry; Retail Trade and Service Industry; Theater and Performing Arts Industry

Summary

The music industry encompasses multiple and diverse for-profit and nonprofit businesses that provide live and recorded music to listeners. Although the sound recording segment makes up a large share of the industry, concerts, music publishing and licensing, artist management, and fine arts outlets such as symphony orchestras all play important roles in the field. Industry products include both tangible goods, such as compact discs (CDs) and digital video discs (DVDs), and intangible products, such as electronic music files and concert performances. Musicians also rely on products and services supplied by the musical instrument manufacturing and repair industries, while listeners

obtain physical or electronic recordings through the music retail industry.

History of the Industry

Although people have written and performed music for entertainment and cultural reasons for millennia, today's commercial music industry dates back only to the sheet music and concert industries of the 1700s. For over a century, music listeners consumed popular music exclusively through live performances. Musicians and singers performed at public venues or were hired to appear in private homes, and amateurs relied on printed sheet music to learn and play popular songs.

By the early twentieth century, the invention of the phonograph had changed the music industry dramatically. Standardized discs called records could hold about four-and-a-half minutes of recorded sound, and the sound recording industry had already begun to emerge. The first record companies, known as record labels, issued recordings of classical and popular music. New labels thrived during World War I, but the popularization of radio, which brought music and other programming to a wider audience, had a negative impact on the early record business during the 1920s. In 1931, two early record companies combined to form EMI, beginning a long history of mergers and acquisitions within the industry.

During the 1940s, technological innovations brought the first tape recording, and the perfection of polyvinyl chloride (PVC) led to the development of the familiar vinyl album. Magnetic tape cartridges—first commercially available as eight-track tapes—proved to be a major addition to the industry, allowing many new recording studios to appear throughout the world. For the first time, serious efforts to record lesser-known music began, widely expanding the available catalog of recorded music.

Although the 1950s had begun with only five major record labels, the success of rock-and-roll music during that decade encouraged a spate of new, independent imprints dedicated to the emerging genre. Shifting consumer tastes were influenced by the increasing popularity of rock, particularly after the British Invasion of 1964. Demand for the singer-songwriter-driven sounds of previous decades declined. Instead, music became a force for social protest and change. Cassette tape recording techniques improved, and the format grew in popularity and availability throughout the 1970s. Airwaves offered new sounds such as rock and funk and, later, disco and punk to avid music listeners.

During the 1980s, the dual emergence of Sony's Walkman, a portable personal tape player, and the cable television network MTV contributed to a musical revolution. Music videos became a vital promotional tool for artists—to the extent that the premieres of videos by artists such as Michael Jackson, marketed as "world premiere video" events, became cultural touchstones. Music became mobile for the first time with the Walkman, and the cassette tape enjoyed a brief heyday as the dominant musical format stretching from the late 1970s into the next decade.

The CD emerged as the dominant music format by the beginning of the 1990s, all but replacing the vinyl albums. (Vinyl sales, propelled by both their nostaligic appeal and accurate sound, have increased to 9.7 million album sales in 2018, accounting for 13.7% of all physical sales.) By the end of the century, the rise of the internet had provided listeners with a new source of recorded music: digital music. Today, streaming music services including iTunes, Amazon Music, Apple Music, Sirius, and Spotify are a significant source of revenue for the industry.

Record companies and trade organizations have acted vigorously to halt the flow of illegally downloaded music since the early 2000s, and within a few years, legitimately purchased downloads began to steadily increase. By 2019, digital music sales had grown to encompass about three-fourths of all global music purchases, according to statistics gathered by the International Federation of the Phonographic Industry (IFPI). This trend was even more pronounced in the United States, where digital sources represented about one-third of total sales. R&B/hip-hop music is the most popular genre by far, trailed closely by rock, country and western, respectively.

Small Businesses
Small businesses make up an important segment of the music industry. Nearly any type of business that can exist in the industry is represented in the small business segment. These businesses may

be as small as one person—such as a solo musician, talent manager, agent, or music retailer. Other small businesses may be considerably larger, with twenty or twenty-five employees. Small businesses often gain success by focusing on a certain niche, such as retailers selling specialty products—used equipment or CDs, for example—or agents or venues that book acts only in a specific genre of music. Some music retailers have closed their brick-and-mortar operations and conduct their business solely online.

Because of the wide revenue spread between those working part-time in the industry and those who have become widely successful, such as top-earning acts and agents, a small music business may earn practically no money or millions of dollars each year.

Pros of Working for a Small Business. Many people establish small music businesses for the personal satisfaction of being part of the industry. Small-business owners perform a range of job duties and generally have the freedom to make creative decisions, such as what music to perform, what bands to book, or what albums to release. Music industry business owners and staff often attend live performances for free and may work with famous musicians. Artists have the remote chance of achieving great financial success.

Cons of Working for a Small Business. Small-business owners are often sole proprietors, meaning that all the financial risks of their organizations lie with them. Thus, an event such as a lawsuit for copyright infringement could bankrupt not only a record label, but also its owner. Musicians, whether self-employed or on the staff of a small arts organization, often experience extended periods of unemployment between tours or performing arts seasons. Because musicians typically earn the bulk of their income from performances, this can leave them short of cash or forced to seek alternate employment.

In addition, small retailers and independent record stores are often subject to cost-cutting efforts from large labels. For example, in June of 2009, EMI informed its smaller accounts, mostly small and independent stores, that it was no longer selling its products directly to them, instead directing them to third-party distributors, who sell at higher prices.

Midsize Businesses

Midsize companies and businesses generally employ a few hundred employees and have much higher revenues than do small businesses, with some topping half a billion dollars. Examples of companies at this level include record labels, music venues, and large symphony orchestras, as well as regional, independent music-store chains. During the late twentieth and early twenty-first centuries, mergers and buyouts led to many small and midsize companies becoming subsidiaries of larger corporations. Some of these companies continue to operate largely as independent businesses, while others have been more or less completely subsumed by their parent companies.

Pros of Working for a Midsize Business. The greater scope of a midsize business means that jobs are generally more specialized. This specialization may appeal to those business owners who prefer to handle top-level decision making or management rather than deal with the variety of day-to-day concerns that can occupy much of the time of small-business owners. Midsize businesses typically have higher revenues than small businesses and may offer the opportunity for greater profit. With mergers and acquisitions common in the industry, the owner of a midsize business may receive a substantial sum of money for the sale of that business to a larger company.

Cons of Working for a Midsize Business. For a business owner who enjoys working closely with music listeners or having a direct hand in the differing aspects of the organization, the increased structural hierarchy inherent in a midsize business can be a distinct disadvantage. With larger numbers of employees come higher levels of personnel management, a task that not everyone enjoys. Record labels and music retailers of this size face stiff competition from larger companies, which may have greater financial resources, lower overhead costs, and increased product integration.

Large Businesses

The large businesses of the music industry are few but powerful. In the sound recording segment of the industry, three companies garner about 66 percent of the segment's total revenue. Live Nation dominates the performance segment of the industry, with 2017 sales exceeding $10 billion. These revenues are representative of the massive earning potential at the upper tiers of the industry. As of 2019, Universal Music Group remains the largest music business in the world, with branches dedicated to album production and distribution, artist management, music catalogs and publishing, merchandizing, and digital ventures. Such diversified operations contribute to the immense influence exerted on the global music industry by the industry's large businesses. The largest businesses in the music retail industry are typically big-box retailers such as Wal-Mart, Best Buy, and Target, though digital-only retailer Apple has garnered the top spot through the success of its iTunes Store, which offers music and videos available for download.

Pros of Working for a Large Business. Large businesses in the music industry may offer high salaries and the prospect of working with some of the music world's biggest names. The industry's renowned glamour revolves around the artists and executives attached to major labels, and the prestige level of working at these organizations can be high.

Cons of Working for a Large Business. The overall challenges facing the industry have hit large sound recording companies especially hard. Major record labels often invest hundreds of thousands of dollars in developing freshly signed artists through recording sessions, promotion, and tour support; if an artist fails to achieve widespread success, these outlays may never be repaid. Because of their size, large companies may face government scrutiny before being able to complete proposed mergers. The media typically pay greater attention to the problems experienced at these well-known companies than to those of smaller, less prominent music businesses.

Organizational Structure and Job Roles

Although the types of businesses in the music industry vary depending on their particular industry segment, size, and purpose, most of these companies must address organizational needs in each of the following activities. A few specialized firms, such as music publishing businesses, may not maintain operations in each field. Typically, in small businesses, one person juggles responsibilities in more than one of these areas, while in midsize and large businesses, the increased size allows employees to have a greater degree of specialization in their work.

Variations in the specifics of each broad job category exist primarily among music businesses that fill different industry roles rather than among businesses of different sizes. That is, a small record label has an organizational structure more similar to a large record label than to an equally small performance venue. These differences are explained more thoroughly in the descriptions of the relevant individual categories that follow.

The following umbrella categories apply to the organizational structure of businesses in the music industry:

- Creative Services
- Business Management
- Sales and Marketing
- Design, Technology, and Manufacturing
- Facilities and Security
- Production and Operations
- Distribution
- Human Resources/Artist Recruitment

Creative Services

Artists who provide creative services lie at the heart of the music industry. Creative artists may be responsible for any combination of writing, recording, performing, arranging, or conducting music. Musicians and singers typically have some degree of formal training. Some may have only rudimentary instruction acquired through regular schooling, while others may have years of personal instruction and advanced degrees under their belts. Composers, conductors, and arrangers typically pursue highly specialized studies in addition to normal musical training. All creative services workers rely on extensive practice and on-the-job training to maintain and improve their technical skills. Many have skills on more than one instrument or can perform various styles of music.

According to the BLS, about half of all creative artists in the music industry are self-employed. Of those who work regularly part- or full-time, nearly all work for religious or performing arts organizations. Some musicians and other creative artists belong to labor unions, such as the American Federation of Musicians (AFM) or the American Guild of Musical Artists (AGMA).

Although artists are the most important players in the music industry, they typically operate outside of the business structure that exists to support and profit from their work. For example, a rock musician under contract to a specific record label would have little to no involvement with any of that label's business operations. Music directors, however, may be exceptions to this rule. These individuals are typically the head conductors at performing arts organizations and may work closely with an organization's executive director to select musical programming that fulfills both artistic and business goals.

Creative services occupations may include the following:
- Musician
- Singer
- Songwriter
- Composer
- Arranger
- Music Director
- Conductor
- Music Video Director

Sales and Marketing

Sales and marketing are vital to the success of all segments of the music industry. Small and large record labels must have employees or entire departments dedicated to public relations, marketing, promotions, and sales. Music publishers work to place their artists' songs in films, television programs, video games, and commercials. Performing arts organizations and concert promoters market their events to attract listeners and sell tickets.

Public relations workers are responsible for getting their artists, recordings, and events mentioned in publications. They conduct such activities as writing press releases, contacting journalists, setting up photo shoots, and working with media outlets to secure maximum coverage for a given topic. Closely related to public relations are promotional staff, who work to secure radio or television time for artists, songs, or events. Public relations and promotions employees may work in offices or attend events, and they typically have bachelor's degrees in English, journalism, public relations, or mass communications. Similarly, members of the marketing staff help coordinate these efforts, as well as conduct and analyze market research to help create overall marketing plans.

Artists, record labels, and concert promoters may all build street teams, which are groups of individuals who market artists or events by such activities as hanging flyers, collecting marketing lists on college campuses, or handing out promotional materials. Street team members are often college students or other young people trying to break into the music industry.

Sales and marketing occupations may include the following:
- Public Relations Manager
- Marketing Manager
- Public Relations Representative
- Publicist
- Market Research Analyst
- Sales Representative
- Street Team Member

Outlook

The outlook for this industry shows it to be on the rebound after several years of decline. Music industry growth mainly came from the growing popularity of streaming services that charge a relatively small monthly fee, like Spotify and Apple Music's $9.99 a month, in exchange for unlimited access to a massive variety of music.

The BLS projects rapid growth in the overall field of arts, entertainment, and recreation as both the incomes and the leisure time of American workers increase. However, performing arts fields such as music are expected to remain unchanged. This discrepancy is due to significant growth expected in the other portions of the larger industry. For example, people are increasingly expected to choose to spend money on health-club memberships rather than on recorded music. Because of this shift in consumer tastes, the BLS does not anticipate occupational growth for musicians or singers to outpace the average for all jobs. Moreover, music jobs are anticipated to remain highly competitive because many people desire them.

Despite the challenges facing the music industry as consumer consumption habits shift, the industry offers exciting opportunities for those who love music. The few performers who achieve worldwide success can earn huge sums of money in a short period of time, and the possibility—no matter how remote—of achieving fame and fortune attracts many musicians to the field. However, most musicians work part-time for low pay, simply for the satisfaction of playing an instrument or singing before an appreciative audience. Full-time musicians and their support crews often spend much of their time on the road, making the lifestyle attractive to individuals who enjoy visiting new places.

Famous First

The father of modern music printing was Ottaviano Petrucci, a printer and publisher who was able to secure a twenty-year monopoly on printed music in Venice during the 16th century. His first collection was entitled *Harmonice Musices Odhecaton* and contained 96 polyphonic compositions, mostly by Josquin des Prez and Heinrich Isaac. He flourished by focusing on Flemish works, rather than Italian, as they were very popular throughout Europe during the Renaissance. (Source: Wikipedia.org)

The range of jobs available in the music industry is quite diverse, and many positions exist for nonperformers. Students who love music but prefer not to take on the risks or the extensive training that come with being a performer may enjoy working for a record company, publishing company, or performance venue. Such workplaces may also offer opportunities for staff members to meet well-known stars or attend publicized events.

Vanessa E. Vaughn

PHILANTHROPIC, CHARITABLE, RELIGIOUS, CIVIC, AND GRANT-MAKING INDUSTRY

Snapshot

General Industry: Personal Services

Career Cluster: Human Services

Subcategory Industries: Business, Professional, Labor, Political, and Similar Organizations; Civic and Social Organizations; Grant-Making and Giving Services; Religious Organizations; Social Advocacy Organizations

Related Industries: Counseling Services; Higher Education Industry; Libraries and Archives Industry; Museums and Cultural Institutions Industry; Personal Services; Political Advocacy Industry; Public Elementary and Secondary Education Industry

Summary

The philanthropic, charitable, religious, civic, and grant-making industry is not, strictly speaking, an "industry," but a collection of organizations whose purpose is to provide services and that operate on a not-for-profit basis. This industry is diverse enough to include charities, religious institutions, service organizations, and foundations supporting scholarship, but these organizations have several features in common: Their purposes are to promote ideals and causes, not to make money; they are part of both the private sector and the government; and they are dependent on donations of money and goods and on volunteer labor.

History of the Industry

Philanthropic, charitable, religious, civic, and grant-making organizations have had a long, if not always cherished, place in American history and society. Their purposes have both overlapped and varied, but they have all sought a central place in the social and moral life of American society. Although Americans have always prided themselves on a society characterized by voluntarism, the diverse organizations that have both supported and been supported by this voluntarism were not always regarded with favor. Rather, changing political, social, and economic circumstances, along with competing ideas regarding charity and compassion, have had profound effects on their forms and practices. The overlapping role of the government with private organizations has likewise changed throughout history.

The separation of church and state established in the U.S. Constitution firmly placed religious organizations outside the public sector and contributed to the creation of religious-based private social service organizations. It also influenced the establishment of a partial separation of charitable and philanthropic efforts from religion. Despite the resulting American tradition of volunteerism, responsibility for the social commonweal was considered a public effort, and private charitable and social service efforts did not enjoy widespread approval or support until the mid-nineteenth century. The period before the Civil War was one of massive social challenges resulting from urbanization, immigration, and industrialization, and these challenges only accelerated in the postwar decades. In particular, immigration created not only new challenges but also new promise, as newly arrived groups formed their own religious and ethnicity-based social services organizations.

The late nineteenth century, remembered as a period of unregulated industrial growth, was also the period when modern philanthropy was born, as industrialists sought to do good with their fortunes, resulting in the creation of many still existing foundations. Charity and social services, by then increasingly privatized efforts, were undergoing a shift to a "scientific" approach that emphasized determining "worthiness" and promoting "moral uplift." A burgeoning labor movement and its politically Progressive allies shifted the emphasis to a public and governmental responsibility for societal welfare, resulting in the strengthening and reforming of the public sector during the early twentieth century period known as the Progressive Era.

It was not until the Great Depression, however, that the primary role of the private sector for public welfare was seriously challenged. The New Deal, as well as the postwar efforts culminating in the 1960s Great Society, led to the creation of the modern welfare state, as well as of new roles for nonprofits of various descriptions. From the 1960s onward, these nonprofits created a kind of "shadow state" that had significant influence in shaping government policy. This increased public role for nonprofits, however, led to an increasingly close relationship with the government that included not only the support of public money but also greater regulation regarding permissible activities, financial practices, and even compensation for top executives.

The 1980s would bring further changes to the roles and relationship of public and private nonprofit organizations. Increasing political conservatism and conservative religious revivalism led to a denigration of the welfare state, eventual cutting of public welfare, and an increased emphasis on private charity and voluntarism. However, fiscal conservativism and, later, declining revenues led to decreasing financial support for the same private organizations that were expected to play an increased public role. Paradoxically, although religious organizations were traditionally excluded from government support, recent presidential administrations have sought to change that tradition, first through the 1996 Charitable Choice Act and then through the creation of the Office of Faith-Based and Community Initiatives.

The Industry Today

The public and private nonprofit industry today is the only sector of the American economy that is defined by what it is not—namely, that its primary purpose is not the creation of economic profits. It is also more varied in focus and purpose than ever before and covers numerous diverse categories, including government agencies and private organizations created to promote a sometimes intangible social, intellectual, or spiritual public welfare. In many of these areas, there are overlapping roles for public organizations and private agencies. The notable exception has traditionally involved interaction with religious organizations, where government support is more limited. Nonetheless, religious organizations enjoy tax exemption and other privileges similar to those of secular organizations.

The degree and type of political activity and advocacy practiced by all nonprofit organizations can affect (though not necessarily eliminate) their tax-exempt classification. The public and private nonprofit sectors, therefore, closely interact in a variety of ways, to the point that private nonprofits have come to be regarded as the "third sector" of the American economy, alongside government and private, for-profit industry. For all the popular political emphasis on the importance of private charities, philanthropies, and social services, however, government support has remained an integral part of the functioning of this sector, with all but the smallest organizations required to register with the Internal Revenue Service (IRS) and to accept a certain degree of IRS monitoring. In some cases, this has led to increased conservatism in the purposes and services of many private organizations.

In recent years, there has been a noticeable blurring of lines between for-profit and not-for-profit activity, both in the sense that organizations devoted to the services traditionally provided by nonprofits have experienced unprecedented for-profit competition and in the sense that some for-profit enterprises make social action part of their business. These efforts have naturally been a source of controversy, as have the increasingly close partnerships between for-profit enterprise and not-for-profit organizations. Such partnerships lead to concerns regarding whether nonprofits can maintain a vital degree of independence from private industry and remain noncommercialized.

Corporate sponsorship and support has long been a hallmark of many officially not-for-profit institutions, as has corporate participation on governing boards. Along with the mixed blessings of for-profit collaboration with nonprofits, there has been recent controversy over the increased use of administrative and financial practices from the for-profit sector. In particular, there has been a slow eroding of the social stigma and even legal prohibitions against nonprofit executives accepting the payment and perks of their counterparts in the for-profit sector.

It is argued that restrictions on compensation in particular drive the most talented people to choose careers in the for-profit sector rather than in nonprofit or public service. At the lower level, these expectations can mean poor compensation for employees, especially in organizations that rely heavily on volunteer labor. They can sometimes put charitable organizations at odds with living wage campaigns. Among religious organizations, there are a variety of views and practices concerning compensation for institutional employees. Conversely, pay rates for public employment are usually set either directly or indirectly via legislation and may involve labor agreements with collective bargaining units.

Another significant change in the nonprofit sector has been the increasingly universal use of the internet, as well as the increasing use of social networking sites, such as Facebook. Indeed, not only is fund-raising increasingly conducted via the internet, but there is also a small but growing number of legitimate organizations whose presence on the Web greatly outpaces their brick-and-mortar facilities.

Small Organizations
Small organizations in the nonprofit world include local organizations and foundations, as well as local churches, synagogues, and other religious institutions. In the public sector, they may include local government agencies. Though they vary in size and purpose, most remain small-scale, and many private agencies are heavily dependent on volunteer labor.

Pros of Working for a Small Organization. Working in a small nonprofit organization has many advantages, not the least of which is less bureaucratization and more opportunity to work one-to-one with people of different backgrounds and perspectives. There tends to be a closer relationship among the paid staff and boards, as well as with the community, and there may also be more opportunities to work in multiple areas and for direct involvement with clients and donors alike. Finally, for nonprofit entrepreneurs, small organizations may require only low overhead to start.

Cons of Working for a Small Organization. Although working for a small nonprofit organization can bring much personal and professional satisfaction, it may also involve numerous headaches and disadvantages peculiar to small organizations. First, in a smaller, less formal workplace, office politics have the potential to become personal, especially among the often dedicated and idealistic people who choose nonprofit work. Additionally, because idealism is emphasized and budgets may be limited, small organizations may suffer from a limited leadership pool. Although there are possibilities for advancement and specialization within the organization, they may be limited. Smaller organizations also are likely not only to be more dependent on volunteer labor but also to require greater staff deference to volunteer boards. With limited budgets and infrastructures, not only is pay likely to be poor, but the managerial leadership is also likely to be less professional, providing fewer opportunities for professional development and networking to employees. In short, small organizations have all the problems of nonprofit organizations, exacerbated by small size and budget.

Midsize Organizations

Midsize nonprofit organizations are a varied group that can sometimes be more diverse than either small or large organizations. These organizations may be local, regional, or national private entities or government agencies. In the case of religious institutions, they may include both individual congregations and larger religious organizations.

Pros of Working for a Midsize Organization. Working for a midsize nonprofit organization may offer the best of both small and large organizations. Midsize organizations may be more financially and organizationally stable than small organizations and may have fewer problems with excess bureaucracy than large organizations. There may be better compensation, greater career mobility, and greater opportunities for specialization and professional growth than in small organizations. Plus, midsize organizations are more likely than small organizations to offer the satisfaction of name recognition, and, depending on the type of organization, they may offer better financial and professional resources.

Cons of Working for a Midsize Organization. Although midsize nonprofit organizations may on average have greater financial and organizational viability than their small counterparts, they may nonetheless have fewer resources, and therefore be less likely to survive economic downturns, than large organizations. As with midsize for-profit corporations, their ambitions may outpace their available resources, leading to more frustrated and unfulfilled organizational goals. In addition, they may have less professional management than large organizations, and paid staff may be more dependent on volunteer labor and beholden to volunteer boards.

Large Organizations

Large not-for-profit organizations include the big-name national and international charities and foundations. Although they may be the projects of individuals or families, they are more likely to be broad-based organizations whose identities transcend those of individuals and families. They may also be public agencies or subsectors of government departments.

Pros of Working for a Large Organization. Working for a large nonprofit organization offers a variety of opportunities to associate with and enjoy the prestige of a widely recognized organization. For career changers moving from the for-profit to the not-for-profit sector, large organizations may offer the most opportunities for transference of professional skills and, for all professional employees in the nonprofit sector, may offer the best opportunities for specialization, career advancement, professional development, and networking. They may also offer some categories of nonprofit employees the most glamour in terms of opportunities for interaction with prominent individual and corporate donors. Finally, pay and benefits, especially at the top executive level, are more likely to be generous, though not necessarily approaching those offered by the for-profit sector.

Cons of Working for a Large Organization. As with large for-profit organizations, one chief disadvantage of working for large nonprofit organizations or public agencies is greater bureaucracy, with all of its attendant problems, including the sense of being merely a "cog in the machine." There may be less opportunity for direct client and donor interaction than in smaller organizations. Because large organizations are more likely to work closely with for-profit corporate partners, the effects of commercialization may diminish the sense of organizational idealism. Paradoxically, legal restrictions and social stigmas regarding compensation for nonprofit employees may make jobs at these organizations less attractive to those who have the potential to earn much more in the for-profit sector.

Organizational Structure and Job Roles

Although the not-for-profit industry is regarded as almost synonymous with volunteer work and voluntarism, there are numerous professional roles and opportunities available within this sector. Although some opportunities may require skills and training similar to those required in the for-profit world, some may require more specialized preparation. Similarly, while many professional opportunities with not-for-profit organizations may involve more mundane and less glamorous duties than the voluntary opportunities, other nonprofit professional roles may offer unique opportunities to educate, influence, and even inspire. In the case of religious organizations, there may be significant religious requirements, chief among them faith membership, for entry into certain job categories, while for other job categories, religious requirements may be negligible or nonexistent. On the other hand, in some organizations even low-level support staff may be required to subscribe to the organization's culture and mission. In nearly all of these categories, working conditions and compensation may vary widely, sometimes even for the same type of position. Finally, although it is not true for all job categories, for some nonprofit jobs, it is possible to gain entry to paid positions via volunteer work, and in many cases, previous relevant volunteer work may be considered advantageous.

The following umbrella categories apply to the organizational structure of organizations in the philanthropic, charitable, religious, civic, and grant-making industry:
- Management and Administration
- Client and Donor Services
- Public Relations
- Facilities and Security
- Technology, Research, and Development
- Financial and Legal Services
- Education and Spirituality
- Human Resources

Management and Administration
As in the for-profit economy, good administration and management are vital to the successful operation of philanthropic, charitable, civic, and grant-making organizations. There are notable differences, though, between working for these organizations, whether at the high or low levels of administration, and holding similar jobs in the for-profit sector. To begin with, administrators and their support staff

at all levels are required to maintain at least a minimal adherence to the purpose and mission of the organizations they work for and to understand the differences between performance criteria for nonprofit organizations and those of for-profit enterprises. In high-level administrative positions, this may mean working closely with volunteer boards, organizational members and volunteers, spiritual or religious leaders, or some combination. Depending on the type of position and organization, administrative roles may merely involve responsibility for day-to-day management or may require long-term, visionary leadership.

In numerous instances, administrative occupations may require a careful balance of authority and deference to voluntary boards, as well as a focus on the less "glamorous," nuts-and-bolts aspects of nonprofit organizations. Also, depending on the size of the organization's paid staff, administrative occupations may involve multiple and sometimes diverse responsibilities. There are many entry points to administrative careers in this industry, and in many cases, the required skills and background may be easily transferred from the for-profit world. However, compensation is likely to be significantly less than it is for similar positions in the for-profit sector.

Management and administrative occupations may include the following:
- Executive Director/Chief Executive Officer (CEO)
- Chief Operating Officer (COO)
- Program Officer
- Project Director
- Administrative Assistant
- Receptionist

Client and Donor Services
Among philanthropic, charitable, civic, and grant-making organizations, client services are what stand in for customer service in for-profit enterprises, and donor services constitute a relatively unique department. Combined, they form the lifeblood of nonprofit organizations, most of whose purposes are providing services and advancing social causes. For that reason, working in client relations, donor relations, or both requires a broad set of people skills for dealing with diverse populations that, depending on the organization, might even overlap. In both cases, working in either of these sectors may require specialized knowledge pertaining to the type of organization,

and in some instances may require advanced degrees. Additionally, for some organizations, working in either of these sectors may require an awareness of broader class and economic issues and even political trends. For many organizations, it is also important for specialists in this sector to maintain awareness of changing donor and client pools. Occupations within this sector may also involve coordination and supervision of volunteer labor and, in the case of donor relations, may require knowledge of internet and social networking technology. Notably, client and donor services are both areas where it may be possible to gain entry into professional positions via volunteer experience.

Client and donor relations occupations may include the following:
- Development Director
- Event Coordinator
- Program Director
- Project Director
- Fund-Raising Officer
- Case Worker
- Social Worker
- Psychologist

Public Relations
Public relations and publicity are vital to the workings of philanthropic, charitable, religious, civic, and grant-making organizations, as well as to public agencies. Specialists in this sector may engage not only in promoting the organization and its goals but also in creating the public face of the organization and, in some cases, frequently dealing with the press. In addition, for many private not-for-profit organizations, publicity and public relations are vital to successful fund-raising. Finally, the job of public relations specialists in the nonprofit sector is often to manage the brand of the organization they serve.

In some cases, public relations work may overlap with that of other departments, especially client and donor services. As partnerships between nonprofit organizations and for-profit corporations become more common, especially among larger organizations, public relations specialists may find themselves working in ethically and legally dicey areas and may find that one of their most important roles is to maintain a line between promotion and commercialization of their organization and its services. In addition to the appropriate professional education and background, working in public relations for nonprofit organizations is increasingly likely to require knowledge of internet and even social networking technology. In some cases, skills may be transferable for those from for-profit public relations or journalistic backgrounds.

Public relations occupations may include the following:
- Marketing Director
- Assistant Marketing Director
- Publications Specialist
- Webmaster
- Public Relations Executive
- Press Agent
- Public Affairs Specialist
- Press Secretary
- Media Specialist

Technology, Research, and Development

Beyond the grant-making organizations and agencies that specialize in the support of research and development, technology, research, and development is a broadly categorized department within the philanthropic, charitable, religious, civic, and grant-making industry and may include everything from program and project development to development of internet capacity, as well as research in a variety of areas. Research and development is also important to retroactive assessment of the success of nonprofit programming. This department therefore, may require broad-based technological skills, business skills, specialized knowledge pertinent to the organization's mission, or a combination of these skills. Full-time opportunities in this department are most likely to be available in large organizations, whereas smaller organizations may be more likely to rely on part-time and volunteer labor for some functions and outside consultants for others.

Because of the broad-based nature of this department, there are numerous career entry points, and for potential entrants, technological skills may be most easily transferable from the for-profit sector. Research and development are broad categories but frequently involve financial research skills that may be transferable from the for-profit sector, albeit with necessary refocusing. Additionally, private and public nonprofit organizations that specialize in research grants or social services may require more social-science-based research skills, and offer opportunities for skill transference in this case from higher education.

Technology, research, and development occupations may include the following:
- Management Information Systems Director
- Chief Technology Officer (CTO)
- Special Projects Manager
- Development Director
- Webmaster
- Researcher
- Statistician

Education and Spirituality

Although this segment may be pertinent only to certain sectors of the not-for-profit industry, religious and spiritual leaders, along with religious education and sacred music specialists, play vital roles in religious institutions. In most houses of worship, ministers, priests, rabbis, imams, and other spiritual leaders are the recognized heads of the organizations they serve, yet in some cases they also may be regarded as employees, with little difference from other religious institution personnel. Spiritual leaders of all faiths are increasingly likely to be found working in nonprofit settings other than houses of worship, including charitable and educational institutions. They must meet the requirements of their respective faiths, which frequently include formal ordination by the appropriate religious organization. In addition, depending on the size and type of the institution, job description and compensation may vary, notably in that spiritual leaders may also take on educational and even musical roles. In large institutions, they are more likely to be assisted, especially in musical duties, by specialists in the appropriate sacred music or religious education field. Occupations in these areas, therefore, require specialized education and training and frequently (though not universally) membership in the appropriate faith. Most of these occupations may involve some supervisory duties, and some may involve specialized work with children and youth. Nearly all require some weekend work, and in some cases those who practice these occupations may also be members of or participants in the institution they serve.

Education and spirituality occupations may include the following:
- Minister/Priest/Rabbi/Imam

- Chaplain
- Cantor/Cantorial Soloist/Church Soloist
- Organist/Musician
- Music/Choir Director
- Educational Director
- Religious School Teacher

Outlook

The outlook for the philanthropic, charitable, religious, civic, and grant-making industry appears to be stable, even in hard economic times, although the outlook varies among different subsets of the industry. This variation makes the outlook for the nonprofit industry difficult to compare to those of many for-profit industries, particularly given the different ways of measuring success in the two sectors. In practice, this set of interdependencies means that, while there will definitely be an increased need for the services of many kinds of nonprofit organizations, public, private, and corporate funding sources may be less available.

The continued economic and social presence of nonprofit organizations also does not stop at the borders of the United States. A growing number of organizations, especially the larger ones, are or are becoming international in scope and operation, some with the sponsorship, assistance, and even active management of prominent individuals. Beyond these, however, there are numerous nonprofits

Famous First

On December 20, 1965, Vice President Hubert Humphrey presented a check for $100,000, representing the National Endowment for the Arts' first grant, to the American Ballet Theatre. Humphrey, as a Democratic senator from Minnesota, had been a champion of the Arts Endowment's establishment, in tandem with the New York Republican Jacob Javits. The New York Herald Tribune reported: "The Treasury of the United States has saved a national treasure. Not directly, perhaps, but the taxpayers, through the government's recently established National Council on the Arts, saved the American Ballet Theatre from extinction." (Source: https://www.arts.gov)

and NGOs that play important charitable, cultural, economic, and even diplomatic roles on an international and global scale. Notably, in countries that feature more advanced welfare states than the United States, charitable organizations may not be perceived as playing the same essential role, but they nonetheless remain a significant part of national economies. In other parts of the world, there may be sometimes uncomfortable negotiations between international nonprofits and indigenous organizations, especially regarding control of the disbursement of funds and goods. Nonetheless, the success of internationally focused nonprofits and of NGOs both require and promote international cooperation, providing these organizations with an often unacknowledged role in the global economy.

Susan Roth Breitzer

PUBLIC ELEMENTARY AND SECONDARY EDUCATION INDUSTRY

Snapshot

General Industry: Education and Training

Career Cluster: Education and Training

Subcategory Industries: Disabled Education; Elementary School Education; High School Education; Kindergarten Education; Middle School and Junior High School Education

Related Industries: Corporate Education Services; Day-Care Services; Higher Education Industry; Private Education Industry

Summary

The public elementary and secondary education industry exists worldwide and is the cornerstone of most countries' formal education structure, fulfilling a commitment to provide youths with the skills and knowledge necessary for fully functional members of society. Elementary school is the first formal stage of public education, where children are introduced to core skills of literacy and computation, such as reading, writing, and mathematics. Secondary education follows elementary studies and often is split between middle school and high school study levels. Secondary education provides general, technical, and professional curricula and prepares the higher-achieving students for postsecondary, or "higher," education.

History of the Industry

American formal education has its roots in the British educational tradition. The curriculum applied in American public schools is derived from ancient ideas about education, dating back to the philosophies of Plato and Aristotle in the fourth century BCE and to the medieval schools of the Catholic tradition, grounded in Aristotelian philosophy. The fundamental areas of educational concern today match the liberal arts that ancient and medieval scholars believed to be fundamental to the life of the mind and necessary to full human intellectual development.

American secondary education has its origin in the *artes liberales* of the Middle Ages. These comprise the seven liberal arts, which include the *trivium* (grammar, logic or dialectic, and rhetoric) and the *quadrivium* (arithmetic, geometry, astronomy, and music). In the earliest public schools in America, children began their formal education with grammar, considered the "lowliest of the seven arts," and later advanced to the more difficult subjects and ultimately the *quadrivium*. Sometimes religion was added to the curriculum to provide a moral component to the educational agenda. Religious teachings at the elementary level traditionally focused on moral teachings and biblical study.

In the tradition of European schools, which channeled education through grammar schools, gymnasia, and university colleges, the North American system offered grammar schools, academies, and liberal arts colleges. Given the religious component of public education in the United States and the fact that public schools also could be counted on to produce religious professionals such as priests as well as counselors, diplomats, physicians, and teachers, it is hardly surprising that churches were from the outset allied with the government in the sponsorship of secondary education. Families tended to seek the highest available education for their children, as a means of improving the living standards of the family, but it was not until the mid-nineteenth century that Americans began to acknowledge a distinction between secondary and higher education. This distinction marked the beginning of the modern era in education.

In the early 1820s, free urban public high schools emerged in the United States to provide alternatives to Latin grammar schools and other private and fee-charging schools. These schools were fostered with the expectation that the secondary education of the country's youths would promote economic development. The first public high school opened in Boston in 1821. Other major cities in the Northeast soon followed the example; by 1839, twenty-six high schools had been established in Boston, and the trend had spread to Philadelphia and Baltimore. Before long, Latin grammar schools were well established throughout Massachusetts, New York, Pennsylvania, New Jersey, and Maryland. The teachers in these early schools usually were ministers with dedicated teaching missions. These earliest schools were aimed primarily at preparing students to enter colleges, which were strictly for men. By 1851, an estimated eighty cities had established high schools. The curriculum of the Boston schools was typical, encompassing subjects such as English, geography, history, arithmetic, algebra, geometry, trigonometry, navigation, surveying, and natural and moral philosophy.

After the United States gained independence in 1776, new educational movements arose. Most notably, monitorial schools, an educational tradition imported from England, were opened to provide inexpensive general education for the masses. However, these monitorial schools did not last. By 1840, they had all been closed because they had not produced the results to justify their existence. Another educational innovation of the time was the Sunday School, through which churches aimed at providing rudimentary academic and moral education to the poor. Its pioneer, Robert Raikes of Gloucester, wanted to "rescue children of factory workers from their filth, ignorance, and sin." Free School Societies organized and developed monitorial schools, Sunday Schools, and free public schools in Connecticut and New York, and again, the trend soon spread to other areas of the country.

The Industry Today

Total enrollment in public and private elementary and secondary schools (prekindergarten through grade 12) grew rapidly during the 1950s and 1960s, reaching a peak year in 1971. This enrollment rise reflected what is known as the "baby boom," a dramatic increase in births following World War II. Between 1971 and 1984, total elementary and secondary school enrollment decreased every year, reflecting the decline in the size of the school-age population over that period. After these years of decline, enrollment in elementary and secondary schools started increasing in fall 1985, began hitting new record levels in the mid-1990s, and continued to reach new record levels every year through 2006, after which enrollment declined slightly from its 2006 level. However, in fall 2013 (55.4 million) through fall 2015 (56.2 million) were higher than the fall 2006 record level of 55.3 million. A pattern of annual enrollment increases is projected to continue at least through fall 2027 (the last year for which NCES has projected school enrollment). Total elementary and secondary enrollment is projected to increase 3 percent between fall 2017 and fall 2027, when enrollment is expected to reach 58.2 million.

Between 1985 and 2007, enrollment in public elementary and secondary schools rose by 26 percent, with the fastest growth occurring in elementary levels (prekindergarten through eighth grade). This increase was matched by an increase in teachers; in 2016, the number of full-time teachers was 3.2 million. Another important development in modern American schools is their initiation into the electronic age. The number of computers in public schools has increased dramatically in recent years. In 2018, the 85 percent of public schools had the internet. Almost all schools had computers in 2019, and the average ratio of students to computers is about 10 to 1. The average ratio of students to multimedia computers is 24 to 1.

The structure, administration, and curricula in American schools evolve with changing times and societal needs. Teachers are increasingly becoming specialized experts in their fields, especially in the subject areas of art, speech correction, and counseling, among others. Public schools also are being used as a venue for addressing diverse societal problems, such as poverty and child hunger. Programs that provide federally subsidized or free lunches are available in most public schools. Furthermore, a great variety of extracurricular activities have been introduced in the majority of elementary and secondary schools.

Small Schools
This sector includes traditionally small public schools ranging from elementary to high school. Charter schools, which are supported by public funds, fall in this category. Currently there are few definitive research definitions of a "small" school; typically, they are defined variously by each state based on the number of students in the school. For example, in Chicago, small schools are those having fewer than four hundred students. The number of supervisors and faculty are concomitantly low, with one to two administrators and five to eight faculty members.

Pros of Working for a Small School. Small schools enhance the capacity for interpersonal relations among students and between staff and students. Small class sizes allow teachers to pay more individual attention to students. Smaller schools encourage stronger bonds among principals, teachers, students, and parents, and promote a level of mutual caring that is often lacking in larger schools. In small schools, students tend to demonstrate healthier attitudes toward school, and they have higher attendance rates. Students in small schools often report feeling safer and more secure, partially because the smaller environment replicates the more intimate conditions of home and community life. Moreover, smaller schools tend to command a higher level of parent and community involvement. In the best cases, parents and teachers become allies in fostering students' academic achievement. Local businesses and community organizations also find it easier to collaborate with small schools, providing internships and other collaborative projects. In smaller schools, teachers more often report positive teacher working conditions and greater job satisfaction.

Cons of Working for a Small School. Small schools have greater restrictions on budget and fewer faculty and thus must limit their study offerings to a constricted curriculum, often offering only academic courses geared to the midlevel student, with few opportunities to tailor their programs or curricula to meet the special needs of their gifted or academically challenged students. Often, courses such as music and art must be cut and services for students with disabilities are limited or lacking. Because the staff is limited, each will take on multiple roles. For instance, some teachers may be required to take on administrative duties, serve on school committees, and administer extracurricular activities. Resources and technical assistance are often limited or lacking at small schools.

Midsize Schools

Midsize schools are determined by the number of students enrolled, although the designation varies by each region. For example, Telecommunication Arts High School in Brooklyn, whose enrollment of 1,250 students and 80 teachers would make it a large school in most cities, is considered a midsize school by New York standards. Typically, schools that are considered midsize have between 500 and 900 students and 50 to 100 employees.

Pros of Working for a Midsize School. While small schools might have limited staff, such as only one special education teacher, midsize schools have extensive programs and adequate personnel to cater to a diverse student population. For example, Telecommunication Arts High School in New York has fifteen full-time special education teachers, an on-site staff psychologist, an assistant principal in charge of budgets and security, and services such as occupational and physical therapy for disabled students as of 2010. Foreign-language classes, Advanced Placement courses, and other programs typically lacking in small schools are available in midsize schools. Midsize high schools have much higher graduation rates than large high schools. A 2010 analysis conducted by Center for New York City Affairs concluded that "on average, the city's forty high schools with enrollments between six hundred and fourteen hundred are just as good as or better than smaller schools in terms of graduation rates, attendance and the ability to serve struggling students."

Cons of Working for a Midsize School. Many midsize schools are located in poor, inner-city areas and tend to be underfunded in comparison with larger schools. In 2005, the Kansas Supreme Court ordered the state to spend $285 million more on schools after midsize school districts sued the state for underfunding. Another challenge that midsize schools face is the limited interaction between teachers and students and their parents. Teachers do not get to know all their students well because of the greater student population. Also, not all students know one another in a midsize school.

Large Schools
Typically, large public schools have student populations of more than 900. While some large schools are found at the elementary level, most schools in this class are high schools. The number of teaching staff and other employees varies accordingly, usually between 150 and 250.

Pros of Working for a Large School. Large schools provide a more vibrant school atmosphere. Many of these schools are found in larger cities where they attract students from diverse backgrounds. Large schools provide more academic clubs, after-school programs, special education programs, foreign-language classes, and a host of extracurricular activities. Large schools, especially those in the wealthy neighborhoods, often are well equipped with advanced technology.

Cons of Working for a Large School. Larger schools tend to have larger classes, which in turn affect the degree of interaction and teacher attention that can be afforded to each student. Because of large student populations, some students are likely to miss out on opportunities to develop their leadership skills and participate in school activities. In view of this, students may feel overlooked and less motivated. Safety issues often are a challenge in these large schools as well. The sheer complexity of a large institution, with its vast physical property and myriad working parts, can prove extremely difficult to manage and monitor safely.

Organizational Structure and Job Roles

The organizational structure and jobs roles of elementary and secondary schools are determined by the size and needs of the individual schools. Specific job titles and descriptions vary by district and state. While public schools do have some leeway to affect decision-making, they do not exist as autonomous entities but operate under the supervision of district and state-level administrations.

The following umbrella categories apply to the organizational structure of small, medium, and large elementary and secondary schools:
- District-Level Administration
- School-Based Administration
- Licensed Instructional Faculty
- Student Support Services (Licensed)
- Administrative Support
- Media and Technology Specialists
- Paraprofessionals
- Bus Drivers
- Maintenance and Custodial Services
- School Nutrition

District-Level Administration
District-level administration provides supervision of schools and support with services related to academics, transportation, discipline, technology, safety, finance, facilities, and health and nutrition. Operations such as payroll, purchasing, hiring, curriculum, and training are handled by the district office rather than at the individual school level. Employees in upper-level positions tend to have advanced

degrees. The number of employees at the district administration level varies according to the size and location of the school district.

School-Based Administration

School-based administrators are responsible for the day-to-day operations of individual schools. Duties include overseeing instruction, discipline, transportation (buses), and school budgets. Administrators hold advanced degrees and credentials in school administration. Salaries vary according to the size of the school and years of experience in education. The number of administrators employed at each school varies according to the school size.

Occupations in the area of school-based administration include, but are not limited to, the following:

- Principal
- Assistant Principal
- Dean of Students

Licensed Instructional Faculty

Licensed instructional faculty are responsible for planning, organizing, and presenting instruction that helps students learn content and skills. The major job functions licensed instructional faculty perform include management of instruction time, management of student behavior, instructional presentation, and monitoring of student performance. Instructional faculty are required to hold a bachelor's degree and state credentials (licenses or certifications). Advanced degrees are not required; however, instructional personnel routinely pursue them to enhance content knowledge and pedagogical skills. Elementary teachers do not normally specialize in a particular content area, because they teach all subjects. Middle school and high school teachers, however, specialize in a specific content area, such as English, math, a foreign language, biology, or music. Salaries of instructional personnel are set by the state department of education and are based on level of education and years of experience.

Occupations in the area of licensed instructional faculty include, but are not limited to, the following:
- Elementary School Teacher
- Middle School Teacher
- Special Education Teacher
- High School Teacher (All Content Areas)
- Curriculum Facilitator
- Curriculum Coach
- Literacy Facilitator or Coach
- Teacher Mentor
- Reading Teacher

Occupations in the area of student support services include, but are not limited to, the following:
- Counselor
- Career Development Counselor
- School Psychologist
- School Social Worker
- Speech-Language Therapist
- Student Intervention Specialist
- English as a Second Language Interpreter
- School Nurse
- Physical Therapist
- Occupational Therapist

Media and Technology Specialists

Media and other technology personnel serve a variety of functions in elementary and secondary schools. They oversee the coordination of the activities of the school library and provide technological support for students, administrators, and instructional faculty. Library media specialists are required to hold graduate degrees and licenses or certifications in library science or instructional technology. Technology assistants perform clerical and technical duties related to the maintenance of school computers while also providing support for the school library, computer labs, instructional faculty, and students.

Occupations in the area of media and technology include, but are not limited to, the following:
- Library/Media Specialist
- Library/Media Assistant
- Technology Specialist
- Technology Assistant
- Instructional Technology Specialist/Assistant
- Audiovisual Specialist

Paraprofessionals

Paraprofessionals support teachers and students by carrying out a variety of duties in the classroom. Individuals in these support positions are not licensed to teach, but they are assigned a range of support duties, working closely with the teacher and the students. Because the specific role of the paraprofessional often is loosely defined, the individual needs of the teacher and/or school administrator can require the paraprofessional to play a multitude of roles. The No Child Left Behind Act requires that paraprofessionals be "highly qualified." The specific requirements for this distinction, however, have been left up to individual states and include two years of college, paraprofessional certifications, and a passing score on a paraprofessional examination.

Paraprofessional occupations in elementary and secondary education include, but are not limited to, the following:

- Teacher Assistant
- Special Education Assistant
- Student Intervention Specialist
- Counseling Assistant
- Bilingual Aide
- Tutor

Famous First

Mather School is the oldest public elementary school in North America. It is located in the Dorchester region of Boston, Massachusetts and was named after Richard Mather. The Dorchester Town Records reads the following:

"It is ordered that the 20th of May 1639, that there shal be a rent paid of 20ls yeerely foreur imposed upon Tomsons Iland to bee payd p euy p'son that hat p'prtie in the said Iland according to the p'portion that any such p'son shall fro tyme to tyem injoy and posesse there, and this towards the mayntenance of a schoole in Dorchestr this rent of 20ls yeerly to bee payd to such a schoolemaster as shall undertake to teach English, Latin, and other tongues, and also writing."
(Source: Wikipedia.org)

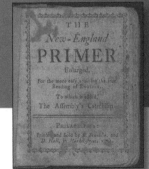

Outlook

This industry's history demonstrates that public education is a stable
area of employment for a great variety of functionaries and experts.
Although school funding varies widely and depends on many factors,
including population demographics, geographical location, and the
economy, teachers and other education personnel always will be
needed to ensure the education of millions of youths. Government
regulations and standards concerning the goals and practices of public
education will be a major factor in determining the employment
outlook and job security of workers in this industry. Among the
major concerns in public elementary and secondary education are
achievement gaps based on race, gender, and socioeconomic status;
raising the achievement of students whose first language is not
English; and improving literacy across the board.

Wendy C. Hamblet, Ruth Omunda/Editor

PUBLISHING AND INFORMATION INDUSTRY

Snapshot

General Industry: Communications

Career Clusters: Arts, A/V Technology, and Communication; Information Technology

Subcategory Industries: Art Publishing; Book Publishing; Calendar Publishing; Directory and Mailing List Publishing; Greeting Card Publishing; News Syndicates; Newspaper Publishing; Periodical Publishing

Related Industries: Advertising and Marketing Industry; Broadcast Industry; internet and Cyber Communications Industry; Motion Picture and Television Industry

Summary

The publishing and information industry mass produces and distributes written materials, including printed books, newspapers, magazines and other periodicals, as well as electronic or digital media that convey the same content, such as e-books and online full-text databases. Published works may convey information, entertain, persuade, or engage in all these activities simultaneously. Databases and guides such as telephone directories also fall within the scope of the industry, which is an important component of the overall information and communications sector.

History of the Industry

Published print was the earliest form of mass communication. Although the written word has been used since ancient times to convey messages to multiple readers or listeners, it was only after the printing press made it possible for a printed text to become standardized that print could become a mass medium. As literacy among the population grew, so did the industry.

Before the advent of the printing press, most writing was done by hand. Producing written materials was a time-consuming and difficult process completed by scribes, often in monasteries. A single copy of the Bible took up to five years to complete. The audience for these manuscripts (often religious or Latin texts) was the educated class and the clergy, as the general population was illiterate. Publishing was revolutionized with the development of the printing press in Germany in 1450 by Johann Gutenberg. Gutenberg's press, the technology of which spread throughout Europe quickly, eliminated the need for manual transcription and made books more accessible to everyone.

In the centuries that followed, the mechanized printing press underwent many improvements, making the mass production of printed material quicker and more affordable. By the eighteenth century, books were widely available throughout the world. Regular publications such as newspapers also began to be produced. As printing technology advanced, making books easier to print, other labor-saving technologies increased the average amount of leisure time and wealth. Now, more people had time to learn how to read and to exercise this ability once they acquired it. Both literacy and printed materials designed to be read during leisure time increased. These societal changes accompanied calls for democratic reforms within the Church and within nations. Thus, the publishing industry became inextricably tied to the democratic notions of a free press, free will, self-actualization, and autonomy.

In many ways, the twentieth century was the golden era of publishing. By the early part of the century, regular publications such as magazines and newspapers were produced in every corner of the world. Even after the advent of other modes of mass communication, such as radio and television, newspapers remained the most popular way for people to find out about current events. The second half of the twentieth century saw a strong trend toward consolidation within the industry. Smaller publishing companies, catering to local markets, increasingly came under corporate control. Part of the reason for this trend was that newer printing equipment was very expensive to purchase and maintain. Many small companies were unable to cover the high cost of equipment upgrades and were forced to sell out to large, cash-rich publishing concerns.

The internet began to influence the publishing industry at the end of the twentieth century. Electronic rather than paper publishing presented opportunities to significantly reduce costs associated with printing and distribution. However, the fact that consumers were beginning to get information online meant decreases in sales, circulation, and advertising revenue for the paper products that had sustained the industry throughout its history.

The Industry Today

The publishing industry continues to face radical challenges and poorly defined opportunities in the twenty-first century. These challenges reflect the impact of the internet. Reading habits are changing, and the industry has had to find ways to adjust to these changes. One of the biggest changes is the rise of self-publishing options, allowing authors to publish without a traditional publishing house. This has led to a change not only in the way that books are published but also the ways that tasks typically undertaken by the publishing house—developmental editing, copyediting, proofreading, design and layout, marketing and promotion, warehousing and distribution—are now the author's responsibility.

Small Businesses

A small business in the publishing industry is likely to have annual revenues between $200,000 and $2 million. It will normally employ ten to fifty people, including distribution staff. Small publishing businesses are often dependent on larger companies to fulfill certain business processes, especially printing, because the costs associated with owning and maintaining modern printing presses are extremely high.

Small presses or independent publishers (known as the "indie press") also fall under this category, although they may also be considered midsize businesses. Generally, small presses—as opposed to small publishing businesses that lack their own presses—have annual revenues of less than $50 million. Small presses are characterized by smaller print runs for titles and can include niche publishers, such as do-it-yourself (DIY) titles, poetry, or collectible books. Small presses typically release about twenty titles each year.

As occurs in the newspaper industry as well, there is a constant cycle of small publishing houses being purchased by larger corporations, and the same concerns about independence and maintaining local editorial control arise. In general, though, because of the opportunities available through multiple media outlets, the publishing industry is constantly renewing itself and new, independent houses spring up when more established small houses are absorbed into larger companies.

A good deal of space in publishing firms is dedicated to the electronic production of printed products. In this space, workers create and manage written content, design ads, and electronically lay out publications. This area is generally not accessible to the public, but some clients may want to work directly with production staff to create their advertisements.

If a small publisher owns its own presses, these may be located in the same building as the offices or at a remote and more industrial location. Printing presses are very large pieces of equipment, and they increase space requirements by several thousand square feet. The printing process is messy, loud, and potentially dangerous. Therefore, the public is generally not admitted to areas dedicated to printing.

Some small presses have begun to offer print-on-demand or publish-on-demand (POD) services. With digital printing capabilities, these companies only need print the number of publications ordered, avoiding costly print runs and warehousing costs. This technology also makes it more feasible for authors to self-publish their works, footing the entire bill for printing costs and selling their publications on their own.

Pros of Working for a Small Publisher. Employees of a small publishing business often have opportunities to learn about all aspects of the business. Smaller companies have freedom to control the content of their products. They also have more flexibility to develop marketing strategies to suit local client needs.

Cons of Working for a Small Publisher. Small publishers have smaller cash reserves than do larger businesses, making them far more vulnerable to market fluctuations. They also have more limited access to new equipment, especially expensive printing presses and other equipment. This can put them at a major competitive disadvantage to larger businesses.

Midsize Businesses

Midsize businesses in the publishing industry are generally defined as those with annual revenues of between $2 million and $50 million. They usually employ between 50 and 250 people, and they are likely to have multiple branches, often within a single geographic region. They generally own at least one printing press, which is sometimes shared by several publications in different communities. Some small presses fall within the category of midsize businesses. These largely independent ventures run fairly lean operations.

Pros of Working for a Midsize Publisher. Midsize publishers have a number of competitive advantages. They tend to have far higher equipment budgets than do small companies. Computer and office equipment is updated on a regular basis, boosting worker efficiency. Having the capital to own and maintain dedicated presses helps such companies control printing costs. Wider circulation in multiple markets allows midsize firms to attract regional and national advertisers in addition to their smaller local clients.

Cons of Working for a Midsize Publisher. Some clients may feel more comfortable dealing with smaller and more local publishing companies than with midsize, regional companies. Larger companies, moreover, tend to have deeper cash reserves, allowing them to weather temporary drops in revenue better than midsize companies can. Moreover, large companies command higher purchasing power with regard to supplies such as paper and ink, so they can better control these costs.

Large Businesses

The publishing industry is increasingly dominated by large businesses, whose revenues range from $50 million to more than $1 billion. Large publishing houses are characterized by the great variety of publications under their control. Large newspaper publishers such as Gannett (*USA Today*) and McClatchy (*Star Tribune* of Minneapolis) publish more than twenty newspapers nationwide. Large periodicals publishers, such as Meredith (*Better Homes and Gardens* and *Family Circle*) and Time Warner (*People*, *Time*, and *Sports Illustrated*) are responsible for a similar number of major publications. Major book publishers, such as Random House and the Penguin Group, publish all over the world and in a variety of media including print, electronic, and audio. Many of these large publishing companies are divisions of even larger multimedia companies. Large publishing businesses employ more than 250 people and compete at a national and international level for revenue. They are often fragmented into regional offices, allowing sales staff to deal directly with local and regional clients.

Pros of Working for a Large Publisher. Larger publishing businesses are among the largest multinational companies in any sector. They are publicly traded and have access to a scale of capital not paralleled elsewhere in the industry. With such massive cash reserves, the largest publishing companies are best positioned to survive industry changes.

Cons of Working for a Large Publisher. Most of the employees of large publishing companies do not have very much decision-making power. Job functions, positions, and even regions of operation may change without local employee input. This situation translates into a kind of job insecurity that many workers find stressful.

Organizational Structure and Job Roles

Regardless of size or products, all publishing companies require similar business activities to function. Division of labor becomes more specialized in larger companies, while employees in the smallest organizations have the broadest range of responsibilities. Duties are conducted on a single floor or building. At larger companies, job functions are executed in isolation from one another.

The following umbrella categories apply to the organizational structure of businesses in the publishing industry:
- Business Management
- Office Management
- Sales and Marketing
- Editorial
- Production
- Printing

Editorial

An editorial department primarily determines product content. Whether working with newspapers, magazines, books, or other publications, members of editorial teams develop the specific character of their companies' products. They come up with the words and images that draw readership. Employees in this category generally have higher degrees in English, journalism, or photography.

Many publishing companies maintain staffs of reporters to investigate noteworthy events or topics. These reporters are responsible for submitting stories to run in their companies' print products. In some companies, written content is provided by contributors rather than reporters. These contributors may be company employees, or they may be freelance writers who are paid per piece. Although some reporters and contributors also take pictures, many publishing companies employ dedicated photographers. These specially trained photojournalists use their skills to capture images that complement written stories.

All potential content is screened and organized by editors. A single publication's staff usually includes a number of different editors. Some specialize in writing headlines, some in selecting photographs, and some work in a single subject area. This latter type of editor may focus on news, sports, or entertainment. All editors within a single office usually report to a chief editor, who is in charge of the day-to-day management of publication content.

All members of an editorial staff answer to a publisher, who is ultimately responsible for the overall content and layout of print products. Publishers may be removed from daily editorial operations, but they serve as conduits between the editorial department and business management staff.

Editorial occupations may include the following:
- Reporter
- Contributor
- Photographer
- Photo Editor
- Headline Editor
- Subject Area Editor
- Chief Editor
- Publisher

Outlook

The outlook for print publications in this industry shows it to be in decline. Readership of serial publications has declined throughout the twentieth century. Many publishers (75%) think that audio, due to podcasting, will become a more important part of their content and commercial strategies.

The Department of Labor projects that book, periodical, and directory publishing will remain relatively stable. However, it notes that even these components of the publishing industry are sensitive to economic fluctuations.

Despite the fact that publishing careers are increasingly unstable, working in this industry is the best way to gain media experience. All forms of media and entertainment rely heavily on talented writers. Individuals with an interest in the written word can gain a level of writing experience in the publishing industry that would be hard to achieve elsewhere. The deadline-driven nature of most publishing companies teaches writers to produce quality copy in a limited time frame. This is a valuable skill for an employee in any business sector to have.

Famous First

Johannes Gensfleisch zur Laden zum Gutenberg (c. 1400–February 3, 1468) was a German blacksmith, goldsmith, inventor, printer, and publisher who introduced printing to Europe with the printing press. His introduction of mechanical movable type printing to Europe started the Printing Revolution and is regarded as a milestone of the second millennium, ushering in the modern period of human history. It played a key role in the development of the Renaissance, Reformation, Age of Enlightenment, and the scientific revolution and laid the material basis for the modern knowledge-based economy and the spread of learning to the masses. (Source: Wikipedia.org)

The publishing industry also remains an excellent place for people who enjoy research. Whether producing newspapers, magazines, or books, publishing businesses rely on investigative talent. Few other jobs can give an individual as many opportunities to hone qualitative research skills.

Perhaps the most attractive reason to consider a career in publishing is precisely that the industry is changing so rapidly. People entering the world of publishing now will have unparalleled opportunities to help shape the future of the industry. Pioneering sustainable business models in the age of the internet will be an incredible challenge, and those involved will be able to define publishing for future generations.

Adam Berger

THEATER AND PERFORMING ARTS INDUSTRY

Snapshot

General Industry: Communications
Career Clusters: Arts, A/V Technology, and Communication
Subcategory Industries: Broadway Musicals; Circuses; Dance Companies; Las Vegas Style Spectacles; Live Performances; Musical Dramas; Opera
Related Industries: Motion Picture and Television Industry; Music Industry

Summary

The theater and performing arts industry includes organizations that produce or organize live presentations involving performances of actors, musicians, dancers, musical groups, and other entertainers. This industry includes the promotion and production of these events as well as providing the artistic and technical skills necessary for the production of events. The group includes a very wide range of businesses and encompasses nonprofit as well as for-profit entities. The group ranges in size from small businesses, including individual freelance performers, to large organizations such as large opera and theater production companies. Many nonprofit organizations are dependent on significant financial support from government and private-foundation grants. The industry is represented in numerous countries and is most developed in metropolitan cities. In the United States, performing artists are more educated on average than the workforce as a whole.

History of the Industry

The practice of presenting live artistic performances dates back to ancient times. Ancient Greek and Roman cultures included dramatic, tragic, and comedic poetry and theater. During the sixteenth century, *commedia dell'arte*, an improvised comic theater with stock characters, flourished in Western Europe. The roots of current repertoires and performing traditions can be traced to the early seventeenth century, when William Shakespeare's plays were written and the first public opera house was opened in 1637 in Venice, Italy. The modern symphony orchestra developed in Germany during the mid-eighteenth century.

Today's large performance organizations, particularly opera companies, originated from the traditions of European royalty. Many modern performing arts organizations were formed during the eighteenth and nineteenth centuries; Italy's famous opera house, La Scala, opened in 1778; the first performing circus in the United States opened in 1793, Broadway musicals began in the early 1800s, the New York Philharmonic was created in 1842, the Boston Symphony Orchestra was created in 1881, and New York's Metropolitan Opera House opened in 1883. In the United States, wealthy patrons started many of the large performing organizations. For example, J. P. Morgan, Andrew Carnegie, and Joseph Pulitzer were important contributors to the New York Philharmonic Orchestra. Numerous artistic leaders and performers were brought from Europe to lead many of the major performing arts organization in the United States.

Many historians identify modern theater's beginnings in 1901 with the founding of the Moscow Art Theatre by Konstantin Stanislavsky. He formulated a revolutionary method of acting and is credited with beginning the modern age of the artistic director in theater.

The modern tradition of ballet dance performance was developed in France by King Louis XIV in the mid-seventeenth century, and in Russia during the mid-eighteenth century. Modern dance traditions departed from ballet in the late nineteenth century. New American theater dance forms such as tap and jazz were developed in the mid-twentieth century.

Major performing arts companies in the United States were aided
in the early twentieth century by the creation of tax-exempt status
for nonprofit organizations. In the United States, a few large
organizations were created in major metropolitan cities on the East
Coast in the late nineteenth and early twentieth centuries; attendance
of performing arts entertainment in the United States grew
rapidly in the post-World War II era. The creation of the National
Endowment for the Arts in 1965 also increased public support for
the performing arts industry. After World War II, an increasingly
educated and wealthy population with more disposable income and
leisure time increased the demand for artistic performances in many
cities. Numerous regional, permanent nonprofit theater companies,
symphony orchestras, and opera companies were subsequently created
in other North American cities.

European higher education institutions employed significant numbers
of performing artists during the nineteenth and early twentieth
centuries. During the mid-twentieth century, American college
and university systems developed another significant segment of
the performing arts industry by forming schools specializing in the
performing arts.

The Industry Today

The performing arts industry today offers several types of
entertainment, including symphony orchestras, theatrical plays
and musicals, operas, dance performances, circuses, and large
multidiscipline spectacle-style shows. Large metropolitan cities
continue to provide the majority of employment opportunities for
performing artists. For-profit performing arts organizations generally
are focused on popular entertainment, such as musical theater
production companies and Las Vegas-style spectacles such as Cirque
du Soleil. Nonprofit organizations generally focus on art performances,
such as symphony orchestras, opera companies, dance companies
(including ballet), and regional theater companies. Performing artists
also are often self-employed as freelance performers and teachers in
private dance and music studios.

Professional symphony orchestras often provide live weekly concerts
in midsize to large cities. Led by a single conductor/music director,
they usually feature a large group of local musicians, often paired with

a single internationally known virtuoso soloist. While some symphony orchestras offer only classical repertoire, many offer both classical and popular repertoire, usually formatted in separate concert series and marketed to different groups of patrons. To attract new audiences, orchestras are using a growing number of new concert formats, including shorter "rush-hour" concerts and concerts with multimedia presentations.

New York's Broadway is the center of the theater world in America. The highest-profile plays and musicals are produced there; sometimes, Broadway shows spawn touring productions that play in large and midsize cities across the country. Productions of Broadway shows also often have extended runs in large cities; New York, Los Angeles, Las Vegas, Toronto, and Chicago are large enough to support several major shows running simultaneously for months or years. Metropolitan communities also may support regional theater companies. Plays and musicals typically employ numerous performers, including instrumentalists, singers, dancers, conductors, and actors; many stage roles require performers to have high-level performance skills in singing, acting, and dancing. Theaters often employ a technical staff that assists in the production of most performing events. Technical theater positions include lighting designers, carpenters, costume designers, stage managers, and technical directors. Large theater companies that produce works with significant commercial appeal are located in major metropolitan cities such as New York, London, and Chicago. Regional theater companies often produce new plays and challenging works that do not have the popular appeal necessary for production on Broadway.

Dance companies are led by an artistic director/choreographer and usually specialize in one tradition—ballet, contemporary, folk, modern, or jazz/tap. Many of the largest dance performance organizations are ballet companies. Dance companies generally have a home theater for most of their performances, although some tour as well. Many ballet companies have an affiliated school that trains young dancers in the distinctive style used by the company.

Large hotels and casinos in Las Vegas and some other gambling and entertainment centers produce live performances of popular music and theater. Well-known performers in rock and roll, country, and popular music perform concerts for large audiences at these venues. Smaller venues in casinos also host performances by local musicians. Casinos and hotels rely on individual contractors to hire performers.

Military organizations in the United States and some other countries are among the largest employers of performing artists. All branches of the United States Armed Forces maintain high-quality music ensembles for ceremonial, entertainment, and educational purposes.

Many corporations that operate cruise ships employ numerous performers, including musicians, dancers, and actors, for the entertainment of cruise patrons. Performers often are employed for contract periods of three to six months. Churches and other religious groups regularly employ trained musicians as organists, pianists, and directors of choirs and other music ensembles. Dance bands, pop, rock-and-roll, and country bands often are employed in nightclubs. Employment generally is for single or weekly engagements at the discretion of managers and owners.

Public and private primary and secondary schools employ performing artists as teachers. Universities employ numerous performing artists as educators and performers. One of the primary goals of many universities is leadership in the arts for the enrichment of their communities; this requires a significant commitment of resources and creates employment for performing artists in music, dance, and theater.

Cooperation between universities and performing arts companies (principally regional theater companies and orchestras) is common in midsize cities. These cooperative agreements to hire performers reduce labor costs and allow the organizations to attract higher-quality performers and artists than they could independently. Performers also may find employment in related industries such as film and the music industry.

The performing arts industry has different primary sources of economic support in different regions of the world. In Europe and Asia, support comes largely from government subsidies. In the United States, the industry is supported by a blend of public ticket sales, private donors, private foundation grants, and government grants. Many large performing arts organizations seek to create a reliable funding source by creating an endowment. Performing arts audiences are dominated by highly educated individuals with high income levels.

The performing arts industry continues to face economic challenges. While the economic efficiency of many industries has increased over time, the performing arts industry has been unable to increase productivity substantially. The performing arts industry remains less efficient economically than other industries because its unique live performances are consumed at the point of production. The solution to the fundamental economic problems facing the performing arts industry continues to be philanthropic support and increasing government subsidies. In the United States, much of the government support comes through the National Endowment for the Arts and each state's arts council.

Small Businesses

Small music ensembles, theater companies, dance ensembles (primarily modern or jazz dance), and some churches typically have only a few employees serving a very small number of patrons. Ticket prices, budgets, and salaries vary, but generally are much lower than those of midsize and large organizations. Some performers act as independent freelance artists or as contractors for other performers, thereby operating as individually owned small businesses.

Pros of Working for a Small Business. Small companies are able to perform (sometimes exclusively) niche repertoires; they possess greater artistic control for performers, in part because of the absence of large administrative structures and artistic staff direction. Performers often enjoy a close-knit working environment; if there is a small staff, they often are friends or family members of the performers.

Cons of Working for a Small Business. Small companies often have relatively low pay and usually do not pay any benefits to performers. For many small companies, the only full-time employee is the executive director or artistic director. Employment for performers often is part-time and can be unpredictable. Sometimes the performers have to take on the business management tasks of the company and can have long periods without employment. Many small nonprofit companies rely on only a few funding sources; the loss of a single grant source or donor can cause serious budget shortfalls.

Midsize Businesses

Midsize performing arts companies typically include music ensembles, theater companies, and dance ensembles (often regional ballet companies). Smaller military bands and Broadway shows, off-Broadway shows, and touring productions of plays or musicals often fall in this category as well. Midsize organizations usually have three types of employees: performers, artistic staff, and management staff. Ticket prices, budgets, and salaries vary widely but generally are much higher than those of small organizations.

Pros of Working for a Midsize Business. Midsize performing arts companies often have greater financial stability compared with smaller companies. The presence of full-time administration allows performers to focus on the artistic work without the other duties they often have in smaller companies. Performers in midsize companies also may be employed part-time or full-time as teachers in higher education.

Cons of Working for a Midsize Business. Midsize companies often have lower pay than large companies. Midsize companies can suffer budget shortfalls that result in loss of compensation. In unionized environments, labor disputes can cause stressful working relationships between management and artistic staff or performers. These contract disputes can last for long periods and may result in the cancellation of performances. The financial support for these midsize organizations often is unpredictable, particularly in cities with shrinking economies or struggling industries.

Large Businesses

Large music ensembles, Broadway productions, popular music tours, military bands, theater companies, and dance ensembles (often ballet companies in the largest cities) typically have three types of employees: performers, artistic staff, and management staff. Unlike the small and midsize companies, large companies often have numerous departments within the management staff, including educational programming, fund-raising/development, and production management. Military bands sometimes are considered part of the large business category. Ticket prices, budgets, and salaries vary widely but generally are much higher than those of midsize organizations.

Pros of Working for a Large Business. Large organizations have significantly higher compensation, higher artistic standards, and greater financial stability compared with midsize organizations. Performers often may find additional related employment in education and/or other performance companies from the perceived prestige and reputation for artistic excellence resulting from employment in a large company.

Cons of Working for a Large Business. Large organizations often create significant pressure for extremely high artistic standards. Performers do not have the desired individual artistic control of their performances. There are a relatively small number of employment opportunities in large organizations and significant competition for employment. Budget shortfalls can cause significant loss of income and uncertain employment.

Organizational Structure and Job Roles

The organizational structure and distribution of tasks within performing arts companies are based on size and for-profit or nonprofit status. Most organizations have a strong functional division between management of the artistic product and the business management of the organization. A board of directors, artistic director, and executive director are likely to handle most of the major management oversight tasks, while the general manager and/or production manager will delegate tasks to other staff. Nevertheless, the tasks themselves generally remain similar throughout the performing arts industry.

The following umbrella categories apply to the organizational structure of small, midsize, and large performing arts companies:
- Business Management
- Administrative Support
- Development and Fund-Raising
- Stage Management
- Personnel Management
- Artistic Management
- Musicians
- Actors
- Dancers
- Costumers
- Composers and Arrangers
- Las Vegas-Style Spectacle Performers

Development and Fund-Raising

Development and fund-raising staff members handle all aspects of fund-raising for the company. These individuals write grant proposals, meet and communicate with donors and potential donors, and report the results to granting agencies. They work with and directly for the board members and the executive director. Some development staff members have academic degrees and/or performance experience, particularly in the company's specific performing art.

Development and fund-raising employees usually are compensated on a salary basis.

Artistic Management

Artistic managers oversee the artistic goals and direction of the company. These individuals program and direct specific repertoire, set artistic norms and standards, decide on the hiring of company and guest performers, and manage all other matters affecting the artistic product and production. They work for the board of directors and in cooperation with the executive director.

For orchestras, the music director often is also the primary conductor. The music director selects repertoire, plans concert series, hires musicians including soloists, rehearses the orchestra and conducts performances. For ballet companies, the ballet master often is the main choreographer for the company, selects repertoire, plans performance series, hires dancers including soloists, and rehearses the company. For theater companies, the director selects repertoire, plans performance series, hires actors and directs the rehearsal process.

Artistic managers usually are hired with multiyear contracts and compensated on a salary basis at a much higher rate than other performers. Occupations in the area of artistic management include the following:
- Music Director
- Ballet Master/Choreographer
- Director

Composers and Arrangers

Composers or arrangers construct musical works for the performances of the company. They work for the artistic manager and in cooperation with the producer, director, or choreographer. Composers usually are hired on a fee basis. Some organizations, including military bands, hire arrangers on a full-time salary basis.

Composers and arrangers also are highly trained professionals skilled in the construction of music for specific performance needs. Occupations in this area include the following:

- Military Band Arranger/Composer
- Orchestral Arranger/Composer
- Film and Television Arranger/Composer

Outlook

Between 1970 and 1990, the number of artists doubled in the United States, growing at twice the rate of the overall labor force. This growth reflects the great expansion of theaters, orchestras, and other venues in the industry and collegiate community. In recent years, the number of performing artists as a percentage of the U.S. population has stabilized and the rate of growth of the industry has been the same as the rate of the overall labor force. The stability of this measure suggests that the performing arts labor force has reached a balancing point in the overall U.S. economy. According to the U.S. Bureau of Labor Statistics (BLS), employment opportunities for most performing artists, including those working in dance, film, music, and theater, are expected to increase by 3–12 percent nationwide between 2016 and 2026.

Performing artists continue to live and work in the largest metropolitan cities, with 20 percent of performing artists living in Los Angeles, New York, Chicago, Washington, D.C., and Boston. Half of all the professional artists in the United States live in thirty metropolitan cities. The Sun Belt cities have the most performers per capita; the western and southern states have seen the largest growth in performing artists recently. One third of performing artists are employed only part of the year, and it is likely that the profession will continue to trend toward seasonal employment. Performing artists are more likely to have college degrees than other members of the labor force; they receive relatively less compensation for their education level and are more likely to be self-employed.

Famous First

The first recorded use of the term "playwright" is from 1605. It appears to have been first used in a pejorative sense by Ben Jonson to suggest a mere tradesman fashioning works for the theatre. Jonson uses the word in his Epigram 49, which is thought to refer to John Marston:

PLAYWRIGHT me reads, and still my verses damns,
He says I want the tongue of epigrams;
I have no salt, no bawdry he doth mean;
For witty, in his language, is obscene.
Playwright, I loath to have thy manners known
In my chaste book; I profess them in thine own.
(Source: Wikipedia.org)

The performing arts industry is reliant on the ability and willingness of consumers to spend disposable income, the ability of individuals and families to give philanthropic gifts, and the support of government agencies and private foundations. The outlook for international opportunities in the performing arts industry varies widely by region.

David Steffens

VIDEO, COMPUTER, AND VIRTUAL REALITY GAMES INDUSTRY

Snapshot

General Industry: Arts and Entertainment

Career Cluster: Arts, A/V Technology, and Communication

Subcategory Industries: Coin-Operated Games Manufacturing; Computer and Peripheral Equipment Manufacturing; Computer Software Games Publishing; Computer Storage Device Manufacturing; Electronic Computer Manufacturing; Electronic Toys and Games Manufacturing; Input/Output Equipment Manufacturing; Software Publishers; Video Game Machines (Except Coin-Operated) Manufacturing

Related Industries: Computer Hardware and Peripherals Industry; Computer Software Industry; Toys and Games Industry

Summary

Dedicated to interactive entertainment, the video, computer, and virtual reality games industry is one of the fastest-growing segments of the entertainment industry. Comprising software, hardware, and peripherals, the electronic game industry provides entertainment experiences ranging from immersive games requiring hundreds of hours of play to casual games popularized by social media and mobile devices. The industry relies on innovative technologies to create entertainment for a global audience ranging in age from toddlers to senior citizens.

History of the Industry

Considerable controversy exists as to what constitutes the first video game. In 1952, Alexander Douglas, a doctoral student at the University of Cambridge, programmed his university's computer to run tic-tac-toe simulations. Some historians attribute the first video game to William Higinbotham, a scientist at Brookhaven National Laboratory. In 1958, Higinbotham prepared for a public open house by programming a table-tennis game to run on a laboratory oscilloscope. His game, *Tennis for Two*, was enthusiastically greeted by the public and was the hit of the open house.

In 1962, the first game available outside a single institute, *Spacewar!*, was created in a Massachusetts Institute of Technology (MIT) computer laboratory after hours by members of MIT's Tech Model Railroad Club. The object of the game was to shoot down one's opponent's spaceship without falling into the Sun. Other programmers who were familiar with academic computers could potentially modify the gameplay of *Spacewar!*, and many did.

The 1970s saw the birth of consumer video games. Instead of being relegated to military bases or universities, video games became coin-operated and were installed in pinball and arcade parlors, pizzerias, and other recreational areas. Clones of *Spacewar!*, based on the original programming at MIT, began appearing in arcades.

In the late 1970s and early 1980s, home video-game consoles began to appear. Manufacturers such as Atari and Magnavox offered simplified versions of coin-operated arcade games playable in consumers' homes, and game consoles sold well. During 1972, the Magnavox Odyssey sold over 100,000 units. These consoles worked with cartridges containing individual games, enabling users to play many different games by purchasing many different cartridges for the same console.

As the decade progressed, consumers became disenchanted with the quality of cartridge-based games, which were noticeably more primitive than the full-sized coin-operated machines found in arcades. Seeking to earn profits quickly, some companies preyed on consumers eager for the latest games by repackaging old games and selling them as new titles. Other companies' game quality dropped precipitously as coin-operated games continued to advance, and consumers became reluctant to purchase titles from an industry that sought only profit.

During this same time period, personal computers (PCs) began to drop in price and become more affordable for families. Personal computers were popular not only for business applications and word processing but also as hubs of game playing. Infocom's *Zork* series and other text-based games formed a genre known as "interactive fiction" that was popular with young adults. As PCs' processing power increased, games with simple graphics became available.

In 1985, the Nintendo Company released the Nintendo Entertainment System (NES), which was sophisticated enough to rekindle interest in game consoles. The Nintendo games were graphically sophisticated for the time, and they introduced a pair of plumbers (the Mario Brothers) and other iconic characters to the gaming public. These characters would become increasingly important as video gaming evolved, because industry sales would come to be driven in part by franchise characters such as the Mario Brothers who would be featured in many different games.

Sega, too, became involved in the console technology race and introduced Sonic the Hedgehog as a franchise character for its Sega Genesis console. While Sega's games were graphically superior to those of Nintendo, the NES had a more aggressive marketing and public relations campaign behind it, and it sold significantly better. In 1999, Sega released the Dreamcast, the first game console with internet access, but even that could not save the company.

At the start of the 2020s, Sony's Playstation 4, Microsoft's Xbox 360, and Nintendo's Switch systems are battling for dominance of the console market, and PCs remain strong contenders for video game dominance. The video gaming industry has grown into a multibillion-dollar industry, one that consistently earns greater revenues than the motion picture industry and that appeals to a wide range of demographics.

The Industry Today

As the video game industry has grown, it has realized the need to open new markets. A significant portion of the industry still caters to "hardcore" gamers, or those seeking the most advanced possible hardware and software features and who play games that require hundreds of hours to solve. However, the overall industry seeks to provide a wide range of games to appeal to all ages, genders, and tastes. As the industry seeks to reach all possible markets, casual gamers have become important alongside hardcore gamers. Casual games do not require the powerful hardware needed to run hardcore games, and they generally require very little time commitment. Throughout the world, then, gaming is becoming more popular, more accessible, and more profitable.

The video, computer, and virtual reality games industry—like most industries reliant on technology—is evolving quickly. Although consoles and PCs are currently the dominant platforms, casual gaming (often played in conjunction with social media) is gaining popularity. Thus, the video game industry consists of more than just first-person shooters and sports simulations. It includes solitaire and other simple one-person games, social-media-based games such as *Farmville* that are played on social networking Web sites, and games featuring immersive worlds such as the *Grand Theft Auto* series, as well as educational games designed for young players.

Casual games do not require the same time commitment that hardcore games do. Players can drop in and drop out of casual games without having to remember complex plots, tactical plans, or anything else. Dropping in to play a casual game has no impact on the player's enjoyment because there is no plot to remember. Hardcore games encourage players to spend dozens, if not hundreds, of hours exploring and mastering them. Generally played on consoles or PCs, these games can cost millions of dollars to make, market, and distribute. Hardcore games run the gamut from sports simulations to realist military simulations to fantasy role-playing games (FRPGs).

Another typical type of hardcore game is the massively multiplayer online role playing game (MMORPG). Players of MMORPGs usually pay a monthly subscription fee to access a shared virtual space simultaneously with other gamers from around the world. These are known as "persistent worlds," because events continue to occur in them even when the player is logged out of the game. Other persistent virtual worlds are free to play but have in-game advertising or charge fees for specific, premium features. Historically, these online games have been played mostly on PCs, but console manufacturers are increasingly aware that their players desire virtual gathering spaces and are building virtual worlds based around their consoles.

The social aspect of gaming is growing quickly. Some players not only want to interact with other players (for example, through MMORPGs and virtual worlds), but also encourage their friends on social networks to play with them. Social games (often played while logged into social networking sites, such as Facebook and MySpace) encourage players to get other members of their social networks involved in them. *Farmville*, *Words with Friends*, and other social games provide casual gaming experiences on social networks.

More serious games have grown into a serious business. Also known as educational or vocational games, these interactive games are increasingly used by businesses and other organizations. Employers have recognized the value of using games to train their employees in a virtual world before letting them loose in the real world, with real profits and losses. The U.S. Army, recognizing the power of gaming, has experimented with using military simulation games as recruiting tools.

With the increasing popularity of video games, especially social and casual games, the way consumers access their games is shifting. In the past, consoles and personal computers (PCs) were the dominant gaming platforms, with handheld consoles such as Nintendo's GameBoy and Sony's Playstation Portable as the third most popular platform. This system of game delivery is changing, however, with the evolution of mobile phones. As mobile phones become more sophisticated and better able to support processor- and graphics-intensive games, they are poised to take over as the most popular gaming platform.

As with other parts of the entertainment industry, video games borrow from and mix with many aspects of popular culture. Film, television, toys, and video games seed one another with concepts and licensed properties: popular video games have made the leap to feature films, and television shows have spawned their own video games. Indeed, many projects that begin as films, television programs, video games, or comic books seek to develop complementary projects in the other media to maximize profitability, particularly so-called genre projects. It has become extremely common for a science-fiction film, for example, to have a novelization, a comic book adaptation, Web-based and mobile-phone-based casual gaming tie-ins, and a hardcore console and PC game adaptation or spin-off. Cooperating companies strive to release all such adaptations around the same time, so that each will increase the audience for the others. This entwining of various media is moving toward a convergence of seemingly all entertainment. Hardware manufacturers for PCs, consoles, handhelds, and mobile phones are readying themselves for their products to allow consumers to communicate, play games, play video, and surf the internet.

Within the video games industry, there are several subindustries. In larger companies, each subindustry may be a subdivision of the same corporation. Game design studios come up with game concepts and details of play (known as game mechanics). The design team creates the conflict, writes the plot, and designs the monsters. Designers create the story that the game publisher will flesh out. Some design teams are subsidiaries of larger game-publishing houses, while others are third-party developers who contract with publishers on a game-by-game basis.

Publishers provide the money and the technical expertise to make a game. They employ programmers to write the code necessary to turn designs into software. Artists take these lines of code and create models, textures, and animation, as well as audio tracks, to turn the raw code into a full audiovisual experience. After analyzing the game for bad code and other quality problems, the publisher gives the go-ahead to mass-produce and distribute the game, either on physical media or as a downloadable file online.

Small Businesses

Small video game businesses typically range from one to ten employees. Many owner-founders began creating video games in their spare time. To break into the video game industry, some small companies act as design studios. They pitch their ideas to video game publishers with a working demo in order to get their game into the hands of consumers. Other small companies provide their games directly to the public on the Web through social networks or as shareware (games freely available for download that require or request fees from players who keep and continue to play them).

Pros of Working for a Small Business. Small businesses have the advantage of being nimble. Instead of spending years on one massive title, a small company can survey the marketplace and focus its efforts precisely. It has the luxury of discovering niches and unusual opportunities that bigger businesses are too unwieldy to explore. Teamwork is also a benefit, as willingness to learn and work multiple roles is expected of all employees.

Cons of Working for a Small Business. Video games are a quickly growing industry, but small businesses are volatile, with many not surviving their first few years. There are also significant start-up costs associated with small businesses specializing in video game development because many require cutting-edge technology. (Because of the life cycle of both games and computer hardware, a game created on an older computer may be obsolete by the time it is released.) Without a steady cash flow or dedicated employees, a small video game company may never fully graduate from a hobby to a business. If owners rely too much on friends and family for assistance, they may also find that their personal relationships suffer if their businesses fail.

Midsize Businesses

In the video game industry, it is difficult to remain a midsize business. Entrepreneurs begin small businesses every day, and large companies grow relatively quickly. Midsize businesses are often on their way to either downsizing to a small business or growing into a large business. Few midsize businesses in the video game industry are planned to remain midsize.

Pros of Working for a Midsize Business. Midsize businesses are generally grown from successful small businesses. With a modest history of success, companies learn what does and does not work. This lends midsize businesses more stability than most small businesses, as well as a more significant cash flow. Midsize companies may also be successful enough to pick and choose their projects, only working on games that interest them. Midsize video game companies are often still small enough that employees are not forced to work only in specific roles but instead may work on a variety of tasks that stretch their skills and build their resumes.

Many midsize companies also have the good fortune to be small enough that every employee works toward a common goal. While larger companies may have too many employees to be personal and small companies' employees may work too hard to constitute a strong team, midsize companies are often just big enough that employees are not overwhelmed by their projects but small enough that everyone is working on the same game, toward the same goal.

Cons of Working for a Midsize Business. As midsize businesses are often contractual partners with larger companies, they may not have as much flexibility as either smaller or larger companies in developing their own game titles. If a large game publisher asks a midsize game design company to assist on a project, the smaller company may have to compromise its creativity and vision in order to fulfill the contract. Midsize companies do not have the same monetary resources that large companies have, so their equipment may be older than that of larger companies. They are also not as nimble as smaller companies and may take too long to change course, if that is what the market dictates.

Large Businesses

Large video game companies are often multinational corporations and are sometimes subsidiaries of parent entertainment companies. Large companies may be design studios or game publishers. Many large publishers establish contracts with third-party designers for game titles, while other corporations keep in-house design staff. In-house designers typically have more money available and greater creative flexibility with their games than do third-party developers.

Pros of Working for a Large Business. Although the video games industry remains volatile, many large video game companies have diversified sufficiently to avoid the danger of overnight financial ruin. Many large companies also have multiple locations, some abroad. Possibilities for transfer exist, and employees may find themselves on localization teams for countries they wish to visit. Large businesses offer more amenities and benefits than smaller corporations, as well as stock options and significant monetary bonuses for completed games.

Large companies also offer the opportunity to work on different types of games within the same corporation. An industry leader such as Electronic Arts publishes titles in several different genres annually, with more always in development. When one game ends, a successful employee may be transferred to a different game to learn new skills or promoted to new responsibilities. Large companies also tend to promote from within, so the more time one spends with a large company, the more likely an employee is to rise through the ranks.

Cons of Working for a Large Business. In large game companies, employees fill specialized roles. This can lead to frustrating layers of bureaucracy and middle-management, as well as rigid sets of job tasks. Additionally, crunch times can last for months on poorly planned and executed projects, greatly increasing employee stress. Large businesses are sometimes also part of larger entertainment companies, which can dismiss otherwise good ideas if they do not fit within the corporate brand. Large companies also rely more on contract labor—employees contracted to work for the company for a specific game title. Independent contractors are often not entitled to the same benefits and protections that regular employees are, and they may not have a job after their titles ship.

Organizational Structure and Job Roles

Video game industry employees are responsible for the entire gaming experience, from the initial concept through marketing and publishing to retail sales. The main three branches of the industry are game design, game production, and retail. The design team is responsible for the initial concepts, story, and visuals. Publishing breathes life into the creations, making the game real, playable, and fun. Marketing and public relations staff, the quality assurance (QA) testers, and sales associates all support and facilitate the success of video game companies. In smaller companies, an individual may fill many roles, while larger companies assign each task to a different employee.

The following umbrella categories apply to the organizational structure of businesses in the video, computer, and virtual reality games industry.

- Management
- Administration and Human Resources
- Marketing and Public Relations
- Retail Stores
- Customer Service
- Amenities and Facilities
- Security
- Game Design
- Production

- Animation/Art
- Audio
- Programming
- Quality Assurance
- Sales and Distribution
- Professional Gamers

Marketing and Public Relations

Marketing is one of the video game industry's most difficult tasks.
While marketing and good public relations can get a game noticed,
an industry research group has found that many casual gamers
prefer to learn about games by word of mouth from their social circle.
Marketing for hardcore gamers also requires a deft touch, as many
passionate gamers resist any sort of organized spin. Viral marketing
for both casual and hardcore games has proven to be successful.

As the public face of a company, a successful marketer requires a
very specific set of skills. A strong candidate for a marketing or public
relations team must have exceptional communication skills (both
oral and in writing) and an ability to connect with mainstream news
outlets and everyday gamers alike. Many marketing managers have
at least a bachelor's degree, and many also have advanced degrees.
Salaries for marketing personnel can range from $50,000 for a public
relations specialist to $110,000 for a marketing manager.

Marketing and public relations occupations may include the following:
- Marketing Director
- Public Relations Manager
- Brand Manager
- Communications Specialist
- Public Relations Specialist

Game Design

Game design is one of the most important parts of the game industry.
Designers provide the initial concepts for games, and their vision
brings those games to fruition. Designers provide story structures,
concepts for the look of characters and items that players will
encounter, dialogue, and paths through each level. They are generally
paid to use their imaginations. Ultimately, designers receive the
kudos (or the blame) for the enjoyability of their games.

Competition for design positions is tough. Many employees on design
teams began their careers in the QA department. Design employees

usually have at least a bachelor's degree, and the majority have spent at least three years in the industry. The starting salary for a new designer is around $45,000, but with industry experience designers can earn over $85,000 per year.

Game design occupations may include the following:
- Design Director
- Lead Designer
- Level Designer
- Interface Designer
- Associate Designer
- Game Writer
- Quest Developer
- World Designer

Animation/Art

The art department is tasked with creating the look of a game. Whether the game takes place within a postapocalyptic wasteland of muted tans and browns or against a hyper-saturated rainbow of colors for a dancing game, the art department must convey the feel of a game visually. Artists must have a strong facility with technology to create electronic reproductions of concept art. Modelers and animators must be familiar with anatomy and physiology in order to ensure an item's movement is appropriate and realistic. Many artists have bachelor's degrees in fine or applied arts. The average salary for an entry-level artist is $45,000, and artists with at least five years of experience in the industry can earn nearly $100,000 per year.

Animation and art occupations may include the following:
- Two-Dimensional Artist
- Three-Dimensional Artist
- Animator
- Concept Artist
- Environment Artist
- Modeler
- Technical Artist
- Texture Artist

Audio

Video game companies' audio departments are responsible for immersing players into their games' virtual worlds. The success of sound effects, musical scores, and character voices all depends on excellent audio teams. Some actors specialize in video game voiceover work and are listed as cast members for dozens of game titles. Many positions in the audio category are independent contractor positions, and some workers may work on several projects at once.

Audio workers usually have bachelor's degrees and some technical experience when entering the video games industry. The entry-level salary is between $40,000 and $50,000 per year, and veterans of the industry can earn more than $85,000 annually.

Audio occupations may include the following:
- Audio Director
- Audio Technician
- Composer
- Sound Designer
- Sound Producer
- Sound Mixer/Editor
- Voiceover Artist

Programming

Programmers write the code that constitutes the core of a video game. Without code, there would be no game. Programmers create the designers' world, allowing artists and audio employees to bring it to life. As code writers, programmers have the most detailed control of the game. Their commands dictate how the world will work and how decisions will play out.

Programmers, in accordance with their status, generally have the highest salaries in the video game industry (outside of upper management). A new programmer, with less than three years' experience in the industry, can earn around $55,000 per year; veterans can nearly double that at $109,000 annually. While a college degree is not strictly necessary for a programming job, familiarity with programming languages is.

Programming occupations may include the following:
- Artificial Intelligence Programmer
- Audio Programmer
- Engine Programmer
- Graphics Programmer
- Interface Programmer
- Lead Programmer
- Networking Programmer
- Physics Programmer

- Quality Assurance Programmer
- Tools Programmer

Famous First

In the 1930s, a story by science fiction writer Stanley G. Weinbaum (*Pygmalion's Spectacles*) contains the idea of a pair of goggles that let the wearer experience a fictional world through holographics, smell, taste, and touch. From today's perspective, the experience Weinbaum describes for those wearing the goggles is uncannily like the modern experience of virtual reality, making him a true visionary of the field. (Source: https://www.vrs.org.uk)

Outlook

The outlook for this industry shows it to be on the rise, with steady growth predicted. The BLS projects that, between 2018 and 2028, the publishing industry will grow by approximately 14 percent. Software publishers make up the lion's share of this growth. In particular, the software publishing job market is forecast to grow by 30 percent, adding nearly 80,000 jobs. Not surprisingly, many of the fastest-growing segments of the software publishing industry are software programmers and system administrators.

Chaunacey Dunklee/Editor

CAREER PROFILES

Advertising, Promotions, and Marketing Managers

Snapshot

Career Cluster(s): Business, Management, and Administration, Hospitality and Tourism, Human Services, Marketing, Sales and Service

Interests: Advertising and marketing, mass media and communications, project management, writing, journalism

Earnings (2018 Median): $132,620 yearly; $63.76 hourly

Employment & Outlook: Faster Than Average Growth Expected

OVERVIEW

Sphere of Work

Advertising and marketing managers work as employees of marketing and advertising agencies within the communication, information, and business sectors. They serve as the main link or point of contact between clients and the agency, and help to manage the interests of clients within the agency. Advertising and marketing managers coordinate print, television, radio, and multimedia advertising campaigns and projects; in

some cases, they may also be responsible for sales and developing new business opportunities.

While advertising and marketing managers contribute to campaign development, they are not technically part of an agency's creative team. Their role is to ensure that campaigns are priced, administered, and executed smoothly and efficiently, and with the client's interests in mind. They ensure that action items and campaign milestones are delivered on time and within budget. Aside from working closely with clients, they coordinate the work activities of personnel such as copywriters, graphic designers, production assistants, art directors, public relations personnel, and market researchers, as well as other project management responsibilities. Advertising and marketing managers are generally supervised by an agency director or client services supervisor.

Work Environment

Advertising and marketing managers work in an office environment within small to large advertising or marketing agencies. Air and car travel may be occasionally required to meet with clients. Evening and weekend work is also often required. Advertising and marketing managers frequently work under pressure and adhere to strict budgets and tight deadlines.

Profile

Interests: Business, Management, and Administration, Hospitality and Tourism, Human Services, Marketing, Sales, and Service
Working Conditions: Work Inside
Physical Strength: Light Work
Education Needs: Bachelor's Degree
Licensure/Certification: Usually Not Required
Physical Abilities Not Required: Not Climb, Not Kneel
Opportunities for Experience: Internship, Apprenticeship, Volunteer Work
Holland Interest Score: AES

* See Appendix A

Occupation Interest

Graduates and professionals with a strong interest in advertising and marketing, mass media and communications, and project management are often attracted to the advertising industry. In particular, the role suits people who have an interest in coordinating multiple activities in a fast-paced environment and who are comfortable working closely with others.

Aside from excellent collaborative, communication, and organizational skills, advertising and marketing managers must also possess strong research and analytical skills and high business acumen. They may be expected to formulate and execute budgets, monitor expenses, and assist with financial reporting. In some instances, they will be expected to make sales calls or develop and present new business proposals.

Successful advertising and marketing managers must be able to speak and write fluently, work with a diverse range of people, adapt to new industries, clients, products and services, and deliver consistent results under pressure. The role also requires considerable tact and diplomacy.

A Day in the Life—Duties and Responsibilities

The typical workday of an advertising and marketing manager includes frequent meetings with staff, clients, and supervisors (generally top-level management or agency owners). The campaign deliverables, which advertising and marketing managers coordinate, are usually subject to tight timeframes and strict deadlines. Therefore, on a daily basis, the role demands excellent organizational and time management skills. Advertising and marketing managers must be adept at multi-tasking, adapting to change, and problem solving.

Advertising and marketing managers generally gain a high level of exposure to different clients, industries, products, and services (although some may specialize in specific industries). The role demands high business (and possibly sales) acumen and the ability to analyze new information quickly and effectively. An advertising and marketing manager is expected to thoroughly research and understand the clients they work with, as well as their client's competitors, and the competitors' competing products and campaigns. This includes developing a deep understanding of the client's industry, customer base, methods and processes, challenges and opportunities, and target markets.

Advertising and marketing managers are expected to have competent computing skills to help them prepare campaign-related and organizational materials, such as financial and marketing reports, client and budget proposals (or "pitches" to acquire new business), and other work-related documents. They may also be expected to develop and manage spreadsheets and databases for project management and accounting purposes.

Duties and Responsibilities

- Preparing advertising and marketing budgets for clients
- Consulting with people in research, creative, and production departments
- Overseeing workers in layout, copy, production, and client services

WORK ENVIRONMENT

Immediate Physical Environment

Office settings predominate. Advertising and marketing managers work for small to large advertising and marketing firms, usually in urban or semi-urban locations. Some travel may be required.

Job security is sometimes tenuous in the advertising industry. Economic or sector downturns, the loss of client accounts, or reduced client spending can lead to layoffs. This tends to create an atmosphere of intense competition.

Human Environment

Advertising and marketing manager roles demand strong collaborative and team skills. Advertising and marketing managers interact with advertising, business, and creative specialists, such as brand and product managers, marketing managers, brand strategists, public relations executives, graphic designers, art directors, multimedia technicians, copywriters, production assistants, and editors. They are likely to work with multiple client contacts, as well as contract or freelance service providers. They usually report to an agency director or owner, or a client services supervisor.

Transferable Skills and Abilities

Communication Skills
- Persuading others

Interpersonal/Social Skills
- Asserting oneself
- Being able to work independently
- Cooperating with others
- Having good judgment
- Motivating others
- Working as a member of a team

Organization & Management Skills
- Managing time
- Meeting goals and deadlines
- Paying attention to and handling details

Unclassified Skills
- Keeping a neat appearance

Technological Environment

Advertising and marketing managers use standard business technologies, including telecommunication and social media tools, presentation tools and software, and financial and database software.

EDUCATION, TRAINING, AND ADVANCEMENT

High School/Secondary

High school students can best prepare for a career as an advertising and marketing manager by taking courses in business, math (with an accounting focus), computer literacy, and communications (for example, journalism or business communications). Courses such as social studies, history, and anthropology will also prepare the student for synthesizing research into written materials. The creative aspects of the advertising industry may be explored through art and graphic design. However, it is important to note that advertising and marketing managers work in an administrative, rather than a creative, capacity. In addition, psychology and cultural studies may provide an understanding of group and individual responses to advertising and other forms of communication.

Students should also become involved in extracurricular school activities and projects that develop business and communication skills to gain hands-on experience prior to graduation. Additionally, serving as a club secretary, treasurer, or other office holder will help to develop organizational skills. Participation in student magazines and newsletters will help to build an understanding of print and multimedia communications.

Suggested High School Subjects
- Applied Math
- Arts
- Business Data Processing
- Business Law
- Business Math
- Composition
- Computer Science
- Economics
- English
- Graphic Communications
- Journalism
- Merchandising
- Statistics

Related Career Pathways/Majors

Business, Management, and Administration Cluster
- Marketing Pathway

Hospitality and Tourism Cluster
- Lodging Pathway
- Travel and Tourism Pathway

Human Services Cluster
- Consumer Services Pathway

Marketing, Sales and Service Cluster
- E-Marketing Pathway
- Management and Entrepreneurship Pathway

Marketing, Sales and Service Cluster
- Marketing Information Management and Research Pathway

Famous First

"Torches of Freedom" was a phrase used to encourage women's smoking by exploiting women's aspirations for a better life during the early twentieth century. Cigarettes were described as symbols of emancipation and equality with men. The term was used by Edward Bernays to encourage women to smoke in public despite social taboos. Bernays hired women to march while smoking their "torches of freedom" in the Easter Sunday Parade of 1929. (Source: Wikipedia.org)

Postsecondary

At the postsecondary level, students interested in or focused on becoming an advertising and marketing manager should work towards earning an undergraduate degree in communications, advertising, marketing, or business administration, or build a strong liberal arts background. Due to strong competition among candidates, a master's degree is sometimes expected, although practical experience is sometimes more highly regarded than formal qualifications.

A large number of colleges and universities offer advertising, marketing, communications, and business degree programs. Some programs offer internships or work experience with advertising agencies. These experiences may lead to entry-level opportunities. Aspiring advertising and marketing managers can also gain entry into the advertising industry via other roles, such as market research, administration, or sales.

Related College Majors
- Advertising
- Business Administration and Management, General
- Journalism
- Marketing Management and Research
- Public Relations and Organizational Communications

Adult Job Seekers

Adults seeking a career transition into or return to an advertising and marketing manager role will need to highlight qualifications, skills, and experience in areas such as business administration, advertising, and marketing. Necessary skills for a successful transition include account coordination, client liaison, and project management. Marketing and advertising experience with a non-agency corporation is often highly regarded because agency firms value employees who understand the client side of the relationship.

Networking is critical—candidates should not rely solely on job boards and advertised positions to explore work opportunities. As with recent college graduates, adult job seekers may wish to consider entry to the advertising industry via an alternative route, such as market research, administration, or sales.

Professional Certification and Licensure

There are no formal professional certifications or licensing requirements for advertising and marketing managers.

Additional Requirements

The most important attributes for advertising and marketing managers are a passion for advertising and marketing communications, coupled with excellent business, organizational, and people skills. Advertising and marketing managers must be skilled and diplomatic coordinators, negotiators, and problem solvers. They should be willing to persist under often heavy workloads and with demanding stakeholders.

EARNINGS AND ADVANCEMENT

Earning potential increases as advancement occurs. Advancement may be quick in corporate ranks, partly because turnover can be high as a result of account success or failure. Many firms provide their employees with continuing education opportunities, either in-house or at local colleges and universities, and encourage employee participation in seminars and conferences.

Median annual wages, May 2018

Marketing managers: $134,290

Advertising, promotions, and marketing managers: $132,620

Advertising, marketing, promotions, public relations, and sales managers: $126,250

Advertising and promotions managers: $117,130

Total, all occupations: $38,640

Note: All Occupations includes all occupations in the U.S. Economy.
Source: U.S. Bureau of Labor Statistics, Employment Projections program

The median annual wage for advertising and promotions managers was $117,130 in May 2018. The median wage is the wage at which half the workers in an occupation earned more than that amount and half earned less. The lowest 10 percent earned less than $57,150, and the highest 10 percent earned more than $208,000.

In May 2018, the median annual wages for advertising and promotions managers in the top industries in which they worked were as follows:

Advertising, public relations, and related services	$134,780
Management of companies and enterprises	$113,210
Information	$103,960
Wholesale trade	$92,800

The median annual wage for *marketing managers* was $134,290 in May 2018. The lowest 10 percent earned less than $69,840, and the highest 10 percent earned more than $208,000.

In May 2018, the median annual wages for marketing managers in the top industries in which they worked were as follows:

Professional, scientific, and technical services	$143,100
Management of companies and enterprises	$142,580
Finance and insurance	$141,410
Manufacturing	$137,610
Wholesale trade	$126,000

Most advertising, promotions, and marketing managers work full-time. Some advertising and promotions managers work more than 40 hours per week.

Fast Fact

Women hold the majority of advertising agency positions, at 60 percent. The same can't be said for African Americans, who hold only five percent of agency jobs.

Source: https://blog.transparentcareer.com/college-students/career-guides/5-facts-world-advertising/

EMPLOYMENT AND OUTLOOK

Advertising and promotions managers held about 27,600 jobs in 2018. Overall employment of advertising, promotions, and marketing managers is projected to grow 8 percent from 2018 to 2028, faster than the average for all occupations. Employment growth will vary by occupation.

Advertising, promotional, and marketing campaigns are expected to continue to be essential as organizations seek to maintain and expand their market share. Advertising and promotions managers will be needed to plan, direct, and coordinate advertising and promotional campaigns, as well as to introduce new products into the marketplace.

However, the newspaper publishing industry, which employs many of these workers, is projected to decline over the next 10 years. The continued rise of electronic media will result in decreasing demand for print newspapers. Despite this decline, advertising and promotions managers are expected to see employment growth in other industries in which they will be needed to manage digital media campaigns that often target customers through the use of websites, social media, or live chats.

Through the Internet, advertising campaigns can reach a target audience across many platforms. This greater reach can increase the scale of the campaigns that advertising and promotions managers oversee. With better advertising management software, advertising and promotions managers can control these campaigns more easily.

Many of the high level jobs are very competitive. College graduates with extensive experience, a high level of creativity, and strong communication skills should have the best job opportunities.

The largest employers of advertising and promotions managers were as follows:

Advertising, public relations, and related services	40%
Information	11%
Management of companies and enterprises	8%
Self-employed workers	6%
Wholesale trade	6%

Marketing managers held about 259,200 jobs in 2018. The largest employers of marketing managers were as follows:

Professional, scientific, and technical services	23%
Management of companies and enterprises	14%
Finance and insurance	10%
Manufacturing	10%
Wholesale trade	8%

Because the work of advertising, promotions, and marketing managers directly affects a firm's revenue, people in these occupations typically work closely with top executives.

The jobs of advertising, promotions, and marketing managers can often be stressful, particularly near deadlines. Additionally, they may travel to meet with clients or media representatives.

Percent change in employment, Projected 2018–28

Marketing managers: 8%

Advertising, promotions, and marketing managers: 8%

Advertising, marketing, promotions, public relations, and sales managers: 6%

Total, all occupations: 5%

Note: All Occupations includes all occupations in the U.S. Economy.
Source: U.S. Bureau of Labor Statistics, Employment Projections program

Related Occupations
- Advertising Director
- Advertising Sales Agent
- Copywriter
- Electronic Commerce Specialist
- Public Relations Specialist

Conversation With . . .
KATHRYN FLYNN

Senior Editor
Dragonfly Editorial, based in Dayton, Ohio
Editor, 32 years

1. What was your individual career path in terms of education/training, entry-level job, or other significant opportunity?

I enrolled in Indiana University's journalism school with the intent of becoming a newspaper reporter, thinking that eventually I might want to cover politics for a large metropolitan daily. I liked reporting but increasingly became passionate about the editing process: developing story ideas, talking about an article's organization, then asking critical questions and fixing errors. I switched my focus and I've never looked back.

My first job after graduating with a BA in journalism and political science was as a copyeditor for a small newspaper in Pennsylvania. I was only there for a year and a half, but starting small was a great way to build on what I had learned in college. By the time I left, I was working as city editor on Friday nights.

I then took a job at *The Capital* in Annapolis, Maryland, working as a copy editor. I quickly went on to become assistant features editor, then features editor, the job I held for most of my 22 years with the paper. Later, I also took on assistant city editor responsibilities.

Relatively early on, I also started freelancing, since newspapers aren't known for their generous salaries. I found that I could use my editing skills on my own schedule—after everybody else was asleep, or on a quiet Sunday afternoon—in my own home.

Meantime, I survived several rounds of layoffs at my newspaper but finally decided to put my abilities to work elsewhere. I took a job as a technical writer and editor for a telecommunications firm until the company was bought out. I thought about freelancing full-time but faced two problems. One, freelance work can come in fits and starts. As a single parent, the prospect of going a week or two without work sets me into a panic. And two, successful full-time freelancing requires a business acumen and drive that I lack. Developing and marketing the business, regularly applying for new work with prospective clients, the timekeeping, invoicing, and quarterly estimated taxes—it's a lot of extra work when I really just want to spend my time working with words.

So, I reached out to the owner of a growing small company I had been freelancing for and told her about my newfound availability. A few weeks later I was working as a full-time, salaried employee at the company, which edits complex documents for companies around the world. I might start out the week working on a report on mergers and acquisitions in the fast food industry, continue on to a document about health programs in Uganda, then write an executive bio for a company newsletter, and finish by editing a proposal response for a government IT support contract. And then I might spend the weekend editing a cookbook for a freelance client.

2. What are the most important skills and/or qualities for someone in your profession?

The most important thing for an editor to possess is a love of the English language, including its complexities, its consistencies, its fluidity. You'll be working with language all day every day, so you really need to love it. Beyond that, an innate curiosity and love of learning will keep you engaged in your work, and attention to detail will help you find errors in everything from punctuation to continuity.

I think it's also important to step back and see the whole picture of what you're editing so you can assess its organization and flow.

And, finally, a good editor will edit and improve a document without losing the author's voice. It's important to make a change because it needs to be made, not just because you can.

3. What do you wish you had known going into this profession?

I wish I would have known that the newspaper journalism I studied and poured so much of my energy into would be so drastically changed by the internet and corporate takeovers that it would border on extinction just a few decades later.

Another thing I didn't realize is how very marketable the ability to write and edit is. There are lots of ways to make a living if you can help an organization communicate clearly.

4. Are there many job opportunities in your profession? In what specific areas?

All sorts of companies and organizations need people who can communicate clearly and there are plenty of opportunities. These jobs exist in health care, nonprofits, higher education, and technical/scientific fields. Good writing and editing make it easy for the reader to understand the intended message, which can help a corporate brand win business, reach potential customers, and improve its reputation.

5. How do you see your profession changing in the next five years? How will technology impact that change, and what skills will be required?

Technology isn't perfect and doesn't replace the necessary skill set, but it can point out inconsistencies or missed mistakes. Editors need to be able to fearlessly adapt to new technology, even as it is being developed at breakneck speed. The ability to work at a distance from clients and coworkers—in my current position, for example, I am in Maryland, my supervisor is in Tennessee, the company is based in Ohio, and our contractors are located throughout the country—opens up new opportunities. It also allows me to work in fuzzy socks.

6. What do you enjoy most about your job? What do you enjoy least about your job?

I love being part of a team of word nerds. We have some interesting conversations, and even though we aren't physically in the same office, we are a good support system for each other. We can draw on each other's strengths and expertise when questions arise. I also love the variety of the content I edit.

I least enjoy the paperwork associated with billable hours for my day job, and invoicing and taxes for my freelance work. I know it's absolutely necessary, but tracking everything is a pain.

7. Can you suggest a valuable "try this" for students considering a career in your profession?

I find reading content out loud to be helpful (and Microsoft Word now has a Read Aloud feature that will do it for you). Some editors read sentences backwards to make sure everything's correct, though that's never worked for me.

More broadly, I would encourage students to work on a publication such as their student newspaper, yearbook, or literary magazine, where they can learn by doing and by being surrounded by other writers and editors. As students continue their education, many professional organizations welcome college students and provide great opportunities for networking and professional development. ACES: The Society for Editing (https://aceseditors.org) is my personal favorite, and it even has a scholarship for student editors.

MORE INFORMATION

Advertising Research Foundation
432 Park Avenue South, 4th Floor
New York, NY 10016-8013
212.751.5656
thearf.org

American Advertising Federation
1101 K Street, NW, Suite 420
Washington, DC 20005-6306
202.898.0089
aaf@aaf.org
www.aaf.org

National Student Advertising
Competition
https://www.aaf.org/AAFMemberR/
Awards_and_Events/Programs_
Events/NSAC.aspx

4A's/American Association of Advertising Agencies
1065 Avenue of the Americas New
York, New York 10018
212.682.2500
OBD@aaaa.org
www.aaaa.org

Association for Women in Communications
1717 E. Republic Rd. Ste A
Springfield, MO 65804
703.370.7436
www.womcom.org

Association of National Advertisers
10 Grand Central
155 E 44th Street
New York, NY 10017
Phone: 212.697.5950
info@ana.net
www.ana.net

Kylie Grimshaw Hughes/Editor

Archivists, Curators, and Museum Workers

Snapshot

Career Cluster(s): Arts, A/V Technology and Communications, Hospitality and Tourism

Interests: History, culture, art, preserving documents, organizing information, research, communication

Earnings (2018 Median): $48,400 yearly; $23.27 hourly

Employment and Outlook: Faster Than Average Growth Expected

OVERVIEW

Sphere of Work

Archivists and curators are preservationists of human culture and history and the natural world. They collect, appraise, organize, and preserve documents, artwork, specimens, ephemera, films, and many other objects for historical and educational purposes. Archivists usually handle documents and records that are of historical value. Curators are more likely

to manage cultural or biological items, such as artwork or nature collections.

Work Environment

Archivists work in libraries, government depositories, universities, and historical museums, while curators are more often employed in art museums, zoos, nature centers, and other cultural or scientific institutions. Each typically divides the workweek between independent projects and interaction with other staff and outsiders, such as dealers, researchers, and the public.

Profile

Interests: Data, People
Working Conditions: Work Inside
Physical Strength: Light Work
Education Needs: Master's Degree, Doctoral Degree
Licensure/Certification: Usually Not Required
Physical Abilities Not Required: Not Climb, Not Kneel, Not Hear and/or Talk
Opportunities for Experience: Internship, Apprenticeship, Volunteer Work, Part-time Work
Holland Interest Score: AES

* See Appendix A

Occupation Interest

People interested in archivist or curator positions value the contributions of humans or the natural world and realize their importance in research. They are scholars who possess good organizational skills and a knack for handling irreplaceable items that are often fragile and extremely valuable. They need to be both detail-oriented and aware of larger cultural, scientific, and/or historical contexts. Other important traits include critical thinking, leadership ability, oral and written communication skills, and a high level of integrity.

A Day in the Life—Duties and Responsibilities

Archivists and curators build on their institution's collections by purchasing items or receiving them as gifts, often the result of bequests. A collection donated by a celebrated author might consist of boxes of unpublished manuscripts and drafts, personal correspondence, publishing contracts, and other printed matter. A collection obtained from a philatelist might include rare postal stamps, philatelic books and journals, microscopes, antique magnifying glasses, and other materials.

The archivist or curator is usually responsible for deciding what items to keep based on physical condition, financial, historical, and cultural value, and relevance to the institution's mission or purpose. While assessing each item, he or she authenticates its provenance (date and origin) and researches the item for any additional relevant information. The archivist or curator also determines how best to preserve and store items. For example, special cabinets may have to be ordered or an item may be given to a conservator for repairs.

Next, the archivist or curator catalogues or classifies items in a database so scholars can access the information. These databases also allow archivists or curators to keep track of their collections, provide reference service, and plan exhibits. Many different classification systems are used, although the most common one in the United States is the Library of Congress Classification System. Some items may be given a taxonomic classification as well as a call number.

Curators and archivists have other tasks in addition to their preservation work. Curators and archivists often write articles, grant proposals, and annual reports. Depending on their work environment, they may give tours and presentations to the public. Curators and archivists may also take care of other administrative duties or oversee assistants who handle some of these responsibilities, or they may do everything themselves.

Duties and Responsibilities

Archivists typically do the following:

- **Authenticate and appraise historical documents and archival materials**
- **Preserve and maintain documents and objects**
- **Create and manage a system to maintain and preserve electronic records**
- **Organize and classify archival records to make them easy to search through**
- **Safeguard records by creating film and digital copies**
- **Direct workers to help arrange, exhibit, and maintain collections**
- **Set and administer policy guidelines concerning public access to materials**
- **Find and acquire new materials for their archives**

Duties and Responsibilities

Curators, museum technicians, and conservators typically do the following:

- **Acquire, store, and exhibit collections**
- **Select the theme and design of exhibits**
- **Design, organize, and conduct tours and workshops for the public**
- **Attend meetings and civic events to promote their institution**
- **Clean objects such as ancient tools, coins, and statues**
- **Direct and supervise curatorial, technical, and student staff**
- **Plan and conduct special research projects**

OCCUPATION SPECIALTIES

Museum Technicians

Museum Technicians prepare specimens for museum collections and exhibits. They preserve and restore specimens by reassembling fragmented pieces and creating substitute pieces.

Art Conservators

Art Conservators coordinate the examination, repair and conservation of art objects.

Historic-Site Administrators

Historic-Site Administrators manage the overall operations of an historic structure or site.

Museum Registrars

Museum Registrars maintain records of the condition and location of objects in museum collections and oversee the movement of objects to other locations.

Archivists preserve important or historically significant documents and records. They coordinate educational and public outreach programs, such as tours, workshops, lectures, and classes. They also may work with researchers on topics and items relevant to their collections. Some archivists specialize in a particular era of history so that they can have a better understanding of the records from that era. Archivists typically work with specific forms of records, such as manuscripts, electronic records, websites, photographs, maps, motion pictures, or sound recordings.

Curators, also known as museum directors, lead the acquisition, storage, and exhibition of collections. They negotiate and authorize the purchase, sale, exchange, and loan of collections. They also may research, authenticate, evaluate, and categorize the specimens in a collection. Curators often perform administrative tasks and help manage their institution's research projects and related educational programs. They may represent their institution in the media, at public events, at conventions, and at professional conferences.

In larger institutions, some curators may specialize in a particular field, such as botany, art, or history. For example, a large natural history museum might employ separate curators for its collections of birds, fish, insects, and mammals.

In smaller institutions with only one or a few curators, one curator may be responsible for a number of tasks, from taking care of collections to directing the affairs of the museum.

Museum technicians, commonly known as registrars or collections specialists, concentrate on the care and safeguarding of the objects in museum collections and exhibitions. They oversee the logistics of acquisitions, insurance policies, risk management, and loaning of objects to and from the museum for exhibition or research. They keep detailed records of the conditions and locations of the objects that are on display, in storage, or being transported to another museum. They also maintain and store any documentation associated with the objects.

Museum technicians may answer questions from the public and help curators and outside scholars use the museum's collections.

Conservators handle, preserve, treat, and keep records of works of art, artifacts, and specimens. They may perform substantial historical, scientific, and archeological research. They document their findings and treat items in order to minimize deterioration or restore them to their original state. Conservators usually specialize in a particular material or group of objects, such as documents and books, paintings, decorative arts, textiles, metals, or architectural material.

Some conservators use x-rays, chemical testing, microscopes, special lights, and other laboratory equipment and techniques to examine objects, determine their condition, and decide on the best way to preserve them. They also may participate in outreach programs, research topics in their specialty, and write articles for scholarly journals.

WORK ENVIRONMENT

Immediate Physical Environment

Archivists and curators tend to work at least part of the time in climate-controlled storage facilities. They may have to wear white gloves or masks to protect items from human contamination. They sometimes deal with dust, mold, and insect infestations. Fieldwork may include visits to off-site locations such as auctions, schools, and private residences.

Human Environment

Archivists and curators usually report to a director and may supervise assistants, volunteers, or interns. In some cases, the curator is the director and reports to a board of administrators. Archivists and curators also interact with clerical staff and fellow preservation professionals, such as librarians, conservators, or museum technicians. They also work with researchers and other members of the public who use their facilities.

Transferable Skills and Abilities

Communication Skills
- Speaking effectively
- Writing concisely

Organization and Management Skills
- Coordinating tasks
- Making decisions

Managing people/groups
- Paying attention to and handling details

Research and Planning Skills
- Analyzing information
- Creating ideas
- Developing evaluation strategies
- Using logical reasoning

Technical Skills
- Performing scientific, mathematical, and technical work

Technological Environment

Archivists and curators rely heavily on computers for research, database management, file sharing, and communication. They also use a variety of digitization equipment for preservation purposes, including digital photography and video cameras. Microscopes are often used for detail work. In many cases, they must be familiar with radio-frequency identifications (RFIDs) and other inventory control and anti-theft systems.

EDUCATION, TRAINING, AND ADVANCEMENT

High School/Secondary

Archivist and curator positions require advanced education. A strong college preparatory program with electives in the areas of professional interest will provide the best foundation for postsecondary studies. History courses are especially important for aspiring archivists and curators. Students interested in becoming a curator of art should take art history and appreciation courses. Botany, zoology, and other natural sciences are important for curators of natural history. Students should also consider volunteering or working part-time in a library, museum, or other similar institution.

Suggested High School Subjects

- Algebra
- Arts
- Biology
- Chemistry
- College Preparatory
- Composition
- English
- Foreign Languages
- History
- Humanities
- Literature
- Social Studies

Related Career Pathways/Majors

Arts, A/V Technology, and Communications Cluster

- Visual Arts Pathway

Hospitality and Tourism Cluster

- Recreation, Amusements, and Attractions Pathway

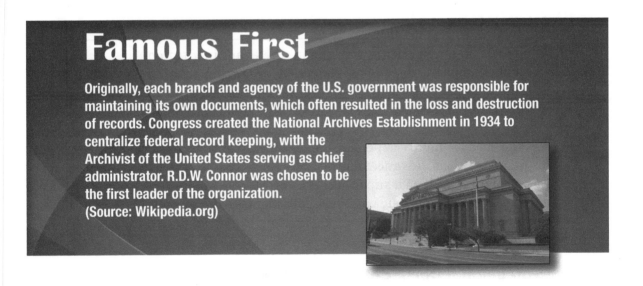

Famous First

Originally, each branch and agency of the U.S. government was responsible for maintaining its own documents, which often resulted in the loss and destruction of records. Congress created the National Archives Establishment in 1934 to centralize federal record keeping, with the Archivist of the United States serving as chief administrator. R.D.W. Connor was chosen to be the first leader of the organization.
(Source: Wikipedia.org)

Postsecondary

A bachelor's degree in history, art history, botany, political science, or other relevant discipline, with additional coursework in archival or museum studies, is the minimum requirement; however, most positions require a master's degree or doctorate in the specialized discipline or a master's degree in library science, archival studies, or museum studies. Business and public administration courses may also be useful. An internship or other work experience in a related institution is typically required for employment. Continuing education courses are expected as part of ongoing professional training.

Related College Majors
- American (U.S.) History
- Art History, Criticism, and Conservation
- Art, General
- Historic Preservation/Conservation and Architectural History
- History
- Library Science/Librarianship
- Museology/Museum Studies
- Public History and Archival Administration

Adult Job Seekers

Adults who have experience working at a relevant institution, researching a particular type of collection, or writing grant proposals or fundraising have an advantage over inexperienced graduates, as maturity and experience are often desired in addition to education.

Advancement is highly dependent upon the size of the institution. In larger institutions, advancement usually takes the form of increasing responsibility, such as a supervisory or directorial position. In government positions, one can move into higher pay grades with proper experience and education. Consulting is also an option for experienced professionals.

Professional Certification and Licensure

Licensing is typically not necessary for archivists and curators, although some employers may require certification by a professional organization, such as the Academy of Certified Archivists (ACA). A master's degree and archival experience are necessary before one can take the ACA written exam for certification. Those interested in becoming certified should consult credible professional associations within the field and follow professional debate as to the relevancy and value of any certification program.

Additional Requirements

Physical strength is needed to lift heavy boxes or other items, and good eyesight is needed for detail work. Membership in professional archivist or curator associations may provide access to networking opportunities and professional development programs.

EARNINGS AND ADVANCEMENT

The median annual wage for archivists, curators, and museum workers was $48,400 in May 2018. The median wage is the wage at which half the workers in an occupation earned more than that amount and half earned less. The lowest 10 percent earned less than $27,190, and the highest 10 percent earned more than $86,480.

Median annual wages, May 2018

Archivists, curators, and museum technicians: $48,400

Librarians, curators, and archivists: $48,020

Total, all occupations: $38,640

Note: All Occupations includes all occupations in the U.S. Economy.
Source: U.S. Bureau of Labor Statistics, Employment Projections program

Median annual wages for archivists, curators, and museum workers in May 2018 were as follows:

Curators	$53,780
Archivists	$52,240
Museum technicians and conservators	$43,020

In May 2018, the median annual wages for archivists, curators, and museum workers in the top industries in which they worked were as follows:

Educational services; state, local, and private	$54,290
Government	$50,070
Museums, historical sites, and similar institutions	$45,350

Most archivists, curators, museum technicians, and conservators work full-time.

Archivists in government agencies and corporations generally work during regular business hours. Curators in large institutions may travel extensively to evaluate potential additions to the collection, organize exhibits, and conduct research. However, for curators in small institutions, travel may be rare. Museum technicians may need to work evenings and weekends if their institutions are open to the public during those times.

EMPLOYMENT AND OUTLOOK

There were approximately 18,000 archivists and curators employed nationally in 2010. They were employed in museums and historical sites; federal, state, and local governments; and public and private educational institutions, mainly college and university libraries. Employment of archivists and curators is expected to grow faster than the average for all occupations through the year 2020, which means employment is projected to increase 20 percent to 28 percent. Demand is expected to increase as public and private organizations emphasize establishing archives and organizing records, especially electronically. Museum and zoo attendance has been on the rise and is expected to continue increasing, which will generate demand for curators.

Employment of archivists is projected to grow 9 percent from 2018 to 2028, faster than the average for all occupations. Demand for archivists is expected to increase as public and private organizations require increasing volumes of records and information to be organized and made accessible. The growing use of electronic records may cause an increase in demand for archivists who specialize in electronic records and records management.

Employment of curators is projected to grow 10 percent from 2018 to 2028, faster than the average for all occupations. Continued public interest in museums and other cultural centers should lead to increased demand for curators and for the collections they manage.

Employment of museum technicians and conservators is projected to grow 9 percent from 2018 to 2028, faster than the average for all occupations. Public interest in science, art, history, and technology is expected to spur some demand for museum technicians and conservators.

Archives and museums that receive federal funds can be affected by changes to the federal budget. When funding is cut, there may be a reduction in the demand for these workers. However, budget surpluses may lead to more job openings.

Candidates seeking archivist, curator, museum technician, or conservator jobs should expect very strong competition because of the high number of qualified applicants per job opening. Graduates with highly specialized training, a master's degree, and internship or volunteer experience should have the best job prospects.

Percent change in employment, Projected 2018–28

Archivists, curators, and museum technicians: 9%

Total, all occupations: 5%

Librarians, curators, and archivists: 3%

Note: All Occupations includes all occupations in the U.S. Economy.
Source: U.S. Bureau of Labor Statistics, Employment Projections program

Related Occupations
- Anthropologist
- Librarian
- Media Specialist
- Research Assistant

Conversation With . . . SAMANTHA NORLING

Archivist, Indianapolis Museum of Art
Indianapolis, Indiana
Archivist, 4 years

1. What was your individual career path in terms of education/training, entry-level job, or other significant opportunity?

My interest in archives took root while I was pursuing a bachelor's degree in American studies and interned at two museums in visitor services. After graduating, I cataloged artifacts part-time at the Scottish Rite of Freemasonry Museum and Library in Washington DC. While researching graduate programs in museum studies, my supervisor (a professional archivist) suggested that I keep library science in mind, which is a common academic path into archival work—many archivist job postings require a library science degree, often with an archives management concentration.

Ultimately, I selected a dual graduate program in public history and library science. Before moving to Indianapolis to begin grad school, I secured a part-time job as Project Archivist at the Indiana Historical Society, which I held throughout graduate school thanks to a work-study partnership between my school and the society. Each summer, I returned to DC for archival internships: first at the Library of Congress, and then at the Association of American Medical Colleges. This practical experience in a variety of settings, along with additional educational opportunities such as conferences, workshops, and webinars, made me a strong applicant for professional positions when I left school. I was offered my current job at the Indianapolis Museum of Art three months after graduating.

2. What are the most important skills and/or qualities for someone in your profession?

Attention to detail and strong organizational skills are necessary when arranging and describing sometimes overwhelmingly large collections of documents, photographs, or other materials. The ability to conduct research effectively is also important, as archivists are often asked to assist others in their research projects, which can reach outside the institution where you work. And strong communication and people skills are a must because, contrary to the popular image of the archivist sitting alone among stacks of books, collaboration with colleagues and interacting with the public are common.

3. **What do you wish you had known going into this profession?**

I cannot stress how important mentorship was in my career path, and that has been true for many early-career archivists that I know. Professors, supervisors, and connections made at conferences can really point students in the right direction and help you establish yourself in the profession before graduating and entering the job market.

4. **Are there many job opportunities in your profession? In what specific areas?**

There are many job opportunities in the archives profession, in a wide variety of organizations: museums, historical societies, public and university libraries, non-profits, city, state and national government, businesses, and more. However, there's a lot of competition for jobs among recent graduates, so it's important to enter the market with both practical experience and theoretical knowledge. It is common for recent graduates to work at least one temporary, grant-funded position (part- or full-time) for a year or longer before securing a permanent position. Taking courses in born-digital preservation and related topics could help give you an edge in the job market. (Born-digital records are those that were originally produced in a digital format, rather than converted from, for instance, print.)

5. **How do you see your profession changing in the next five years? What role will technology play in those changes, and what skills will be required?**

It's an exciting time as archivists face the challenges that born-digital records present and best practices evolve to meet those needs. Because of the digital nature of many records collected by archives today, technology in many forms is becoming more central to archival work. Knowledge of a wide variety of digital file formats, along with the systems and tools to help ingest and preserve those files long-term, will likely be a requirement for archivists in the not-so-distant future.

6. **What do you enjoy most about your job? What do you enjoy least about your job?**

I love when I get the chance to collaborate with colleagues in other departments of the museum. Creating exhibitions, selecting and implementing a new digital asset management system for the museum, and creating an online portal allowing the public to access our digitized collections are examples of cross-departmental projects I've worked on.

My least favorite part of the job is that I often work alone because I'm the only archivist in my institution. This is known as a "lone arranger" in the profession, and is somewhat common, though the majority of archivists work with other archivists on a daily basis.

7. Can you suggest a valuable "try this" for students considering a career in your profession?

Visit a local archives (believe me, there are many in every city!) and talk the archivists. If possible, go with a research need in mind, perhaps a collection that the archives hold that you would like to look through. Students should find an opportunity to conduct primary source research in an archives for an assignment—most colleges and universities have special collections and university archives right on campus.

MORE INFORMATION

Academy of Certified Archivists (ACA)
230 Washington Avenue, Suite 101
Albany, NY 12203
518.694.8471
ww.certifiedarchivists.org

Certifies archivists:
https://www.certifiedarchivists.org/
get-certified/

American Association for State and Local History
2021 21st Ave S., Suite 320
Nashville, TN 37212
Phone: 615-320-3203
info@AASLH.orgwww.aaslh.org
https://aaslh.org/

American Alliance of Museums (AAM)
2451 Crystal Drive, Suite 1005
Arlington, VA 22202
202.289.1818
www.aam-us.org

American Institute for Conservation (AIC) and Foundation for Advancement In Conservation
727 15th St., NW, Suite 500
Washington, DC 20005
www.culturalheritage.org

Association for Art Museum Curators (AAMC)
174 East 80th Street
New York, NY 10075
646.405.8065
www.artcurators.org

Provides grants for students and professional development:
www.artcurators.org/?page=Grants

Association of Moving Image Archivists (AMIA)
1313 North Vine Street
Hollywood, CA 90028
323.463.1500
AMIA@amianet.org
www.amianet.org

Provides scholarships and fellowships:
www.amianet.org/events/scholarship.
php

Offers the Silver Light Award for "career achievement in moving image archiving":
http://www.amianet.org/events/
awardsilver.php

National Association of Government Archives and Records Administrators (NAGARA)
444 N. Capitol Street, NW
Suite 237
Washington, DC 20001
202.508.3800
info@nagara.org
https://www.nagara.org/

National Council on Public History

Cavanaugh Hall 127
425 University Boulevard
Indianapolis, IN 46202-5140
317.274.2716
ncph@iupui.edu
www.ncph.org

National Trust for Historic Preservation

The Watergate Office Building
2600 Virginia Avenue NW,
Suite 1100
Washington, DC 20037
202.588.6000
https://savingplaces.org/

Organization of American Historians

112 N. Bryan Avenue
Bloomington, IN 47408-4141
812.855.9854
oah@oah.org
www.oah.org

Society for History in the Federal Government

P.O. Box 14139
Benjamin Franklin Station
Washington, DC 20044
www.shfg.org

Society of American Archivists (SAA)

17 North State Street, Suite 1425
Chicago, IL 60602-3315
312.606.0722
www2.archivists.org

Maintains a directory of postsecondary archival programs:
www2.archivists.org/dae

Sally Driscoll/Editor

Clergy

Snapshot

Career Cluster(s): Human Services
Interests: Theology, public speaking, listening, supporting others, communicating with others
Earnings (2018 Median): $56,250
Employment and Outlook: Average Growth Expected

OVERVIEW

Sphere of Work

Clergy are trained spiritual leaders in a community of faith. They conduct religious rites and ceremonies such as weddings and funerals, devise and oversee religious education programs, offer comfort to those who are suffering illness or grief, and counsel people troubled by family or personal problems. Most clergy work in a house of worship. Some work in the military, medical facilities, prisons, private corporations, or social service agencies, or choose to teach in seminaries and religious schools.

Work Environment

Clergy are usually on call at all times. A member of the clergy can be called upon at any time to perform their ministerial duties. Clergy thus must be flexible and adaptable, able to work with changing situations as they arise. As the standard office schedule is usually not possible, clergy often take two days off during the week. Depending upon the size of the worship institution and its ability to provide secretarial assistance, there may be extensive administrative and financial records to maintain in addition to scholarly and caregiving duties.

Profile

Interests: Data, People
Working Conditions: Work Inside
Physical Strength: Light Work
Education Needs: Bachelor's Degree, Master's Degree
Licensure/Certification: Usually Not Required
Physical Abilities Not Required: Not Climb, Not Kneel, Not Handle, Not See
Opportunities for Experience: Military Service, Volunteer Work
Holland Interest Score: SAI

* See Appendix A

Occupation Interest

Individuals interested in pursuing a career in religion should be adept at understanding the theology of their specific faith tradition and applying it in practical situations, and should also possess a strong sense of compassion. Because clergy need to be comfortable interacting with people on an individual basis, in small numbers, and in large groups, they should be both good listeners and skilled public speakers. Some background in psychology and social services is also helpful, as clergy need to be able to deal calmly with unexpected emergencies.

A Day in the Life—Duties and Responsibilities

The typical workday for members of clergy varies greatly, often depending on the size and location of the religious institution in which they are employed. Clergy in small houses of worship may find themselves as the only paid staff members, so a great deal of administrative office work must be included in the schedule, even with volunteer secretarial help that is sometimes offered. Clergy in larger institutions often have a more specific focus. They may specialize in youth ministry, visitation of the sick and bereaved, financial and administrative planning for expansion of the institution, or scholarly message preparation and delivery on a weekly basis.

All clergy study sacred texts, interpret religious laws, follow current religious and social events, provide instruction and counseling, care for the needy, lead prayer, and perform religious ceremonies as requested. Participation in local community events may also be required.

In group settings such as committee meetings, clergy must interact diplomatically with a variety of people who may hold strong opinions on sensitive subjects. On an individual basis, clergy act as trustworthy counselors who may hear extremely personal and confidential information. In rare instances, such as cases of child or spousal abuse, they may be required to contact law enforcement officials.

Duties and Responsibilities

- Tending to the needs of sick and impoverished members
- Teaching and counseling congregation members
- Visiting hospitals or shut-in members
- Doing work for charitable organizations
- Organizing youth activities
- Following the directions of their supervisors

WORK ENVIRONMENT

Immediate Physical Environment

Much of the work of clergy is performed in an office or study setting; however, clergy are on-call professionals who must have reliable and accessible means of transport, as they need to respond quickly when emergencies occur.

Transferable Skills and Abilities

Communication Skills
- Listening attentively
- Speaking effectively
- Writing concisely

Interpersonal/Social Skills
- Being able to remain calm
- Being patient
- Counseling others
- Providing support to others
- Teaching others
- Working as a member of a team

Organization and Management Skills
- Handling challenging situations
- Making decisions
- Managing people/groups
- Managing time
- Organizing information or materials

Research and Planning Skills
- Solving problems
- Using logical reasoning

Human Environment

In large institutions, clergy interact with other staff members and laity, requiring the use of diplomatic and administrative abilities. In smaller institutions, where clergy may be the only paid staff, a slower pace and less human interaction is common, and personal scheduling and work discipline become even more important. In hospitals, military bases, and secular colleges, chaplains should be prepared to work with people from various religions, as well as those who have no religious background.

Technological Environment

Fewer houses of worship are able to provide professional secretarial assistance, which means that clergy are increasingly required to be familiar with software programs for word processing, desktop publishing, presentations, and financial transactions (especially with regard to taxation regulations for nonprofit institutions).

EDUCATION, TRAINING, AND ADVANCEMENT

High School/Secondary

High school students who wish to become clergy can best prepare by studying English, history, languages, philosophy, and psychology. Since many public schools do not offer courses in religion, interested high school students may wish to request credit for courses taken at a local college or an independent high school of the student's faith tradition. Volunteer work with a nonprofit organization or hospital is also helpful preparation.

Suggested High School Subjects
- Business and Computer Technology
- College Preparatory
- English
- History
- Humanities
- Literature
- Philosophy
- Political Science
- Psychology
- Social Studies
- Sociology
- Speech
- Theatre and Drama

Related Career Pathways/Majors

Human Services Cluster
- Family and Community Services Pathway

Famous First

For 20 years, Father Fulton John Sheen (later Monsignor) hosted the nighttime radio program *The Catholic Hour* before moving to television and presenting *Life Is Worth Living*. Sheen's final presenting role was on the syndicated *The Fulton Sheen Program*. For this work, Sheen twice won an Emmy Award for Most Outstanding Television Personality and was featured on the cover of *Time Magazine*. (Source: Wikipedia.org)

Postsecondary

If possible, prospective clergy should take specific seminary preparatory courses at a college founded by the faith in which the student seeks ordination. However, counseling, psychology, and philosophy courses at universities offering no religious studies also provide a solid background. Those interested in military chaplaincy should obtain ROTC training as well, and education courses are necessary for students interested in ministry at a private school or college.

While some independent worship organizations do not require an advanced degree in theology or divinity, many do. Unlike most graduate schools, however, faith seminaries may not require a Graduate Record Exam (GRE) score. Because the requirements for a traditional divinity degree are diverse, students seeking to be a chaplain at the university level may want to consider a more focused degree in their faith's theology and history or in counseling, subjects that are more commonly available for doctoral degrees. Many universities include teaching requirements in a chaplain's job description, and thus prefer applicants who hold or are candidates for a doctoral degree.

Related College Majors
- Bible/Biblical Studies
- Biblical and Other Theological Languages and Literatures
- Pastoral Counseling and Specialized Ministries

- Religion/Religious Studies
- Religious Education
- Theology/Theological Studies

Adult Job Seekers

Life experience is a valuable asset in this field, which requires empathy for the struggles of daily life. Volunteer administrative positions in churches or other institutions of faith provide valuable background. Many seminaries offer courses and degrees online, with varying amounts of on-campus requirements. For work in hospitals, chaplains are usually required to have extensive Clinical Pastoral Education (CPE) preparation, in which candidates participate in volunteer training under the supervision of senior staff hospital chaplains. Teaching and youth counseling experience is important in religious schools and in university settings. Similarly, those seeking employment as corporate chaplains will want to be at familiar with business career activities. Adults seeking clergy positions should familiarize themselves with the requirements of the organizations where they wish to work.

Professional Certification and Licensure

Denominational ordination is usually required at some point, often after a trial period of employment, and certification by the state is necessary in order to officiate at weddings and funerals. In some states, it is possible to be ordained by the state itself, without specific religious affiliation. Chaplains may obtain certification from the Association of Professional Chaplains, National Association of Catholic Chaplains, or National Association of Jewish Chaplains.

Additional Requirements

Clergy are often called upon to provide counseling in sensitive situations; confidentiality in these cases is extremely important, as is the ability to ascertain when professional psychological help is needed, and, on rare occasions, when law enforcement should be notified. Some faiths have lifestyle requirements, such as celibacy or vows of poverty, for their clergy members.

EARNINGS AND ADVANCEMENT

Earnings vary greatly depending on the type of religion and can also be influenced by the experience of the clergy and the geographic location of the congregation.

Roman Catholic priests earn a salary. With further training and experience, they can rise in the ranks of administration of the Catholic Church. Diocesan priests had median annual earnings of $35,824 in 2018. Priests take a vow of poverty and are supported by their religious order. Any personal earnings are given to the order. Their vow of poverty is recognized by the Internal Revenue Service, which exempts them from paying federal income tax.

Most Protestant ministers are paid a salary, although a few are paid from the offering collections or even serve as a volunteer. Some denominations are tightly organized and have a rigid hierarchy through which one may advance, while in other denominations ministers may advance to a top position more quickly. Median annual earnings of Protestant ministers were $50,356 in 2018. In large, wealthier denominations, Protestant ministers often earned significantly higher salaries than those in smaller congregations.

Rabbis earn a salary. Since there is no formal hierarchy among congregations, rabbis can advance to head rabbis of well-established congregations, serve in the military, or teach in Rabbinical seminaries. Median annual earnings of rabbis were $140,000 in 2018.

Clergy usually receive a package of benefits that may include paid vacations, holidays, and sick days; life and health insurance; a car allowance; free housing; travel and education allowances; and a retirement plan. On occasion, clergy may earn extra money through teaching, writing or officiating at ceremonies, such as weddings

EMPLOYMENT AND OUTLOOK

There were approximately 432,559 clergy serving congregations nationally in 2018. Employment is expected to grow about as fast as the average for all occupations through the year 2020, which means employment is projected to increase 8 percent. Most job openings will stem from the need to replace clergy who leave the ministry, retire, or die.

Related Occupations
- Educational Counselor
- Marriage and Family Therapist
- Religious Activities and Education Director

Related Military Occupations
- Chaplain

Fast Fact

The Church used dramas during the Middle Ages to teach acceptable thought and behavior to the generally illiterate masses. Case in point: *Everyman*, which tells the tale of a man facing death who cannot find anyone but his good deeds to usher him to heaven.

Source: ancient.eu.

Conversation With . . . REV. DR. JO ANN DEASY

Director of Institutional Initiatives and Student Research
The Association of Theological Schools
Pittsburgh, Pennsylvania
Pastor and theological academic/
administrator, 24 years

1. What was your individual career path in terms of education/training, entry-level job, or other significant opportunity?

I grew up in a nominally Catholic home, stopped attending church in second grade, and got involved in an evangelical group in high school, where I had a conversion experience. I felt I wanted to give my life to that kind of work. The church was conservative and didn't really know what to do with a smart woman. At 17, I internalized a lot of that and had to take a slower path to figure out what I was called to do, because it didn't fit what they were hoping women would do.

I started with a bachelor's degree in engineering at the University of California at Berkeley, but knew that was not what I wanted to do with my life. So, after working in engineering for a year, I tested out work in church ministry, first as a counselor at a Christian summer camp, and then in a two-year internship in youth ministry.

I decided to pursue a graduate degree in theological education and earned my Master of Divinity at Gordon Conwell Theological Seminary in South Hamilton, Massachusetts. After graduating, I became minister of education for a church in Duluth and was ordained in the Evangelical Covenant Church. Two years later, I returned to North Park Theological Seminary in Chicago, where I had spent my final year of graduate school, now as dean of students. I stayed seven years, and left to finish my doctorate at Garrett-Evangelical Theological School in Evanston, Illinois. The stock market crashed just before I graduated in 2010, so it took a long time to find work. I also had not studied a classical discipline; I studied the sociology of churches. I took a number of part-time jobs until one of them, pastor of a congregation, finally became a full-time position. Five years ago, I began my job here.

I have been told I have a natural talent for writing, especially being able to write about complex concepts in a very accessible way. Thinking back, divinity school was a trial by fire because suddenly I was writing twenty-five-page papers, after engineering studies and its five-page papers. By my doctorate, I was writing one-hundred-page papers. I didn't get training in writing but what I did do was read classic authors such as Victor Hugo and Jane Austen.

When I started my doctorate, I honed my writing skills by starting a blog, writing theological reflections on my travel around the world, or weekly devotions during Advent. Being a youth minister required writing skills in marketing and publicity for different events. And there are so many different philosophies about how to prepare a sermon. Some traditions say create an outline, then listen to the Holy Spirit. Others say write down everything. Early on, I wrote every word but when it comes to public speaking, I learned that I needed to let go of that manuscript to do a good job. I learned to create the flow of an argument to organize my thoughts.

Now my job requires me to write in a number of capacities. I write shorter articles for publication. When I translate our myriads of research to come up with a couple of articles that are accessible to people, it's all about distilling that information. What are you really trying to say? Writing forces me to do that. I also do grant writing and reporting, advertising for my webinars, and scripts for presentations. About once a year I write a longer scholarly article for an academic journal. I also write reports and do postings for Listservs.

2. What are the most important skills and/or qualities for someone in your profession?

An ability to write articles to share data, resources, or theological reflections for a broad audience; program management and event planning skills; public speaking skills; and intercultural capacity. I find in writing and speaking publicly that you also need both humility and strength of character. You are putting your ideas out there and have to receive criticism, critique, and opposing arguments graciously. You have to walk a fine line that allows you to be both confident in your own voice and willing to listen to the input of others.

3. What do you wish you had known going into this profession?

I wish I had been more strategic in my doctoral program. I followed my interests and passions but did not make choices that would have made it easier to find a job. I did not connect with the right mentors, present at the right conferences, publish any scholarly articles, or choose a major that fit with current openings at theological schools for teaching positions.

I wish I had understood how much time would be given to administration. It seems that once you choose a path in administration in higher education it is difficult to get back into teaching.

4. Are there many job opportunities in your profession? In what specific areas?

Those with doctoral degrees similar to mine, in practical theology and/or sociology of religion, often need to be creative and pair administrative skills with other areas of expertise. I am serving in academic administration but am doing so at an accrediting agency. Others are serving in similar nonprofit, grantmaking, and resource organizations or teaching in all different types of organizations. Some are serving as pastors, ministers, or in other types of ministries.

5. **How do you see your profession changing in the next five years? How will technology impact that change, and what skills will be required?**

I need to be able to think about technological systems and structures that allow me to communicate, gather data, and disseminate data in ways that are efficient for both myself and the end users. There is an increasing need to make data and communication customized to individual users. There is also an increased need to learn how to communicate in ways that effectively get through the overwhelming amount of input everyone receives. There is a need to work with increasingly diverse and polarized groups of people.

I am constantly moving between big picture/industry thinking and needs of individual clients.

6. **What do you enjoy most about your job? What do you enjoy least about your job?**

I most enjoy talking with people about their own career passions, advocating for those on the margins, and writing all sorts of articles about my work, from short news pieces on events to executive summaries of data to deeper theological reflection articles.

I least enjoy office politics, sexism and patriarchy, and the relentless pace of my work.

7. **Can you suggest a valuable "try this" for students considering a career in your profession?**

Serve in student government, create a website or blog where you write regularly, or teach a course, workshop or Sunday school class.

MORE INFORMATION

Association for Clinical Pastoral Education
55 Ivan Allen Jr. Boulevard,
Suite 835
Atlanta, GA 30308
404.320.1472
acpe@acpe.edu
www.acpe.edu

Catholic Campus Ministry Association
1292 Long Hill Road
Stirling, NJ 07980
908.360.5110
info@ccmanet.org
www.ccmanet.org

Chaplaincy Institute
Interfaith Ordination Program
941 The Alameda
Berkeley, CA 94707
510.843.1422
www.chaplaincyinstitute.org

Corporate Chaplains of America
1300 Corporate Chaplain Drive
Wake Forest, NC 27587
919.570.0700
www.chaplain.org

Reconstructing Judaism
1299 Church Road
Wyncote, PA 19095
215.576.0500
https://www.reconstructingjudaism.org/

Military Chaplains Association
P.O. Box 7056
Arlington, VA 22207-7076
703.533.5890
www.mca-usa.org

National Council of Churches of Christ in the USA
110 Maryland Ave, NE, Suite 108
Washington, DC 20002
202.544.2350
https://nationalcouncilofchurches.us/

Copywriters

Snapshot

Career Cluster(s): Arts, A/V Technology and Communications, Business, Management, and Administration
Interests: Writing, being creative, current events, research, analyzing data, communicating with others
Earnings (2018 Median): $47,838 yearly
Employment and Outlook: Average Growth Expected

OVERVIEW

Sphere of Work

Copywriters work within the communication and information sectors. They research and prepare the written words that accompany advertising, promotional, and marketing materials. These include brochures, print advertising, press releases, scripts for television and radio commercials, websites, direct mail pieces, and any other communications that call for an ability to write engaging and persuasive content.

Copywriters are often employed by marketing and advertising agencies, but they may also work as independent freelancers. Copywriting is a highly collaborative role, which usually demands working with a team of creative colleagues and supervisors. Copywriters interact with other communication specialists, such as marketers, brand strategists, advertising executives, public relations executives, graphic designers, art directors, multimedia technicians, and editors. They are also likely to work with clients and business specialists across a broad range of industries, topics, products, and services.

Work Environment

Copywriters work in an office environment, although the role is sufficiently flexible to accommodate working from any place where computer and telecommunication technologies are readily available. Freelance copywriters may work remotely, from a home office or other setting.

Full-time copywriters generally work for marketing and advertising agencies or within other communication outlets. A full-time employee may expect to work forty hours per week during normal office hours. They may be required to work longer hours, as needed.

Profile

Interests: Data,
Working Conditions: Work Inside
Physical Strength: Light Work
Education Needs: Bachelor's Degree
Licensure/Certification: Usually Not Required
Physical Abilities Not Required: Not Climb, Not Kneel, Not Hear and/or Talk
Opportunities for Experience: Internship, Volunteer Work, Part-time Work
Holland Interest Score: ASI

* See Appendix A

Occupation Interest

Copywriting attracts graduates and professionals who have a strong grounding in written communications. This occupation suits people with an interest in writing and a flair for creative expression and engaging an audience. Copywriters must be able to write fluently on a broad range of topics and to manage multiple projects concurrently. They usually have a strong interest in trends and markets.

In addition to having excellent writing skills, copywriters must possess strong research and analytical abilities. They must have advanced oral communication and collaboration skills and the ability to produce creative work under pressure. Copywriting demands good organizational, prioritization, and time management skills. Copywriters must also be able to respond positively to constructive criticism and feedback about the work they produce.

A Day in the Life—Duties and Responsibilities

The copywriter's day is characterized by periods of independent and collaborative work. As a member of a creative team, copywriters meet with their colleagues, supervisors, and clients on a daily basis to brainstorm and present ideas as well as develop, analyze, and critique creative strategies and solve problems. Copywriters spend solitary time researching, drafting advertising and promotional materials, and revising content as needed. Research may entail activities like referring to consumer surveys or conducting interviews. The solitary aspects of the occupation demand high levels of self-discipline and self-motivation. This is especially important for freelance copywriters who spend much of their time working alone and managing their own workloads.

The copywriter's daily output includes written content and concepts for brochures, print advertising, billboards, press releases, scripts for television and radio commercials, websites, direct mail pieces, and other marketing materials. The copywriter may find that the projects and assignments they work on are subject to tight timeframes and strict deadlines. It is a daily challenge for copywriters to produce high quality creative work under pressure.

Copywriters may be expected to contribute within their workplaces more widely. This may include some administrative duties, such as tracking project hours.

Duties and Responsibilities

- Coming up with creative concepts that will sell a product or idea
- Developing a central theme for a campaign
- Promoting your work to agencies, clients or upper management

WORK ENVIRONMENT

Immediate Physical Environment

Office settings predominate. Copywriters in full-time employment generally work for small to large marketing and advertising firms or in other corporate contexts. Freelance copywriters often work from home.

Transferable Skills and Abilities

Communication Skills
- Expressing thoughts and ideas
- Persuading others
- Writing concisely

Interpersonal/Social Skills
- Being able to remain calm
- Being able to work independently
- Respecting others' opinions

Managing people/groups
- Paying attention to and handling details

Organization and Management Skills
- Managing time
- Meeting goals and deadlines

Research and Planning Skills
- Creating ideas

Human Environment

Copywriting demands strong collaborative skills. Copywriters interact with other communication and creative specialists, such as marketers, brand strategists, advertising executives, public relations executives, graphic designers, art directors, multimedia technicians, and editors. They are also likely to work with clients and business specialists across a broad range of industries.

Technological Environment

Copywriters use technologies that range from telephone, email, and the Internet to word processing software. Copywriters may also be expected to work with web content management systems and blogging software. Advanced computing skills and an understanding of multimedia, social media, and emerging media technologies are considered an advantage.

EDUCATION, TRAINING, AND ADVANCEMENT

High School/Secondary

High school students can best prepare for a career in copywriting by taking courses in English literature, language and composition, social studies, journalism, and business communications. The creative nature of copywriting may be explored through art and graphic design; the business aspects through business studies, accounting and entrepreneurship; and the technology aspects through computer literacy. Courses such as history and anthropology can also prepare the student for synthesizing research into written materials. Psychology and cultural studies may provide an understanding of group and individual responses to written and visual messaging. Extracurricular school activities that involve writing can also provide students with an opportunity to develop their writing skills and learn from others prior to graduation. Such activities might include entering writing competitions and writing for school newspapers or club newsletters.

Suggested High School Subjects
- Applied Communication
- Composition
- English
- Foreign Languages
- Journalism
- Literature
- Psychology

Related Career Pathways/Majors

Arts, A/V Technology, and Communications Cluster
- Journalism and Broadcasting Pathway

Business, Management, and Administration Cluster
- Marketing Pathway

Famous First

The first female copywriter, Helen Lansdowne, was inducted into the Advertising Hall of Fame in 1967, three years after her death. Her 1911 line "A skin you love to touch" for a soap ad is considered to be the first use of sex appeal in advertising. (Source: https://www.aaaa.org)

Postsecondary

Graduates from a diverse range of disciplines can become copywriters. The most common pathway to copywriting is by obtaining an undergraduate degree in communications, advertising, marketing, or journalism. Coursework in the social sciences can also be helpful preparation for writing persuasive content. A large number of colleges and universities offer courses in copywriting. There are also an increasing number of certified and non-certified copywriting programs, seminars, and workshops offered by private companies, academies, and professional associations.

Postsecondary students interested in a career in copywriting are also encouraged to become involved in extracurricular, club, or volunteer roles where they can develop their writing skills and begin to build a writing portfolio.

Related College Majors
- Advertising
- Communications, General
- English Language and Literature, General
- Liberal Arts and Sciences/Liberal Studies
- Marketing Management and Research
- Public Relations and Organizational Communications

Adult Job Seekers

Adults seeking a career transition into copywriting are advised to develop copywriting experience and a portfolio through part-time or volunteer work for a charity, non-profit organization, local club, or association. Writing a personal blog is another way to build a portfolio while also developing the daily discipline of writing.

An increasing number of copywriting opportunities are advertised on non-traditional job sites. The proliferation of web-based freelance writing sites allows people with little or no previous copywriting experience to upload their own articles for sale or bid for writing projects.

Taking writing courses may assist with networking and portfolio development. Self-guided learners may also benefit from reading "how to" books about copywriting or by undertaking short courses, seminars, or workshops.

Professional Certification and Licensure

There are no required professional certifications or licenses for copywriting. Practical experience generally outweighs formal qualifications in this occupation. Some professional associations provide certifications in the field. The American Marketing Association offers the Professional Certified Marketer (PCM) certification, which requires association membership and completion of a written exam. Consult credible professional associations within the field and follow professional debate as to the relevancy and value of any certification program.

Additional Requirements

The most important attribute for prospective copywriters is a love of writing combined with interest in a broad range of topics. In addition to advanced writing skills, copywriters must possess strong social and cultural awareness, an understanding of trends and markets, and the ability to write about products and services in emotionally engaging terms. A portfolio of writing samples is essential.

EARNINGS AND ADVANCEMENT

Copywriters can become copy supervisors or creative supervisors within an organization. Earnings for copywriters vary greatly depending on the specific job and the size, prestige and location of the company. Copywriters working in large organizations in urban areas can demand higher annual earnings. Median annual earnings of copywriters were $47,838 in 2018.

Copywriters may receive paid vacations, holidays, and sick days; life and health insurance; and retirement benefits. These are usually paid by the employer.

EMPLOYMENT AND OUTLOOK

Writers, of which copywriters are a specialty, held about 123,200 jobs nationally in 2018. About one-half of salaried writers worked in the information sector, which includes advertising; newspaper, periodical, book, and directory publishers; radio and television broadcasting; software publishers; motion picture and sound recording industries; Internet service providers, web search portals, and data processing services; and Internet publishing and broadcasting.

Employment is expected to grow as fast as average for all occupations through the year 2028, which means employment is projected to increase 8 percent. Turnover is relatively high in this occupation. Freelancers often leave the field because they cannot earn enough money.

Related Occupations

- Advertising and Marketing Manager
- Advertising Director
- Advertising Sales Agent
- Electronic Commerce Specialist
- Journalist
- Public Relations Specialist
- Radio/TV Announcer and Newscaster
- Technical Writer
- Writer and Editor

Fast Fact

Writers' words to know: mogigraphia means "writer's cramp" – which occurs in the muscles of the hand - and colygraphia, which means the dreaded writers' block.

Source: academicwritingexperts.com.

Conversation With . . . LAURA A. WILLIAMSON

President, LWM Communications, Inc.
Washington, D.C.
Journalist or freelance communications
consultant, 30 years

1. What was your individual career path in terms of education/training, entry-level job, or other significant opportunity?

For as long as I can remember, the written word has held power for me. Whether I was buried in a book, journaling, or writing poems and stories, disappearing into words on a page was something that made me feel good. I wasn't sure how to turn that into a living, but I knew somehow I would.

I earned my BA from Georgetown University's Honors English program, then went to work as a fact checker for a woman who was writing a book about former U.S. Secretary of Defense Robert S. McNamara. I learned a lot about the writing process and about the endless hours of research (years, even) involved in writing a book. It was a fantastic experience.

When this job concluded, I ended up getting a full-time job at the Urban Institute, a Washington, D.C. think tank, where I ran the clearinghouse. It was a job and it paid the bills. It wasn't a career. However, during this time I happened upon an ad for a travel writing workshop and signed up. A few hours later, armed with the name of a travel editor and a whole lot of inspiration, I phoned some friends in Canada looking for an easy travel destination. Together, we came up with the idea of writing about petroglyphs near their home in Winnipeg. The editor agreed to buy my story if he liked it—and he did. I was off and running.

Motivated by the sale of my first story—and first byline!—I applied to the Master's program at the University of Maryland College Park's journalism school. I wrote for the campus newspaper, and during a semester break, I walked into the offices of the Lynchburg (Va.) *News & Advance*, located the city editor, and told him that I wanted to work for him. He hired me as an intern on the spot. The *N&A* ultimately became my first full-time newspaper job.

Over the next four years, I moved up through two more newspapers, each larger than the last, while covering healthcare. Then I got on board at the *Atlanta Journal and Constitution*. I started out in the suburbs covering local government and worked my way up to the central newsroom and back into healthcare. I was the health and welfare reporter during welfare reform in the early to mid-90s.

I became more passionate about health and science, got married, and wanted to start a family. Like many before me, I decided to make the natural shift from journalism into public relations. But I swore then (and have kept this promise to myself) that I would only work for organizations whose mission I believed in. I freelanced for a progressive P.R. firm and for the Campaign for Tobacco-Free Kids, where I had the privilege of writing extensively for them during the tobacco legislation battles of the 1990s. I went on to work for Environmental Media Services, a progressive PR firm that also allowed me to work part-time when I was pregnant.

After my child was born, I decided to work part-time from home. I had significant contacts who continued to send me writing or editing assignments, which I worked in around my child's needs. As he grew older, I was able to work during his school hours. My consulting business grew alongside my child. And it grew 100 percent through referrals, which continues to be true today.

Even though there are now multiple platforms for communication, organizations still rely heavily upon the written word to get their message out. So, the work I do involves writing in many capacities.

I write whatever the client needs, and in most cases, I'm explaining science. Some clients need web content, some need press releases, and some need content for annual reports, highlighting their major achievements for the year. I write white papers, which are persuasive pieces that make an argument for change, typically in policy or business strategy. I also write messaging points, op-eds, so-called "Hill drops" that provide information for members of Congress, speeches, newsletters or Facebook/Twitter feeds.

2. What are the most important skills and/or qualities for someone in your profession?

Being able to write well and to do so quickly, capturing the essence of your client's message and communicating it clearly. Being able to write in an organization's (or individual's) voice other than your own. And for the science, the ability to translate research findings into everyday language, which often involves interviewing scientific investigators to clarify what they found.

You need to be able to think for yourself and take initiative because clients are outsourcing this work to save themselves time. They rely upon you to take the ball and run with it, to understand their needs and deliver a product that fits those needs.

You need to be organized and disciplined in order to get a large project finished by a certain date. You also need to know how to do research.

3. What do you wish you had known going into this profession?

How to set up an S Corporation sooner than I did. How to do my own accounting/taxes. Both would have saved me some money.

4. Are there many job opportunities in your profession? In what specific areas?

Yes. every business and organization needs well-written content.

5. How do you see your profession changing in the next five years? How will technology impact that change, and what skills will be required?

For me, technology changes mainly impact how I communicate with clients and deliver my final product. Writing is writing. The changes are more around how we handle conference calls or how we exchange documents. You need to be willing and able to learn new systems and applications.

6. What do you enjoy most about your job? What do you enjoy least about your job?

I love being able to turn complex science into language the rest of the world can understand and use. It's challenging and rewarding to write about the latest research in cancer treatments, cardiology, or diabetes.

As a consultant, I love the flexibility—I can work from anywhere and during whichever hours I choose. I work in bed in my pajamas. Or dressed and at my desk. Sometimes I work from other cities, states, or countries. It's up to me, as long as I meet my clients' deadlines.

I least like not having paid vacation or sick time, or company-provided health insurance. If I don't work I don't get paid. Also, I don't know how much work I will have from month to month and I often have to wait a month or more for payment. Being a consultant is not for everyone, and certainly not for someone who is risk averse.

7. Can you suggest a valuable "try this" for students considering a career in your profession?

If you know you can write well, what you need to find out is how well you can write quickly and under pressure. The best way to do that is to get an internship. I highly recommend doing this in a newsroom environment, where you will learn more about everything you need to know to survive in this business than anywhere else. It's trial by fire, and it's the best training you can get. It will also train you to write clearly and to avoid jargon. I do not recommend going straight into public relations without this experience.

MORE INFORMATION

Advertising Research Foundation
432 Park Avenue South, 4th Floor
New York, NY 10016-8013
212.751.5656
thearf.org

American Advertising Federation
1101 K Street, NW, Suite 420
Washington, DC 20005-6306
202.898.0089
aaf@aaf.org
www.aaf.org

National Student Advertising
Competition
https://www.aaf.org/AAFMemberR/
Awards_and_Events/Programs_
Events/NSAC.aspx

4A's/American Association of Advertising Agencies
1065 Avenue of the Americas New
York, New York 10018
212.682.2500
OBD@aaaa.org
www.aaaa.org

American Marketing Association
311 South Wacker Drive, Suite 5800
Chicago, IL 60606
800.262.1150
info@ama.org
www.marketingpower.com

American Society of Magazine Editors
28-07 Jackson Ave.
New York, NY 11101
212.872.3737
asme@magazine.org
www.magazine.org/editorial/asme

Association for Women in Communications
1717 E. Republic Rd. Ste A
Springfield, MO 65804
417.888.8606
www.womcom.org

Association of National Advertisers
10 Grand Central
155 E 44th Street
New York, NY 10017
Phone: 212.697.5950
info@ana.net
www.ana.net

Dow Jones Newspaper Fund, Inc.
P.O. Box 300
Princeton, NJ 08543-0300
609.452.2820
djnf@dowjones.com
www.newsfund.org

International Association of Business Communicators
649 Mission Street, 5th Floor
San Francisco, CA 94105
800.776.4222
service_centre@iabc.com
www.iabc.com

Public Relations Society of America
120 Wall Street, 21st Floor
New York, NY 10005
212.460.1400
membership@prsa.org
www.prsa.org

Society for Technical Communication
3251 Old Lee Highway, Suite 406
Fairfax, VA 22030
703.522.4114
www.stc.org

Kylie Grimshaw Hughes/Editor

Court Reporters

Snapshot

Career Cluster(s): Business, Management, and Administration
Interests: Legal system, current events, written communication
Earnings (2018 Median): $57,150 yearly; $27.48 hourly
Employment and Outlook: Average Growth Expected

OVERVIEW

Sphere of Work

Court reporters, also referred to as court stenographers, certified shorthand reporters, court monitors, or deposition reporters, record court proceedings for local, state, and federal courts. Court reporters create accurate verbatim transcripts of legal proceedings, meetings, judges' speeches, and conversations between lawyers and judges.

Court reporters are responsible for creating the written legal record that documents and preserves court proceedings. During court proceedings, they also assist judges, lawyers, juries, and defendants by locating specific information or records in the court record or transcript and by providing

closed-captioning and real-time translating services to those in need of speech and hearing related services.

Work Environment

Court reporters spend their workdays creating legal transcripts for both civil and criminal court proceedings within local, state, and federal court systems. Court reporters work in administrative offices and courtrooms. Freelance court reports may work from home offices, captioning televised or webcast legal proceedings. Court reporters generally work forty-hour weeks or more. Court reporters may find the pace of the work and expectations of accuracy challenging.

Profile

Interests: Data, Things
Working Conditions: Work Inside
Physical Strength: Light Work
Education Needs: Junior/Technical/
  Community College, Bachelor's Degree
Licensure/Certification: Required
Physical Abilities Not Required: Not
  Climb, Not Kneel
Opportunities for Experience:
  Internship, Military Service
Holland Interest Score: CSE

* See Appendix A

Occupation Interest

Individuals drawn to the court reporter profession tend to be intelligent and detail oriented. The most successful court reporters display traits such as focus, excellent hearing, hand-eye coordination, time management, initiative, and concern for individuals and society. Court reporters should enjoy working within the legal system. They should also stay abreast of the news and trends in the greater community.

A Day in the Life—Duties and Responsibilities

The court reporter's area of job specialization and work environment determine his or her daily occupational duties and responsibilities. Court reporting specialties include stenographic recording, real-time captioning, electronic reporting, voice writing, and webcasting.

During legal proceedings, court reporters record testimony from all witnesses, legal objections and motions, instructions and questions asked between the judge and the jury, ruling, sentencing, appeals, and other events and conversations. They may use shorthand, computerized equipment, or a stenotype machine to capture these events. Court reporters ask all legal participants to restate or clarify speech or information which is inaudible, unclear, or spoken too quietly to be understood. They also provide real-time translation or captions for deaf or hearing-impaired people involved in legal proceedings and ensure that all captioning complies with federal regulations.

When a proceeding is over, the court reporter creates transcripts from all recordings. This involves creating the computer dictionary used to translate keystroke codes or voice files into written text, correcting grammar and spelling errors in the resulting text, and generating copies of the new transcript. These copies must be compared regularly with the original to ensure accuracy. The original transcript must be filed in a timely manner, since it will be requested by participants in the proceedings and become public record. Rulings mentioned in the transcript are verified with the presiding judge as a further accuracy check. When people request copies of the legal transcript or want to read the original, the court reporter is responsible for complying with those requests in a timely manner as well.

In addition to these duties, court reporters must maintain all court reporting equipment, including stenotype machine, analog tape recorders, digital equipment, and voice silencing microphones. They also develop personalized methods for storing and accessing stenographic data, audio recording, and voice files.

Court reporters play a critical role in legal proceedings, which require an exact record of what was said. They are responsible for producing a complete, accurate, and secure legal transcript of courtroom proceedings, witnesses' testimonies, and depositions.

Court reporters in the legal setting also help judges and lawyers by capturing, organizing, and producing the official record of the proceedings. The official record allows users to efficiently search for important information contained in the transcript. Court reporters also index and catalog exhibits used during court proceedings. Some court reporters, however, do not work in the legal setting or in courtrooms. These reporters primarily serve people who are deaf or hard-of-hearing by transcribing speech to text as the speech occurs.

Broadcast captioners are court reporters who provide captions for television programs (called closed captions). These reporters transcribe dialogue onto television monitors to help deaf or hard-of-hearing viewers or others viewing television programs in public places. Some broadcast captioners may translate dialogue in real time during broadcasts; others may caption during the postproduction of a program.

Communication access real-time translation (CART) providers are court reporters who work primarily with deaf or hard-of-hearing people in a variety of settings. They assist clients during board meetings, doctors' appointments, and any other events in which real-time translation is needed. For example, CART providers may caption the dialogue of high school and college classes and provide an immediate transcript to students with hearing problems or who are learning English as a second language. Although some court reporters may accompany their clients to events, many broadcast captioners and CART providers work remotely. An Internet or phone connection allows them to hear and type without having to be in the room. Court reporters who work with deaf or hard-of-hearing people turn speech into text. For information on workers who help deaf or hard-of-hearing people through sign language, cued speech, or other spoken or gestural means, see the profile on interpreters and translators.

Duties and Responsibilities

- Attend depositions, hearings, proceedings, and other events that require written transcripts
- Capture spoken dialogue with specialized equipment, including stenography machines, video and audio recording devices, and covered microphones
- Report speakers' identification, gestures, and actions
- Read or play back all or a portion of the proceedings upon request from the judge
- Ask speakers to clarify inaudible or unclear statements or testimony
- Review the notes they have taken, including the names of speakers and any technical terminology
- Provide copies of transcripts and recordings to the courts, counsels, and parties involved
- Transcribe television or movie dialogue to help deaf or hard-of-hearing viewers
- Provide real-time translation in classes and other public forums for the deaf or hard-of-hearing population

WORK ENVIRONMENT

Immediate Physical Environment

The immediate physical environment of court reporters varies based on their specialization. Court reporters spend their workdays recording and transcribing legal proceedings in business offices, home offices, local courts, state courts, federal courts, government agencies, and prisons.

Transferable Skills and Abilities

Communication Skills
- Editing written information
- Expressing thoughts and ideas
- Speaking effectively
- Writing concisely

Interpersonal/Social Skills
- Cooperating with others
- Working as a member of a team

Organization and Management Skills
- Managing time
- Meeting goals and deadlines
- Paying attention to and handling details
- Performing routine work

Research and Planning Skills
- Using logical reasoning

Human Environment

Court reporters work with a wide variety of people and should be comfortable interacting with court clerks, court administrators, incarcerated people, lawyers, judges, defendants, plaintiffs, witnesses, and juries.

Technological Environment

Court reporters may use different methods for recording speech, such as stenotype machine recording, steno mask recording, and electronic recording. Court reporters use stenotype machines to record dialogue as it is spoken. Stenotype machines work like keyboards, but create words through key combinations rather than single characters, allowing court reporters to keep up with fast-moving dialogue. Key combinations entered on a stenotype machine are recorded in a computer program. The program uses computer-assisted transcription to translate the key combinations into the words and phrases they represent, creating real-time, readable text. The court reporter then reviews the text for accuracy and corrects spelling and grammatical errors.

Court reporters also may use steno masks to transcribe speech. Court reporters who use steno masks speak directly into a covered microphone, recording dialogue and reporting gestures and actions. Because the microphone is covered, others cannot hear what the reporter is saying. The recording is sometimes converted by computerized voice-recognition software into a transcript that the court reporter reviews for accuracy, spelling, and grammar.

For both stenotype machine recording and steno mask recording, court reporters must create, maintain, and continuously update an online dictionary that the computer software uses to transcribe the key presses or voice recordings into text. For example, court reporters may put in the names of people involved in a court case, or the specific words or technical jargon typically used in that type of legal proceeding.

Court reporters also may use digital recorders in their job. Digital recording creates an audio or video record rather than a written transcript. Court reporters who use digital recorders operate and monitor the recording equipment. They also take notes to identify the speakers and provide context for the recording. In some cases, court reporters use the audio recording to create a written transcript.

EDUCATION, TRAINING, AND ADVANCEMENT

High School/Secondary

High school students interested in pursuing a career as a court reporter should prepare themselves by developing good study habits. High school-level study of typing, foreign languages, political science, sociology, shorthand, and psychology will provide a strong foundation for postsecondary-level study in the field. Due to the diversity of court reporter specialties, high school students interested in this career path may benefit from seeking internships or part-time work that expose them to the legal system.

Suggested High School Subjects
- Business and Computer Technology
- Composition
- English
- Government
- Keyboarding
- Shorthand

Related Career Pathways/Majors

Business, Management, and Administration Cluster
- Court Reporter

Famous First

Court reporting can be traced back to 63 BCE when a man named Marcus Tullius Tiro worked for Roman philosopher and lawyer Cicero. Tiro took dictation and managed Cicero's financial matters. In order to transcribe speeches, he developed a system of notation symbols and abbreviations. Tiro's shorthand system consisted of over 4,000 signs. This notation system became known as Tironian notes and was later taught in European monasteries during the Medieval period. The notes eventually expanded to over 13,000 signs, but its use declined after 1100 CE. (Source: https://connorreporting.com)

Postsecondary

Postsecondary students interested in becoming court reporters should work towards an associate's degree or bachelor's degree in pre-law, criminology, or a related field. Vocational and technical schools also offer formal court reporter training programs. Coursework in education, psychology, and foreign languages may also prove useful in their future work. Postsecondary students can gain work experience and potential advantage in their future job searches by securing internships or part-time employment within the legal system.

Related College Majors
- Court Reporter

Adult Job Seekers

Adults seeking employment as court reporters should have, at a minimum, a high school diploma or associate's degree. Some court reporting organizations and specialties require extensive court reporting experience, on-the-job training, bachelor's degrees, or second language proficiency. Adult job seekers should educate themselves about the educational and professional license requirements of their home states and the organizations where they seek employment. They may benefit from joining professional associations to help with networking and job searching. Professional court reporting associations, such as the National Court Reporters Association and the United States Court Reporters Association, generally offer job-finding workshops and maintain lists and forums of available jobs.

Professional Certification and Licensure

Many states require court reporters who work in legal settings to be licensed or certified by a professional association. Licensing requirements vary by state and by method of court reporting.

The National Court Reporters Association (NCRA) offers certification for court reporters, broadcast captioners, and communication access real-time translation (CART) providers. Currently, about half of states accept or use the Registered Professional Reporter (RPR) certification in place of a state certification or licensing exam.

Digital and voice reporters may obtain certification through the American Association of Electronic Reporters and Transcribers (AAERT), which offers the Certified Electronic Reporter (CER) and Certified Electronic Transcriber (CET) designations.

Voice reporters also may obtain certification through the National Verbatim Reporters Association (NVRA). As with the RPR designation, some states with certification or licensing requirements will accept the NVRA designation in place of a state license.

Certification through the NCRA, AAERT, and NVRA all require the successful completion of a written test, as well as a skills test in which applicants must type, record, or transcribe a minimum number of words per minute with a high level of accuracy.

In addition, all associations require court reporters to obtain a certain amount of continuing education credits in order to renew their certification.

Additional Requirements

After completing their formal program, court reporters must undergo a few weeks of on-the-job training. This typically includes training on the specific types of equipment and more technical terminology that may be used during complex medical or legal proceedings.

Individuals who find satisfaction, success, and job security as court reporters will be knowledgeable about the profession's requirements, responsibilities, and opportunities. Court reporters must demonstrate integrity and professional ethics as they have access to confidential legal information. Membership in professional court reporting associations is encouraged among all court reporters as a means of building professional community and networking.

EARNINGS AND ADVANCEMENT

Court reporters' salaries vary widely by type of court, geographic location, skill, experience and level of responsibility. The median annual wage for court reporters was $57,150 in May 2018. The median wage is the wage at which half the workers in an occupation earned more than that amount and half earned less. The lowest 10 percent earned less than $28,150, and the highest 10 percent earned more than $104,460.

In May 2018, the median annual wages for court reporters in the top industries in which they worked were as follows:

State government, excluding education and hospitals	$66,430
Local government, excluding education and hospitals	$60,450
Business support services	$46,020

Freelance court reporters are paid for their time, but can also sell their transcripts per page for an additional profit.

Court reporters who work in a court setting typically work full-time recording events and preparing transcripts. Freelance reporters have more flexibility in setting their work schedules.

Court reporters may receive paid vacations, holidays, and sick days; life and health insurance; and retirement benefits. These are usually paid by the employer. Freelance court reporters working for large firms often receive similar benefits. In some locations, court reporters are provided with recording equipment, and in other locations court reporters must provide their own equipment. Freelance court reporters must usually purchase their own recording equipment.

EMPLOYMENT AND OUTLOOK

Court reporters held about 15,700 jobs in 2018. The largest employers of court reporters were as follows:

Business support services	34%
Local government, excluding education and hospitals	31%
State government, excluding education and hospitals	28%
Self-employed workers	5%

Many court reporters work in courts or legislatures. Many also work as freelance reporters and are hired by law firms or corporations for pretrial depositions and other events on an as-needed basis.

Many court reporters must travel to various courthouses or offices in different locations. However, some broadcast captioners and communication access real-time translation (CART) providers work remotely from either their home or a central office.

Because of the speed and accuracy required to capture a verbatim record and the time-sensitive nature of legal proceedings, court reporting positions may be stressful.

More than half worked for state and local governments. Employment of court reporters is expected to grow faster than average for all occupations through the year 2028, which means employment is projected to increase 7 percent. Demand for court reporters will be spurred by the continuing need for accurate transcription of court proceedings and in pretrial depositions, and by the growing need to create captions of Internet programming, live, or pre-recorded television and other technologies, and to provide other realtime translating services for the deaf and hard-of-hearing community.

Federal legislation mandates that all new television programming must be captioned for deaf and hard-of-hearing persons. Additionally, the Americans with Disabilities Act gives deaf and hard-of-hearing students in colleges and universities the right to request access to real-time translation in their classes.

Related Occupations
- Legal Secretary
- Medical Transcriptionist
- Secretary
- Word Processor

Related Military Occupations
- Legal Specialist and Court Reporter

Fast Fact

Scribes, as they were called, were present at the founding of the nation, including when the Declaration of Independence and the Bill of Rights were drafted. Less than a century later, President Lincoln entrusted scribes to record the Emancipation Proclamation.

Source: phoenixdepositionservices.com

Conversation With . . .
MICHAEL HENSLEY, RDR

President
MPH Stenography
Dublin, California
Court reporter/stenographer, 4 years

1. What was your individual career path in terms of education/training, entry-level job, or other significant opportunity?

I first wanted to be a high school music teacher and spent thirteen years as a marching band coach. However, my financial situation changed after two-and-a-half years at the University of Southern California and I couldn't finish my degree. That meant I wouldn't reach my full earnings potential. I worked administrative jobs to make ends meet.

One day I happened to see a post from a friend on Facebook about court reporting and asked her about it. Our conversation prompted me look into the field, and every single bit of information I read convinced me that this work was for me. The opportunities are endless, and I enjoy the high level of professionalism.

As a second career seeker, my fulltime job working a graveyard shift at a call center had to come first. I started school at age 30 and took four years to earn my associate's degree in court reporting from Sage College, which unfortunately has since closed because its accrediting institution closed. The program trained me to write more than 200 words per minute on a stenotype machine among other critical skills involved in taking verbatim testimony for a court trial.

I started work as a scheduling manager for a court reporting agency before I graduated, then freelanced for a number of agencies, and now own my own company. Right now, I'm the only employee—as many freelancers and consultants are—but am in a position to grow my firm. I've also served as the district director for the California Court Reporters Association and am active in the National Court Reporters Association.

I focus on freelance deposition reporting. My primary clients are attorneys I connect with through court reporting agencies. I go to doctors' offices, attorneys' offices, and business locations to take deposition and testimony. I'm in court very little, probably five percent of my time. I don't generate content and I don't formulate questions. I just hear what's being spoken and polish it for a transcript. I typically work 40–50 hours a week but can scale it up or back as needed. I partner with about fifteen different court reporting agencies and my next goal is to market directly to attorneys. I've also been able to present at state and national conferences, as well as do motivational speaking and mentor students so they have a guided start in the industry.

This is a specialized skill. I have a stenograph machine—called "a writer"—and carry a laptop and several microphones as backup. I use specialized transcription software.

2. What are the most important skills and/or qualities for someone in your profession?

Attention to detail. When editing a transcript, you need to make sure it's punctuated correctly and sometimes a comma makes all the difference.

You also need a strong curiosity for learning various subject matter. In school, you learn medical and legal terminology. Beyond that, I've been exposed to topics ranging from computer programming to woodworking to dairy and agriculture.

3. What do you wish you had known going into this profession?

I wish I had known about it sooner. As I look back, my biggest fear was that I didn't want to get stuck. I have a skillset that translates to other areas in this field.

4. Are there many job opportunities in your profession? In what specific areas?

Yes. Job placement out of school is close to 100 percent. This field offers four different areas: freelance deposition work; court reporting as a salaried employee in a courthouse; captioning for TV, video or other media that might be done in a studio or from home; and CART, which stands for Communication Access Real-Time Translation for the deaf and hard of hearing community. A CART provider captions in a variety of settings, such as a business meeting or a school or church.

5. How do you see your profession changing in the next five years? How will technology impact that change, and what skills will be required?

Court reporters are trained to capture 96–97 percent accuracy at first pass, and with computers we get to 99.9 percent. The technology still on the horizon will get us that last .1 percent. Artificial intelligence will enhance, not replace, our ability. Computers rely on patterns and predictive scenarios and human speech does not operate in that way. We hear tone of voice or see a subtle shrug of shoulders. There is a need for a human to discern what is being said. For instance, "I don't know." Or, "I don't, no."

As equipment becomes more robust regarding video and audio transmissions, the number of proceedings captured remotely will continue to expand. You could be doing an arbitration in China from your home office in Detroit.

6. **What do you enjoy most about your job? What do you enjoy least about your job?**

Every day is a new story, and that's what's really exciting for me. One day is about forensic accounting, the next is about video game design. I enjoy the legal field, and I enjoy that I create something that is historical. I've been involved with the Veterans History Project, where we record interviews with war veterans that are held in a database in the Library of Congress.

I do miss having work friends that I would see on a daily basis by going to the same office. As a freelance deposition reporter, I'm a lone wolf.

7. **Can you suggest a valuable "try this" for students considering a career in your profession?**

The NCRA and state associations are rolling out a program that includes a free, six-week introductory course where you can learn the stenography alphabet (https://www.ncra.org/home/students-teachers/careers-in-court-reporting-captioning/DiscoverSteno-A-to-Z-program-dates-and-locations). Or go to a courthouse when proceedings are open to the public. As you listen, imagine how it is to catch each and every word. It's a very different type of listening, to capture every single word as it is spoken.

MORE INFORMATION

American Association of Electronic Reporters and Transcribers
P.O. Box 9826
Wilmington, DE 19809
302.765-3510
sherry@aaert.org

National Center for State Courts
300 Newport Avenue
Williamsburg, VA 23185-4147
800.616.6164
webmaster@ncsc.dni.us
www.ncsc.org

National Court Reporters Association
12030 Sunrise Valley Drive
 Suite 400
Reston, VA 22182-3808
800.272.6272
https://www.ncra.org/home

Simone Isadora Flynn/Editor

Dancers and Choreographers

Snapshot

Career Cluster(s): Arts, A/V Technology, and Communications
Interests: Dance, performing arts, physical activity, exercise, music
Earnings (2018 Median): $18.70 hourly
Employment and Outlook: Little or No Growth Expected

OVERVIEW

Sphere of Work

Dancers and choreographers work in the performing arts field, usually in collaboration with other dancers, a director of choreography, musicians, and composers. Dancers use their bodies to create movements and poses that evoke a feeling or idea befitting the accompanying music or drama. Choreographers arrange and teach all dancers' movements and gestures in a given work. Both dancing and choreography are highly competitive fields requiring a high degree of personal and

professional commitment. Many dancers transition into careers as choreographers when they stop dancing professionally.

Work Environment

Dancers and choreographers work in a variety of environments, but almost all of them work in dance studios as part of a group of dancers in preparation for performance. Depending on the type of organization they work for, and the imagined setting for a particular piece, performances could take place in a theatre, a public location, or on a film set. In academic settings, choreographers are also responsible for educating their dancers on the history of different types of dance, including lessons on specific techniques, pivotal figures in the field, innovations in choreography, and contemporary dance theory.

Profile

Interests: Data, People
Working Conditions: Work Inside, Work Both Inside and Outside
Physical Strength: Heavy Work
Education Needs: Junior/Technical/ Community College, Apprenticeship, Bachelor's Degree
Licensure/Certification: Usually Not Required
Physical Abilities Not Required: Not Handle
Opportunities for Experience: Apprenticeship, Volunteer Work, Part-time Work
Holland Interest Score: AER, AES

* See Appendix A

Occupation Interest

Working as a dancer or choreographer appeals to those with a strong interest in the performing arts who enjoy the idea of highly disciplined, creative, collaborative work. Prospective dancers should have an innate love of dance and the drive to pursue their inclinations, as dance is an intensely competitive field and employment can be both sporadic and financially challenging. Because it is physically demanding, people interested in pursuing dance careers should be exceptionally fit and possess great agility, balance, stamina, and muscle coordination. Dance and choreography are both careers in which networking is key to success, due to relatively slow job growth and intense competition for available jobs.

A Day in the Life—Duties and Responsibilities

It is difficult for most dancers to find enough work in their chosen field to earn an adequate living. Many dancers and choreographers supplement their dancing income with jobs in academia, and many of them spend part of their day teaching. This may include teaching younger dancers new techniques in a dance studio or educating them on dance theory in a classroom by watching videos of past performances, reading essays, and discussing the correlation between dance and other artistic movements.

Dancers and choreographers should expect to attend almost daily rehearsals for a performance in the evenings while a piece is in production. During rehearsals, the choreographer is responsible for directing the group's attention toward particular sections of a dance that need work. Early in the development of a work, choreographers arrange each section of the dance separately, which allows them to analyze each dancer's movements and help coordinate exact body movements to certain parts of the music. After several rehearsals, all sections of the dance will be performed in sequence and the group will attempt to run through the entire piece at once, working on making smooth transitions between the different sections.

Dance is a career that encompasses more than just working hours. Dancers carefully control their weight, paying strict attention to diet and exercise. Most live in or close to major cities where large dance companies are financially viable. There is a tremendous amount of personal discipline required to succeed as a dancer. Moreover, because the career of a dancer typically only lasts into his or her thirties, there is pressure to make the most of the years when he or she is physically able to compete with other dancers.

Choreographers also experience work-related stress, because their field is highly competitive and tied to geography. However, choreographers are not under the intense pressure to maintain a specific body weight that affects dancers, and they usually do not spend as much time practicing and exercising.

Duties and Responsibilities

Dancers typically do the following:

- Audition for a part in a show or for a job within a dance company
- Learn complex dance movements that entertain an audience
- Rehearse several hours each day to prepare for their performance
- Study new and emerging types of dance
- Work closely with instructors, choreographers, or other dancers to interpret or modify their routines
- Attend promotional events, such as photography sessions, for the production in which they are appearing

Choreographers typically do the following:

- Put together moves in a sequence to create new dances or interpretations of existing dances
- Choose the music that will accompany a dance routine
- Audition dancers for a role in a show or within a dance company
- Assist with costume design, lighting, and other artistic aspects of a show
- Teach complex dance movements
- Study new and emerging types of dance to design more creative dance routines
- Help with the administrative duties of a dance company, such as budgeting

WORK ENVIRONMENT

Immediate Physical Environment

Dancers and choreographers usually work indoors, either in a dance studio or a theatre, preparing a piece for performance with other dancers. Sometimes they perform outdoors during the summer months. Dance takes a toll on a person's body, so on-the-job injuries are common in dancers. In fact, dancers have one of the highest rates of injuries and illnesses of all occupations. Many dancers stop performing by the time they reach their late thirties because of the physical demands of their work. Nonperforming dancers may continue to work as choreographers, directors, or dance teachers.

Transferable Skills and Abilities

Communication Skills
- Expressing thoughts and ideas

Creative/Artistic Skills
- Being skilled in art, music, or dance

Interpersonal/Social Skills
- Asserting oneself

Organization and Management Skills
- Paying attention to and handling details

Research and Planning Skills
- Analyzing information
- Creating ideas
- Gathering information

Technical Skills
- Performing scientific, mathematical, and technical work

Human Environment

Dancers and choreographers work in a highly collaborative environment. They should be thick-skinned and assertive, and should be comfortable contributing to a group. Choreographers will have to decide how much they are willing to allow for dancer interpretation and improvisation in the composition of their dance.

Technological Environment

Working in a studio or theatre can help choreographers familiarizing themselves with basic sound, video, and lighting equipment. Dancers and choreographers watch past performances on DVD and on computers. They wear special shoes and clothing designed to maximize flexibility of movement.

EDUCATION, TRAINING, AND ADVANCEMENT

High School/Secondary

Because dancers' careers tend to peak in their twenties, parents should enroll interested children in classes as early as possible. High school students wishing to pursue a career as a dancer or choreographer should take as many courses as possible in their high school's dance department. Many have their first auditions during their high school years. Involvement in the arts, particularly music and theatre, will also provide valuable experience in on-stage performance and strengthen their understanding of rhythm. Courses in literature will also be helpful, as a major part of choreography deals with dramatic concerns. Literature courses can help young dancers improve their ability to interpret dramatic roles using dance techniques.

Suggested High School Subjects
- Arts
- English
- Humanities
- Instrumental and Vocal Music
- Physical Education
- Theatre and Drama

Related Career Pathways/Majors

Arts, A/V Technology, and Communications Cluster
- Performing Arts Pathway

Famous First

At the end of the nineteenth century, the dancer Vladimir Stepanov developed his own method of documenting choreography, which he later detailed in his book *L'Alphabet des Mouvements du Corps Humain*. In 1893, Stepanov proposed a project to the St. Petersburg Imperial Ballet School to record the choreography of the company's repertory for posterity. Stepanov's first demonstration of the effectiveness of his method was the notation of the one-act ballet *La Flûte magique*. (Source: Wikipedia.org)

Postsecondary

At the university level, students interested in becoming a dancer or choreographer should major in dance; some may choose to focus on choreography within the major or take as many courses as possible in choreography and theory. Students should take a wide range of performing arts and humanities courses, studying literature, theatre, and music as elective courses. They may even choose to pursue one of these subjects as an additional major or minor. Most importantly, college students wishing to pursue a career as a dancer or choreographer should take advantage of dance and choreography opportunities wherever available. Dancers may want to consider taking a basic business or mathematics course or spend some time researching other career options, because most will need to transition into a second career at the end of their dancing career.

Dancers planning to move into a teaching career at some point will need to earn a Master of Fine Arts degree (MFA) in dance.

Related College Majors
- Dance
- Visual and Performing Arts

Adult Job Seekers

The job market for professional dancers and choreographers is extremely competitive. Typically, only the most hardworking and talented dancers are able to make a living as dancers. Finding a job as a choreographer for a successful dance company is also highly competitive, and many dancers and choreographers pursue jobs in public or private education. Adult dancers face a dilemma similar to that faced by professional athletes, in that their careers tend to peak before they reach middle age.

Professional Certification and Licensure

There are no professional certificates or licenses required to work as a dancer or a choreographer, although employers look upon college-level education favorably.

Additional Requirements

Successful dancers and choreographers are disciplined, diligent, persistent, and committed. They should be extremely talented, agile, graceful, and physically fit, with strong feet that have healthy arches. They must be physically flexible, have excellent stamina, and have realistic expectations about the field they are about to enter. In addition to these qualities, prospective dancers may choose to plan for their future by learning different job skills, as age and injury will limit their career longevity as professional dancers.

EARNINGS AND ADVANCEMENT

Earnings depend on the place of employment, geographic location, unionization, and the dancer's ability. Earnings of many professional dancers are governed by union contracts. The unions and producers sign basic agreements specifying minimum salary rates, hours of work, benefits, and other conditions of employment.

The median hourly wage for choreographers was $22.98 in May 2018. The median wage is the wage at which half the workers in an occupation earned more than that amount and half earned less. The lowest 10 percent earned less than $10.26, and the highest 10 percent earned more than $46.93.

Median annual wages, May 2018

Choreographers: $22.98

Entertainers and performers, sports andrelated workers: $20.64

Total, all occupations: $18.58

Dancers and choreographers: $18.17

Dancers: $16.31

Note: All Occupations includes all occupations in the U.S. Economy.
Source: U.S. Bureau of Labor Statistics, Employment Projections program

The median hourly wage for dancers was $16.31 in May 2018. The lowest 10 percent earned less than $9.35, and the highest 10 percent earned more than $40.08.

In May 2018, the median hourly wages for choreographers in the top industries in which they worked were as follows:

Educational services; state, local, and private	$23.99
Performing arts companies	$20.62

In May 2018, the median hourly wages for dancers in the top industries in which they worked were as follows:

Educational services; state, local, and private	$25.59
Performing arts companies	$17.89
Spectator sports	$15.14

Schedules for dancers and choreographers vary with where they work. During tours, dancers and choreographers have long workdays, rehearsing most of the day and performing at night.

Choreographers who work in dance schools may have a standard workweek when they are instructing students. They also spend hours working independently to create new dance routines.

Dancers under union contracts receive full life and health insurance and are covered by pension plans.

EMPLOYMENT AND OUTLOOK

Dancers held about 13,900 jobs in 2018. The largest employers of dancers were as follows:

Self-employed workers	30%
Performing arts companies	27%
Educational services; state, local, and private	9%
Spectator sports	6%

Choreographers held about 7,200 jobs nationally in 2018. The largest employers of choreographers were as follows:

Educational services; state, local, and private	48%
Self-employed workers	30%
Performing arts companies	16%

Dancers and choreographers worked in a variety of industries, such as dance studios and schools, as well as colleges and universities; food services and drinking establishments; performing arts companies, which includes dance, theater, and opera companies; and amusement and recreation venues, such as casinos, cruise ships and theme parks.

Most major cities serve as home to major dance companies; however, many smaller communities across the nation also support home-grown, full-time professional dance companies.

Employment of dancers is projected to show little or no change from 2018 to 2028. Employment of choreographers is projected to decline 3 percent from 2018 to 2028.

Positions in large dance companies are competitive, so dancers may find positions in smaller companies or in companies that stage professional dance competitions. There may be better opportunities for dancers and choreographers in large cities, such as New York and Las Vegas, or for dancers who join a traveling company.

A continued interest in dance and in pop culture may provide opportunities in venues outside of dance companies, such as TV or movies, casinos, and theme parks, or as judges in dance competitions. Many dancers and choreographers, nonetheless, struggle to find opportunities to express themselves; dance companies rely on word of mouth, grants, and public funding.

Dancers and choreographers face intense competition, and the number of applicants is expected to vastly exceed the number of job openings. Dancers who attend schools or conservatories associated with a dance company may have a better chance of finding work at that company than other dancers have.

Related Occupations
- Actor
- Director/Producer
- Model
- Musician and Composer

Conversation With . . . ROBERT MOSES

Artistic Director, Robert Moses' Kin
San Francisco, California
Choreographer/dancer, 30+ years

1. What was your individual career path in terms of education/training, entry-level job, or other significant opportunity?

I entered college with the thought that I might go into business—my family had a small store in the Philadelphia neighborhood I grew up in—and though I had begun dancing before enrolling and loved it greatly, I wasn't quite sure how to make a career of it. I had taken a gym class in dance and performed in high school.

I was lucky to have great teachers who were also mentors. They insisted I do my homework and learn as much about the profession as I could. With their help, I was able to decide to become a concert choreographer and dancer. During my first two years at Orange Coast College, I studied everything available, danced in my first professional company, and began a lifelong love of all-things-called-dance.

I went on to California State University, Long Beach, home to one of the West Coast's best dance programs, and found a fair amount of work in Los Angeles—commercial work, this play, that video. I danced with a lot of little companies that, though small, were significant. After graduation, I came to San Francisco and worked with ODC/Dance, then went on to dance with Twyla Tharp, then the American Ballet Theatre in New York. Then I started my own company, Robert Moses' Kin. I have choreographed pieces for companies ranging from Alvin Ailey American Dance Theater to the Cincinnati Ballet, and taught in numerous residencies and master classes both in the U.S. and abroad, including a post as Choreographer in Residence at Stanford University from 2005 to 2016.

When you work for someone else, you work for someone else. It becomes clear that what you really want to do as an artist, you have to do yourself. When I choreograph a work, it's based on what's in the room as an idea unfolds. You have to be deliberate, but you can't turn off the spigot.

2. What are the most important skills and/or qualities for someone in your profession?

Dancers need strength of will as well as body, a heart and mind to hold their self-respect and love of self, and a few good friends for when that audition doesn't go the way it should.

3. What do you wish you had known going into this profession?

I knew this was a choice for a profession but I did not quite understand it was a life choice as well—that people I met at 18 would still be friends in my 50s—or that the world can be both enormous and incredibly personal at the same time.

Say you're a senior and a junior kind of looks up to you. Twenty years later, you run into them, they say they've been following you and are going to bring their class to see you. You realize your roots mean something. Or, sometimes people's fortunes are up and down and you can give someone a hand up by giving them a word about a job. And then there are the people who are just there for your entire life.

4. Are there many job opportunities in your profession? In what specific areas?

Yes, there are opportunities but, in dance, creating the next new thing is part of the art. Artists are creatives and willfully create their careers. There is no waiting here.

Figure out where you can live, then look for the work. Your life is going to be more important than the job that may or may not work out. Do your homework. Look at the size of a company's budget and see if you can make a decent living. Are there other opportunities if for some reason this isn't what you thought it might be? Talk with the dancers in a company: Are you happy working with these people? They'll tell you.

Audition. I recently met with 100 kids and only two of them emailed or called to say, "Hey, we talked." Those are the two that are going to stick in my head. In fact, we have a tour to Mexico coming up and one of the two is a very good dancer and I think she'll fit in. I'm going to give her a call.

Get over your shyness or insecurity. You don't have to have a lot of ego, but you do have to put yourself out there because otherwise people won't know you're there.

5. How do you see your profession changing in the next five years? What role will technology play in those changes, and what skills will be required?

Technology has already changed the field so much. We no longer add it to performance as an afterthought. Artists use it to broaden their options and abilities. Today I create my own music, sketch costumes, write text, stage, choreograph and more using technology. Where it goes from here is anyone's guess.

6. What do you enjoy most about your job? What do you enjoy least about your job?

Getting to work with amazing individuals full of life, each of whom has different points of view on every moment we share, is very exciting. Regarding the least favorite part, I hold the idea that there is so much that is positive and available that the tough times are only bumps. But, being practical: continually raising funds is a bummer.

7. Can you suggest a valuable "try this" for students considering a career in your profession?

If you are a dancer or a choreographer, go to a different teacher one out of every four classes, or watch and learn about dance making from a form you know nothing about. If you're a ballet dancer, watch an expert tap dancer and deal with rhythm in the way they do. Or if you are a choreographer, watch theater and try to convey meaning without word and with words. The point is to always stretch.

When you learn from different people, one teacher will tell you have a fantastic line; another will say your approach to style is good, and someone else will tell you your rhythmic sense is strong or lacking. The best teachers give you information about yourself to help you grow.

MORE INFORMATION

American College Dance Association
15 West Montgomery Avenue, Suite 301
Rockville, MD 20850
240.428.1736
info@acda.dance
www.acdfa.org/

American Dance Guild, Inc.
320 West 83rd Street, Apt. 7D
New York, NY 10024
www.americandanceguild.org

American Dance Therapy Association
10632 Little Patuxent Parkway, Suite 108
Columbia, MD 21044
410.997.4040
info@adta.org
www.adta.org

American Guild of Musical Artists
1430 Broadway, 14th Floor
New York, NY 10018
212.265.3687
agma@musicalartists.org
www.musicalartists.org

American Guild of Variety Artists
363 Seventh Avenue, 17th Floor
New York, NY 10001-3904
212.675.1003
agva@agvausa.com
www.agvausa.com

Career Transition for Dancers
The Caroline and Theodore Newhouse Center for Dancers
165 W. 46th Street, Suite 701
New York, NY 10036
212.764.0172
info@careertransition.org
www.careertransition.org

Dance/USA
1029 Vermont Ave NW, Suite 400
Washington, DC 20005
202.833.1717
www.danceusa.org

National Association of Schools of Dance
11250 Roger Bacon Drive, Suite 21
Reston, VA 20190-5248
703.437.0700
info@arts-accredit.org
nasd.arts-accredit.org/index.jsp

Mark Boccard/Editor

Editors

Snapshot

Career Cluster(s): Arts, A/V Technology, and Communications, Information Technology

Interests: Theater, film, planning events, coordinating tasks

Earnings (2018 Median): $59,480 yearly; $28.60 hourly

Employment and Outlook: Declining Growth Expected

OVERVIEW

What Editors Do

Editors plan, coordinate, and revise material for publication in books, newspapers, or periodicals or on websites. Editors review story ideas and decide what material will appeal most to readers. During the review process, editors offer comments to improve the product and suggest titles and headlines. In smaller organizations, a single editor may do all the editorial duties or share them with only a few other people.

The following are examples of types of editors:

Assistant editors are responsible for a particular subject, such as local news, international news, feature stories, or sports. Most assistant editors work for newspaper publishers, television broadcasters, magazines, book publishers, or advertising and public relations firms.

Copy editors proofread text for errors in grammar, punctuation, and spelling and check for readability, style, and agreement with editorial policy. They suggest revisions, such as changing words and rearranging sentences and paragraphs to improve clarity or accuracy. They also may carry out research, confirm sources, and verify facts, dates, and statistics. In addition, they may arrange page layouts of articles, photographs, and advertising.

Executive editors oversee assistant editors and generally have the final say about which stories are published and how those stories are covered. Executive editors typically hire writers, reporters, and other employees. They also plan budgets and negotiate contracts with freelance writers, who are sometimes called "stringers" in the news industry. Although many executive editors work for newspaper publishers, some work for television broadcasters, magazines, or advertising and public relations firms.

Managing editors typically work for magazines, newspaper publishers, and television broadcasters and are responsible for the daily operations of a news department.

Publication assistants who work for book-publishing houses may read and evaluate manuscripts, proofread uncorrected drafts, and answer questions about published material. Assistants on small newspapers or in smaller media markets may compile articles available from wire services or the Internet, answer phones, and proofread articles.

Work Environment

Editors held about 118,300 jobs in 2018. The largest employers of editors were as follows:

Newspaper, periodical, book, and directory publishers	38%
Self-employed workers	14%
Professional, scientific, and technical services	9%
Religious, grantmaking, civic, professional, and similar organizations	8%
Other information services	7%

Most editors work in offices, whether onsite with their employer or from a remote location. They often use desktop or electronic publishing software, scanners, and other electronic communications equipment.

Jobs are somewhat concentrated in major media and entertainment markets—Boston, Chicago, Los Angeles, New York, and Washington, DC—but improved communications and Internet capabilities are allowing editors to work from a greater variety of locations.

Overseeing and coordinating multiple writing projects simultaneously is common among editors and may lead to stress or fatigue.

Self-employed editors face the added pressures of finding work on an ongoing basis and continually adjusting to new work environments.

Work Schedules

Most editors work full-time, and their schedules are generally determined by production deadlines and type of editorial position. Editors typically work in busy offices and have to deal with production deadline pressures and the stresses of ensuring that the information they publish is correct. As a result, editors often work many hours, especially at those times leading up to a publication deadline. These work hours can be even more frequent when an editor is working on digital material for the Internet or for a live broadcast.

Fast Fact

The Scotts Magazine, thought to be the oldest consumer magazine still in print, dates back to 1739.

Source: ed2010.com.

Duties and Responsibilities

- Read content and correct spelling, punctuation, and grammatical errors
- Rewrite text to make it easier for readers to understand
- Verify facts cited in material for publication
- Evaluate submissions from writers to decide what to publish
- Work with writers to help their ideas and stories succeed
- Develop story and content ideas according to the publication's style and editorial policy
- Allocate space for the text, photos, and illustrations that make up a story or content
- Approve final versions submitted by staff

HOW TO BECOME AN EDITOR

A bachelor's degree in communications, journalism, or English, combined with previous writing and proofreading experience, is typically required to be an editor.

Education

Employers generally prefer candidates who have a bachelor's degree in communications, journalism, or English. Candidates with other backgrounds who can show strong writing skills also may find jobs as editors. Editors who deal with specific subject matter may need related work experience. For example, fashion editors may need expertise in fashion that they gain through formal training or work experience.

Work Experience in a Related Occupation

Many editors start as editorial assistants, writers, or reporters. Those who are particularly skilled at identifying good stories, recognizing writing talent, and interacting with writers may be interested in editing jobs.

Important Qualities

Creativity

- Editors must be imaginative, curious, and knowledgeable in a broad range of topics. Some editors must regularly come up with interesting content or story ideas and attention-grabbing headlines.

Detail oriented

- Editors must be meticulous to ensure that material is error free and matches the style of a publication.

Good judgment

- Editors decide whether certain stories are ethical and whether there is enough evidence to publish them.

Interpersonal skills

- In working with writers, editors must have tact and the ability to guide and encourage them in their work.

Writing skills

- Editors ensure that all written content has correct grammar, punctuation, and syntax. Editors must be able to write clearly and logically.

Other Experience

Editors can gain experience by working on high school and college newspapers and for magazines, radio and television stations, advertising and publishing companies. Magazines and newspapers may have offer student internships. For example, the American Society of Magazine Editors offers a Magazine Internship Program to qualified full-time students in their junior or senior year of college. Interns may write stories, conduct research and interviews, and gain general publishing experience.

Editors need to be proficient in computer use, including electronic publishing, graphics, Web design, social media, and multimedia production.

Advancement

Some editors hold management positions and must make decisions related to running a business. For them, advancement generally means moving up to publications with larger circulation or greater prestige. Copy editors may move into original writing or substantive editing positions or become freelancers.

PAY

The median annual wage for editors was $59,480 in May 2018. The median wage is the wage at which half the workers in an occupation earned more than that amount and half earned less. The lowest 10 percent earned less than $31,500, and the highest 10 percent earned more than $117,810.

In May 2018, the median annual wages for editors in the top industries in which they worked were as follows:

Religious, grantmaking, civic, professional, and similar organizations	$67,230
Professional, scientific, and technical services	$67,220
Other information services	$63,460
Newspaper, periodical, book, and directory publishers	$55,390

JOB OUTLOOK

Employment of editors is projected to decline 3 percent from 2018 to 2028. Despite some job growth in online media, decreases in traditional print magazines and newspapers will cause a decline in overall employment of editors.

Median annual wages, May 2018

Total, all occupations: 5%

Media and communication workers: 4%

Editors: -3%

Note: All Occupations includes all occupations in the U.S. Economy.
Source: U.S. Bureau of Labor Statistics, Employment Projections program

Competition for jobs with established newspapers and magazines will be particularly strong because employment in the publishing industry is projected to decline. Editors who have adapted to online media and are comfortable writing for and working with a variety of electronic and digital tools will have the best prospects in finding work. Although the way in which people consume media has changed, editors will continue to add value by reviewing and revising drafts and keeping the style and voice of a publication consistent.

Famous First

America's first woman newspaper editor, Ann Franklin (1696-1763)—wife of printer James Franklin and sister-in-law to Benjamin Franklin— learned the newspaper business soon after her marriage in 1723. After serving a jail term for the "wicked" articles he published in *The New England Courant*, James moved to Rhode Island where he and Ann published its first newspaper, *The Rhode Island Gazette*. When James died in 1735, Ann took over the paper and did many commercial printing jobs in her first year to supplement her income. She became the General Assembly of Rhode Island's official printer, a position she held until her death.
(Source: http://www.womenhistoryblog.com)

Conversation With . . .
JOE EVANS

Editor in Chief
Chesapeake Bay Magazine/Chesapeake Bay Media
Annapolis, Maryland
Communications and content development
business, 30 years

1. What was your individual career path in terms of education/training, entry-level job, or other significant opportunity?

I grew up in and around a television station. My father ran the CBS affiliate in Charleston, South Carolina, and from time to time, I was the unpaid labor. During elections, for example, I was a runner from phone banks delivering a precinct's vote count. I graduated from the University of North Carolina at Chapel Hill with a communications degree focusing on radio, television, and motion pictures, and I minored in American studies and folklore. I really enjoyed storytelling and the Carolinas is a great place for that.

Then I left to do something else—race sailboats. I won a lot of races regionally and had Olympic dreams. I came to Annapolis for a clinic at the U.S. Naval Academy. It turned out I was in the second tier of sailors. Also, this was 1980, the year the U.S. boycotted the Olympics. However, I stayed in the industry. I taught at and managed a sailing school for three years. I made sails, sold boats, fixed boats, then built boats at my own company, J Hamilton Yacht Co., which I operated for sixteen years. I got a good dose of business management. I also realized when I saw people the age I am now that there was a physical limit, given the exposure to lead, paint dust, and hard physical labor. I always had a personal commitment that I would not ask someone else to do something I wasn't willing to do.

I'd always been interested in outdoor pursuits and, during these years, I freelanced about fishing and hunting, and I produced video for outlets such as National Geographic Today, ESPN, and Bass Pro's Outdoor World. I partnered with an outdoor sporting artist to do stories around the world for magazines such as *Sporting Classics*, *Flyfishing in Saltwater*, *Shooting Sportsman*, and the like. I became a fly-fishing guide, then regional business manager for the Orvis Company and promotions and marketing manager for Bass Pro Shops.

Along the way, I squeezed out a media production master's degree at American University in Washington, D.C. It was great to learn from a mentor, and to make the commitment of time and money to do nothing but understand the visual media business and proper formats for story treatments, production planning, and telling a story.

I became founding editor of a regional boating magazine, and later, a Maryland Dept. of Natural Resources public information officer. Then, I got the call to become the *Chesapeake Bay Magazine* editor-in-chief and steer the venerable publication through its transition to become a modern multimedia operation.

At the end of the day, I have had the rare luck to marry all of my passions into a career. By doing what I loved, I met people who knew my background and skillset, and those contacts grew into a network that helped me move through my career.

2. What are the most important skills and/or qualities for someone in your profession?

Empathy. Tenacity. Credibility. Imagination. Integrity. Courage. Solid work ethic and habits. Research skills, and a firm grip on grammar and style.

3. What do you wish you had known going into this profession?

I just wish I had known earlier how much fun this business can be.

4. Are there many job opportunities in your profession? In what specific areas?

With the digital revolution, the old, buttoned-down, 9-to-5, desk-bound writing jobs have substantially dried up, and that may be a good thing, as the opportunities for storytelling and self-guided exploration and distribution are now limitless. Anyone can publish these days, and if it's good, someone will read it, and you might even get paid for it. However, modern professional storytellers must be multifunctional. This means being able to provide complete packages suitable for all platforms. A complete writer should be able to provide useable photography. Some basic video production skills are also valuable. Keep in mind that your story might flow well into a podcast, which means having a sense of how audio recording works. All of these skills interconnect in modern media. Old-school (staid) publications that have not evolved into becoming vibrant multimedia content providers are either fading fast or already gone. At what point are we totally digital? Everybody in this industry is wondering when it's going to happen. The good news is that most of the raw material is collected on a smart phone and then finished and published using a laptop. Boom.

If none of that appeals to you, then go into sales, make more money, and maybe become the publisher someday. Those jobs are pretty much always open.

5. How do you see your profession changing in the next five years? How will technology impact that change, and what skills will be required?

Industry insiders knew a digital content revolution was coming as far back 1999 with the advent of digital consumer video recording (TiVo), whereby consumers could choose their own content and avoid the random and irrelevant material and advertising being thrown out by the networks. The digital content revolution accelerated with the introduction of the iPhone in 2007. I don't anticipate any great changes to this landscape in the next five years.

The fundamental elements of good journalism and content development remain as they ever were. (See question 2.) Crummy, sloppy, and unethical content will persist as it always has, and a few readers will continue to eat it up inside various echo chambers of paranoia and angst. But the good stuff will persevere and thrive through limitless digital networks and platforms. The cost of participating is relatively low, and the action is free-flowing and immediate.

6. What do you enjoy most about your job? What do you enjoy least about your job?

I enjoy seeing how great stories make an impact by engaging, entertaining, and informing people. The bonus is how effective storytelling brightens the outlook for the people we write about and the readers who are somehow moved.

The fact that the work never stops is my minor complaint. A mixed blessing.

7. Can you suggest a valuable "try this" for students considering a career in your profession?

Write, photograph, video or record something every day. Learning to write is like learning to play the banjo. You need to practice to become proficient, and you shouldn't do it in public until you've got the hang of it.

Finished product, whether video, audio, or written content, starts and ends with effective writing. In order to write well, you need to read well.

If you are serious about doing this, read *The Art of Readable Writing* (1949) by Rudolf Flesch. You'll probably have to buy a cheap, used copy at abebooks.com. Same for Joseph Mitchell's *My Ears are Bent* (1938). Also, pick up a copy of *Dreyer's English* (2019) and snap off a page or two before you go to sleep each night. It will make you smile, and you'll get more comfortable with the ever-changing opinions on grammar and style.

Conversation With . . .
AMY SHARPE

Bourne MA
Technical Editor, 11 years

1. What was your individual career path in terms of education/training, entry-level job or other significant opportunity?

I got my degree in journalism from the University of North Carolina and went to work for the *Cape Cod Times* in Hyannis, Massachusetts, as a copy editor. I was really fortunate that when I was in college I knew I wanted to be a copy editor. It was easier for copy editors to get jobs than reporters. I stayed at the *Times* for 18 years, editing stories on everything from breaking news to a description of the best beaches on the Cape.

My next job was working as a copy editor for AOL.com in its content division. The writers had been hired to enter data into a database and didn't know anything about writing in a journalistic style, using neutral language or providing balance. I took out a lot of adjectives. After two years I went back to newspapers, working at the *Providence Journal* as a copy editor.

I stayed there four years and went to work editing e-newsletters for a company called SmartBrief in Washington, D.C. on a variety of industry news and subjects. I edited newsletters targeted to the gambling industry, environmental concerns, insurance companies, financial institutions and other industries. I worked there four years and during that time I started a freelance career as a technical editor.

I sometimes write abstracts for technical reports. An abstract is a summary of an academic or scientific report and is usually 300 to 400 words. Since abstracts are often translated into other languages, technical writers and editors need to be careful about their word choice to make sure the abstract translates well. You learn that technical publishers don't like the words "once," "namely" and "thus," for instance.

I also write summaries of reports for technical publishers covering the electric power industry that are meant to be read by people who work in that industry. It's highly scientific, very dry. It's sort of the opposite of a newspaper. But it requires the same attention to detail that I learned working for newspapers.

2. What are the most important skills and/or qualities for someone in your profession?

Technical writers and editors need to have an appreciation of English language and grammar, of style, spelling, and usage. You need to be able to spot errors and question things. You need to be proficient in using Word and the tracking feature in Word so clients can see the changes that are made.

You also have to be able to manage your time and be able to communicate with engineers and other technical people. They're very concerned that someone who is not a subject matter expert is going to change something and make them sound stupid. Most of them are really nice, and they are very grateful for the help.

It's important to pay attention to detail and be consistent. Some technical writers work on how-to manuals—they have to remember the proper order of the steps and make sure they make sense.

3. What do you wish you had known going into this profession?

I wish I had known more about the use of formatting, Excel, spreadsheets, doing tables and things like that. I've learned by trial and error and it's been hard sometimes. I think if I had more skills like that, I could do more work. If I knew how to do video it would open doors for more work.

4. Are there many job opportunities in your profession? In what specific areas?

I feel there's more opportunity for freelance work than there used to be. There are fewer technical publishing companies than there used to be, and a lot of companies that had a publishing component are outsourcing or have smaller staff.

5. How do you see your profession changing in the next five years? How will technology impact that change, and what skills will be required?

Being able to work remotely—from home or anywhere—has been a huge advantage of technology.

Technology also is allowing reports to include more complicated graphics now, especially online. Reports will sometimes have videos embedded in them and PowerPoint slides. There's an effort to make them more user-friendly.

6. What do you enjoy most about your job? What do you enjoy least?

I really like that I can set my own hours and work from different locations. I have deadlines, but it's up to me how to meet them. If you want to work from midnight to 4 a.m. you can do it. I also enjoy having the opportunity to learn about different topics. In this job, you are always learning. I like the variety and the flexibility. But the content isn't always as interesting as when I worked for newspapers.

7. Can you suggest a valuable "try this" for students considering a career in your profession?

Get involved in the school newspaper. Read and learn the elements of writing. The *Elements of Style* by Strunk and White is still a classic. You can go to college and graduate school to learn a specific skill, like nursing or engineering, and earn a certificate in technical writing if you like to write.

MORE INFORMATION

ACES: The Society for Editing
PO Box 1090
Gardnerville, NV 89410
https://aceseditors.org/

**American Society of Magazine
Editors**
28-07 Jackson Ave.
New York, NY 11101
212.872.3737
asme@magazine.org
www.magazine.org/editorial/asme

**Radio Television Digital News
Association (RTDNA)**
529 14th St NW #1240
Washington, DC 20045
https://www.rtdna.org/

Film and Video Editors and Camera Operators

Snapshot

Career Cluster(s): Arts, A/V Technology, and Communications

Interests: Art, filmmaking, photography, design, communicating with others

Earnings (2018 Median): $53,747 yearly; $29.54 hourly

Employment and Outlook: Faster Than Average Growth Expected

OVERVIEW

Sphere of Work

Film and video editors, along with camera operators, define and help guide the photographic style or look of a motion picture. Camera operators ensure that the director's vision for the film, such as its mood and appearance, is achieved. They receive guidance from directors on how photographic shots should be created, and work with other set personnel to design and frame shots appropriately. Film and video

editors have a strong knowledge of lighting, special effects, and other important pieces of filmmaking technology that are being used on the set. Many camera operators are also specialized, and only focus on areas such as special effects or location shots.

Work Environment

Camera operators work on the movie set under the guidance of the cinematographer or director, directing the cameras in such a way that the best shot is framed and taken. Such sets are busy and complex, with different groups working together to render a scene. This work environment is often tense, particularly in light of budget concerns and production deadlines. Film and video editors also work in studio offices and production studios, where they coordinate with writers, directors, producers, and other key artistic and technical professionals in the filmmaking process. Camera operators generally work long and erratic hours. Their work hours may vary based on the production deadlines and the amount of film direction with which they are charged. The work itself can be draining both physically and psychologically, particularly as it may call for multiple shots, angles, and camera mountings in order to achieve the best take.

Profile

Interests: Data, Things
Working Conditions: Work Both Inside and Outside
Physical Strength: Light Work
Education Needs: Bachelor's Degree
Licensure/Certification: Usually Not Required
Physical Abilities Not Required: Not Climb, Not Hear and/or Talk
Opportunities for Experience: Internship, Apprenticeship, Military Service
Holland Interest Score: ASE

* See Appendix A

Occupation Interest

Film and video editors are critical components of the filmmaking field. They work closely with film directors and producers to make their artistic dreams a reality. They are also senior-level managers on the set, and must be effective communicators as they direct camera operators and many other production personnel to create the ideal shot. Camera operators are exceptional students of film, having studied a wide range of past and present techniques and even developing innovative new approaches to filmmaking.

A Day in the Life—Duties and Responsibilities

Film and video editors and camera operators manipulate images that entertain or inform an audience. Camera operators capture a wide range of material for TV shows, movies, and other media. Editors arrange footage shot by camera operators and collaborate with producers and directors to create the final content.

Many camera operators supervise one or more assistants. The assistants set up the camera equipment and may be responsible for its storage and care. Assistants also help the operator determine the best shooting angle and make sure that the camera stays in focus.

Likewise, editors often have one or more assistants. The assistants support the editor by keeping track of each shot in a database or loading digital video into an editing bay. Assistants also may do some of the editing tasks.

Duties and Responsibilities

- Shoot and record television programs, motion pictures, music videos, documentaries, or news and sporting events
- Organize digital footage with video-editing software
- Collaborate with a director to determine the overall vision of the production
- Discuss filming and editing techniques with a director to improve a scene
- Select the appropriate equipment, such as the type of lens or lighting
- Shoot or edit a scene based on the director's vision

WORK ENVIRONMENT

Immediate Physical Environment

Film and video editors and camera operators and directors of photography work primarily at movie studios and sets. These are complex locations with a wide range of working parts, departments, and individuals. Sets are often in large, enclosed, and ventilated studios and lots, or on location throughout the country and world. Depending on the set and the film needs, a cinematographer may work outdoors in a variety of weather conditions.

Human Environment

Cinematographers are senior-level managers, directing the actions of camera operators and equipment operators on a movie set. They also coordinate directly with other important figures on the set and in the studio, including directors, producers, set and costume designers, special effects crews, screenwriters, and actors.

Transferable Skills and Abilities

Creative/Artistic Skills
- Being skilled in art, music or dance

Interpersonal/Social Skills
- Cooperating with others
- Working as a member of a team

Technical Skills
- Working with machines, tools or other objects

Unclassified Skills
- Being physically active

Technological Environment

Cinematographers interact with many pieces of technical equipment while directing photography on the set. Most operators prefer using digital cameras because the smaller, more inexpensive instruments give them more flexibility in shooting angles. In addition, drone cameras give operators an opportunity to film in the air, or in places that are hard to reach. Film and video editors also must keep up with the changing filmmaking technology available on the market.

EDUCATION, TRAINING, AND ADVANCEMENT

High School/Secondary

High school students are encouraged to take classes in photography, film, drama, and art. They must also study communications, computer science, and graphics. Interested high school students should also get involved in school audio-visual departments and clubs.

Suggested High School Subjects
- Applied Communication
- Arts
- Audio-Visual
- English
- Literature
- Mathematics
- Photography
- Theatre and Drama

Related Career Pathways/Majors

Arts, A/V Technology, and Communications Cluster
- Performing Arts Pathway

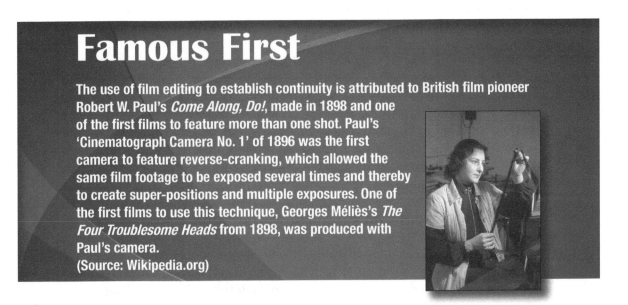

Famous First

The use of film editing to establish continuity is attributed to British film pioneer Robert W. Paul's *Come Along, Do!*, made in 1898 and one of the first films to feature more than one shot. Paul's 'Cinematograph Camera No. 1' of 1896 was the first camera to feature reverse-cranking, which allowed the same film footage to be exposed several times and thereby to create super-positions and multiple exposures. One of the first films to use this technique, Georges Méliès's *The Four Troublesome Heads* from 1898, was produced with Paul's camera.
(Source: Wikipedia.org)

Postsecondary

Most editors and camera operators have postsecondary degrees from colleges or film schools. Many colleges offer bachelor's degrees in film studies and in fine arts, while a number of vocational and technical schools offer associate's degrees in specialized fields related to filmmaking. A large number of independent institutions, like the American Film Institute (AFI), offer similar specialized training in cinematography. The majority of the most popular programs are located in cities with thriving film and broadcast industries, such as Los Angeles and New York.

Related College Majors
- Film-Video Making/Cinema and Production
- Photography

Adult Job Seekers

Film and video editors and camera operators attain high-level jobs after gaining considerable experience in the film industry. Qualified adults who seek to rise in their profession should therefore be willing to work as a gaffer, camera operator assistant, or similar role. This work experience helps build an aspiring cinematographer's qualifications and set management skills. They may also seek a job as an assistant by directly contacting film producers and studios. Film and video editors and camera operators may also find opportunities by joining and networking through professional associations, such as the American Society of Cinematographers or the International Cinematographers Guild.

Professional Certification and Licensure

There is no licensure requirement for film and video editors and camera operators. However, many individuals seek additional training and certification in cinematography from accredited universities, such as New York University's Certificate in Cinematography program. Such programs give job candidates highly valuable training that may enhance their job appeal.

Additional Requirements

Film and video editors and camera operatorsshould have strong artistic vision and capabilities. They must also demonstrate attention to detail and composition.

As shooting a scene often requires multiple takes, angles, and camera mounts, a camera operator should have patience and persistence. As set managers, they should be comfortable working with and directing people on the set. Finally, they must be able to meet the demands of producers and directors.

EARNINGS AND ADVANCEMENT

The number of Internet-only platforms, such as streaming services, is likely to increase, along with the number of shows produced for these platforms. This growth may lead to more work for editors and camera operators.

In broadcasting, the consolidation of roles—such as editors who determine the best angles for a shoot, the use of robotic cameras, and the increasing reliance on amateur film footage—may lead to fewer jobs for camera operators. However, more film and video editors are expected to be needed because of an increase in special effects and overall available content.

Film and video editors and camera operators will face strong competition for jobs. Most job openings are projected to be in entertainment hubs such as New York City and Los Angeles because specialized editing workers are in demand there. Those with experience at a TV station or on a film set should have the best prospects. Video editors may improve their prospects by developing skills with different types of specialized editing software.

Film and video editors and camera operators may receive paid vacations, holidays, and sick days; life and health insurance; and retirement benefits. These benefits are usually paid by the employer.

EMPLOYMENT AND OUTLOOK

Film and video editors and camera operators, held about 29,400 jobs in 2018. Employment of cinematographers is expected to faster slower than the average for all occupations through the year 2028, which means employment is projected to increase 14 percent to 9 percent. While overall job growth in the entertainment industry is expected to be slow, an increase in special effects in motion picture industry may increase the need for these workers.

Related Occupations
- Cinematographer
- Motion Picture Projectionist
- Motion Picture/Radio/TV Art Director
- Photographer

Related Occupations
- Audiovisual and Broadcast Director

Fast Fact

The first digitally edited feature film was produced in 1992, using a program called the Avid/1Media Composer. *Let's Kill All the Lawyers* broke ground because up until then, hard drive capacity limited digital editing to shorter projects such as music videos and commercials.

Source: premiumbeat.com

Conversation With . . .
ADAM EPSTEIN

Videographer, Sports Radio Host, and Editor
WJFK 106.7 The Fan
Associate Producer, Podcast Village
Washington, D.C.
Videographer and multimedia, 5 years

1. **What was your individual career path in terms of education/training, entry-level job, or other significant opportunity?**

I knew in high school I wanted to be a sports broadcaster and did my own show on the school's morning TV. I earned my degree in mass communications from Virginia Commonwealth University in Richmond. As a junior, I interned with 106.7 FM The Fan and as a senior, with NBC4. Both stations are in Washington, D.C.

I started applying for jobs before graduation and interviewed with 106.7 and Sirius XM. Sirius hired me as a part-time newsroom audio editor for 20 hours a week. That involved watching and listening to games and cutting highlights and putting them into a database, and I worked 8 p.m. to 2 a.m. I was living with my parents and making ends meet as a waiter at Uncle Julio's.

Months later, I heard from 106.7. They knew my background at school was video and they had just started video production for their online stream. Basically, I technically directed a TV show online for them—adding graphics, switching cameras. This was also a part-time job. But I was able to stop working at Uncle Julio's and move out of my parents' house.

Over time, the Sirius job started to feel like a dead end and, long story short, through a connection I went to work part-time for the Washington Redskins as a videographer, where I was cameraman for practice and interviews, and created highlights and packages. I also started working on the "Redskins Coaches Show" for the Redskins Broadcast Network that aired once a week on NBC 4.

Now, I am a host, editor, and videographer for WJFK 106.7 for 25 hours a week, and part of my job is being video producer for their show, *The Sports Junkies*. Through that job, I met the owners of Podcast Village, a startup in D.C. So I also work at Podcast Village editing made-for-TV podcasts that are released on YouTube for 20 hours a week. I do think video podcasts are the future, but you need to know what you're doing. If the microphones are good quality, or if there's a studio echo—I hear that immediately.

As I get more established in my career, I'm figuring out that making connections and building your own brand is the most important thing. We're getting to the point where the network you work for doesn't matter as much as who you are. To build that brand, I also do a podcast, "Play to Win," on my own website—P2Wradio.com—that I run with a couple of friends. We do podcasts, videos, and post events where we do live reporting. It's almost like a concert. My goal is to build the website and draw advertisers who, for example, could sponsor an article.

The Redskins opened me up to do a lot of freelancing, and now I also own my own camera equipment. That's a big thing because I can sell myself as a one-man band, and that's the direction my industry is moving. My end goal is to become a host/talent at a national company like ESPN or Fox Sports.

2. What are the most important skills and/or qualities for someone in your profession?

Being able to do a little bit of everything. Having skills to do basic audio and video editing. Being familiar with operating a camera for pictures and a video camera for long feature videos. Since I hope to become a host/talent one day, I would say having good public speaking abilities is important.

3. What do you wish you had known going into this profession?

I wish someone had told me that the first five years out of college would be mostly working for minimum wage or volunteering for experience (which you shouldn't be afraid to do, at least for short periods of time). I wish someone told me I would most likely have to leave my market to one day return and be successful. If, for example, your end goal is to host in Washington, D.C., your best bet is to go to a smaller market where you can become recognizable and then work your way up through bigger markets until you can come back to D.C. with that experience. I wish someone taught me Adobe skills like Photoshop and Premiere pro while I was in high school.

4. Are there many job opportunities in your profession? In what specific areas?

There are plenty of entry-level positions and full-time positions as producers. I've also seen plenty of openings for cameramen. Companies are specific in their searches. They may be looking for a sports cameraman, or hard news anchor, or morning producer. You have to nail down which position you want. You must be able to adapt. Talent/hosting gigs are the hardest job to find.

5. How do you see your profession changing in the next five years? How will technology impact that change, and what skills will be required?

In the next five years, more and more networks/companies will be looking for "one-man bands." Someone who can shoot, edit, produce, write, and record. Someone who can go to an event, create a story, produce the story, write the story, and post it on the company website. More and more people in the industry will have to learn and be efficient with Photoshop, Canva, Ripl, and other applications that help you make graphics and social media posts. Be aware now that your employer will be all over all of your social media accounts! They will be judging your work on social media but also judging the decisions, pictures, and stories you post on your personal social media feed. So be very cautious with how many "partying" photos you've posted.

6. What do you enjoy most about your job? What do you enjoy least about your job?

I most enjoy the freedom and creativity. I never feel like I've worked a normal hard day of work because I'm always getting a chance to bring my ideas to life. I really enjoy editing and all things sports videography. Basically, if it involves sports, I'm in a good mood. The part of my job I enjoy the least is the hours. I'm up every day at 5 a.m.! On the weekends, I get to sleep in, but you need to be prepared for work any hours.

7. Can you suggest a valuable "try this" for students considering a career in your profession?

Students interested in a sports broadcasting career should try to create their own brand. Start a YouTube channel with videos you edit and produce. Start a podcast that you host and edit. And create social media accounts connected with your brand where you can post, design, and network to grow your skills.

MORE INFORMATION

**American Society of
Cinematographers**
1782 N Orange Drive
Los Angeles, CA 90028
323.969.4333
office@theasc.com
www.theasc.com

**International Cinematographers
Guild**
7755 Sunset Boulevard
Hollywood, CA 90046
323.876.0160
www.cameraguild.com

Offers the Emerging Cinematographer
Awards:
www.ecawards.net

Publishes the ICG Magazine:
www.icgmagazine.com

**National Association of Broadcast
Employees and Technicians**
501 3rd Street NW, 6th Floor
Washington, DC 20001
nabet-cwa-union.org
https://www.nabetcwa.org/

New York Film Academy
17 Battery Place, 1st Floor,
New York, NY 10004
212.674.4300
www.nyfa.edu

Michael P. Auerbach/Editor

Grant Writers

Each year, public and private foundations award billions of dollars in grants, sums of money that are intended to advance a specific objective. Grant writers help to match funders with projects they want to support.

What they do

Grant writers research, draft, and submit proposals that help organizations or individuals receive grant funding. To be eligible for funding, an organization or individual must have an objective that aligns with a grant's specifications. Many grant writers work for nonprofit or charitable organizations. Others are self-employed and take on projects from a variety of sources, such as museums and schools. No matter whom they work for, most of these writers research grants, write proposals, and have other tasks.

Researching grants

To find available funding, grant writers identify grants that match the objective of the organization or individual seeking money. They often scour detailed lists, databases, and donor websites. Part of researching grants is determining which ones are not worth pursuing.

Writing proposals

Grant proposals often require a variety of documents, such as a cover letter, project narrative, and supporting information, which might include things like letters of endorsement from members of the community. Through these documents, grant writers explain why a cause is important and how the funds will be used. For example, grant writers might describe the past, present, and planned activities of the grant-seeking individual or organization. In drafting the proposal, writers must follow the grant's guidelines, such as ensuring that the organization meets eligibility requirements, and provide a budget that outlines how the grant money would be spent.

Incorporating all of these elements into a successful proposal takes time and expertise—especially when there are hundreds, sometimes thousands, of organizations competing for the same funds.

Other tasks

Grant writers' other tasks may include responding to funders' questions about a proposal, developing relationships with prospective donors, and documenting a grant's impact at the conclusion of a project.

Some grant writers have other roles within their organization.

What It's like

Grant writing offers opportunities to earn a paycheck while helping a cause. But as with all occupations, the work has its challenges, too. Part of writing is meeting deadlines—and that's among the most difficult parts of the work. Making sure it all comes together at the same time can be stressful. Getting rejections, also part of the job, can be discouraging.

Self-employed grant writers face additional challenges, such as finding enough work and running their own business. Income is often inconsistent, especially when they're starting out.

Grant writers enjoy unique rewards too, though, such as the independence to choose a variety of projects for causes they believe in. Often, that project variety becomes its own perk.

EMPLOYMENT AND WAGES

Much of the employment and wage information about grant writers is anecdotal, because the U.S. Bureau of Labor Statistics (BLS) does not collect data specific to this occupation.

BLS counts many grant writers among other types of writers and authors. But a worker who does more than write grants may be counted in other occupations, including social and community service managers and postsecondary teachers.

Many grant writers are self-employed. Self-employed grant writers usually charge a flat fee or an hourly rate for their services. Anecdotal information suggests that self-employed grant writers charge fees of between hundreds and thousands of dollars per project, while hourly rates range from $20 to $100, depending on experience and other factors.

HOW THEY PREPARE

Grant writers usually have a range of skills, a college degree, and other training or experience.

Skills

Research and writing skills are essential for grant writers. Research helps writers find grant opportunities. Good writing expresses ideas clearly and succinctly, with creativity and persuasiveness helping a proposal stand out.

Interpersonal skills are important, too, because grant writers interact with clients, colleagues, and donors to gather and relay information.

Grant writers also need to be detail oriented and have multitasking and organizational skills. These skills allow them to juggle multiple grant applications and adhere to each grant's guidelines and deadlines.

Education and training

Grant writers, like other types of writers and authors, typically need a bachelor's degree to qualify for entry-level jobs. Often, the field of study doesn't matter, but helpful courses include marketing and English.

Some colleges and universities offer programs specifically in grant writing. Classes and workshops are also available through community colleges and professional associations. But many grant writers learn from online resources, books, and on-the-job training. And years of practice help them develop the skills for writing successful grant proposals.

Experience and more

Experience in a related occupation is generally not required for entry-level grant writing jobs, but it can be helpful to have. For example, many grant writers start out in another role in an organization before transitioning to grant writing. A background in communications, fundraising, or budgeting is valuable.

Gaining experience isn't limited to employment, however. Networking with other grant writers and doing some unpaid work may help you learn more about the occupation.

Experienced grant writers also might opt to earn certification, which demonstrates a level of proficiency and could improve their employment options.

And, although success is not guaranteed, grant writers have a better chance of writing a good proposal if they're passionate about the causes for which they seek funds.

Famous First

The first secretary of the Rockefeller Foundation, one of the oldest grant making foundations in the U.S., was Jerome Davis Greene, former secretary of Harvard University, who wrote a "memorandum on principles and policies" for an early meeting of the trustees that established a rough framework for the foundation's work. On December 5, the board made its first grant of $100,000 to the American Red Cross to purchase property for its headquarters in Washington, D.C.
(Source: Wikipedia.org)

Fast Fact

Among the most celebrated grants are the so-called "genius grants" issued by the MacArthur Foundation. McArthur Fellows excel in a range of creative and intellectual pursuits and receive a $625,000 stipend—no strings attached.

Source: macfound.org.

Conversation With . . .
ROSEMARIE RESNIK

Rosemarie Resnik & Associates
Osterville, Massachusetts
Consultant and grant writer for nonprofits, 12 years

1. **What was your individual career path in terms of education/training, entry-level job or other significant opportunity?**

In high school, I was chairman of the prom committee and a class officer for four years and have chaired my class reunions. I was always interested in event management and fundraising. After going to Assumption College in Worcester. I went to work for Harvard University/Radcliffe College in Cambridge and managed all the reunions and class committees.

My next employer was the Massachusetts Institute of Technology, where I was director of alumni activities. The job combined fundraising with alumni relations. I ran telethons, parent fundraisers and oversaw MIT alumni clubs around the world. I worked there nine years and traveled all over the world. I turned an entry-level job into a great career by relying on mentors, taking advantage of professional development opportunities and never thinking I knew more than I did!

When I married my husband, I moved from the Boston area to the much quieter region of Cape Cod. I took a job for six years as director of resource development for the International Fund for Animal Welfare, which is headquartered in Yarmouthport.

I left to start a consulting firm—that was my dream job for the next stage of my career. Cape Cod turned out to be the perfect place to start a business offering consulting services to non-profit organizations. There are many nonprofits here that are too small to have their own development office, so my firm takes on that role. We will help with your annual fundraising appeals, development plans, capital campaigns and marketing.

Writing is a big part of the job—we write grant applications, pamphlets, direct mail and other marketing material and help nonprofits write their mission statements, strategic plans and cases for support. A case for support tells donors why they should support the nonprofit.

We write, and we design. I have a staff of four people including myself and a designer. I think I've been very successful because I've put a great team around me. My network of mentors and colleagues is huge, too. If I have a question, I can call 25 people and ask what they think.

2. What are the most important skills and/or qualities for people specializing in grant writing?

You have to be a strategic thinker. You have to be analytical and be able to read budgets and data. In my firm, we also write pamphlets and direct mail appeals. We include statistics in those marketing materials, but we also tell a story about the organizations we represent. It's a little like feature writing in journalism.

Grant writing is more nuts and bolts. The grant writer identifies a problem and the impact of the problem and describes a solution, while also coming up with a budget and measurable outcomes. The problem could be anything from food shortages among people with disabilities to an unmet need for quality day care.

Writing for state and federal grants is more time consuming than appealing to private foundations. The government requests a lot of data.

Grant writers also have to have people skills. You can't lock yourself in a room like a machine. You have to go out and cultivate major donors—pick up the phone, call them, offer to take them on a tour of your organization. Fundraising—and, increasingly, grant writing—is about building relationships.

3. What do you wish you had known going into this profession?

I didn't realize that my first love—event planning—would turn out to be a burnout job. It wasn't fulfilling in the way that raising money for nonprofits is. Also, at first I didn't realize how much of a role data analysis would play in grant writing. Data tells a story. There's accountability. You need to show fundraisers how you spent their money.

4. Are there many job opportunities going into your profession? In what specific areas?

Larger institutions have one to five grant writers on staff. In smaller organizations, grant writing might be just part of a fundraiser's job. More family foundations are popping up every day, and they increasingly are underwriting the operational budget of nonprofit organizations—including fundraising jobs like grant writing.

Grant writing is part of every fundraising plan. You're not going to get a grant writing job at 21. Go to work for a hospital, university or other non-profit organization to see what part of fundraising you're interested in. That's where you're going to learn. Maybe one year you'll be a grant writer, and the next year you will work on major appeals.

5. How do you see your profession changing in the next five years? How will technology impact that change and what skills will be required?

Writing grant applications online has changed the process. You used to be able to include marketing materials in the grant application package. Now you go online and have a limited number of characters with which to write the application. You have to tell your story in a succinct way.

Social media keeps donors and members up to date, but when it comes to big fundraisers, print is still king. People like to touch it, feel it. The future will continue to integrate direct mail and social media. At the end of the day, it's about building relationships and demonstrating why donors should fund you.

6. What do you enjoy most about your job? What do you enjoy least?

I love seeing the dollars raised through fundraising making a difference in people's lives. In this job, you meet great, wonderful, caring people who are trying to make a difference in their community.

What I don't like is when boards of nonprofits don't realize fundraising is a marathon, not a short race. People want to give up after one grant application fails. You've got to keep going.

7. Can you suggest a valuable "try this" for students considering a career in your profession?

Get an internship with a nonprofit organization. Take a communications class in high school. Take a marketing class if your school offers it. Always take writing classes, and get feedback on your writing.

Graphic Designers

Snapshot

Career Cluster(s): Arts, A/V Technology, and Communications, Business, Management, and Administration, Information Technology

Interests: Visual arts, advertising, marketing, being creative, communicating with others

Earnings (2018 Median): $50,370 yearly; $24.21 hourly

Employment and Outlook: Slower Than Average Growth Expected

OVERVIEW

Sphere of Work

Graphic designers create visually appealing products and promotional materials that range from simple logos or business cards to entire corporate branding campaigns. Their work is intended to convey a commercial message or otherwise draw attention to an idea, which they accomplish mostly with sophisticated graphic design and animation software. Traditional artistic mediums, such as printmaking or painting, continue to be used, but sporadically. A designer interested in a long-term career must also learn skills in animation, digital video

production, copywriting, web design, or marketing, or collaborate frequently with people who possess these skill sets or perform these job functions.

Work Environment

Graphic designers work mostly in the publishing, advertising, and marketing industries, but some work for graphic design firms or government agencies. Many are self-employed. They spend much of their time working on computers, but may also have access to a full art studio. If self-employed, they interact heavily with clients. If employed in a design firm or design department, they interact with a team of professionals and staff and have less direct contact with clients; however, some customer service is necessary when choosing the final design—a process that can take anywhere from a couple of days to several weeks.

Profile

Interests: People, Things
Working Conditions: Work Inside
Physical Strength: Light Work, Medium Work
Education Needs: Bachelor's Degree
Licensure/Certification: Usually Not Required
Physical Abilities Not Required: Not Climb, Not Kneel, Not Hear and/or Talk
Opportunities for Experience: Part-time Work
Holland Interest Score: AES

* See Appendix A

Occupation Interest

People who are attracted to graphic design tend to be creative thinkers who are interested in solving problems with images or in making the world more visually interesting. They are artistic and have a good eye for detail, but are also capable of seeing the big picture and being flexible in their presentation of multiple design ideas for a single project. They must have excellent interpersonal and communication skills since they almost always work closely with members of a team. They must be able to handle criticism and work under pressure to meet deadlines.

A Day in the Life—Duties and Responsibilities

Graphic designers are responsible for planning and carrying out projects that fulfill their clients' needs. A major specialty today is branding, in which the designer works with a team of writers, artists, market researchers, and others to create a company's image, including a recognizable logo, stylized advertisements, catchy slogans, and high-tech trade show displays. The designer will suggest colors, images, fonts, and other artistic elements, then create several sample designs for each element of the branding campaign.

Graphic designers create the covers and interior layout for magazines, books, brochures, newspapers, and other print materials. Typically, they work with editors to acquire the articles and advertisements, and then fit them into the allotted space in the most appealing manner. Graphic designers select fonts, graphics, and other design elements (in collaboration with the client or author if the project is a book) and also design internal advertisements that are presented with the final product.

Study of graphic design discipline includes the option to learn website design skills, so some graphic designers specialize in web design and are able to earn a living without working on any print design projects. Some graphic designers collaborate with programmers to create computer games, with authors to create graphic novels, with interior decorators to plan the interiors of businesses, or with architects to design public spaces.

Self-employed graphic designers must also spend some of their time marketing their services, billing customers, preparing contracts, and handling other administrative and business management tasks.

Duties and Responsibilities

- Designing images that convey a message or identify a product or organization
- Creating designs by hand or using computer software
- Meeting with clients to determine their needs
- Deciding on the message that a design should portray
- Giving advice to clients on ways to reach an audience through visual means

OCCUPATION SPECIALTIES

Cartoonists

Cartoonists draw political cartoons, newspaper comics, or comic books.

Fashion Artists

Fashion Artists draw stylish illustrations of new clothing fashions for newspapers or related advertisements.

Illustrators

Illustrators create pictures for books, magazines, billboards, posters and record albums.

Medical and Scientific Illustrators

Medical and Scientific Illustrators draw precise illustrations of machines, plants, animals, or parts of the human body or animal bodies for business and educational purposes.

Set Illustrators

Set Illustrators build and decorate sets for movies, television, and theatrical productions.

Motion Picture Cartoonists

Motion Picture Cartoonists draw series of pictures for animated films shown on TV and in movies.

WORK ENVIRONMENT

Immediate Physical Environment

Graphic designers usually work in studios or offices surrounded by art samples and design reference materials. If a project has a tight deadline, the graphic designer can expect to work some evening hours or work on the design from their home computer until the project is done.

Human Environment

In larger design firms and departments, a graphic designer is often one member of a creative team comprised of photographers, illustrators, web developers, and others who collaborate on projects under the supervision of a creative director. Designers may also work with market researchers, architects, interior designers, content editors, clients, authors, and other professionals outside the firm.

Transferable Skills and Abilities

Communication Skills
- Expressing thoughts and ideas
- Speaking effectively
- Writing concisely

Creative/Artistic Skills
- Being skilled in art, music or dance

Interpersonal/Social Skills
- Being able to work independently
- Perceiving others' feelings

Organization and Management Skills
- Managing time
- Meeting goals and deadlines

Technological Environment

Graphic designers most often use Adobe Creative Suite software (Photoshop, Illustrator, and InDesign) for cover design, manipulating and creating illustrations, page layout design, editing and placing digital photographs, and other purposes. They also use digital photography and video cameras, scanners, printmaking equipment, printing and publishing equipment, and other tools. Each design project is different and may require different resources, so graphic designers should enjoy learning new skills.

EDUCATION, TRAINING, AND ADVANCEMENT

High School/Secondary

Students should pursue a comprehensive college-preparatory program that includes courses in art, graphic design, computer science, and the social sciences. Other relevant courses include film, new media, photography, and industrial arts. Awareness of contemporary graphic design, web design, and animation software programs is extremely important. Most college admissions programs require a portfolio of artistic work, which might include digital designs, as well as hand-drawn sketches or paintings, sculpture, and other sample work.

Suggested High School Subjects
- Applied Communication
- Applied Math
- Arts
- Composition
- Computer Science
- English
- Graphic Communications
- Industrial Arts
- Literature
- Metals Technology
- Pottery
- Woodshop

Related Career Pathways/Majors

Arts, A/V Technology, and Communications Cluster
- Audio and Video Technologies Pathway
- Printing Technologies Pathway
- Visual Arts Pathway

Business, Management, and Administration Cluster
- Marketing Pathway

Information Technology Cluster
- Marketing Pathway

Famous First

Graphic designs of animals by prehistoric social groups in the Chauvet Cave, in France, were created earlier than 30,000 BCE and many other rock or cave paintings in other parts of the world show that graphic art emerged very early in the development of prehistoric human cultures. This history— along with that of writing, which had begun at least by the late 4th millennium BCE—together constitute the foundation of graphic design.
(Source: Wikipedia.org)

Postsecondary

Most entry-level positions require a bachelor's degree from an art school or program. Graphic design programs include courses in studio art, design, computer graphics, printing, and other graphic design specialties. Programs should include the option to work an internship. A general awareness of contemporary design is also helpful. The development of a portfolio for use in future job searches is essential, so many graphic design students make an effort to obtain freelance work.

Related College Majors
- Design and Visual Communications
- Graphic Design/Commercial Art and Illustration
- Industrial Design

Adult Job Seekers

Adults with a background in fine art, illustration, photography, typography, or another creative discipline can learn the fundamentals of graphic design and update their skills by taking graphic arts courses, which some schools offer in the evenings and on weekends to accommodate adult professionals. A portfolio can be assembled independently and/or in conjunction with classes.

Advancement for graphic designers comes with experience or taking classes in new software or techniques to supplement current skills. Some designers choose to establish their own firms. Advanced degrees can help experienced designers begin to obtain design work in a different specialty, such as web animation.

Professional Certification and Licensure

There are no licenses or nationally recognized certificates required for graphic designers; however, the idea of professional certification has gained popularity, so it is advisable to follow the issue as it progresses. Adult education programs and computer software companies offer their own certificates upon satisfactory completion of their courses.

Additional Requirements

Graphic artists must have good eyesight, be extremely creative, enjoy art and design, and find satisfaction in continuing professional development. They should be willing to follow trends in advertising, web media, and design, and should enjoy brainstorming for a single project. Although creativity is a plus, graphic designers must be able to distance themselves from their work enough to accept a client's criticism and revisions of design ideas. Excellent people skills are a must in this collaborative field, which can be highly competitive and requires the ability to make and maintain good contacts with clients and colleagues.

EARNINGS AND ADVANCEMENT

The median annual wage for graphic designers was $50,370 in May 2018. The median wage is the wage at which half the workers in an occupation earned more than that amount and half earned less. The lowest 10 percent earned less than $29,610, and the highest 10 percent earned more than $85,760.

In May 2018, the median annual wages for graphic designers in the top industries in which they worked were as follows:

Advertising, public relations, and related services	$51,380
Specialized design services	$51,320
Newspaper, periodical, book, and directory publishers	$43,450
Printing and related support activities	$40,170

Graphic designers on salary may receive paid vacations, holidays, and sick days; life and health insurance; and retirement benefits. These are paid by the employer. Self-employed graphic designers must arrange for their own ways of meeting these costs.

EMPLOYMENT AND OUTLOOK

Graphic designers held about 290,100 jobs in 2018. The largest employers of graphic designers were as follows:

Self-employed workers	22%
Specialized design services	10%
Advertising, public relations, and related services	8%
Printing and related support activities	7%
Newspaper, periodical, book, and directory publishers	5%

Graphic designers generally work in studios, where they have access to equipment such as drafting tables, computers, and software. Although many graphic designers work independently, those who work for specialized graphic design firms are often part of a design team. Many graphic designers collaborate with colleagues or work with clients on projects.

Graphic designers' schedules vary depending on workloads and deadlines. Those who are self-employed may need to adjust their workday to meet with clients in the evenings or on weekends. In addition, they may spend some of their time looking for new projects or competing with other designers for contracts.

Related Occupations
- Art Director
- Designer
- Electronic Commerce Specialist
- Floral Designer
- Industrial Designer
- Interior Designer
- Medical and Scientific Illustrator
- Multimedia Artist and Animator
- Online Merchant
- Software Developer
- Web Developer

Related Military Occupations
- Graphic Designer and Illustrator

MORE INFORMATION

American Institute of Graphic Arts
222 Broadway
New York, NY 10038
212.807.1990
www.aiga.org

Graphic Artists Guild
31 West 34th Street, 8th Floor
New York, NY 10001
212.791.3400
communications@gag.org
www.graphicartistsguild.org

National Art Education Association
901 Prince Street
Alexandria, VA 22314
800.299.8321
info@arteducators.org
https://www.arteducators.org/

National Association of Schools of Art & Design
11250 Roger Bacon Drive, Suite 21
Reston, VA 20190-5248
703.437.0700
info@arts-accredit.org
nasad.arts-accredit.org/index.jsp

Society for Environmental Graphic Design
1900 L Street NW, Suite 710
Washington, DC 20036
202-638-5555
segd@segd.org
https://segd.org/

Society of Publication Designers
27 Union Square W., Suite 207
New York, NY 10003
212.223.3332
mail@spd.org
www.spd.org/

Sponsors student photography and design competitions:
www.spd.org/student-outreach/

Sally Driscoll/Editor

Historians

Snapshot

Career Cluster(s): Arts, A/V Technology, and Communications, Information Technology

Interests: Writing, story-telling, research, communicating with others

Earnings (2018 Median): $61,140 yearly; $29.40 hourly

Employment and Outlook: As Fast As Average Growth Expected.

OVERVIEW

Historians conduct research and analysis for governments, businesses, individuals, nonprofits, historical associations, and other organizations. They use a variety of sources in their work, including government and institutional records, newspapers, photographs, interviews, films, and unpublished manuscripts, such as personal diaries, letters, and other primary source documents. They also may process, catalog, and archive these documents and artifacts.

Many historians present and interpret history in order to inform or build upon public knowledge of past events.

They often trace and build a historical profile of a particular person, area, idea, organization, or event. Once their research is complete, they present their findings through articles, books, reports, exhibits, websites, and educational programs.

In government, some historians conduct research to provide information on specific events or groups. Many write about the history of a particular government agency, activity, or program, such as a military operation or space missions. For example, they may research the people and events related to Operation Desert Storm.

In historical associations, historians may work with archivists, curators, and museum workers to preserve artifacts and explain the historical significance of a wide variety of subjects, such as historic buildings, religious groups, and battlegrounds. Workers with a background in history also may go into one of these occupations. Many people with a degree in history also become high school teachers or postsecondary teachers.

Duties and Responsibilities

Historians typically do the following:

- Gather historical data from various sources, including archives, books, and artifacts
- Analyze and interpret historical information to determine its authenticity and significance
- Trace historical developments in a particular field
- Engage with the public through educational programs and presentations
- Archive or preserve materials and artifacts in museums, visitor centers, and historic sites
- Provide advice or guidance on historical topics and preservation issues
- Write reports, articles, and books on findings and theories

WORK ENVIRONMENT

Historians may spend much of their time researching and writing reports.

Historians work in museums, archives, historical societies, and research organizations. Some work as consultants for these organizations while being employed by consulting firms, and some work as independent consultants.

Work Schedules

Most historians work full-time during regular business hours. Some work independently and are able to set their own schedules. Historians who work in museums or other institutions open to the public may work evenings or weekends. Some historians may travel to collect artifacts, conduct interviews, or visit an area to better understand its culture and environment.

HOW TO BECOME A HISTORIAN

Although most historian positions require a master's degree, some research positions require a doctoral degree. Candidates with a bachelor's degree may qualify for some entry-level positions, but most will not be traditional historian jobs.

Education

Historians need a master's degree or PhD for most positions. Many historians have a master's degree in history or public history. Others complete degrees in related fields, such as museum studies, historical preservation, or archival management.

Transferable Skills and Abilities

Analytical skills

- Historians must be able to examine various types of historical resources and draw clear and logical conclusions based on their findings.

Communication skills

- Historians must communicate effectively when collecting information, collaborating with colleagues, and presenting their research to the public through written documents and presentations.

Foreign language skills

- Historians may need to review primary source materials that are not in English. This makes knowledge of the other language useful during research.

Problem-solving skills

- Historians try to answer questions about the past. They may investigate something unknown about a past idea, event, or person; decipher historical information; or identify how the past has affected the present.

Research skills

- Historians must be able to examine and process information from a large number of historical resources, including documents, images, and material artifacts.

In addition to coursework, most master's programs in public history and similar fields require an internship as part of the curriculum.

Research positions within the federal government and positions in academia typically require a PhD Students in history PhD programs usually concentrate in a specific area of history. Possible specializations include a particular country or region, period, or field, such as social, political, or cultural history.

Candidates with a bachelor's degree in history may qualify for entry-level positions at museums, historical associations, or other small organizations. However, most bachelor's degree holders usually work outside of traditional historian jobs—for example, jobs in education, communications, law, business, publishing, or journalism.

Other Experience

Many employers recommend that prospective historians complete an internship during their formal educational studies. Internships offer an opportunity for students to learn practical skills, such as handling and preserving artifacts and creating exhibits. They also give students an opportunity to apply their academic knowledge in a hands-on setting.

Famous First

Systematic historical thought emerged in ancient Greece, whose historians contributed to the development of historical methodology. The earliest known critical historical works were *The Histories*, composed by Herodotus of Halicarnassus (484–425 BCE), known as the "father of history." Herodotus attempted to distinguish between more and less reliable accounts, and personally conducted research by travelling extensively. (Source: Wikipedia.org)

PAY

The median annual wage for historians was $61,140 in May 2018. The median wage is the wage at which half the workers in an occupation earned more than that amount and half earned less. The lowest 10 percent earned less than $29,270, and the highest 10 percent earned more than $110,670.

Median annual wages, May 2018

Social scientists and related workers: $78,650

Historians: $61,140

Total, all occupations: $38,640

Note: All Occupations includes all occupations in the U.S. Economy.
Source: U.S. Bureau of Labor Statistics, Employment Projections program

In May 2018, the median annual wages for historians in the top industries in which they worked were as follows:

Federal government, excluding postal service	$97,840
Professional, scientific, and technical services	$61,680
State government, excluding education and hospitals	$50,040
Local government, excluding education and hospitals	$30,980

Most historians work full-time during standard business hours. Some work independently and are able to set their own schedules. Historians who work in museums or other institutions open to the public may work evenings or weekends. Some historians may travel to collect artifacts, conduct interviews, or visit an area to better understand its culture and environment.

JOB OUTLOOK

Employment of historians is projected to grow 6 percent from 2018 to 2028, about as fast as the average for all occupations.

Percent change in employment, Projected 2018–28

Social scientists and related workers: 11%

Historians: 6%

Total, all occupations: 5%

Note: All Occupations includes all occupations in the U.S. Economy.
Source: U.S. Bureau of Labor Statistics, Employment Projections program

Many organizations that employ historians, such as historical societies and historical consulting firms, depend on donations or public funding. Thus, employment growth from 2018 to 2028 will depend largely on the amount of funding available.

Historians may face very strong competition for most jobs. Because of the popularity of history degree programs, applicants are expected to outnumber positions available. Those with a master's degree or PhD should have the best job opportunities.

Practical skills or hands-on work experience in a specialized field such as collections, fundraising, or exhibit design also may be beneficial. Jobseekers may gain this experience through internships, related work experience, or volunteering. Positions are often available at local museums, historical societies, government agencies, or nonprofit and other organizations.

Because historians have broad training and education in writing, analytical research, and critical thinking, they can apply their skills to many different occupations. Thus, many people with history degrees do not compete for the limited number of historian positions.

Fast Fact

History's sources are often its "winners," not its "losers." After all, winners want to tout their heroic victories.

Source: historians.org

Conversation With . . . CHARLES J. QUILTER II, PhD

Airdale & Chrunschi LLC
Laguna Beach, California
Historian, 53 years

1. What was your individual career path in terms of education/training, entry-level job, or other significant opportunity?

I grew up in a Marine Corps aviation family, enlisted in the Marine Corps Reserve when I was 17, and then went into the University of California, Berkeley to get my undergraduate degree in history. My focus was East Asian studies, and I also studied three semesters in Japan. After graduation, I went straight on to active duty for six years as a fighter-attack pilot in Vietnam; I've had a lifelong fascination with flying and went on to spend 30 years as a commercial pilot, finally retiring as a Delta Air Lines captain at the federally-mandated age of 60. I still fly at 78.

The Marine Corps didn't really care what our degrees were in, and a lot of guys were English literature and history majors, including many fighter pilots. In its history program, the Corps wants an accurate accounting of the operations it's been involved in, which is generally not interpretive but a recitation of straight facts.

All units are required to produce a command chronology, which is basically collecting all the relevant names, dates, statistics, and notable events such as combat. The narrative part is written for the commanding officer's signature. Thanks to my degree in history, I was assigned that additional duty while flying in combat with my squadron in Vietnam in 1967-68. That was my first "official" work as a historian.

I remained in the Marine Corps Reserve during my civilian career and towards the end of my military career wound up in command of all the field historians and combat artists at the Marine Corps Historic Center. We deployed to various locations where combat and contingency operations were taking place. That got me into Desert Shield and Desert Storm in 1990-91 and to the Bosnia conflict in 1994. I retired from the Reserve that year, but was called back in 2003, where I was sent to Kuwait and Iraq where I was the oldest Marine to serve.

There are relatively few slots in the active Marine establishment for historians. The guys I commanded in the 80s and 90s all came out of combat arms and had degrees in history. Although official military history is a relatively dry recitation of straight facts, one of the innovative things the Marine Corps did was start an oral history program. In doing so, they discovered a valuable tool for getting into Marines' heads by asking, "What's going on? What are your main concerns right now?" We had great latitude of how we got around in a theater of operations to do this. You learn techniques to draw them out. I set up a small HD camera on a tripod over my shoulder with a map in the background. They open up to you because you're a fellow Marine, and many of us historians had been in combat situations before. I also collected written records and worked to get them declassified.

After I retired from the airline—which was one year before Iraq—I looked forward to going to graduate school. I wanted the discipline of going through the academic process and eventually received my master's in history from UC Irvine and, later, a doctorate from the same institution. For the doctorate, I studied German at our local community college because the sources for my dissertation topic were all in that language. We were required to focus on two major fields for the PhD, and mine were Modern Europe and transnational systems in world history.

My small publishing business started with an autobiographical work about the Korean War that had previously been self-published by a colorful and controversial Marine aviator named John Verdi. Although I had published a few articles, I'd never tackled a biography. Verdi was certainly one of the most innovative squadron commanders of his era and played an influential role in the development of Marine aviation. Verdi was killed in 1991, and after much urging by other Marines who had known him, I got permission to re-publish an annotated version of his Korea memoir. Working with a fellow squadronmate, this was followed with a second volume to tell the rest of his story. After shopping them to a couple of university and institutional presses to no avail, we decided to publish it ourselves and sell it on Amazon. I'm about to do the ebook, and our firm welcomes submissions of Marine Corps history and aviation.

2. What are the most important skills and/or qualities for someone in your profession?

A historian needs training in critical analysis and theory; cogent writing skills; languages and living/studying abroad; effective research techniques; as well as cross-studies in economics and cultural anthropology. You've got to get out there—travel and experience some life—as well as understand when to stop researching and get the work done.

3. What do you wish you had known going into this profession?

I kind of backed into the writing and publishing business and am fortunate to have other sources of income. That's allowed me to follow my passion. I've had an unusual career as a historian, that's for sure.

4. Are there many job opportunities in your profession? In what specific areas?

In terms of being a published historian and being able to live from it, I think the prospects are meager. Teaching can put bread on the table, but grants and publishing opportunities at the university level are probably the most secure. There are a handful of successful writers of popular history. Historical fiction is chancier but probably more lucrative. One unheralded area is the intelligence services and career government positions (which are non-political) where academic achievements and critical thinking skills constitute valuable expertise, and historian-type positions may be available.

5. How do you see your profession changing in the next five years? How will technology impact that change, and what skills will be required?

Anybody can write anything and see it be "published" by Amazon and similar outfits. One can earn as much as two or three cents an hour doing this. One consequence is that the business of just getting something read by an editor or publisher has become very difficult. Another aspect has been the shortened attention spans of many people who now get their information in short bites or even by memes from social media. These can be written in a few minutes but can have immense influence in the right circumstances. They also can be utterly false and malicious. On the other hand, a serious, fact-based article can take weeks and months to research and produce. A book can take a year or more. And who will pay to get this done? In some ways, this represents an existential crisis for truth, and I don't have any clear insight regarding how this can be fixed. Better education will help in the long term.

6. What do you enjoy most about your job? What do you enjoy least about your job?

Like artists and composers, there can be great deal of personal satisfaction at creating a written work even if it will be cruelly handled in the marketplace. In this sense, I feel a certain pride in having added to the historical record. I can't recommend that to everybody, but personally I was happy enough to pay the price.

7. Can you suggest a valuable "try this" for students considering a career in your profession?

Read a lot. Critically.

MORE INFORMATION

American Association for State and Local History
021 21st Avenue South
Ste. 320
Nashville, TN 37212
615.320.3203
info@aaslh.org
aaslh.org

American Historical Association
777 6th St. NW, 11th Floor
Washington, DC 20001
202.544.2422
info@historians.org
https://www.historians.org/

National Council on Public History
Cavanaugh Hall 127
425 University Blvd.
Indianapolis, IN 46202-5140
317.274.2716
https://ncph.org/

Organization of American Historians
112 N. Bryan Avenue
Bloomington, Indiana 47408-4141
812.855.7311
oah@oah.org
https://www.oah.org/

Interpreters and Translators

Snapshot

Career Cluster(s): Business, Management, and Administration, Hospitality and Tourism

Interests: Languages, foreign cultures, writing, working with people, communicating with others

Earnings (2018 Median): $49,930 yearly; $24.00 hourly

Employment and Outlook: Much Faster Than Average Growth Expected

OVERVIEW

Sphere of Work

Interpreters and translators facilitate communication between people who speak different languages or hearing and deaf people. While the terms are commonly thought to be interchangeable, translators and interpreters work in different media. A translator translates written materials, usually into his or her native language, while an interpreter translates oral communication and may switch between languages. Some do both types of work. Among the most popular

languages being translated into English today are Spanish, Arabic, Chinese, and American Sign Language (ASL).

Work Environment

Translators often work by themselves at home, where they receive assignments via the Internet or mail. Interpreters work in a variety of settings, such as hospitals, courtrooms, schools, airports, and government offices. They may work alone with just their clients or with partners. In some cases, a translator or interpreter might work the night shift or odd hours, especially when communicating with people who live and work in other time zones. Some interpreters work with reporters in combat zones, risking their lives to do so.

Profile

Interests: Data, People
Working Conditions: Work Inside
Physical Strength: Light Work
Education Needs: Bachelor's Degree, Master's Degree
Licensure/Certification: Recommended
Physical Abilities Not Required: Not Climb, Not Kneel
Opportunities for Experience: Military Service, Volunteer Work
Holland Interest Score: ESA, ISC, SCE

* See Appendix A

Occupation Interest

Interpreting and translating attract those who are linguistically gifted and enjoy foreign cultures. Translators tend to be introverts who enjoy reading and writing and prefer solitary work, while interpreters tend to be extroverts who love being around people, have excellent hearing and listening skills, and are quick thinkers. Translators must manage deadlines while interpreters comply with variable schedules. In either case, the work demands strong cognitive skills and a sharp memory. Sign language interpreters also need excellent hand dexterity.

A Day in the Life—Duties and Responsibilities

A translator spends most of his or her day translating documents at a computer. A job might be as simple as a few paragraphs in a blog, to a book or transcript hundreds of pages long. The translator takes time to reflect on what he or she reads. The translator then tries to communicate the message with as much of its natural rhythm and nuances intact as possible. Such work requires full knowledge of each language, including slang, subject-specific jargon, colloquialisms, as well as a deep understanding of each culture. Usually a translator has several dictionaries and style guides at his or her disposal, as grammar and punctuation are extremely important.

Interpreters work closely with their clients, in person or via phone, videophone, or microphone. Interpretation may be simultaneous or consecutive. Simultaneous interpreting involves listening to a speaker and translating orally, or signing, at the same time. In some cases, the interpreter is given a written speech or paper to consult in advance for general ideas and language. In other cases, there is no time to think! Consecutive interpreting involves listening to a speaker complete a few words or a sentence and then translating it orally. Depending on the speaker's pace, the interpreter might have time to consider various interpretations of a word or phrase.

Interpreters at United Nations conventions or other types of conferences often sit in the audience and whisper their translations into a microphone. Sign language interpreters sometimes use videophones and a computer to communicate with the deaf.

Self-employed translators and interpreters spend part of the day keeping up with marketing, billing, and other administrative tasks.

Interpreters and translators aid communication by converting messages or text from one language into another language. Although some people do both, interpreting and translating are different professions: interpreters work with spoken communication, and translators work with written communication.

Interpreters convert information from one spoken language into another—or, in the case of sign language interpreters, between spoken language and sign language. The goal of an interpreter is to have people hear the interpretation as if it were the original language. Interpreters usually must be fluent speakers or signers of both languages, because they communicate back and forth among people who do not share a common language.

There are three common modes of interpreting: simultaneous, consecutive, and sight translation:

Simultaneous interpreters convey a spoken or signed message into another language at the same time someone is speaking or signing.

Simultaneous interpreters must be familiar with the subject matter and maintain a high level of concentration to convey the message accurately and completely. Due to the mental fatigue involved, simultaneous interpreters may work in pairs or small teams if they are interpreting for long periods of time, such as in a court or conference setting.

Consecutive interpreters convey the speaker's or signer's message in another language after they have stopped to allow for the interpretation. Note taking is generally an essential part of consecutive interpreting.

Sight translation interpreters provide translation of a written document directly into a spoken language, for immediate understanding, but not for the purposes of producing a written translated document.

Translators convert written materials from one language into another language. The goal of a translator is to have people read the translation as if it were the original written material. To do that, the translator must be able to write in a way that maintains or duplicates the structure and style of the original text while keeping the ideas and facts of the original material accurate. Translators must properly transmit any cultural references, including slang, and other expressions that do not translate literally.

Translators must read the original language fluently. They usually translate into their native language.

Nearly all translation work is done on a computer, and translators receive and submit most assignments electronically. Translations often go through several revisions before becoming final.

Translation usually is done with computer-assisted translation (CAT) tools, in which a computer database of previously translated sentences or segments (called a "translation memory") may be used to translate new text. CAT tools allow translators to work more efficiently and consistently. Translators also edit materials translated by computers, or machine translation. This process is called post-editing.

Interpretation and translation services are needed in virtually all subject areas. Although most interpreters and translators specialize in a particular field or industry, many have more than one area of specialization.

The following are examples of types of interpreters and translators:

Community interpreters work in community-based environments, providing vital language interpretation one-on-one or in group settings. Community interpreters often are needed at parent–teacher conferences, community events, business and public meetings, social and government agencies, new-home purchases, and many other work and community settings.

Conference interpreters work at conferences that have non-English-speaking attendees. The work is often in the field of international business or diplomacy, although conference interpreters can interpret for any organization that works with speakers of foreign languages. Employers generally prefer more experienced interpreters who can convert two languages into one native language—for example, the ability to interpret from Spanish and French into English. For some positions, such as those with the United Nations, this qualification is required.

Conference interpreters often do simultaneous interpreting. Attendees at a conference or meeting who do not understand the language of the speaker wear earphones tuned to the interpreter who speaks the language they want to hear.

Health or medical interpreters and translators typically work in healthcare settings and help patients communicate with doctors, nurses, technicians, and other medical staff. Interpreters and translators must have knowledge of medical terminology and of common medical terms in both languages. They may translate research material, regulatory information, pharmaceutical and informational brochures, patient consent documents, website information, and patients' records from one language into another.

Healthcare or medical interpreters must be sensitive to patients' personal circumstances, as well as maintain confidentiality and ethical standards. Interpretation may also be provided remotely, either by video relay or over the phone.

Liaison or escort interpreters accompany either U.S. visitors abroad or foreign visitors in the United States who have limited English proficiency. Interpreting in both formal and informal settings, these specialists ensure that the visitors can communicate during their stay. Frequent travel is common for liaison or escort interpreters.

Legal or judicial interpreters and translators typically work in courts and other legal settings. At hearings, arraignments, depositions, and trials, they help people who have limited English proficiency. Accordingly, they must understand legal terminology. Many court interpreters must sometimes read documents aloud in a language other than that in which they were written, a task known as sight translation. Legal or judiciary interpreters and translators must have a strong understanding of legal terminology.

Literary translators convert journal articles, books, poetry, and short stories from one language into another language. They work to keep the tone, style, and meaning of the author's work. Whenever possible, literary translators work closely with authors to capture the intended meaning, as well as the literary and cultural characteristics, of the original publication.

Localizers adapt text and graphics used in a product or service from one language into another language, a task known as localization. Localization specialists work to make it appear as though the product originated in the country where it will be sold. They must not only know both languages, but also understand the technical information they are working with and the culture of the people who will be using the product or service. Localizers make extensive use of computer and web-based localization tools and generally work in teams.

Localization may include adapting websites, software, marketing materials, user documentation, and various other publications. Usually, these adaptations are related to products and services in information technology, manufacturing and other business sectors.

Sign language interpreters facilitate communication between people who are deaf or hard of hearing and people who can hear. Sign language interpreters must be fluent in English and in American Sign Language (ASL), which combines signing, finger spelling, and specific body language. ASL is a separate language from English and has its own grammar.

Some interpreters specialize in other forms of interpreting for people who are deaf or hard of hearing.

Some people who are deaf or hard of hearing can lip-read English instead of signing in ASL. Interpreters who work with these people do "oral interpretation," mouthing speech silently and very carefully so that their lips can be read easily. They also may use facial expressions and gestures to help the lip-reader understand.

Other modes of interpreting include cued speech, which uses hand shapes placed near the mouth to give lip-readers more information; signing exact English; and tactile signing, which is interpreting for people who are blind as well as deaf by making hand signs into the deaf and blind person's hand.

Trilingual interpreters facilitate communication among an English speaker, a speaker of another language, and an ASL user. They must have the versatility, adaptability, and cultural understanding necessary to interpret in all three languages without changing the fundamental meaning of the message.

Duties and Responsibilities

- Listening through earphones to what is being said
- Convert concepts in the source language to equivalent concepts in the target language
- Compile information and technical terms into glossaries and terminology databases to be used in their oral renditions and translations
- Speak, read, and write fluently in at least two languages, one of which is usually English
- Relay the style and tone of the original language
- Render spoken messages accurately, quickly, and clearly
- Apply their cultural knowledge to render an accurate and meaningful interpretation or translation of the original message

WORK ENVIRONMENT

Immediate Physical Environment

Interpreters tend to work in diverse interior and exterior environmental conditions, including potentially dangerous or unhealthy job sites. Travel is often required. Translators, on the other hand, work in offices with less variable conditions or at home.

Transferable Skills and Abilities

Communication Skills
- Expressing thoughts and ideas
- Speaking effectively
- Writing concisely

Interpersonal/Social Skills
- Cooperating with others
- Working as a member of a team

Organization and Management Skills
- Making decisions

Research and Planning Skills
- Creating ideas
- Developing evaluation strategies
- Using logical reasoning

Human Environment

Unless self-employed, translators and interpreters report to supervisors or directors and usually interact with various office staff and professionals. Their clients may change from day to day. Interpreters also interact with the public at conventions or while touring cities with their clients.

Technological Environment

A translator uses translation software on a computer and might use a transcription machine. An interpreter sometimes uses a microphone and might rely on a smart phone, tablet computer, or laptop to access the Internet or a computerized dictionary. Some sign language interpreters use a videophone along with a video relay service (VRS) or video interpreting service.

EDUCATION, TRAINING, AND ADVANCEMENT

High School/Secondary

Achieving proficiency in a foreign language takes many years. A college-preparatory program with four years of at least one foreign language, along with courses in English, speech, and the social sciences (political science, anthropology, and world cultures), will provide the best foundation for a career in interpretation or translation. Those students interested in translating technical material should consider additional courses in science and technology. Foreign exchange programs and travel, volunteer work with ethnic organizations, and other independent educational experiences can prove invaluable.

Suggested High School Subjects
- College Preparatory
- Composition
- English
- Foreign Languages
- Literature
- Speech

Related Career Pathways/Majors

Business, Management, and Administration Cluster
- Human Resources Pathway

Hospitality and Tourism Cluster
- Travel and Tourism Pathway

Famous First

Simultaneous interpretation using electronic equipment was introduced at the Nuremberg trials in 1945. The equipment facilitated large numbers of listeners, and interpretation was offered in French, Russian, German, and English. The technology arose in the 1920s and 1930s when American businessperson Edward Filene and British engineer Alan Gordon Finlay developed simultaneous interpretation equipment with IBM.
(Source: Wikipedia.org)

Postsecondary

While a bachelor's degree is the minimum requirement for most jobs, the selection of a major is a personal decision based on the type of work desired. Students might consider double majoring in a foreign language and in another subject, such as computer science, English literature, engineering, nursing, or pre-law, or in two foreign languages, such as Spanish and French. Some translators and interpreters need an advanced degree to translate subject-specific concepts and vocabulary.

Study abroad programs, foreign travel, and participation in international clubs are some ways to gain important hands-on experience. An internship might be needed for some jobs; some employers offer on-the-job-training.

Related College Majors
- Communication Disorders, General
- Foreign Languages Teacher Education
- Linguistics
- Sign Language Interpretation

Adult Job Seekers

Bilingual adults should be able to transition well into an interpreting or translating career, especially with relevant experience. For example, a bilingual nurse would have an advantage translating or interpreting in a medical setting. Continuing education courses can refresh or teach new skills. Prospective interpreters and translators should expect to be tested in their language abilities as a prerequisite for employment.

Advancement is highly dependent on experience. Advancement opportunities might include better work hours, higher pay, or more interesting assignments. Those with experience may also consider moving into editorial positions or starting their own companies.

Professional Certification and Licensure

States do not license interpreters or translators. Professional certification is voluntary, although many employers only hire those who are certified in a particular subject or specialty. Professional associations, such as the American Translators Association and the International Association of Conference Interpreters, offer certification. Translators typically must pass a written examination.

Additional Requirements

Interpreters and translators who wish to work for government agencies must pass a civil service exam while freelancers need good business skills as well as experience in the field. Interpreters and translators should consider membership in professional associations, which often provide opportunities for networking and professional development. Work experience or certification is required for membership in some organizations.

EARNINGS AND ADVANCEMENT

Earnings of interpreters and translators depend on the type of work done and the language spoken, as well as the education, experience and skill of the individual. Median annual earnings of interpreters and translators were $45,893 in 2012. The lowest ten percent earned less than $24,327, and the highest ten percent earned more than $91,595.

Full-time interpreters and translators employed by multinational companies may receive paid vacations, holidays, and sick days; life and health insurance; and retirement benefits. These are usually paid by the employer. Interpreters working for the United Nations earn tax-free salaries. In addition, international organizations often pay supplementary living and family allowances. Freelance work in this field offers less in fringe benefits.

EMPLOYMENT AND OUTLOOK

Interpreters and translators held about 76,100 jobs in 2018.

Percent change in employment, Projected 2018–28

Interpreters and translators: 19%

Total, all occupations: 5%

Media and communication workers: 4%

Note: All Occupations includes all occupations in the U.S. Economy.
Source: U.S. Bureau of Labor Statistics, Employment Projections program

The largest employers of interpreters and translators were as follows:

Professional, scientific, and technical services	33%
Self-employed workers	22%
Educational services; state, local, and private	18%
Hospitals; state, local, and private	8%
Government	6%

Employment of interpreters and translators is projected to grow 19 percent from 2018 to 2028, much faster than the average for all occupations. Employment growth reflects increasing globalization and a more diverse U.S. population, which is expected to require more interpreters and translators.

Demand will likely remain strong for translators of frequently translated languages, such as French, German, Portuguese, Russian, and Spanish. Demand also should be strong for translators of Arabic and other Middle Eastern languages; for the principal Asian languages including Chinese, Japanese, Hindi, and Korean; and for the indigenous languages from Mexico and Central America such as Mixtec, Zapotec, and Mayan languages.

Demand for American Sign Language interpreters is expected to grow due to the increasing use of video relay services, which allow people to conduct online video calls and use a sign language interpreter.

In addition, growing international trade and broadening global ties should require more interpreters and translators, especially in emerging markets such as Asia and Africa. The ongoing need for military and national security interpreters and translators should result in more jobs as well.

Computers have made the work of translators and localization specialists more efficient. However, many of these jobs cannot be entirely automated, because computers cannot yet produce work comparable to the work that human translators do in most cases.

Job prospects should be best for those who have at least a bachelor's degree and for those who have professional certification. Those with an advanced degree in interpreting and/or translation also should have an advantage.

Job prospects for interpreters and translators should also vary by specialty and language. For example, interpreters and translators of Spanish should have good job prospects because of expected increases in the population of Spanish speakers in the United States. Similarly, job opportunities should be plentiful for interpreters and translators specializing in healthcare and law, because of the critical need for all parties to understand the information communicated in those fields.

Interpreters for the deaf will continue to have favorable employment prospects because there are relatively few people with the needed skills.

Related Occupations
- Intelligence Officer
- Interpreter and Translator
- Radio Intelligence Officer

Fast Fact

The word "translation" derives from the Latin word *translatio*, or *translationis*, which means "to change venue," or "transporting or transferring something."
Source: rosettatranslation.com.

Conversation With . . .
FRANÇOISE MASSARDIER-KENNEY

Professor of French
Director for Institute for Applied Linguistics
Kent State University, Kent, Ohio
Translator and educator, 30 years

1. What was your individual career path in terms of education/training, entry-level job, or other significant opportunity?

I grew up in Eastern France. I was interested in English for family reasons: my parents and grandparents were involved in the resistance movement during World War II so obviously they were very happy when the British and Americans got involved. There was a sense that this was a really good culture and, by extension, language. Also at that time, American rock and British music was omnipresent.

I earned my undergraduate degree in English comparative literature at the Université de Besançon, France, came to the United States to be (and, for personal reasons, stayed) in the U.S. I earned my master's and finished my doctoral degree, both in English and both at Kent State. At the same time, I trained in education and became certified to teach English and French. I taught at five different schools in seven years, which was very good because it taught me to understand how the American education system worked. I taught at public, private, senior and junior high schools while at the same time freelancing as a translator. There is a lot of local industry here with an international reach. I had a mentor at the time who taught me that if you stay in one area you are going to have to do everything. I even translated messages.

At the time, Kent State's president was very interested in partnerships with Eastern Bloc countries. One partnership was with a university that had a sophisticated applied linguistics institute and he decided the university should have that. That's how this institute started. He looked for people who could teach in that program and I was hired in 1989. In 2005 I became director.

In my work I have written or co-edited a number of books and translated a number of works, perhaps most notably George Sand's *Valvèdre*. It can take up to two years to translate a book and I've been very lucky because I had a job in a university so I could select what I wanted to do.

2. What are the most important skills and/or qualities for someone in your profession?

Knowing more than one language, excellent research skills, willingness to constantly learn in diverse fields, comfort with new technologies

3. What do you wish you had known going into this profession?

The importance of networking with others in the same profession and keeping abreast of new resources.

4. Are there many job opportunities in your profession? In what specific areas?

The language industry includes all the countries in the business of providing translation or adapting software that involves language but also culture. It is a huge industry because the Web is very international. Most jobs are in language project management, editing machine translation output, and localization (adapting software for foreign markets). In some language pairs, the work is plain translation.

Any company that does international business has huge translation needs. If, for example, a business needs a three-million-word document translated in two weeks, that project obviously requires a big team. The team provides translation of texts used by a segment of industry using consistent terminology, as well as quality assurance. I expect to see major changes in the next five years.

5. How do you see your profession changing in the next five years? How will technology impact that change, and what skills will be required?

The development of neural machine translation and artificial intelligence is changing the field. A lot of translation work is going to be done by machine, but machine output is rarely perfect. You still need a human to go through the translation, just as you still need a doctor to go back and see if scans or X-rays are accurate. People working in the language industry will need to know more than languages; they will need to have some training in computer science also. They will need to follow the fast pace of technological developments and understand the principles driving software development.

6. What do you enjoy most about your job? What do you enjoy least about your job?

What I enjoy most: Learning new things all the time. What I enjoy least: the uncertainty about what is coming next.

7. Can you suggest a valuable "try this" for students considering a career in your profession?

Try this: Select a one-page text in your non-native language—known as B language (specialized and/or idiomatic) and translate it into your own language. Time it. Then take the same short text and run it through an open source machine translation system. Then edit the machine-translated text and time it. Compare the time and skills it took to translate using both methods.

MORE INFORMATION

American Association of Language Specialists
3051 Idaho Avenue N.W. # 425
Washington, D.C. 20016
https://www.taals.net/

American Translators Association
225 Reinekers Lane, Suite 590
Alexandria, VA 22314
703.683.6100
ata@atanet.org
www.atanet.org
Certifies translators:
www.atanet.org/certification/aboutcert_
overview.php

Offers honors and awards:
www.atanet.org/membership/
honorsandawards.php

National Security Education Program
4800 Mark Center Drive, Suite 08F09-02
Alexandria, VA 22350-7000
571.256.0711
nsep@nsep.gov
www.nsep.gov

Sponsors scholarships and fellowships
www.nsep.gov/initiatives

Registry of Interpreters for the Deaf
333 Commerce Street
Alexandria, VA 22314
703.838.0030
www.rid.org

Sponsors sign language interpreter
scholarships and awards:

www.rid.org/aboutRID/schol_awards/
index.cfm

Offers sign language certification and
professional development:
www.rid.org/education/overview/index.
cfm

Sally Driscoll/Editor

Journalists

Snapshot

Career Cluster(s): Arts, A/V Technology, and Communications
Interests: Writing, story-telling, research, solving problems, communicating with others
Earnings (2018 Median): $43,490 yearly; $20.91 hourly
Employment and Outlook: Decline Expected

OVERVIEW

Sphere of Work

The field of journalism involves reporting news, events, and ideas to a wide audience through various media, including print (newspapers and magazines), broadcasting (television and radio), or the Internet (news websites and blogs). Journalists usually start out as reporters, covering anything from sports and weather to business, crime, politics, and consumer affairs. Later, they may become editors, helping to direct the process of gathering and presenting stories.

Journalists can operate on many different levels local, regional, national, or international. It is common for a journalist to start out working on the local or regional level and then move up

the ladder as his or her career progresses. Journalists spend the bulk of their time investigating and composing stories, observing events, interviewing people, taking notes, taking photographs, shooting videos, and preparing their material for publication or broadcast. This work can happen in a matter of minutes, or it can take days or weeks to gather information and build a story.

Work Environment

A journalist's work environment is fast-paced and competitive, subject to tight and changing deadlines, irregular work hours, and pressure to get breaking news on the air or on-line before other news organizations. Journalists covering "hard news"—current events that directly affect people's lives, such as crime, politics, or natural disasters—typically work with stories that are moving and changing constantly; their challenge is to present as much relevant and verifiable information as possible under the circumstances. Journalists covering less pressing subjects, like economic and social trends, popular culture, or "human interest" stories, are subject to less immediate time pressures, but are under no less of an obligation to get their facts straight.

Journalists must therefore be able to adapt to unfamiliar places and a variety of people. They must be accustomed to interruptions and have the ability to pick up and process new information at all times.

Profile

Interests: Data, People
Working Conditions: Work Both Inside and Outside
Physical Strength: Light Work
Education Needs: Bachelor's Degree, Master's Degree
Licensure/Certification: Usually Not Required
Physical Abilities Not Required: Not Climb, Not Kneel
Opportunities for Experience: Internship, Apprenticeship, Military Service, Volunteer Work, Part-time Work
Holland Interest Score: EAS

* See Appendix A

Occupation Interest

Successful journalists are curious by nature and can work comfortably with a wide variety of subjects. They enjoy writing and presenting stories, and they have a great respect for principals that define a free society. These principals include the public's right to know and to question government, business, and social institutions. They also respect an individual's desire to feel connected to what is going on in society. Journalists have to be adept at dealing with people, and successful journalists often have a competitive nature that drives them to try to get the "scoop" before other journalists.

Journalism can be multifaceted work—it can be a low-key, local position for a community newspaper, or it can involve travel and a myriad of settings. Reporting can be a fast-paced in- or out-of-office experience driven by publication editors or broadcast producers.

Finally, journalists have to exhibit tenacity and a tough skin, able to pursue a story to its natural end with a commitment to fair and accurate reporting, even when dealing controversial topics or evasive interview subjects.

A Day in the Life—Duties and Responsibilities

On any given day, journalists are researching and developing story ideas, checking facts, writing articles for publication, all on a tight deadline. Journalists uncover news, information, statistics, and trends that they incorporate into news stories, broadcasts, feature stories, and editorials. They meet regularly with editors and get assignments based on the day's or week's happenings. Depending where a journalist works, a typical day can vary.

Daily newspapers and newswire services, with very short lead times, have journalists working at all times, around the clock, following ongoing news stories. Weekly newspapers, and weekly and monthly magazines, have longer lead times, and so deadlines are less frequent.

Some journalists work in the field as correspondents, perhaps traveling with a camera crew and conducting "man-on-the-street" interviews, or gathering information about rapidly developing events, which they then submit electronically to newspaper editors or radio or television producers. Since the rise of the Internet, the distinction between print and broadcast journalism has become less sharp: newspaper websites today often include video feeds, and television news stations have websites where their stories appear in text form.

The most important part of a journalist's job is making sure that the stories he or she presents are based on solid, verifiable facts, rather than rumors or misinformation. Inaccuracies can creep into news stories in many ways honest mistakes, the reporter's own conscious or unconscious biases, and sources attempting to deceive the public are just a few. For this reason, journalists must invest a good deal of time in making sure their stories are correct before they reach the public.

Reporters and correspondents often work for a particular type of media organization, such as a television or radio station, newspaper, or website. Those who work in television and radio set up and conduct interviews, which can be broadcast live or recorded for future broadcasts. These workers are often responsible for editing interviews and other recordings to create a cohesive story and for writing and recording voiceovers that provide the audience with the facts of the story. They may create multiple versions of the same story for different broadcasts or different media platforms.

Journalists for print media conduct interviews and write articles to be used in newspapers, magazines, and online publications. Because most newspapers and magazines have print and online versions, reporters typically produce content for both versions. This requires that they stay up to date with new developments of a story so that the online editions can be updated with the most current information.

Outlets are increasingly relying on multimedia journalists to publish content on a variety of platforms, such as a video content on the website of a daily newspaper. Multimedia journalists typically record, report, write, and edit their own stories. They also gather the audio, video, or graphics that accompany their stories.

Reporters and correspondents may need to maintain a presence on social media networking sites. Many use social media to cover live events, provide additional information for readers and viewers, promote their stations and newscasts, and engage with their audiences.

Some journalists, particularly those in large cities or large news organizations, cover a particular topic, such as sports, medicine, or politics. Journalists who work in small cities, towns, or organizations may need to cover a wider range of subjects.

Reporters who cover international news often live in another country and report news for a specific region of the world.

Some reporters—particularly those who work for print news—are self-employed and take freelance assignments from news organizations. Freelance assignments are given to writers on an as-needed basis. Because freelance reporters are paid for the individual story, they work with many organizations and often spend some of their time marketing their stories and looking for their next assignment. Reporters also may collaborate with editors, photographers, videographers, and other journalists when working on a story.

Some people with a background as a reporter or correspondent work as postsecondary teachers and teach journalism or communications at colleges and universities.

Broadcast news analysts, also called anchors, lead news shows on television or radio. Others are news commentators, who analyze and interpret news stories and offer opinions. Some news commentators come from fields outside of journalism and have expertise in a particular subject—for example, politics, business, or medicine—and are hired on a contract basis to provide their opinion on the subjects being discussed.

Duties and Responsibilities

- Researching public records
- Interviewing people
- Writing stories on computer relay terminals
- Specializing in one or more fields of news
- Covering news in a particular location
- Taking photographs
- Writing headlines
- Laying out pages
- Editing wire service copy
- Writing editorials
- Investigating leads and news tips

OCCUPATION SPECIALTIES

News Writers

News Writers write news stories from notes recorded by reporters after evaluating and verifying the information, supplementing it with other material and organizing stories to fit formats.

Reporters and Correspondents

Reporters and Correspondents gather and assess information, organize it and write news stories in prescribed style and format. They may also take photographs for stories and give broadcast reports, or report live from the site of events.

Columnists

Columnists analyze news and write columns or commentaries based on personal knowledge and experience with the subject matter. They gather information through research, interviews, experience, and attendance at functions such as political conventions, news meetings, sporting events, and social activities.

Critics

Critics write critical reviews of literary, musical, or artistic works and performances.

Editorial Writers

Editorial Writers write comments on topics of reader interest to stimulate or mold public opinion in accordance with the viewpoints and policies of publications.

WORK ENVIRONMENT

Immediate Physical Environment

A journalist's work environment can be anywhere, from a crime scene to a press conference to a desk in an office. News outlets usually house journalists in large, well-lit rooms filled with work stations, computer equipment, and the sounds of keyboards and printers. "Boots-on-the-ground" reporting can take a journalist anywhere, though: embedded war correspondents may travel with a military unit right into battle; a journalist reporting on the fishing industry may spend several days on a fishing boat at sea; the next week, that same journalist may tour a farm or a factory or a school to get the next story.

Transferable Skills and Abilities

Communication Skills
- Speaking effectively
- Writing concisely

Interpersonal/Social Skills
- Asserting oneself
- Being flexible
- Being persistent
- Cooperating with others
- Working as a member of a team

Organization and Management Skills
- Managing time
- Meeting goals and deadlines
- Paying attention to and handling details

Research and Planning Skills
- Analyzing information
- Gathering information
- Solving problems

Unclassified Skills
- Discovering unusual aspects of stories

Human Environment

Journalists deal with people. They are constantly interviewing people and collecting and analyzing information; therefore, they can usually be found speaking with anyone who has something to do with the story at hand, be it politicians, company officials, protesters, or an average person.

Technological Environment

Today, journalists submit their stories electronically and can therefore be anywhere in the world, collecting information. They often carry their technology on their back, with just a laptop computer and camera, or travel with a crew of broadcast professionals who can put the journalist on the air live at any time.

EDUCATION, TRAINING, AND ADVANCEMENT

High School/Secondary

High school students can prepare to be a journalist by working for the school newspaper or yearbook, volunteering with local broadcasting stations, and participating in internships with news organizations. Coursework should include a strong focus on writing and communication, through classes such as English, social studies, political science, history, and psychology. Knowledge of foreign languages can also be highly useful in many journalism jobs.

Practical experience is highly valued and can be found through part-time or summer jobs, summer journalism camps, work at college broadcasting stations, and professional organizations. Work in these areas can help in obtaining scholarships, fellowships, and assistantships for college journalism majors.

Local television stations and newspapers often offer internship opportunities for up-and-coming journalists to improve their craft by reporting on town hall meetings or writing obituaries and human-interest stories.

Suggested High School Subjects
- Business
- College Preparatory
- Composition
- Computer Science
- Economics
- English
- Government
- Journalism
- Keyboarding
- Literature
- Photography
- Political Science
- Social Studies
- Speech

Related Career Pathways/Majors

Arts, A/V Technology, and Communications Cluster

- Journalism and Broadcasting Pathway

Famous First

Sir William Howard Russell was an Irish reporter with *The Times*, and is considered to have been one of the first modern war correspondents. He spent 22 months covering the Crimean War, including the Siege of Sevastopol and the Charge of the Light Brigade. He later covered events during the Indian Rebellion of 1857, the American Civil War, the Austro-Prussian War, and the Franco-Prussian War.
(Source: Wikipedia.org)

Postsecondary

Most, but not all, journalists have a bachelor's degree in journalism, English, or another liberal arts-related field. There are many journalism schools within colleges and universities across the country. Many schools also offer master's and doctoral degrees, which are especially useful for those interested in journalistic research and teaching.

Bachelor degree program coursework should include broad liberal arts subjects, a general overview of journalism, and then specialty courses that correspond with the highly important requirements for good writing and communication. These can include classes in social media, broadcast writing, news editorial writing, magazine writing, copyediting, interviewing, media ethics, blogging, feature writing, news reporting, and news photography.

All college and university students should make the effort to use career centers, academic counselors, and professors when seeking opportunities for advancement through volunteering or interning.

Related College Majors
- Broadcast Journalism
- Journalism

Adult Job Seekers

Almost anyone can become a journalist if they can find a local
newspaper willing to let them try writing a story. Adults can seek
continuing journalism education and ongoing opportunities to
volunteer in various capacities, perhaps by writing guest newspaper
columns, or helping produce a local newsletter, or writing for a blog.
These options mean it is entirely viable to seek journalism jobs after
having been out of the workplace for a while. Prospective journalists
will need to have updated resumes, preferably with portfolios showing
relevant work.

More experience leads to more specialized and challenging
assignments. Large publications and news stations prefer journalists
with several years of experience. With more experience, journalists
can advance to become columnists, correspondents, announcers,
reporters, or publishing industry managers.

Becoming adept at freelancing—where reporters work independently
by selling stories to any interested media outlet—is another way to
stay involved in the journalism field.

Professional Certification and Licensure

In the United States, professional certification is not necessary to
be a journalist; however, involvement in the Society of Professional
Journalists or other professional organizations can help journalists
network and raise their profile.

Additional Requirements

It is extremely useful for journalists to have experience
with computer graphics and desktop skills, as well as
proficiency in all forms of multimedia. Familiarity with
databases and knowledge of news photography is an
added plus.

EARNINGS AND ADVANCEMENT

The median annual wage for broadcast news analysts was $66,880 in May 2018. The median wage is the wage at which half the workers in an occupation earned more than that amount and half earned less. The lowest 10 percent earned less than $27,370, and the highest 10 percent earned more than $200,180..

Median annual wages, May 2018

Broadcast news analysts: $66,880

Media and communication workers: $57,530

Reporters, correspondents, and broadcast news analysts: $43,490

Reporters and correspondents: $41,260

Total, all occupations: $38,640

Note: All Occupations includes all occupations in the U.S. Economy.
Source: U.S. Bureau of Labor Statistics, Employment Projections program

The median annual wage for reporters and correspondents was $41,260 in May 2018. The lowest 10 percent earned less than $23,490, and the highest 10 percent earned more than $100,930.

In May 2018, the median annual wages for broadcast news analysts in the top industries in which they worked were as follows:

Radio and television broadcasting	$64,600
Educational services; state, local, and private	$41,210

In May 2018, the median annual wages for reporters and correspondents in the top industries in which they worked were as follows:

Other information services	$59,720
Radio and television broadcasting	$48,220
Newspaper, periodical, book, and directory publishers	$35,860

Most reporters, correspondents, and broadcast news analysts work full-time. Reporters may need to work additional hours or change their schedules in order to follow breaking news. Because news can happen at any time, journalists may need to work nights and weekends. Broadcast news analysts may also work nights and weekends to lead news programs or provide commentary.

Journalists may receive paid vacations, holidays, and sick days; life and health insurance; and retirement benefits. These are usually paid by the employer.

EMPLOYMENT AND OUTLOOK

Percent change in employment, Projected 2018–28

Total, all occupations: 5%

Media and communication workers: 4%

Broadcast news analysts: 1%

Reporters, correspondents, and broadcast news analysts: -10%

Reporters and correspondents: -12%

Note: All Occupations includes all occupations in the U.S. Economy.
Source: U.S. Bureau of Labor Statistics, Employment Projections program

Broadcast news analysts held about 6,900 jobs in 2018. The largest employers of broadcast news analysts were as follows:

Radio and television broadcasting	71%
Self-employed workers	13%
Educational services; state, local, and private	3%

Reporters and correspondents held about 42,800 jobs in 2018. The largest employers of reporters and correspondents were as follows:

Newspaper, periodical, book, and directory publishers	44%
Radio and television broadcasting	28%
Self-employed workers	14%
Other information services	9%

Overall employment of reporters, correspondents, and broadcast news analysts is projected to decline 10 percent from 2018 to 2028. Employment of reporters and correspondents is projected to decline 12 percent, while employment of broadcast news analysts is projected to show little or no change from 2018 to 2028. Declining advertising revenue in radio, newspapers, and television will negatively affect the employment growth for these occupations.

Readership and circulation of newspapers are expected to continue to decline over the next decade. In addition, television and radio stations are increasingly publishing content online and on mobile devices. As a result, news organizations may have more difficulty selling traditional forms of advertising, which is often their primary source of revenue. Some organizations will likely continue to use new forms of advertising or offer paid subscriptions, but these innovations may not make up for lost print-ad revenues.

Declining revenue will force news organizations to downsize and employ fewer journalists. Increasing demand for online news may offset some of the downsizing. However, because online and mobile ad revenue is typically less than print revenue, the growth in digital advertising may not offset the decline in print advertising, circulation, and readership.

News organizations also continue to consolidate and increasingly are sharing resources, staff, and content with other media outlets. For example, reporters are able to gather and report on news for a media outlet that can be published in multiple newspapers owned by the same parent company. As consolidations, mergers, and news sharing continue, the demand for journalists may decrease. However, in some instances, consolidations may help limit the loss of jobs. Mergers may allow financially troubled newspapers, radio stations, and television stations to keep staff because of increased funding and resources from the larger organization.

Reporters, correspondents, and broadcast news analysts are expected to face strong competition for jobs. Those with experience in the field—experience often gained through internships or by working for school newspapers, television stations, or radio stations—should have the best job prospects.

Multimedia journalism experience, including recording and editing video or audio pieces, should also improve job prospects. Because stations and media outlets are increasingly publishing content on multiple media platforms, particularly the web, employers may prefer applicants who have experience in website design and coding.

Related Occupations
- Copywriter
- Radio/TV Announcer and Newscaster
- Technical Writer
- Writer and Editor

Fast Fact

Pioneering investigative journalist Nellie Bly faked mental illness for ten days to investigate conditions in the insane asylum at New York's Blackwell's Island. After the *New York World* published her six-part series, New York City budgeted $1 million to care for the mentally ill

Source: womenshistory.org and crazyfacts.com.

Conversation With . . . DAN CASEY

Columnist, Roanoke Times
Roanoke, Virginia
Journalist, 35 years

1. What was your individual career path in terms of education, entry-level job, or other significant opportunity?

I wasn't your typical college student. It took me eight years to earn a four-year degree at the University of Maryland. One of the jobs I had was working as a bicycle messenger in Washington, D.C. A majority of our clients were newspapers, wire services, public relations companies. It was exciting work, especially on certain days—such as when John Hinckley tried to assassinate President Reagan, or when a jetliner loaded with people crashed into the 14th Street Bridge during an ice storm. That excitement totally hooked me on the news business and its importance in our daily lives. When I finally managed to earn a college degree (in English) I took a job for $210/week at a weekly newspaper in the Washington suburbs. I got some good stories, then six months later moved on to a larger weekly. Two years later, I was at *The Capital*, a daily in Annapolis, Maryland. After seven years there, I moved to *The Roanoke Times*. Here, I've done just about everything in the newsroom—reporting, editing, copy editing, managing local news, and now I write three columns a week.

The messenger job focused me on a career path, but every job I've had since age 11 has helped me in this business. I delivered newspapers, washed dishes, made pizzas, did roofing, jockeyed gasoline, sold shoes, and performed maintenance and repairs at a large apartment complex. Experiences like those helped me understand how things worked in the world and how to relate to people from all walks of life.

2. Are there many job opportunities in your profession? In what specific areas?

The job opportunities in newspapers are fading quickly. But that's not true of the larger media. There's plenty of opportunity and growth in online news media, especially sites such as Talking Points Memo, and Raw Story. Basic skills such as gathering information fast and presenting it coherently are more in demand than ever because the traditional news cycle is shorter than ever.

3. What do you wish you had known going into this profession?

This is generally a low-paid profession, with no law degree or medical license or scientific credentials necessary. Publishers take advantage of that, wage-wise. They'll try to hire you as inexpensively as possible and keep wages low. This doesn't mean you can't make a decent living or even a lot of money working in news. You can, if you're willing to work hard, get good stories, and jump to newer, higher-paying jobs as quickly as you can. Don't spend more than two years in one place. Do this early in your career and you'll have a lot more satisfaction later on.

4. How do you see your profession changing in the next five years? What role will technology play in those changes, and what skills will be required?

I'm close to retirement and wondering if my employer's print edition will be around for five more years. That's kind of a backwards way of saying, whatever you do, DON'T plan a career in traditional newspapers and magazines. If you want to work in news, it's OK to get some experience at a paper or magazine, but get out as fast as you can and head for online news outlets.

The traditional skills in the news business are 1) news-gathering ability and 2) writing, in that order. As the media morphs more and more into online only, those will remain very important. But they're not nearly enough. Skills in photography, video, online presentation, and social media will be at least as important.

5. Do you have any general advice or additional professional insights to share with someone interested in your profession?

The biggest trap I've witnessed many reporters fall into is losing sight of who their client is. The client is ALWAYS your reader. It is NEVER your sources. Still, a lot of people in this profession spend great deals of time trying hardest to please their sources, as if they fear their ability to gather information will dry up if they make their sources unhappy. The truth is, your sources need you more than you need them.

6. What do you like most about your job, and what do you like least about your job?

As a columnist, I have enormous freedom to write about what interests me. I never have to get bogged down in tedious subjects like a beat reporter might have to. The thing I like least is the grind. The column runs on Tuesdays, Thursdays, and Sundays. That means I have ironclad deadlines every Monday, Wednesday and Friday afternoon. That keeps me constantly planning: What are the topics for the next three columns? How much reporting will those require? What sources do I need to talk to, and when? Figuratively, it's a treadmill that never stops.

7. **Can you suggest a valuable "try this" for students considering a career in your profession?**

Few people naturally have a writer's voice. A voice is developed, not ingrained. So develop yours. Find a variety of writers whose voices you admire and read them a lot. Analyze passages you particularly admire. What makes a particular passage so good? And then play around, outside the confines of writing on deadline. Ask yourself: How would Hemingway, or Hunter Thompson or Mike Royko (or whoever) write this story? What lead would they write? Do it over and over again. Eventually you'll find your own voice.

Conversation With . . . SIRI CARPENTER

Freelance science journalist
Editor-in-chief, The Open Notebook
Madison, Wisconsin
Journalist, 20 years

1. What was your individual career path in terms of education/training, entry-level job or other significant opportunity?

I got my bachelor's degree from the University of Wisconsin-Madison and my master's and PhD in social psychology from Yale University. Writing had always interested me, but prior to graduate school I didn't know the field of science journalism existed. My graduate advisor supported my interest, and enabled me to pursue journalism internships during two summers I would have otherwise spent in the lab.

The first internship was at the *Richmond Times-Dispatch* in Virginia for the American Association for the Advancement of Science Mass Media Fellowship Program. The summer after that, I interned at *Science News* magazine in Washington, D.C.

The internships taught me the basics of what it means to be a science journalist: How to find worthwhile science stories, how to report stories through research and interviews and how to engage readers from start to finish.

After a few years, I became self employed as a freelance writer. The freedom and flexibility appealed to me—I could work for publications anywhere, from my own cozy office in Wisconsin. Eventually I became an editor, first for *Discover* magazine and then, as a freelance editor, for other publications such as *bioGraphic* and *Science News for Students*.

In 2010 my friend and colleague Jeanne Erdmann and I co-founded The Open Notebook, a nonprofit organization whose mission is to help science writers improve their skills. TON—as we lovingly call it—has now published hundreds of articles focused on the craft of science writing, tackling subjects as varied as how to weather difficult or dangerous field reporting conditions to how to spot "shady" statistics in scientific papers.

2. What are the most important skills and/or qualities for someone in your profession?

Curiosity.

Sure, it's good to have some understanding of science and statistics and to be able to craft good sentences and spin irresistible stories. Multimedia and data visualization skills are also great. All of these skills can be learned in school or on the job. Curiosity comes from within. People who are naturally curious about the world around them will most easily learn to be good science reporters and writers—and derive the most joy from this profession.

A commitment to factual accuracy and good time management skills also are imperative. Science writers who can reliably turn in stories on deadline will seldom be out of work.

3. What do you wish you had known going into this profession?

I wish I had realized earlier that it's normal to feel lost when tackling a new topic, and that when it comes time to face the blank page and start writing, almost all writers flail for a while.

If you can put up with some periods of despair, then the payoff is the flood of joy that comes when you've finally mastered whatever confused you, or when you've finally pounded a draft into submission and can hit "send."

4. Are there many job opportunities in your profession? In what specific areas?

Science writing is an extremely broad field. Some science writers and editors are freelance or staff journalists for media outlets such as newspapers, magazines, journalism websites and radio and TV. Others work for universities, medical centers, museums, scientific societies and government agencies.

Science writers also include nonfiction book authors, podcasters, YouTubers, textbook and curriculum writers and even event planners. Many science writers do some mix of these or other jobs.

5. How do you see your profession changing in the next five years? How will technology impact that change and what skills will be required?

There are fewer science print journalism jobs than there once were. But new publications—mainly online—have sprung up and the number of freelancers is growing.

As technologies for producing and editing video evolves, science writers can take new approaches to stories that once would have taken the form of printed words on a page.

Improvements in online communications have made it easier for teams of people to work together remotely on platforms such as Slack, Dropbox, Google Docs and Zoom to create "newsrooms" that might be dispersed across many time zones.

6. What do you enjoy most about your job? What do you enjoy least?

What I enjoy most is the variety in my job. As a freelance writer, editor, and head of a nonprofit organization, I am rarely doing the same thing for two days in a row. On any given day, I might be digging into research on carnivorous plants or the hazards of vaping or ways of combating cyberattacks.

What I enjoy least about the job is how sedentary it is. I spend most of my work hours sitting down at a desk or on a sofa with my laptop.

7. Can you suggest a valuable "try this" for students considering a career in your profession?

Find an article on a scientific topic that interests you in a publication such as *Science News*, *National Geographic*, *The Atlantic*, *the New York Times*, *Quartz*, *Outside*, or *Slate*. Read the article three times. The first time, read it casually, to learn and enjoy. The second time, take note of a few things you found interesting or memorable—a startling statistic or a gripping moment of drama.

The third time you read the story, think about what steps the writer might have taken to achieve the things you found memorable. How might they have found the information used in the statistics? Do you think the writer personally witnessed the dramatic scene that captured your imagination, or might they have reconstructed it based on interviews?

If you find that digging deep into science stories to figure out what makes them tick is enjoyable, then a career in science writing just might be for you.

MORE INFORMATION

Accrediting Council on Education in Journalism and Mass Communications (ACEJMC)
201 Bishop Hall, P.O. Box 1848
University, MS 38677-1848
662.915.5550
pthomps1@olemiss.edu
https://www.acejmc.org/

Association for Women in Communications
1717 E. Republic Rd. Ste A
Springfield, MO 65804
703.370.7436
www.womcom.org

Dow Jones Newspaper Fund, Inc.
P.O. Box 300
Princeton, NJ 08543-0300
609.452.2820
djnf@dowjones.com
www.newsfund.org

National Association of Broadcasters
1771 N Street NW
Washington, DC 20036
202.429.5300
nab@nab.org
www.nab.org

National Federation of Press Women
140B Purcellville Gateway Dr. Suite 120
Purcellville, VA 20132
571.295.5900
www.nfpw.org

National Newspaper Association
101 S. Palafox, Unit 13323
Pensacola, FL 32591
850.542.7087
https://www.nnaweb.org/

National Press Club
529 14th Street NW, 13th Floor
Washington, DC 20045
202.662.7500
www.press.org

News Media Alliance
4401 N. Fairfax Dr., Suite 300
Arlington, VA 22203-1867
571.366.1000
info@newsmediaalliance.org
https://www.newsmediaalliance.org/

Newspaper Guild-CWA
501 Third Street NW, 6th Floor
Washington, DC 20001-2797
202.434.7177
guild@cwa-union.org
www.newsguild.org

Poynter Institute
801 3rd Street S.
St. Petersburg, FL 33701
727.821.9494
www.poynter.org

Society of Professional Journalists
Eugene S. Pulliam National Journalism Center
3909 N. Meridian Street
Indianapolis, IN 46208
317.927.8000
www.spj.org

Judges and Hearing Officers

Snapshot

Career Cluster(s): Law, Public Safety and Security

Interests: Law, research, writing, dealing with conflict, listening to others, communicating with others

Earnings (2018 Median): $117,190 yearly; $56.34 hourly

Employment and Outlook: Slower Than Average Growth Expected

OVERVIEW

Sphere of Work

A judge is a public official who oversees the legal process in the courtroom. The judge serves as the chief administrator of a court proceeding. He or she sets the tone of the proceeding by advising attorneys, plaintiffs, and defendants on the rules and procedures of the hearing or trial, ruling on the relevance of testimony, determining whether evidence is admissible, and settling disputes between opposing attorneys during the proceedings. A judge also meets with litigants outside of the courtroom to determine whether a trial or hearing is necessary at all. Once a jury

has ruled on a defendant's liability or guilt, the judge will apply the sentence or award damages based on the law.

Work Environment

Judges work in office settings (known as "chambers"), where they meet with attorneys and other legal professionals, study evidence, and legal precedents, write opinions, and organize the procedures for court cases. They also work in the courtroom, overseeing proceedings in civil and criminal courts. Judges may be found in a wide range of courts, such as municipal and superior courts, appellate courts, state supreme courts, federal district courts and the highest court in the country, the U.S. Supreme Court. Judges work with a large and diverse number of people, including lawyers, accused criminals, security and law enforcement professionals, victims of crime, and the general public.

Profile

Interests: Data, People
Working Conditions: Work Inside
Physical Strength: Light Work
Education Needs: Doctoral Degree
Licensure/Certification: Required
Physical Abilities Not Required: Not Climb, Not Kneel
Opportunities for Experience: Military Service, Volunteer Work, Part-time Work
Holland Interest Score: ESA

* See Appendix A

Occupation Interest

A judge is a leading figure in the application and interpretation of laws. The judge is the highest authority in a courtroom, setting the rules, allowing or excluding evidence, ruling on objections and courtroom conduct, and controlling other important aspects of the courtroom proceedings. A judge is the individual who works to ensure that the hearing proceeds in such a way that it is truly fair and equitable for both defendants and plaintiffs.

Outside of the courtroom, a judge is also an expert on the law. He or she may offer opinions on new laws, pending lawsuits, and even the tenets of the Constitution. A judge's opinion may answer pivotal questions about whether a business or government policy is compliant with the law and concurrent with the best interests of society.

A Day in the Life—Duties and Responsibilities

Most judges spend much of their workday in chambers, hearing attorney arguments and either arbitrating a legal dispute or determining whether a case should go to trial. Their discussions also cover issues such as the admissibility of evidence, witnesses, and other elements of a case. Judges write legal opinions and organize trial and hearing rules while in their chambers or locating information in law libraries. They also supervise their staff members, including administrative and clerical personnel. When they are called into court, judges work to ensure that the proceeding is fair, including instructing the jurors on which information to retain, disciplining unruly parties in the courtroom, and monitoring evidence to ensure that no inadmissible material is introduced that could bias jury members.

Federal judges share many of the responsibilities of municipal and regional judges, but they focus on issues that have more far-reaching or national implications. Appellate court judges and Supreme Court justices will often hear arguments regarding cases on which other judges at a more local level have already ruled—it is the responsibility of these judges to weigh whether the previous ruling was legal and/or constitutional.

Duties and Responsibilities

- Research legal issues
- Read and evaluate information from documents, such as motions, claim applications, and records
- Preside over hearings and listen to and read arguments by opposing parties
- Determine if the information presented supports the charge, claim, or dispute
- Decide if the procedure is being conducted according to the rules and law
- Apply laws or precedents to reach judgments and to resolve disputes between parties
- Write opinions, decisions, and instructions regarding cases, claims, and disputes

OCCUPATION SPECIALTIES

Appellate-Court Judges

Appellate-Court Judges review cases handled by the lower courts and administrative agencies, and if they determine that errors were made in a case and if legal precedent does not support the judgment of the lower court, they may overturn the verdict of that court.

Juvenile Court Judges

Juvenile Court Judges arbitrate, advise, and administer justice in matters dealing with youth and young adults.

Municipal Court Judges

Municipal Court Judges preside over cases within a city. Traffic violations, misdemeanors, small claims cases and pretrial hearings constitute the bulk of their work.

Probate Judges

Probate Judges arbitrate, advise, and administer justice in estate matters and the registration and certification of official documents such as last wills and testaments.

Justices of the Peace

Justices of the Peace are magistrates with jurisdiction over a small district or part of a county that decides cases, pretrial hearings and can perform marriages.

Magistrates

Magistrates are state court judges that preside over cases only within a certain jurisdiction with limited judicial powers.

Hearing Officers

Hearing Officers are employed by government agencies to make decisions about appeals of agency administrative decisions, such as eligibility for social assistance benefits.

WORK ENVIRONMENT

Transferable Skills and Abilities

Communication Skills
- Expressing thoughts and ideas
- Speaking effectively
- Writing concisely

Interpersonal/Social Skills
- Cooperating with others
- Counseling others
- Providing support to others
- Working as a member of a team

Organization and Management Skills
- Making decisions

Research and Planning Skills
- Developing evaluation strategies
- Using logical reasoning

Technical Skills
- Performing scientific, mathematical, and technical work

Immediate Physical Environment

Judges spend the majority of their time working in their chambers or in a courtroom or hearing room, both of which are typically located in secure government buildings and/or courthouses. The office setting is professional and orderly, with administrative staff researching laws, preparing opinions, and drafting court documents. The courtroom is highly organized and orderly: each individual present is tasked with specific duties, and the jury is legally bound to follow the rules and instructions of the judge.

Human Environment

Judges work with a wide variety of people, such as litigants (the plaintiff and defendant), legal counsel for each side, court reporters, witnesses, security personnel, the public in attendance and, of course, the members of the jury. Supreme Court (state and federal) justices and appeals court judges (who may sit on three-judge panels or en banc) also collaborate to formulate collective opinions on legal and constitutional issues.

Technological Environment

Judges often use computers to write opinions and organize court procedures for each case. Courtrooms tend to employ simple technology, including microphones and television monitors used for the presentation of evidence.

EDUCATION, TRAINING, AND ADVANCEMENT

High School/Secondary

High school students who aspire to become judges should study political science and government, social studies, history, and philosophy. English and communications courses are also extremely useful to build research, writing, analysis, and public speaking skills. An awareness of current events on a local and national level is of benefit as well. Students should also pursue activities that allow them to gain experience outside the classroom, such as involvement in Student Council and other leadership organizations.

Suggested High School Subjects
- Algebra
- College Preparatory
- Composition
- Economics
- English
- Government
- History
- Humanities
- Literature
- Political Science
- Psychology
- Sociology
- Speech

Related Career Pathways/Majors

Law, Public Safety and Security Cluster
- Legal Services Pathway

Famous First

The first Chief Justice of the United States was John Jay; the Court's first docketed case was Van Staphorst v. Maryland (1791), and its first recorded decision was West v. Barnes (1791). Perhaps the most controversial of the Supreme Court's early decisions was Chisholm v. Georgia, in which it held that the federal judiciary could hear lawsuits against states. Soon thereafter, responding to the concerns of several states, Congress proposed the Eleventh Amendment, which granted states immunity from certain types of lawsuits in federal courts. The Amendment was ratified in 1795.
Source: Wikipedia.org)

Postsecondary

Aspiring judges must have an undergraduate degree in a related field (with a pre-law focus), such as political science, English, or history. In addition to undergraduate training, most judges are required to have a degree in law, such as an LLB or a JD. This training gives students exposure to a wide range of significant legal rulings and helps them become fully versed in the law, its application, and interpretation.

Related College Majors
- Law (LLB, JD)

Adult Job Seekers

State and federal judges are usually appointed by senior government officials, such as governors or, in the case of federal judges, the president. Municipal and regional judges are elected by the public. Those having hopes for a judicial appointment or election should practice law for several years, building a positive reputation within the legal community and the community in which they live. Since politicians and the voting public determine who will become a judge, prospective judges must be self-promoters and knowledgeable about how to use the media to their advantage.

Professional Certification and Licensure

In addition to earning his or her law degree, a judge must pass the bar examination of the state in which he or she works. Judges may also join a professional legal association, such as the American Bar Association.

Additional Requirements

Judges should have prior experience as lawyers, as well as an exceptional understanding of the law and the U.S. Constitution. They should have strong analytical and communication skills, which help them apply the law or the tenets of the Constitution to the issues brought before them by the litigants. Ideally, judges should be even-handed and decisive, especially in light of the strong emotions that can arise during arbitration and court proceedings.

EARNINGS AND ADVANCEMENT

The median annual wage for administrative law judges, adjudicators, and hearing officers was $99,850 in May 2018. The median wage is the wage at which half the workers in an occupation earned more than that amount and half earned less. The lowest 10 percent earned less than $45,120, and the highest 10 percent earned more than $169,640.

Median annual wages, May 2018

Judges, magistrate judges, and magistrates: $133,920

Judges and hearing officers: $117,190

Administrative law judges, adjudicators, and hearing officers: $99,850

Legal occupations: $80,810

Total, all occupations: $38,640

Note: All Occupations includes all occupations in the U.S. Economy.
Source: U.S. Bureau of Labor Statistics, Employment Projections program

The median annual wage for judges, magistrate judges, and magistrates was $133,920 in May 2018. The lowest 10 percent earned less than $34,790, and the highest 10 percent earned more than $193,330.

In May 2018, the median annual wages for administrative law judges, adjudicators, and hearing officers in the top industries in which they worked were as follows:

Federal government	$129,920
State government, excluding education and hospitals	$82,910
Local government, excluding education and hospitals	$77,470

In May 2018, the median annual wages for judges, magistrate judges, and magistrates in the top industries in which they worked were as follows:

State government, excluding education and hospitals	$151,900
Local government, excluding education and hospitals	$87,440

Some courthouses have evening and weekend hours. In addition, judges have to be on call during nights or weekends to issue emergency orders, such as search warrants and restraining orders.

Judges may receive paid vacations, holidays, and sick days; life and health insurance; and retirement benefits. These are usually paid by the employer. Judges may also receive a cost-of-living allowance, travel and library allowances and payment of state bar or other association dues.

EMPLOYMENT AND OUTLOOK

Administrative law judges, adjudicators, and hearing officers held about 15,200 jobs in 2018. The largest employers of administrative law judges, adjudicators, and hearing officers were as follows:

State government, excluding education and hospitals	49%
Federal government	33%
Local government, excluding education and hospitals	17%

Judges, magistrate judges, and magistrates held about 29,800 jobs in 2018. The largest employers of judges, magistrate judges, and magistrates were as follows:

State government, excluding education and hospitals	55%
Local government, excluding education and hospitals	45%

Employment of judges and hearing officers is projected to grow 3 percent from 2018 to 2028, slower than the average for all occupations.

Percent change in employment, Projected 2018–28

Legal occupations: 7%

Total, all occupations: 5%

Judges, magistrate judges, and magistrates: 3%

Judges and hearing officers: 3%

Administrative law judges, adjudicators, and hearing officers: 2%

Note: All Occupations includes all occupations in the U.S. Economy.
Source: U.S. Bureau of Labor Statistics, Employment Projections program

These workers play an essential role in the legal system, and their services will continue to be needed into the future. However, budgetary constraints in federal, state, and local governments may limit the ability of these governments to fill vacant judge and hearing officer positions or authorize new ones. If there are governmental budget concerns, this could limit the employment growth opportunities of hearing officers and administrative law judges working for local, state, and federal government agencies, despite the continued need for these workers to settle disputes.

The prestige associated with becoming a judge, and the fact that many need to be elected or nominated into the position, will ensure continued competition for these positions. Most job openings will arise as a result of judges and hearing officers leaving the occupation because of retirement, to teach, or because their elected term is over.

Related Occupations
- Lawyer

Related Military Occupations
- Lawyer

Conversation With . . .
THE HON. JERRY A. BROWN

Bankruptcy Judge, 22 years

1. What was your individual career path in terms of education/training, entry-level job, or other significant opportunity?

I always wanted to be a lawyer, and I had a couple of uncles who encouraged me to be a lawyer. I went to Murray State College in Western Kentucky; there wasn't a pre-law program but I majored in history and social sciences and was on the debate team. Tulane University Law School, back in the early '50s, offered regional scholarships and I received one. I wanted to go in the Army first and fulfill my military obligation and Tulane was very clear: you go do your military duty and we'll hold the scholarship.

When I graduated, I was a law clerk for Judge John Minor Wisdom. He was an outstanding judge on the U.S. Fifth Circuit Court of Appeals, a wonderful person to work for, a great writer. He was a legal giant, well known for his influential votes during the Civil Rights era. That's when I first got the urge to be a judge.

I was in private practice with one of the fine old law firms, Monroe and Lemann, for 30 years. I did commercial law, business law, defense work, and some reorganization work, which is a specialized portion of bankruptcy. I left in 1990 and went with a boutique bankruptcy firm, Bronfin and Heller. Not quite two years later, I applied and was appointed to the Bankruptcy Court of the Eastern District of Louisiana by the Fifth U.S. Circuit Court of Appeals. I served one 14-year term, another five-year abbreviated term, then retired but was recalled twice for a total of six years.

2. What are the most important skills and/or qualities for someone in your profession?

Being able to write well and being able to analyze and solve problems in writing. So much of legal problems is decided on the written word. Oral argument has been curtailed a great deal. For a judge, writing and a command of the English language is all-important.

3. What do you wish you had known going into this profession?

I wish I'd known how to write better. I was assistant editor at Tulane Law Review and did a lot of legal writing as a lawyer, but it's a different style and a different approach when you're a judge. As a lawyer you advocate your point. As a judge, you've got to weigh both sides and come to a just decision.

4. Are there many job opportunities in your profession? In what specific areas?

Judgeships open up from time to time. Some people retire, and some people don't get reappointed for various reasons. There are always openings in the judiciary but they come at odd times.

5. How do you see your profession changing in the next five years? What role will technology play in those changes, and what skills will be required?

It's changing dramatically, primarily because of electronic filing and computers. In 2002, we in the bankruptcy court were one of the first in this area to make electronic filing compulsory. Almost all federal courts now have electronic filing and case management, and state courts are going that way. Some judges are proficient enough to listen to an argument or witness testimony and at the same time be pulling cases or other research up on the computer. The big problem is the temptation of judges and law clerks to get on the computer and get information that is not in evidence.

6. What do you enjoy most about your job? What do you enjoy least?

I enjoy being in court. Some judges want to do everything through briefs or the written word but I enjoy the interchange with lawyers. I still enjoy trying cases and doing research. The thing I enjoy most is solving problems and reaching a just and fair solution that helps people that is permitted by the law involved.

The thing I enjoy least is probably arguments about attorney's fees. I also don't like a lying witness or fraud. Fortunately, we don't have too much of that.

7. Can you suggest a valuable "try this" for students considering a career in your profession?

Most judges will welcome students into their courtroom, and maybe into their chambers. Find out if there's an interesting trial or hearing going on and go in and listen. I also suggest that a young person try to get a lawyer or judge to mentor them, perhaps through a college or law school program.

The other thing is you should concentrate on learning English. It's a sad story that many lawyers do not write well enough and cannot formulate a logical English sentence.

MORE INFORMATION

American Bar Association
321 N. Clark Street
Chicago, IL 60654-7598
800.285.2221
www.americanbar.org

American Judges Association
300 Newport Avenue
Williamsburg, VA 23185-4147
757.259.1841
aja.ncsc.dni.us

**Association of American Law
Schools**
1614 20th St NW
Washington, DC 20009-1001
202.296.8851
www.aals.org

Federal Bar Association
1220 N. Fillmore Street, Suite 444
Arlington, VA 22201
571.481.9100
www.fedbar.org

Law School Admission Council
662 Penn Street
Newtown, PA 18940
215.968.1101
lsacinfo@lsac.org
www.lsac.org

**National Council of Juvenile and
Family Court Judges**
P.O. Box 8970
Reno, NV 89507
775.507.4777
contactus@ncjfcj.org
www.ncjfcj.org

U.S. Supreme Court
1 First Street NE
Washington, DC 20543
202.479.3000
www.supremecourt.gov

Michael P. Auerbach/Editor

Lawyers

Snapshot

Career Cluster(s): Government and Public Administration, Law, Public Safety and Security

Interests: Law, business, writing, research, resolving conflict, communicating with others, helping others

Earnings (2018 Median): $120,910 yearly; $58.13 hourly

Employment and Outlook: Average Growth Expected

OVERVIEW

Sphere of Work

Lawyers (also called attorneys) work within the legal system. They represent the rights and interests of individuals, corporations, and other entities under federal, state, and even international law. Lawyers work in a wide array of areas, such as regulatory compliance, criminal law, lobbying, business and industries, probate, and human rights. Attorneys work in law offices, business offices, government agencies, and courtrooms. Over one-quarter of attorneys are self-employed, either working in their own practices or as partners in a law firm. To some, attorneys act as counsels, providing advice on everyday business and personal activities. For others, lawyers act as an advocate, speaking on their behalf in court during criminal or civil proceedings.

Work Environment

Lawyers typically work in office environments. Large law firms are often fast-paced, with lawyers meeting with clients, preparing and filing paperwork, conducting research, and performing other legal tasks. Attorneys at smaller firms or practices must often perform more tasks than their counterparts at larger firms or practices. Government agencies and major business corporations typically retain or employ attorneys who perform research, write position papers, and issue recommendations for changes in action based on new law and regulations.

Lawyers usually work long and sometimes erratic hours, including late nights and weekends. They should expect to work within a highly competitive environment, both during and after their job search. Private law firms and government law offices may be strikingly different in terms of financial resources, and tend to offer different rates of compensation. Different lawyers may also specialize in different areas of the law, such as corporate law, environmental law, or malpractice cases.

Profile

Interests: Data, People
Working Conditions: Work Inside
Physical Strength: Light Work
Education Needs: Doctoral Degree
Licensure/Certification: Required
Physical Abilities Not Required: Not Climb, Not Kneel
Opportunities for Experience: Military Service, Part-time Work
Holland Interest Score: ESA

* See Appendix A

Occupation Interest

Although the work of an attorney is often very challenging, it can also be exciting and rewarding. Lawyers are considered experts in the field of law, and use this expertise to help others conduct business, deal with legal troubles, protect the environment, and write legislation. Many attorneys become judges or politicians, while others use their knowledge to help a business grow and profit in the marketplace.

A Day in the Life—Duties and Responsibilities

An attorney's daily responsibilities vary based on the type of law in which the individual works or specializes in. A staff attorney or legal counsel for a major business corporation spends much of his or her day analyzing regulations and legislation, researching legal precedents, studying tax codes, meeting with government officials, writing legal correspondence, attending negotiations, and drafting contracts and other legal documents. Private lawyers may perform these activities as well, although in the absence of large numbers of co-workers, they may also perform administrative tasks, including billing and office management.

Lawyers who work as advocates in the court system perform many of the tasks as other attorneys, but also focus on proceedings in the courts. They research previous judicial decisions, interview witnesses and litigants, meet with judges and opposing attorneys, prepare courtroom questions and comments, review testimony, file motions, select juries and, during hearings and trials, present evidence on their clients' behalf.

In addition to their work on behalf of clients, many attorneys perform a number of other activities. For example, they often perform academic work, teaching at law schools and other universities, and write scholarly papers for law journals and similar periodicals. Many attorneys work with the poor or impoverished, assist in disputes between clients and property owners, and provide advice on personal financial decisions.

Lawyers, also called attorneys, act as both advocates and advisors. As advocates, they represent one of the parties in a criminal or civil trial by presenting evidence and arguing in support of their client. As advisors, lawyers counsel their clients about their legal rights and obligations and suggest courses of action in business and personal matters. All attorneys research the intent of laws and judicial decisions and apply the laws to the specific circumstances that their clients face.

Lawyers may have different titles and different duties, depending on where they work. In law firms, lawyers, sometimes called associates, perform legal work for individuals or businesses. Those who represent and defend the accused may be called criminal law attorneys or defense attorneys.

Attorneys also work for federal, state, and local governments. Prosecutors typically work for the government to file a lawsuit, or charge, against an individual or corporation accused of violating the law. Some may also work as public defense attorneys, representing individuals who could not afford to hire their own private attorney.

Others may work as government counsels for administrative bodies and executive or legislative branches of government. They write and interpret laws and regulations and set up procedures to enforce them. Government counsels also write legal reviews of agency decisions. They argue civil and criminal cases on behalf of the government.

Corporate counsels, also called in-house counsels, are lawyers who work for corporations. They advise a corporation's executives about legal issues related to the corporation's business activities. These issues may involve patents, government regulations, contracts with other companies, property interests, taxes, or collective-bargaining agreements with unions.

Public-interest lawyers work for private, nonprofit organizations that provide legal services to disadvantaged people or others who otherwise might not be able to afford legal representation. They generally handle civil cases, such as those having to do with leases, job discrimination, and wage disputes, rather than criminal cases.

In addition to working in different industries, lawyers may specialize in particular legal fields. Following are examples of types of lawyers in these fields:

Environmental lawyers deal with issues and regulations that are related to the environment. For example, they may work for advocacy groups, waste disposal companies, or government agencies to help ensure compliance with relevant laws.

Tax lawyers handle a variety of tax-related issues for individuals and corporations. They may help clients navigate complex tax regulations, so that clients pay the appropriate tax on items such as income, profits, and property. For example, tax lawyers may advise a corporation on how much tax it needs to pay from profits made in different states in order to comply with Internal Revenue Service (IRS) rules.

Intellectual property lawyers deal with the laws related to inventions, patents, trademarks, and creative works, such as music, books, and movies. For example, an intellectual property lawyer may advise a client about whether it is okay to use published material in the client's forthcoming book.

Family lawyers handle a variety of legal issues that pertain to the family. They may advise clients regarding divorce, child custody, and adoption proceedings.

Securities lawyers work on legal issues arising from the buying and selling of stocks, ensuring that all disclosure requirements are met. They may advise corporations that are interested in listing in the stock exchange through an initial public offering (IPO) or in buying shares in another corporation.

Duties and Responsibilities

- Interviewing clients and witnesses
- Advising clients as to legal rights and responsibilities
- Gathering evidence to commence legal action or form a defense
- Examining and cross-examining witnesses
- Summarizing cases to juries
- Writing reports and legal briefs
- Representing clients in court and before other agencies of government
- Preparing various documents such as wills, property titles and mortgages
- Acting as trustee, guardian or executor

WORK ENVIRONMENT

Immediate Physical Environment

Lawyers work primarily in office settings, such as law firms, government agencies, corporate headquarters, and similar business environments and home offices. They also attend hearings and trials in courtrooms, conduct research in law libraries, and meet with clients and other individuals at their homes or at other locations, including prisons.

Transferable Skills and Abilities

Communication Skills
- Persuading others
- Speaking effectively
- Writing concisely

Interpersonal/Social Skills
- Being honest
- Cooperating with others
- Providing support to others
- Working as a member of a team

Organization and Management Skills
- Organizing information or materials
- Paying attention to and handling details
- Performing duties which change frequently

Research and Planning Skills
- Analyzing information
- Developing evaluation strategies
- Gathering information
- Using logical reasoning

Human Environment

Lawyers work with a wide variety of other people. During legal and civil cases, these individuals interact with clients and opposing litigants, judges, witnesses, law enforcement officials, and courtroom professionals. Outside the courtroom, lawyers interact with business executives, elected and government officials, paralegals, labor representatives, and administrative personnel.

Technological Environment

Lawyers will rely on office computer systems and related software to prepare cases, draft motions, and write correspondence. They may use presentation equipment, such as laptop projectors, video units, and similar equipment, for presenting courtroom evidence and for offsite presentations.

EDUCATION, TRAINING, AND ADVANCEMENT

High School/Secondary

High school students who plan to become lawyers are encouraged to take courses that help build their understanding of the law, such as history, political science, social studies, business, and economics. They would also benefit from taking courses that build communication and writing skills, such as composition and public speaking classes.

Suggested High School Subjects
- Algebra
- Business Law
- College Preparatory
- Composition
- Economics
- English
- Foreign Languages
- Government
- History
- Literature
- Political Science
- Psychology
- Social Studies
- Sociology
- Speech

Related Career Pathways/Majors

Government and Public Administration Cluster
- Revenue and Taxation Pathway

Law, Public Safety and Security Cluster
- Legal Services Pathway

Famous First

Rome developed a class of specialists who were learned in the law, known as jurisconsults (iuris consulti)—wealthy amateurs who dabbled in law as an intellectual hobby, which meant that the Romans were the first to have a class of people who spent their days thinking about legal problems. Until Claudius legalized the profession, any citizen could call himself an advocate. By the start of the Byzantine Empire, the legal profession had become well established, heavily regulated, and highly stratified. (Source: Wikipedia.org)

Postsecondary

Aspiring attorneys need a bachelor's degree in a related field, such as history, political science, government, or public safety, with a focus on pre-law studies. After they receive their undergraduate degree, they must enter an accredited law school, where they will pursue their juris doctoral degree.

Related College Majors
- Law (LLB, JD)
- Pre-Law Studies

Adult Job Seekers

Many adults find employment as a lawyer through their law school's placement office. Attorneys who seek employment positions with the government may apply through government websites. Professional associations such as the American Bar Association (ABA) also offer resources on how to pursue a job in the legal field.

Professional Certification and Licensure

In addition to their law degrees, lawyers must pass the bar examination of the state or states in which they work. They may also join a professional legal association such as the ABA or similar state organizations.

Additional Requirements

Lawyers must have excellent analytical, research, and communications skills. They must have strong understanding of the law (particularly in the areas in which they work) and the U.S. Constitution, and tend to be both driven and highly organized. Lawyers often work long hours, and should be comfortable dealing with conflict. Furthermore, lawyers must often work with accused criminals, which can lead to tension and confrontations with such people if the case is not proceeding as desired. Because they are legally bound to protect clients' privacy regardless of guilt or innocence, lawyers must sometimes be willing to subordinate personal ethical feelings to the demands of their job.

EARNINGS AND ADVANCEMENT

The median annual wage for lawyers was $120,910 in May 2018. The median wage is the wage at which half the workers in an occupation earned more than that amount and half earned less. The lowest 10 percent earned less than $58,220, and the highest 10 percent earned more than $208,000:

Median annual wages, May 2018

Lawyers: $120,910

Legal occupations: $80,810

Total, all occupations: $38,640

Note: All Occupations includes all occupations in the U.S. Economy.
Source: U.S. Bureau of Labor Statistics, Employment Projections program

In May 2018, the median annual wages for lawyers in the top industries in which they worked were as follows:

Federal government	$145,160
Legal services	$122,150
Local government, excluding education and hospitals	$94,490
State government, excluding education and hospitals	$86,900

Lawyers who own their own practices usually earn less than those who work in law firms or other business establishments. Occupational Employment Statistics (OES) survey wage data only includes lawyers working in business establishments.

The majority of lawyers work full-time and many work more than 40 hours per week. Lawyers who are in private practice and those who work in large firms often work additional hours, conducting research and preparing and reviewing documents.

Lawyers may receive paid vacations, holidays, and sick days; life and health insurance; and retirement benefits. These are usually paid by the employer.

EMPLOYMENT AND OUTLOOK

Lawyers held about 823,900 jobs in 2018. The largest employers of lawyers were as follows:

Legal services	48%
Self-employed workers	20%
Local government, excluding education and hospitals	7%
State government, excluding education and hospitals	6%
Federal government	5%

Employment of lawyers is projected to grow 6 percent from 2018 to 2028, about as fast as the average for all occupations. Demand for legal work is expected to continue as individuals, businesses, and all levels of government require legal services in many areas.

Percent change in employment, Projected 2018–28

Legal occupations: 7%

Lawyers: 6%

Total, all occupations: 5%

Note: All Occupations includes all occupations in the U.S. Economy.
Source: U.S. Bureau of Labor Statistics, Employment Projections program

Despite this need for legal services, more price competition over the next decade may lead law firms to rethink their project staffing in order to reduce costs to clients. Clients are expected to cut back on legal expenses by demanding less expensive rates and scrutinizing invoices. Work that was previously assigned to lawyers, such as document review, may now be given to paralegals and legal assistants. Also, some routine legal work may be outsourced to other, lower cost legal providers located overseas.

Although law firms will continue to be among the largest employers of lawyers, many large corporations are increasing their in-house legal departments in order to cut costs. For many companies, the high cost of hiring outside counsel lawyers and their support staffs makes it more economical to shift work to their in-house legal department. This shift will lead to an increase in the demand for lawyers in a variety of settings, such as financial and insurance firms, consulting firms, and healthcare providers.

The federal government is likely to continue to need lawyers to prosecute or defend civil cases on behalf of the United States, prosecute criminal cases brought by the federal government, and collect money owed to the federal government. However, budgetary constraints at all levels of government, especially the federal level, will likely moderate employment growth.

Despite the projected growth in new jobs for lawyers, competition for jobs should continue to be strong because more students are graduating from law school each year than there are jobs available. According to the American Bar Association's National Lawyer Population Survey, a compilation of data collected by state bar associations or licensing agencies, there were over 1.3 million resident and active attorneys as of December 2016. Some law school graduates who have been unable to find permanent positions turn to temporary staffing firms that place attorneys in short-term jobs. These firms allow companies to hire lawyers as needed and permit beginning lawyers to develop practical experience. Many other law school graduates and licensed lawyers end up finding work in other occupations or industries due to the difficulty in finding jobs with traditional legal employers.

Because of the strong competition, a law school graduate's willingness to relocate and his or her practical experiences are becoming more important. However, to be licensed in another state, a lawyer may have to take an additional state bar examination.

Related Occupations
- Human Resources Specialist/Manager
- Judge
- Paralegal

Related Military Occupations
- Lawyer

Fast Fact

The author of *Mother Goose's Fairy Tales* was attorney Charles Perrault, who published the beloved children's classic after losing his job as King Louis XIV's finance minister in 1685.

Source: teris.com.

Conversation With . . .
JOSHUA T. GILLELAN II

Appellate Attorney
Washington D.C.
Lawyer, 46 years

1. What was your individual career path in terms of education/training, entry-level job, or other significant opportunity?

I didn't decide I wanted to be a lawyer until after I graduated from St. John's College in Annapolis, MD. At the time, I was teaching in the Baltimore City Public Schools and quickly despaired of making the difference I had wanted to make in that role. I began to consider a career as a public official and thought I needed to go to law school to do that, so I took the LSAT. I scored in the 98th percentile, which helped make my decision to apply to law school. In the first year appellate moot court competition at the University of Maryland School of Law, I realized that I had found my niche and should be an appellate litigator.

That's because I realized the job of an appellate lawyer is synthesizing the precedential decisions and analytically fitting the present case into the favorable side of existing decisions. This is done in a written brief to the court. Reading and writing is about 95 percent of this job.

Upon graduation, although offered other opportunities for more money—one a clerkship for a judge and one a non-appellate government position—I found a job with the U.S. Dept. of Labor that had me arguing my first case in a federal court of appeals about six weeks after I was sworn into the bar. My career at the Labor Department lasted 31 years, and I retired as a senior appellate attorney having briefed and argued over 200 cases in the U.S. courts of appeals. I also did a substantial amount of work in U.S. Supreme Court cases. In 2004, I opened my own practice and continue to advocate on behalf of injured maritime, offshore oil, and overseas defense contractor employees.

One early lesson: I found out that oral argument, which can be ten minutes or, at best, a half hour to further explanation to a panel of judges, is the most exciting part of this job. It is kind of a payoff for the many hours in front of the computer.

2. What are the most important skills and/or qualities for someone in your profession?

As an appellate specialist, you need a linear and reasoned thought process. You need to be articulate. You also need to be able to write. This is very cerebral writing that shows the logical steps you are taking to reach a conclusion and urging the judges to follow. It's a form of writing that does not seek to entertain or educate, but to persuade. Appellate judges are the rare audience equipped with a long attention span.

Any attorney who sets foot in any courtroom needs the ability to step back from his or her own understanding of the case and hear where the judge is coming from and provide the best response to that point of view.

3. What do you wish you had known going into this profession?

I wish I'd known the extent to which court-imposed deadlines can interfere with family and personal life. For instance, I had a case at the Supreme Court with deadlines that meant I worked virtually throughout the holiday season and even through New Year's Eve and Day. Much of that time was spent writing, re-writing, and editing.

4. Are thee many job opportunities in your profession? In what specific areas?

This is a booming profession—total receipts of the law profession continue to grow—but law schools are cranking out a surplus of applicants for the available legal jobs. Try very hard to avoid graduating in the bottom half of your law school class.

5. How do you see your profession changing in the next five years? What role will technology play in those changes, and what skills will be required?

Already a great deal of legal work has been transferred from lawyers to paralegals and now some document analysis is being outsourced to South Asia—India, mostly. In addition, technology has changed the face of legal research, which used to involve moldy old books and now is online. The law office, in general, is going paperless and case files are now digitized. Most of the federal courts require only e-filing a digital copy of most documents.

The way things are moving, the future may hold more and more binding arbitration of disputes that may not go to court. My own view is that this is a terrible thing because the public pays for impartial adjudicators. Whether I think it's gotten them or not, I trust that process more than the selection of a corporate arbitrator.

6. What do you like most about your job, and what do you like the least about your job?

What I find most fulfilling is to receive a favorable decision from an appellate court that establishes precedent that will govern—and thereby produce the same favorable outcome—in thousands of other cases. The greatest challenge is appearing before judges who have a philosophical disagreement with the purposes of the applicable statute.

7. Can you suggest a valuable "try this" for students considering a career in your profession?

To see if you're interested in becoming an appellate lawyer, go online and find a federal court of appeals decision, or a U.S. Supreme Court case, on a subject that interests you. Read the briefs to which the court's decision responded. See if you think you'll be able to think and write that way, because that's what's required. It's not like any other kind of writing. It's formal and it tends toward the abstract.

MORE INFORMATION

American Bar Association
321 N. Clark Street
Chicago, IL 60654-7598
800.285.2221
www.americanbar.org

Association of American Law Schools
1614 20th St NW
Washington, DC 20009-1001
202.296.8851
www.aals.org

Association of Corporate Counsel
1001 G Street NW
Suite 300W
Washington, D.C. 20001
202.293.4103
www.acc.com

Commercial Law League of America
3005 Tollview Drive
Rolling Meadows, Illinois 60008
312.240.1400
info@clla.org
www.clla.org

Federal Bar Association
1220 N. Fillmore Street, Suite 444
Arlington, VA 22201
571.481.9100
www.fedbar.org

Law School Admission Council
662 Penn Street
Newtown, PA 18940
215.968.1101
lsacinfo@lsac.org
www.lsac.org

National District Attorneys Association
1400 Crystal Drive, Suite 330
Arlington, VA 22202
703.549.9222
www.ndaa.org

Michael P. Auerbach/Editor

Librarians

Snapshot

Career Cluster(s): Education and Training, Health Science
Interests: Reading, research, arranging information, communicating with others, helping others
Earnings (2018 Median): $59,050 yearly; $28.39 hourly
Employment and Outlook: As Fast As Average Growth Expected

OVERVIEW

Sphere of Work

A librarian is an information specialist who helps patrons locate various kinds of information quickly and effectively within a library setting. He or she is responsible for the selection, organization, and circulation of library materials, including print media, books, magazines and periodicals, and digital and electronic media. A librarian also manages non-print materials, including films, tapes, CDs, maps, and microfiche. He or she generally performs administrative, technical, and customer service tasks.

Work Environment

A librarian assists patrons in finding and reaching books and information sources. A librarian usually works in a public or academic library, as well as in a school library media center or special library. In all cases, a librarian works in a pleasant, comfortable environment, either independently or under the supervision of a library director. A librarian generally works a standard thirty-five to forty-hour workweek and may be required to work during the evenings or on weekends.

Profile

Interests: Data, People
Working Conditions: Work Inside
Physical Strength: Light Work
Education Needs: Bachelor's Degree, Master's Degree, Doctoral Degree
Licensure/Certification: Required
Physical Abilities Not Required: Not Climb, Not Kneel
Opportunities for Experience: Internship, Volunteer Work, Part-time Work
Holland Interest Score: ESA

* See Appendix A

Occupation Interest

People looking to become librarians should find satisfaction in learning about the ways in which ideas and information are communicated within modern society. They should be passionate about working with people and helping them locate and obtain various kinds of information effectively and accurately. Librarians often work alone or with a small staff and must be comfortable managing and overseeing all aspects of a public or private library. Aspiring librarians should be extremely organized, with a passion for cataloging and arranging information systematically.

A Day in the Life—Duties and Responsibilities

Librarians primarily manage the day-to-day operations of the libraries in which they work. Most librarians select and procure print, audiovisual, and electronic information sources for the various sections of the library. They organize, classify, and maintain library materials according to physical or electronic catalogs and databases. They assist library patrons and respond to any reference questions patrons may have. In smaller libraries, librarians are responsible for checking out and receiving materials.

Librarians often act as teachers, transferring library skills to customers or groups of customers. They sometimes hold regular tutoring sessions, which orient new patrons to the library. Some librarians schedule a daily or weekly storytelling or literacy meeting to read aloud to groups of small children visiting the library. In larger libraries, librarians specialize in a specific subject area and must coordinate with other librarians and library staff to make sure each section or department runs smoothly. Librarians also take on various administrative tasks, such as preparing budgets and other reports and maintaining employee and circulation records. In many cases, librarians hire, train, and supervise other library personnel.

In recent years, technology has begun to decrease the public's reliance on print and hardcopy materials. As a result, librarians are now responsible for remote and electronic databases, Internet research and cataloging, and web content management. They also instruct patrons on the use of various electronic library systems.

Duties and Responsibilities

- Help library patrons conduct research and find the information they need
- Teach classes about information resources
- Help patrons evaluate search results and reference materials
- Organize library materials so they are easy to find, and maintain collections
- Plan programs for different audiences, such as storytelling for young children
- Develop and use databases of library materials
- Research new books and materials by reading book reviews, publishers' announcements, and catalogs
- Choose new books, audio books, videos, and other materials for the library
- Research and buy new computers and other equipment as needed for the library
- Train and direct library technicians, assistants, other support staff, and volunteers
- Prepare library budgets

OCCUPATION SPECIALTIES

The following are examples of types of librarians:

User services librarians

User services librarians help patrons conduct research using both electronic and print resources. They teach patrons how to use library resources to find information on their own. This may include familiarizing patrons with catalogs of print materials, helping them access and search digital libraries, or educating them on Internet search techniques. Some user services librarians work with a particular audience, such as children or young adults.

Technical services librarians

Technical services librarians obtain, prepare, and organize print and electronic library materials. They arrange materials to make sources easy for patrons to find information. They are also responsible for ordering new library materials and archiving to preserve older items.

Administrative services librarians

Administrative services librarians manage libraries, hire and supervise staff, prepare budgets, and negotiate contracts for library materials and equipment. Some conduct public relations or fundraising for the library.

Academic librarians

Academic librarians assist students, faculty, and staff in postsecondary institutions. They help students research topics related to their coursework and teach students how to access information. They also assist faculty and staff in locating resources related to their research projects or studies. Some campuses have multiple libraries, and librarians may specialize in a particular subject.

Public librarians

Public librarians work in their communities to serve all members of the public. They help patrons find books to read for pleasure; conduct research for schoolwork, business, or personal interest; and learn how to access the library's resources. Many public librarians plan programs for patrons, such as story time for children, book clubs, or other educational activities.

School librarians

School librarians, sometimes called school media specialists, work in elementary, middle, and high school libraries, and teach students how to use library resources. They also help teachers develop lesson plans and find materials for classroom instruction.

Special librarians

Special librarians work in settings other than school or public libraries. They are sometimes called information professionals. Law firms, hospitals, businesses, museums, government agencies, and many other groups have their own libraries that use special librarians. The main purpose of these libraries and information centers is to serve the information needs of the organization that houses the library. Therefore, special librarians collect and organize materials focused on those subjects. Special librarians may need an additional degree in the area of specialization.

The following are examples of special librarians:

Corporate librarians

Corporate librarians assist employees in private businesses in conducting research and finding information. They work for a wide range of businesses, including insurance companies, consulting firms, and publishers.

Government librarians

Government librarians provide research services and access to information for government staff and the public.

Law librarians help lawyers, law students, judges, and law clerks locate and organize legal resources. They often work in law firms and law school libraries.

Medical librarians

Medical librarians, also called health science librarians, help health professionals, patients, and researchers find health and science information. They may provide information about new clinical trials and medical treatments and procedures, teach medical students how to locate medical information, or answer consumers' health questions.

WORK ENVIRONMENT

Transferable Skills and Abilities

Communication Skills
- Expressing thoughts and ideas
- Speaking effectively
- Writing concisely

Interpersonal/Social Skills
- Cooperating with others
- Working as a member of a team

Organization and Management Skills
- Coordinating tasks
- Making decisions
- Managing people/groups
- Paying attention to and handling details
- Performing duties which change frequently

Research and Planning Skills
- Developing evaluation strategies

Immediate Physical Environment

Most librarians work in clean, quiet, and well-ventilated library spaces. They maintain a library's level of calm and serenity by monitoring patrons' behavior to ensure their compliance with library rules and regulations.

Human Environment

Librarians regularly interact with library patrons, including young children, adolescents, college students, teachers, and members of community organizations. They report to a library supervisor or director and often manage library assistants, technicians, administrative staff members, and janitorial personnel.

Technological Environment

Librarians use a wide variety of tools and equipment to help them organize information. They regularly work with paper and electronic card catalogs, microforms, the Internet and e-mail, and computer programs. They also use projection equipment, audiovisual devices, and fax machines.

EDUCATION, TRAINING, AND ADVANCEMENT

High School/Secondary

High school students who wish to become librarians should focus on college preparatory courses that deal with business, communications, language and literature, technology, and public speaking. Students may also benefit from studying at least one foreign language. Interested students should spend time in their high school and local libraries, familiarizing themselves with current information systems and cataloging procedures as well as the structure of a library.

Suggested High School Subjects
- Arts
- Audio-Visual
- Business
- Business Data Processing
- College Preparatory
- Composition
- Crafts
- English
- Foreign Languages
- Government
- History
- Humanities
- Keyboarding
- Literature
- Mathematics
- Photography
- Political Science

- Science
- Social Studies
- Speech

Related Career Pathways/Majors

Education and Training Cluster
- Professional Support Services Pathway

Health Science Cluster
- Health Informatics Pathway

Famous First

The first recorded librarian was Zenodotus of Ephesus, holding that post from the end of Ptolemy I's reign. He introduced an organization system whereby texts were assigned to different rooms based on their subject matter. Within their subjects, Zenodotus organized the works alphabetically by the first letter of the name of their author. Library staff attached a tag to the each scroll with information on each work's author, title, and subject so that materials could be easily returned to the correct room and so that library users did not have to unroll each scroll in order to see what it contained. This was the first recorded use of metadata. (Source: Wikipedia.org)

Postsecondary

After high school, prospective librarians must obtain a bachelor's degree, preferably in library science. Employers generally give preference to students who graduate from American Library Association (ALA)-accredited schools. At the college level, students should prepare for a career in library science by studying librarianship, children's and adult literature, archival methods, humanities, science and technology, and subject reference and bibliography, among other subjects.

In order for a librarian to work in a public, academic, or special library, he or she must obtain a master's degree in library science

(MLS) after completing an undergraduate degree. Graduate programs in library science usually cover the foundations of information science, censorship, user services, and automated circulation systems, in addition to other supplemental and elective courses. Though not required, some librarians choose to obtain a doctorate in library and information science.

Related College Majors
- Library Assistant Training
- Pre-Law Studies

Adult Job Seekers

Many aspiring librarians begin by volunteering or working part-time in local libraries. Those enrolled in an undergraduate or graduate program may also be able to participate in a work-study program or internship with a participating library. Prospective librarians can apply for employment directly with a library, through library associations, or through school placement services.

Experienced librarians may advance to supervisory or teaching positions. These positions may require more budgetary, administrative, and managerial skills and duties. Advancement is often dependent on seniority, education, and library size.

Professional Certification and Licensure

Librarians who work in public schools or local libraries are usually required to be certified. Certification and licensure requirements vary by state. Many states also require librarians to acquire teacher certifications, and some states require librarians to pass a comprehensive examination. Interested individuals should research and fulfill the education and certification requirements of their home state.

Librarians who specialize in certain subject areas, such as law, medicine, or the sciences, may also need to earn an advanced degree in their desired subject. For example, twenty states require school librarians to have an advanced degree in library science or education.

Additional Requirements

Librarians are responsible for maintaining large databases of information and must therefore be extremely organized and detail-oriented. They must also be passionate about information systems and interested in the changing trends in and improvements to those systems. They should enjoy continually learning about new research methods and classification technology.

EARNINGS AND ADVANCEMENT

The median annual wage for librarians was $59,050 in May 2018. The median wage is the wage at which half the workers in an occupation earned more than that amount and half earned less. The lowest 10 percent earned less than $34,630, and the highest 10 percent earned more than $93,050.

In May 2018, the median annual wages for librarians in the top industries in which they worked were as follows:

Colleges, universities, and professional schools; state, local, and private	$64,130
Elementary and secondary schools; state, local, and private	$60,780
Information	$56,970
Local government, excluding education and hospitals	$53,060

Most librarians work full-time. Public and academic librarians often work on weekends and evenings, and may work holidays. School librarians usually have the same work and vacation schedules as teachers, including summers off. Special librarians, such as law or corporate librarians, typically work normal business hours, but may need to work more than 40 hours per week to help meet deadlines. Compared with workers in all occupations, librarians have a higher percentage of workers who belong to

EMPLOYMENT AND OUTLOOK

Librarians held about 134,800 jobs in 2018. The largest employers of librarians were as follows:

Elementary and secondary schools; state, local, and private	33%
Local government, excluding education and hospitals	31%
Colleges, universities, and professional schools; state, local, and private	18%
Information	7%

Employment of librarians is projected to grow 6 percent from 2018 to 2028, about as fast as the average for all occupations.

Percent change in employment, Projected 2018–28

Librarians: 6%

Total, all occupations: 5%

Librarians, curators, and archivists: 3%

Note: All Occupations includes all occupations in the U.S. Economy.
Source: U.S. Bureau of Labor Statistics, Employment Projections program

Communities are increasingly turning to libraries for a variety of services and activities. Therefore, there will be a continuous need for librarians to manage libraries and help patrons find information. Parents value the learning opportunities that libraries present for children because libraries are able to provide children with information they often cannot access from home. In addition, the increased availability of electronic information is also expected to increase the demand for librarians in research and special libraries, where patrons will need help sorting through the large amount of digital information. However, budget limitations, especially in local government and educational services, may limit growth for libraries and librarians.

A degree from an American Library Association accredited program and work experience may lead to more job opportunities. Candidates who are able to adapt with the rapidly changing technology will have better prospects.

There may be good prospects later in the decade as older library workers retire and generate openings.

Related Occupations
- Archivist and Curator
- Computer and Information Systems Manager
- Library Technician
- Media Specialist
- Research Assistant

Conversation With . . . AUDREY CHURCH

President, American Association of School Librarians
Chicago, Illinois
Library sciences, 36 years

1. What was your individual career path in terms of education/training, entry-level job, or other significant opportunity?

I was a public school librarian for 20 years—three years at the primary school level and 17 years at the high school level. I completed my student teaching in both high school English and library science and loved both, but my first job offer was for the primary school librarian position, and the rest is history. I absolutely loved my time working as a school librarian. In fact, the only job better than being a school librarian is teaching people to be school librarians—which is what I do now as a professor of school librarianship at Longwood University in Farmville, Virginia.

School librarianship crosses two fields of study, education and library science. Most states require that school librarians first earn a teaching license. My initial teaching license is in Secondary English, but people come to the school librarianship career with teaching licenses in varied fields, from elementary education to social studies to physical education. In order to become a certified school librarian, I completed a master's degree in education with a concentration in school librarianship. People who have a master's degree in library science, and who perhaps have a background as a public librarian or an academic librarian but do not hold a teaching license must complete required education coursework.

I also serve as president of the American Association of School Librarians.

2. What are the most important skills and/or qualities for someone in your profession?

The most important qualities for a school librarian are a desire to work with children, the ability to work well with others, and the willingness to be a lifelong learner. Strong communication and leadership skills are also necessary, as are good organizational skills and proficiency with technology.

3. What do you wish you had known going into this profession?

I wish I had known the variety of jobs and roles that school librarians play on a daily basis: teacher, instructional partner, information specialist, instructional leader, technology integrator, professional development provider, program administrator. No two days are alike, and it is never boring. It would be difficult to describe a "normal" day in a twenty-first-century school library.

4. Are there many job opportunities in your profession? In what specific areas?

In some areas of the United States, due to budget crises, school librarian positions have been cut. In other areas, however, there is a shortage of qualified persons to fill open positions. In some areas where jobs were previously cut (for example, in California and in Washington, DC), we now see the restoration of positions as budget situations improve.

5. How do you see your profession changing in the next five years? What role will technology play in those changes, and what skills will be required?

While school librarians will continue to work with print resources, more and more resources will be available in digital format. The teaching role of the librarian will become even more critical as school librarians continue to teach students digital literacy skills. Technology plays a key role as librarians help students and staff become effective users of ideas and information. Critical thinking and problem solving skills will be required, as will flexibility and adaptability.

6. What do you enjoy most about your job? What do you enjoy least about your job?

The facets of my job that I enjoy the most are working with people, helping students and staff gain the skills that they need to be independent, information-literate lifelong learners. I enjoy helping students become critical thinkers, enthusiastic readers, skillful researchers, and ethical users of information. I love the fact my job continues to evolve as technology and education change. I enjoy the opportunity to work with all students in the school, all teachers, administrators, parents, and community members.

The facet of my job that I enjoy the least is that there are never enough hours in the day to complete all the tasks that need to be done.

7. Can you suggest a valuable "try this" for students considering a career in your profession?

I would encourage students considering a career as a school librarian to spend time observing an elementary school library, a middle school library, and a high school library. Many people have very traditional views of what a school librarian does, believing that the library is still a place of books and quiet. While we certainly still have books, the library is a hub of information, inquiry, and instruction. It is an active and interactive place of learning.

MORE INFORMATION

American Association of Law Libraries
105 W. Adams Street, Suite 3300
Chicago, IL 60603-6225
312.939.4764
support@aall.org
www.aallnet.org

American Association of School Librarians
50 E. Huron Street
Chicago, IL 60611
800.545.2433
aasl@ala.org
www.aasl.org

American Library Association
50 E. Huron Street
Chicago, IL 60611
800.545.2433
www.ala.org

American Society for Information Society & Technology
8555 16th Street, Suite 850, Silver Spring, Maryland 20910, USA
301-495-0900
asist@asist.org www.asis.org
https://www.asist.org/

Library of Congress
101 Independence Avenue SE
Washington, DC 20540
202.707.5000
www.loc.gov

Medical Library Association
225 West Wacker Drive, Suite 650
Chicago, IL 60606-1210
312.419.9094
websupport@mail.mlahq.org
www.mlanet.org

Special Libraries Association
7918 Jones Branch Drive, Suite 300
McLean, Virginia 22102 USA
703.647.4900
www.sla.org

Briana Nadeau/Editor

Multimedia Artists and Animators

Snapshot

Career Cluster(s): Arts, A/V Technology, and Communications
Interests: Art, illustration, web design, current trends, being competitive, communicating with others
Earnings (2018 Median): $72,520 yearly; $34.87 hourly
Employment and Outlook: As Fast As Average Growth Expected

OVERVIEW

Sphere of Work

Commercial artists may design artwork for product packaging, billboards, media advertisements, and other marketing tools, or create illustrations for magazines, books, and other forms of media. Some are self-employed, working from home offices, while others work for advertising and design agencies of varying sizes.

Work Environment

Commercial artists often work in settings such as design firms, advertising companies, and corporate offices for manufacturers, in environments that are generally clean and comfortable. Their hours vary based on the size and scope of the project on which they are working, as well as the time constraints established in a contract. Smaller companies and independent, self-employed artists tend to work longer hours to manage not only their projects, but also the issues associated with a small business.

Profile

Interests: Data, People, Things
Working Conditions: Work Inside
Physical Strength: Light Work
Education Needs: On-The-Job Training, Junior/Technical/Community College, Apprenticeship, Bachelor's Degree
Licensure/Certification: Usually Not Required
Physical Abilities Not Required: Not Climb, Not Kneel, Not Hear and/or Talk
Opportunities for Experience: Internship, Apprenticeship, Military Service, Volunteer Work, Part-time Work
Holland Interest Score: AEI

* See Appendix A

Occupation Interest

Commercial artists must combine a talent for art and creative thinking with good research and communication skills, close attention to detail, and the ability to meet deadlines and work in a competitive atmosphere, all while remaining true to the needs of the client. They should be aware of general public attitudes and keep up with current trends. Many independent commercial artists set their own hours and act as small business entrepreneurs as well as creative artists.

A Day in the Life—Duties and Responsibilities

Multimedia artists and animators often work in a specific medium. Some focus on creating animated movies or video games. Others create visual effects for movies and television shows. Creating computer-generated images (known as CGI) may include taking images of an actor's movements and then animating them into three-dimensional characters. Other animators design scenery or backgrounds for locations.

Artists and animators can further specialize within these fields. Within animated movies and video games, artists often specialize in characters or in scenery and background design. Video game artists may focus on level design: creating the look, feel, and layout for the levels of a video game.

Animators work in teams to develop a movie, a visual effect, or an electronic game. Each animator works on a portion of the project, and then the pieces are put together to create one cohesive animation.

Some multimedia artists and animators create their work primarily by using computer software or by writing their own computer code. Many animation companies have their own computer animation software that artists must learn to use. Video game designers also work in a variety of platforms, including mobile gaming and online social networks.

Other artists and animators prefer to work by drawing and painting by hand and then translating the resulting images into computer programs. Some multimedia artists use storyboards or "animatics," which look like a comic strip, to help visualize the final product during the design process.

Many multimedia artists and animators put their creative work on the Internet. If the images become popular, these artists can gain more recognition, which may lead to future employment or freelance work.

Duties and Responsibilities

- Use computer programs and illustrations to create graphics and animation (images that appear to move)
- Work with a team of animators and artists to create a movie, game, or visual effect
- Research upcoming projects to help create realistic designs or animation
- Edit animation and effects on the basis of feedback from directors, other animators, game designers, or clients
- Meet with clients, other animators, games designers, directors, and other staff (which may include actors) to review deadlines and development timelines

WORK ENVIRONMENT

Transferable Skills and Abilities

Communication Skills
- Expressing thoughts and ideas
- Persuading others
- Speaking effectively
- Writing concisely

Interpersonal/Social Skills
- Being able to remain calm
- Respecting others' opinions

Organization and Management Skills
- Making decisions
- Paying attention to and handling details

Research and Planning Skills
- Analyzing information
- Creating ideas
- Gathering information

Technical Skills
- Performing scientific, mathematical, and technical work
- Working with machines, tools or other objects

Unclassified Skills
- Performing work that produces tangible results

Immediate Physical Environment

Commercial artists work primarily in design firms, studios, or office spaces in marketing and advertising companies. These environments are well lit and well ventilated, with computers and Internet access. Many commercial artists are independent consultants who work from studios and office spaces in their own private residences.

Human Environment

Depending on their areas of expertise, commercial artists meet and interact with a wide range of individuals. These parties include marketing and advertising professionals, business executives, editors, decorators, medical professionals, and other specialized commercial artists.

Technological Environment

Commercial artists might use computer programs such as desktop publishing and graphics editing software. A fax machine or scanner may be necessary in order to send prospective designs to clients. Other materials used can include art media such as pencils, pens, inks, and paints; designers' tools such as T-squares and parallel rules; and books of type styles and other reference sources.

EDUCATION, TRAINING, AND ADVANCEMENT

High School/Secondary

High school students should study art, including drawing, photography, and design; math, including geometry; and computer science, including graphic design and drafting. They should also take advantage of any subject areas of interest to them as artists; for example, future medical illustrators are advised to take anatomy and physiology classes.

Suggested High School Subjects
- Applied Math
- Arts
- College Preparatory
- Composition
- Computer Science
- Crafts
- Drafting
- English
- Graphic Communications
- Literature
- Photography
- Pottery
- Woodshop

Related Career Pathways/Majors

Arts, A/V Technology, and Communications Cluster
- Visual Arts Pathway

Famous First

Charles-Émile Reynaud further developed his projection praxinoscope into the *Théâtre Optique* with transparent hand-painted colorful pictures in a long perforated strip wound between two spools, patented in December 1888. From October 1892 to March 1900, Reynaud gave over 12,800 shows to more than 500,000 visitors at the Musée Grévin in Paris. His Pantomimes *Lumineuses* series of animated films each contained 300 to 700 frames that were manipulated back and forth to last 10 to 15 minutes per film. A background scene was projected separately. Piano music, song and some dialogue were performed live, while some sound effects were synchronized with an electromagnet.
(Source: Wikipedia.org)

Postsecondary

Aspiring commercial artists may pursue a bachelor's degree in fine art, design, or a similar field. Alternatively, they may enroll in art or design institutes for programs with more studio time and a greater focus on graphic design, photography, or publishing art. Further education may be warranted depending on how a commercial artist chooses to specialize. For example, a prospective art director may also study management or art administration, while somebody interested in medical or scientific illustration would be well served by a master's degree in a relevant science.

Related College Majors
- Art, General
- Crafts, Folk Art, and Artisanry
- Educational/Instructional Media Design
- Educational/Instructional Media Technology
- Fine/Studio Arts
- Graphic Design/Commercial Art and Illustration
- Painting
- Printmaking
- Visual and Performing Arts

Adult Job Seekers

An internship or apprenticeship is a good way to gain necessary experience. Individuals looking for work can apply directly to the art or advertising director of a particular company, and may also find opportunities through professional organizations such as the American Institute of Graphic Arts (now known as AIGA). Any potential commercial artist must have a portfolio showing his or her best work.

Professional Certification and Licensure

Some organizations provide certification programs to help commercial artists become specialists in their particular fields. For example, the International Association for Identification offers a forensic artist certification program. Such certification can provide a competitive edge for job candidates.

Additional Requirements

Commercial artists should be both creative and extremely knowledgeable of the wide range of media options available to them to meet a client's needs. They should be willing to listen to and communicate with clients who may or may not agree with their ideas. Commercial artists must have self-discipline and a strong work ethic, especially in light of the fact that many are self-employed.

EARNINGS AND ADVANCEMENT

Earnings of multimedia artists and animators depend on skill, education, and the type, size, and geographic location of the employer. Earnings of freelance multimedia artists and animators may vary with the artists' individual fees and reputation, as well as the nature and amount of work sold.

The median annual wage for multimedia artists and animators was $72,520 in May 2018. The median wage is the wage at which half the workers in an occupation earned more than that amount and half earned less. The lowest 10 percent earned less than $40,870, and the highest 10 percent earned more than $124,310.

In May 2018, the median annual wages for multimedia artists and animators in the top industries in which they worked were as follows:

Software publishers	$82,360
Motion picture and video industries	$77,860
Computer systems design and related services	$76,920
Advertising, public relations, and related services	$67,330

Earnings for self-employed multimedia artists and animators vary widely. Those struggling to gain experience and build a reputation may be forced to charge only small fees for their work. Well-established free-lancers may earn much more than salaried artists.

Multimedia artists and animators may receive paid vacations, holidays, and sick days; life and health insurance; and retirement benefits. These are usually paid for by the employer.

EMPLOYMENT AND OUTLOOK

Multimedia artists and animators held about 71,600 jobs in 2018. The largest employers of multimedia artists and animators were as follows:

Self-employed workers	59%
Motion picture and video industries	12%
Computer systems design and related services	6%
Software publishers	5%
Advertising, public relations, and related services	3%

Employment of multimedia artists and animators is projected to grow 4 percent from 2018 to 2028, about as fast as the average for all occupations. Projected growth will be due to increased demand for animation and visual effects in video games, movies, and television. Job growth may be slowed, however, by companies hiring animators and artists who work overseas. Studios may save money on animation by using lower paid workers outside of the United States.

Percent change in employment, Projected 2018–28

Total, all occupations: 5%

Multimedia artists and animators: 4%

Art and design workers: 2%

Note: All Occupations includes all occupations in the U.S. Economy.
Source: U.S. Bureau of Labor Statistics, Employment Projections program

Consumers will continue to demand more realistic video games, movie and television special effects, and three-dimensional movies. This will create demand for newer computer hardware, which will enhance the complexity of animation and visual effects. Additional multimedia artists and animators will be required to meet this increased demand.

Further, an increased demand for computer graphics for mobile devices, such as smart phones, will lead to more job opportunities. Multimedia artists will be needed to create animation for games and applications for mobile devices.

Despite positive job growth, there will be competition for job openings because many recent graduates will be interested in entering the occupation. In addition to having a robust portfolio, those who specialize in a specific type of animation or in a specific skill, such as drawing or computer programming, should have the best opportunities.

Related Occupations
- Art Director
- Designer
- Graphic Designer
- Industrial Designer
- Interior Designer
- Medical and Scientific Illustrator
- Merchandise Displayer
- Photographer
- Sign Painter and Letterer
- Software Developer
- Web Developer

Related Military Occupations
- Graphic Designer and Illustrator

Conversation With . . .
JOHNNY CHEW

Director/Animator, Self-employed
johnnychew.com
Los Angeles, California
Multimedia Artist and Animator for 10 years

1. What was your individual career path in terms of education/training, entry-level job, or other significant opportunity?

I've always loved and been fascinated by animation. In high school, I taught myself how to use Adobe Flash, doing some simple animations. At the end of high school, an art teacher connected me with a small studio outside of Boston where I began interning two days a week. That eventually turned into a full-time position and I ended up working there for two years. After that I attended the Massachusetts College of Art and Design, where I really got interested in multimedia art and doing less traditional animation.

Once I graduated, I worked at another studio in Boston for a year before deciding that the studio life wasn't for me. I quit that job and did freelance work and ended up teaching animation at my alma mater for a year. I got connected to a director's rep and made the move out to Los Angeles. I'm now doing freelance work ranging from editing and post-effects to directing and animating. I've worked for Nintendo, Toyota, Cinemax, Capitol Records, PBS, Audi and lots of various record labels doing lyric videos and editing. I've worked on television commercials, music videos, title sequences, documentaries and video games.

2. What are the most important skills and/or qualities for someone in your profession?

I think the most important skill to have in animation and multimedia art is to be creative within limitations. Time, budget, and facilities are all limitations that you'll face constantly. The ability to work creatively and to work around problems and issues within those limits is a difficult but important skill set to learn. Being able to design a project with a three-day turn around and still make something striking and something that is your own has been invaluable in my experience.

3. What do you wish you had known going into this profession?

That there is no singular path to follow to success. Going into this field, a lot of my friends and I thought there was some sort of checklist of steps to follow in order to "break in." That couldn't be further from the truth. There is no one way to go about it besides trying things out and trusting your gut. Your path may be different from your friend's path and that's OK.

4. Are there many job opportunities in your profession? In what specific areas?

There are tons of job opportunities in multimedia art. Most projects involve lots of people, so there are many positions that open up with each new project. It's also a field that's constantly growing, so even when one studio closes, another will pop up to take its place. It's a newer form of content that the internet has made very popular, so there are lots of people and companies looking to do it.

5. How do you see your profession changing in the next five years? What role will technology play in those changes, and what skills will be required?

I think the internet will continue to change the way multimedia art is consumed and distributed. It's going to keep moving towards alternative forms of distribution like Netflix or Hulu, creating much more opportunity for a wide variety of work to be created and seen. I think that because of these newer channels for distribution, we're going to see a wider range of style and content of work being shown. A good web presence and a unique, individual style of work is going to be invaluable going forward.

6. What do you enjoy most about your job? What do you enjoy least about your job?

The novelty of making an image or video from scratch still hasn't worn off for me. Animating something moving and then going back and watching it still feels like magic to me. The least favorite part of the job is how little the outside world knows about what goes into it. You'll have to spend more time than you'd imagine trying to communicate why something can or cannot be done.

7. Can you suggest a valuable "try this" for students considering a career in your profession?

The best thing you can do if you're thinking about getting into multimedia art or animation is to find free or trial animation software, or just get a ton of paper and dive in head first. There's certainly a learning curve to the software and traditional animation, but the big test is whether you enjoy sitting and drawing or creating frame after frame for hours only to end up with five seconds of footage after a full day's worth of work. Don't worry about learning all the ins and outs before you start creating; just go for it and focus on whether or not you're having fun while you're doing it. If you are, this might be the right field for you.

MORE INFORMATION

American Institute of Graphic Arts
222 Broadway
New York, NY 10038
212.807.1990
www.aiga.org

Color Marketing Group
1908 Mount Vernon Avenue
Alexandria, VA 22301
703.329.8500
www.colormarketing.org

Design Management Institute
38 Chauncy Street, Suite 800
Boston, MA 02111
617-338-6380
www.dmi.org

Graphic Artists Guild
31 West 34th Street, 8th Floor
New York, NY 10001
212.791.3400
communications@gag.org
www.graphicartistsguild.org

National Art Education Association
901 Prince Street
Alexandria, VA 22314
703.860.8000
info@arteducators.org
www.naea-reston.org

**National Association of Schools of
Art & Design**
11250 Roger Bacon Drive, Suite 21
Reston, VA 20190-5248
703.437.0700
info@arts-accredit.org
nasad.arts-accredit.org/index.jsp

Society of Publication Designers
27 Union Square West, Suite 207
New York, NY 10003
212.223.3332
www.spd.org

Michael P. Auerbach/Editor

Music Directors and Composers

Snapshot

Career Cluster(s): Arts, A/V Technology, and Communications
Interests: Music, musical instruments, entertaining and performing, composing or arranging music, recording, promotion
Earnings (2018 Median): $49,630 yearly; $22.86 hourly
Employment and Outlook: Little Or No Growth Expected

OVERVIEW

Sphere of Work

Musicians and composers, considered entertainers regardless of their genre or stature, express themselves through the use of instruments and/or voice. While many musicians write their own music, recognition as a composer is usually reserved for those who compose original works meant to be performed by other musicians. They each tend to specialize in a particular musical genre, although crossovers are common. In addition to contemporary compositions, musicians and composers are

able to draw on a vast collection of music in the public domain for new arrangements and interpretations.

Work Environment

Musicians compose and practice in studios, often located in their homes, and perform in diverse environments, from cruise ships, nightclubs, and churches to large concert halls and stadiums. Some perform outdoors when weather permits. Performance makes up only a fraction of the musician's workweek, with the bulk of their time taken up by practice, rehearsals, composing, travel, and other responsibilities, including recording, if they are a recording artist. With the exception of orchestra members, church organists, and a few others, most musicians and composers are self-employed. Musicians have the highest chance of succeeding professionally if they live near major cities, where the greatest number of employment opportunities can be found.

Profile

Interests: Data, People
Working Conditions: Work Inside
Physical Strength: Light Work
Education Needs: High School Diploma or GED, Junior/Technical/Community College, Bachelor's Degree
Licensure/Certification: Usually Not Required
Physical Abilities Not Required: Not Climb, Not Kneel
Opportunities for Experience: Apprenticeship, Military Service, Volunteer Work, Part-time Work
Holland Interest Score: ASE

* See Appendix A

Occupation Interest

Most people who choose to become a professional musician or composer do so after becoming proficient at one or more instruments. They enjoy expressing themselves creatively in this "nonverbal language," and, in the case of musicians, enjoy performing for an audience. While they have certainly learned that practice is the key to success, they demonstrate other necessary qualities as well, including creativity, stamina, confidence, and the ability to cooperate with other musicians.

A Day in the Life—Duties and Responsibilities

Music directors, also called conductors, lead orchestras and other musical groups during performances and recording sessions.

Composers write and arrange original music in a variety of musical styles.

Music directors lead orchestras, choirs, and other musical groups. They ensure that musicians play with one coherent sound, balancing the melody, timing, rhythm, and volume. They also give feedback to musicians and section leaders on sound and style. Music directors may work with a variety of musical groups, including church choirs, youth orchestras, and high school or college bands, choirs, or orchestras. Some work with orchestras that accompany dance and opera companies.

Composers write music for a variety of types of musical groups and users. Some work in a particular style of music, such as classical or jazz. They also may write for musicals, operas, or other types of theatrical productions. Some composers write scores for movies or television; others write jingles for commercials. Many songwriters focus on composing music for audiences of popular music. Some composers use instruments to help them as they write music. Others use software that allows them to hear a piece without musicians.

Some music directors and composers give private music lessons to children and adults. Others teach music in elementary, middle, or high schools.

A successful professional composer may be offered commissions to write advertising jingles, film scores, orchestral works, or other types of music. Some composers are also hired to arrange music— that is, take an existing work and have it performed in a novel way. For example, a composer might take a pop song and turn it into an orchestral work. When not busy with their creative work, composers meet with clients and spend time promoting their talents.

Musicians may also set aside time for composing music or writing songs. They also listen to recordings by other musicians and keep abreast of new equipment and technologies. Because the field is so competitive, making a living as a full-time musician or composer is difficult. Therefore, many musicians and composers also hold day jobs that divide their attentions even further.

Duties and Responsibilities

Music directors typically do the following:

- Select musical arrangements and compositions to be performed for live audiences or recordings
- Prepare for performances by reviewing and interpreting musical scores
- Direct rehearsals to prepare for performances and recordings
- Choose guest performers and soloists
- Audition new performers or assist section leaders with auditions
- Practice conducting to improve their technique
- Meet with potential donors and attend fundraisers

Composers typically do the following::

- Write original music that orchestras, bands, and other musical groups perform
- Arrange existing music into new compositions
- Write lyrics for music or work with a lyricist
- Meet with orchestras, musical groups, and others who are interested in commissioning a piece of music
- Study and listen to music of various styles for inspiration
- Work with musicians to record their music

Fast Fact

Wolfgang Amadeus Mozart and Joseph Haydn were real-life pals and possible influences on each other, despite Haydn being Mozart's elder by twenty-four years. They apparently used to jam on violins/violas together.

Source: pianotv.net, nytimes.com.

OCCUPATION SPECIALTIES

Instrumental Musicians

Instrumental Musicians play musical instruments as soloists or as members of a musical group, such as an orchestra or band, to entertain audiences.

Choral Directors

Choral Directors conduct vocal music groups, such as choirs and glee clubs.

Orchestra Conductors

Orchestra Conductors lead instrumental music groups, such as orchestras and dance bands.

Musical Directors

Musical Directors plan and direct the activities of personnel in studio music departments and conduct studio orchestras.

Singers

Singers entertain by singing songs on stage, radio, and television or in nightclubs.

Arrangers

Arrangers transcribe musical compositions or melodic lines to adapt them to or create a particular style.

Orchestrators

Orchestrators write musical scores for orchestras, bands, choral groups or individuals.

WORK ENVIRONMENT

Immediate Physical Environment

Music directors commonly work in concert halls and recording studios, and they may spend a lot of time traveling to different performances. Composers can work in offices, recording studios, or their own homes.

Jobs for music directors and composers are found all over the country. However, many jobs are located in cities in which entertainment activities are concentrated, such as New York, Los Angeles, Nashville, and Chicago.

Transferable Skills and Abilities

Communication Skills
- Expressing thoughts and ideas

Creative/Artistic Skills
- Being skilled in art, music or dance

Research and Planning Skills
- Analyzing information

Research and Planning Skills
- Creating ideas

Human Environment

Musicians interact with many different people, most notably their audiences and other musicians or singers. A session musician will also work closely with studio technicians, a touring artist may travel with his staff and stage crew, and a church organist will collaborate with the music director and minister. Composers often work closely with a film director, advertising team, choreographer, and other professionals.

Technological Environment

Musicians playing instruments that are not electric or electronic, including string, wind, and other traditional instruments, are concerned mainly with the operation and maintenance of those instruments, although any performing artist typically needs to work with microphones, amplifiers, and other electrical equipment. Additional musical technologies are involved in working with electric guitars, keyboards, and the like, and for recording artists there is a world of sound recording technology with which to become familiar.

EDUCATION, TRAINING, AND ADVANCEMENT

High School/Secondary

Music directors and composers today generally need at least a high school diploma. Most will want to pursue a strong college preparatory program, with electives in music and courses specific to their interests, such as creative writing, electronics, or film studies. Private lessons, summer music camps, and extracurricular performance opportunities are extremely important. Proficiency on one or more instruments will be required for admission to a college music program or conservatory.

Suggested High School Subjects
- Arts
- English
- Foreign Languages
- Humanities
- Instrumental and Vocal Music
- Mathematics

Related Career Pathways/Majors

Arts, A/V Technology, and Communications Cluster
- Performing Arts Pathway

Famous First

The *Hurrian* Songs are a collection of music inscribed in cuneiform on clay tablets excavated from the ancient Amorite-Canaanite city of Ugarit, which dates to approximately 1400 BCE. One of these tablets, contains the Hurrian Hymn to Nikkal (known variously as the Hurrian Cult Hymn, A Zaluzi to the Gods, or simply h.6), making it the oldest surviving substantially complete work of notated music in the world. While the composers' names of some of the fragmentary pieces are known, h.6 is an anonymous work.
(Source: Wikipedia.org)

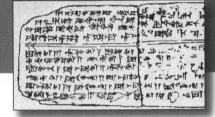

Postsecondary

In general, Music directors and composers must find the balance of formal and informal education that best meets their needs. An unusually talented musician may choose to forego college and move directly into their performing career. On the other hand, some musicians benefit from at least a bachelor's degree in music. Music programs include courses in theory, composition, arranging, and performance. Instead of music, one might consider majoring in music education, audio engineering, or even double majoring in music and business. Continuing education courses in piano tuning, instrument repair and construction, or other related courses might be good choices as well.

Related College Majors
- Music Conducting
- Music General Performance
- Music History and Literature
- Music Piano and Organ Performance
- Music Theory and Composition
- Music Voice and Choral/Opera Performance
- Music, General

Adult Job Seekers

Adults who take up an instrument later in life face stiff competition; however, it is common for a musician to become a composer later in adulthood, and for musicians to switch instruments later in life. Although Music directors and composers can work part-time, the hours, and often the pay, are not always conducive to parenting and other adult responsibilities.

Advancement opportunities are limited and, in most cases, highly dependent on one's level of success. They include chaired positions or opportunities for solos, more lucrative recording contracts, performance fees, or commissions, and/or the ability to hire a manager to take care of business responsibilities, thus opening up more time for creative pursuits. Only a very small percentage of musicians and composers reach celebrity status.

Job seeks might consider joining professional organizations such as the American Federation of Music directors and composers, considered to be the largest such organization dedicated to furthering the careers of professional musicians, to seek career advancement opportunities.

Professional Certification and Licensure

There are no certificates or licenses needed for most performers or composers, although a few organizations offer certification that may be required for jobs in that specialty, such as the American Guild of Organists.

Additional Requirements

Music directors and composers are usually artists with a passion for their craft, but forging a professional career in this field is no easy task. Aspiring professional musicians need to be prepared for all the financial hazards of freelance work, including an inconsistent income (or backup income from another source) that needs to be spread over periods of no musical work. As with any fine arts career, passion and persistence are often the most important qualifications.

EARNINGS AND ADVANCEMENT

Earnings of multimedia artists and animators depend on skill, education, and the type, size, and geographic location of the employer. The median annual wage for music directors and composers was $49,630 in May 2018. The median wage is the wage at which half the workers in an occupation earned more than that amount and half earned less. The lowest 10 percent earned less than $21,640, and the highest 10 percent earned more than $112,820.

Median annual wages, May 2018

Music directors and composers: $49,630

Entertainers and performers, sports and related workers: $42,940

Total, all occupations: $38,640

Note: All Occupations includes all occupations in the U.S. Economy.
Source: U.S. Bureau of Labor Statistics, Employment Projections program

In May 2018, the median annual wages for music directors and composers in the top industries in which they worked were as follows:

Elementary and secondary schools; state, local, and private	$53,970
Performing arts companies	$53,830
Religious, grantmaking, civic, professional, and similar organizations	$39,920

Rehearsals and recording sessions are commonly held during business hours, but performances take place most often on nights and weekends. Because music writing is done primarily independently, composers may be able to set their own schedules.

EMPLOYMENT AND OUTLOOK

Music directors and composers held about 64,700 jobs in 2018. The largest employers of music directors and composers were as follows:

Religious, grantmaking, civic, professional, and similar organizations	59%
Self-employed workers	28%
Elementary and secondary schools; state, local, and private	5%
Performing arts companies	4%

Music directors, composers, musicians, singers, and related workers are employed in a variety of settings, such as religious, civic, professional or other similar organizations; professional orchestras, small chamber music groups, opera companies, musical theater companies, and ballet troupes. Musicians and singers also perform in nightclubs and restaurants and for weddings and other events. Well-known musicians and groups may perform in concerts, appear on radio and television broadcasts, and make recordings and music videos. The Armed Forces also offer careers in their bands and smaller musical groups.

Employment of music directors and composers is projected to show little or no change from 2018 to 2028. Music directors will be needed to lead orchestras for concerts and musical theater performances. They also will conduct the music that accompanies ballet troupes and opera companies. In addition, there will likely be a need for composers to write original music and arrange known works for performances. Composers will be needed as well to write film scores and music for television and commercials.

Percent change in employment, Projected 2018–28

Total, all occupations: 5%

Entertainers and performers, sports and related workers: 5%

Music directors and composers: 1%

Note: All Occupations includes all occupations in the U.S. Economy.
Source: U.S. Bureau of Labor Statistics, Employment Projections program

However, orchestras, opera companies, and other musical groups can have difficulty getting funds. Some music groups are nonprofit organizations that rely on donations and corporate sponsorships, in addition to ticket sales, to fund their work. These organizations often have difficulty finding enough money to cover their expenses. In addition, growth may be limited for music directors in schools due to struggles with school funding, and music programs may be cut.

Tough competition for jobs is anticipated because of the large number of people interested in entering this field. In particular, there will be considerable competition for full-time music director and composer positions. Candidates with exceptional musical talent and dedication should have the best opportunities.

Music directors and composers may experience periods without work. During these times, they may work in other occupations, give music lessons, attend auditions, or write music.

Related Occupations
- Actor
- Dancer/Choreographer
- Sound Engineer

Related Military Occupations
- Music Director
- Musician

Conversation With . . . JONATHAN NEWMAN

Director of Composition & Coordinator of New Music
Associate Professor of Composition
Shenandoah Conservatory, Winchester, Virginia
Professional composer, 25 years

1. What was your individual career path in terms of education/training, entry-level job, or other significant opportunity?

I became very focused quite early on. As a child, I played piano, and always created little pieces for myself to play. Later I played trumpet, and then trombone, and got interested in jazz. All through school, I played in bands and orchestras and sang in choruses nearly every day of the week. When I started writing pieces for those student ensembles and for my friends and myself to play, I realized I was composing. I attended a summer composition program and looked up composition degrees for college. I received my undergraduate degree in music from the Boston University School for the Arts (now the College of Fine Arts), and my Master's at The Juilliard School in New York. Both degrees were in music composition. It is most common now for young composers to receive a doctorate, but my role models at the time did not. After graduating with my Master's, I lived in New York and supported myself with various jobs working at box offices and concert halls, at a major music publisher, and most especially as a freelance music copyist, which is kind of like being an assistant to other composers. I helped to prepare their performance materials for premieres and worked with music publishers to prepare music publications. During this decade, I wrote for musicians and ensembles for various concerts until my performances and commissions got to the point where I felt I could be a composer full time. After another 10 years or so, I added in teaching full-time at a university. I have been at the Shenandoah Conservatory for five years, where I run the composition program, direct the new music ensemble, and curate our new music performing arts series.

2. What are the most important skills and/or qualities for someone in your profession?

Composers possess an unquenchable desire to figure out how music works and how it is put together. Much as an engineer wants to take apart a mechanical device to see how it works, a composer searches out scores to do exactly the same.

Composition is very much a collaborative art and working with other musicians as well as artists in other fields is an essential skill.

Composers also tend to be very detail-oriented people focused on the minutiae that go into putting a musical score together.

In addition, composers also are self-driven. They tend to be people who aren't interested in something like an office-job type life. The career doesn't have weekends or vacations or set hours. It's all project-based and quite entrepreneurial, with months of non-stop work—all managed by yourself alone.

3. **What do you wish you had known going into this profession?**

Time-management issues were the biggest surprise for me. If you self-publish your works as I do—and as many do now—you need business and administrative skills. While they are fairly simple to master, the larger challenge is the time management required to execute business tasks such as invoicing, licenses, inventory management, and correspondence, while protecting the large swaths of time required to write music. If, like me, you have a family and a teaching position, that becomes more complicated. I finally hired an assistant, who also manages my self-publishing business.

4. **Are there many job opportunities in your profession? In what specific areas?**

It's important to understand that there is no such thing as a "job" as a composer. Rather, it is a career. As with all careers in music, one's complete income comes from a variety of sources. A composer might write a work on commission for a fee, receive earnings from publishing existing pieces and licensing them, and also have work rehearsing or conducting those pieces. S/he might also play in an ensemble, teach piano lessons, or teach at a university. The most common path for a concert music composer is to write while also teaching at the college level, and because of the staggering number of composers qualified to do exactly that, those specific opportunities are rare, extremely competitive, and challenging to secure.

5. **How do you see your profession changing in the next five years? How will technology impact that change, and what skills will be required?**

Technology has already drastically changed my profession so much that as long as computers and software remain relatively the same kind of construct (rather than say, something sci-fi like being implanted into your head), I don't expect the field to change much more. Music notation software is so sophisticated that I can open a score from a young composer and instantly tell if the work was written on computer (rather than conceived of on paper, and then later copied to computer for clarity). The artistic issues of that notwithstanding, available software options can be useful tools, and fluency with them, as well as with sound editing, sequencing, and recording software and equipment, will continue to be essential for composers. I also expect social media will become even more of a publishing venue for composers.

6. What do you enjoy most about your job? What do you enjoy least about your job?

Nothing beats the experience of creating something from nothing—of conceiving an idea, and then hearing that idea made real by musicians in a live performance. It never gets old, and it makes the months—and sometimes years—of long, detailed work worthwhile. I also really enjoy working with musicians; making music together in a group or ensemble is the single best thing about being a musician.

I least enjoy the pile of self-promotion tasks essential for the entrepreneurial twenty-first-century musician, including promoting through social media, mailings to ensembles and conductors, promotional recordings, traveling to promote one's performances and catalog. These are crucial but drain my energies. I often wish I could just write.

7. Can you suggest a valuable "try this" for students considering a career in your profession?

If you have some friends who play instruments, or sing, try writing them something to play! Rather than composing something for a computer to play (which is quite easy to do and very common), conceive of what you'd like to hear, look at scores of pieces you'd like to emulate, sketch out the ideas and keep honing them down until they become a musical work you'd like to hear. Prepare a score and parts and rehearse the work with your friends. If possible, arrange for a live performance! There is no better learning experience. The key is to write for people you know, who can give you feedback, and with whom you enjoy collaborating. If you like the experience, you can simply do it again and again and again...and then you're a composer!

MORE INFORMATION

American Federation of Musicians (AFM)
1501 Broadway, Ninth Floor
New York, NY 10036
212.869.1330
www.afm.org

Lists a variety of scholarships:
www.afm.org/young-musicians/
scholarships

American Guild of Musical Artists
1430 Broadway, 14th Floor
New York, NY 10018
212.265.3687
agma@musicalartists.org
www.musicalartists.org

American Guild of Organists
475 Riverside Drive, Suite 1260
New York, NY 10115
212.870.2310
info@agohq.org
www.agohq.org

American Guild of Variety Artists
363 7th Avenue, 17th Floor
New York, NY 10001-3904
212.675.1003
agva@agvausa.com
www.agvausa.com

American Society of Composers, Authors, and Publishers (ASCAP)
250 West 57th Street
New York, NY 10107
212.621.6000
www.ascap.com

American Society of Music Arrangers and Composers (ASMAC)
5903 Noble Avenue
Van Nuys, California 91411
818.994.4661
www.asmac.org

Sponsors scholarships:
www.asmac.org/478590

Offers masterclasses:
www.asmac.org/478577

League of American Orchestras
33 West 60th Street, 5th Floor
New York, NY 10023
212.262.5161
www.americanorchestras.org

National Association for Music Education
1806 Robert Fulton Drive
Reston, VA 20191
800.336.3768
www.menc.org

Sponsors the Tri-M Music Honor Society for secondary students:
www.menc.org/resources/view/tri-m-music-honor-society

Presents information about music careers:
www.menc.org/careers

Music Publishers Association of the United States
243 5th Avenue, Suite 236
New York, NY 10016
212.327.4044
admin@mpa.org
www.mpa.org

National Association of Schools of Music
11250 Roger Bacon Drive, Suite 21
Reston, VA 20190-5248
703.437.0700
info@arts-accredit.org
nasm.arts-accredit.org/index.jsp

Sally Driscoll/Editor

Paralegal and Legal Assistants

Snapshot

Career Cluster(s): Business, Management, and Administration, Law, Public Safety and Security

Interests: Law, legal system, research, political science, investigation, administrative tasks

Earnings (2018 Median): $50,940 yearly; $24.49 per hour

Employment and Outlook: Faster Than Average Growth Expected

OVERVIEW

Sphere of Work

Paralegals are professionals who provide background research and other forms of assistance to attorneys. Paralegals help attorneys prepare for judicial hearings, trials, and corporate or client meetings, in addition to other legal tasks. Much of their preparatory work involves researching laws and legal decisions, preparing briefs, contracts, and agreements, and assembling other documents, legal or otherwise, for use during the trial process or other function (such as a real estate

transaction). Paralegals generally begin their careers performing basic research and administrative tasks. As they become more experienced, their responsibilities expand significantly to the point that they advise attorneys on the best course of action, attend trials and hearings, and prepare arguments.

Work Environment

Paralegals typically work a standard forty-hour week as employees of private law firms, government agency offices, and corporations. During their workdays, paralegals often manage multiple tasks, as the caseload requires. In addition to their work in an office setting, paralegals may spend a great deal of time in law libraries, researching judicial decisions, statutes, and other legal information. As they become more experienced, paralegals may be drawn into more time-consuming and high-profile casework. Such work may require that they travel for business, conduct client interviews, and attend hearings and off-site meetings.

Profile

Interests: Data, People
Working Conditions: Work Inside
Physical Strength: Light Work
Education Needs: Junior/Technical/ Community College
Licensure/Certification: Recommended
Physical Abilities Not Required: Not Climb, Not Kneel
Opportunities for Experience: Military Service, Part-time Work
Holland Interest Score: SEC

* See Appendix A

Occupation Interest

Paralegals are seen as important contributors to the legal field. Although paralegals are prohibited from practicing law, much of their work is viewed as similar to the work that attorneys perform. Paralegals are, therefore, part of the dynamic world of law without the requirement of a law degree. Individuals who are interested in becoming paralegals typically enjoy research, studying and working within the legal system, and helping others.

A Day in the Life—Duties and Responsibilities

Depending on the field of law in which they work, paralegals may have a very diverse set of responsibilities. As they help attorneys prepare for trials, paralegals collect and organize all of the case facts, locate relevant case laws and past court decisions, assist with depositions, and obtain affidavits (or sworn testimony). Paralegals often prepare this information in the form of detailed reports for the attorneys' use. They also draft litigation documents and notes for arguments. More experienced paralegals may join the attorney in the courtroom, keeping his or her documentation readily available.

Outside of the courtroom, paralegals assist in creating a wide range of legal documents, including patent papers, mortgages, contracts, and divorce settlement or separation papers. In corporate settings, paralegals are responsible for compiling employee benefits, shareholder agreements, and other packages of relevance to the business. A paralegal who works in a government office or in a legal services office that provides legal assistance to the poor may prepare law guides, provide non-legal guidance to clients, and file legal documents.

Paralegals use technology and computer software for managing and organizing the increasing amount of documents and data collected during a case. Many paralegals use computer software to catalog documents, and to review documents for specific keywords or subjects. Because of these responsibilities, paralegals must be familiar with electronic database management and be current on the latest software used for electronic discovery. Electronic discovery refers to all electronic materials obtained by the parties during the litigation or investigation. These materials may be emails, data, documents, accounting databases, and websites.

Paralegals' specific duties often vary depending on the area of law in which they work. The following are examples of types of paralegals and legal assistants:

Corporate paralegals, for example, often help lawyers prepare employee contracts, shareholder agreements, stock-option plans, and companies' annual financial reports. Corporate paralegals may monitor and review government regulations to ensure that the corporation is aware of new legal requirements.

Litigation paralegals maintain documents received from clients, conduct research for lawyers, retrieve and organize evidence for use at depositions and trials, and draft settlement agreements. Some litigation paralegals may also help coordinate the logistics of attending a trial, including reserving office space, transporting exhibits and documents to the courtroom, and setting up computers and other equipment.

Paralegals may also specialize in other legal areas, such as personal injury, criminal law, employee benefits, intellectual property, bankruptcy, immigration, family law, and real estate.

Specific job duties may also vary by the size of the law firm. In small firms, paralegals' duties tend to vary more. In addition to reviewing and organizing documents, paralegals may prepare written reports that help lawyers determine how to handle their cases. If lawyers decide to file lawsuits on behalf of clients, paralegals may help draft documents to be filed with the court. In large organizations, paralegals may work on a particular phase of a case, rather than handling a case from beginning to end. For example, paralegals may only review legal material for internal use, maintain reference files, conduct research for lawyers, or collect and organize evidence for hearings. After gaining experience, a paralegal may become responsible for more complicated tasks. Unlike the work of other administrative and legal support staff employed in a law firm, the paralegal's work is often billed to the client.

Paralegals may have frequent interactions with clients and third-party vendors. In addition, experienced paralegals may assume supervisory responsibilities, such as overseeing team projects or delegating work to other paralegals.

Because paralegals are not required to pass the bar exam, they are not permitted to provide legal guidance directly to clients, provide arguments in the courtroom, or authorize any legal tasks. However, many consider the work of the paralegal to be just as demanding and important as a practicing attorney. In fact, many paralegals eventually use their knowledge of the law and the legal system to enter law school and become practicing attorneys. Other paralegals continue on to managerial-level positions within their organizations.

Duties and Responsibilities

- Investigate and gather the facts of a case
- Conduct research on relevant laws, regulations, and legal articles
- Organize and maintain documents in paper or electronic filing systems
- Gather and arrange evidence and other legal documents for attorney review and case preparation
- Write or summarize reports to help lawyers prepare for trials
- Draft correspondence and legal documents, such as contracts and mortgages
- Get affidavits and other formal statements that may be used as evidence in court
- Help lawyers during trials by handling exhibits, taking notes, or reviewing trial transcripts
- File exhibits, briefs, appeals and other legal documents with the court or opposing counsel
- Call clients, witnesses, lawyers, and outside vendors to schedule interviews, meetings, and depositions

WORK ENVIRONMENT

Immediate Physical Environment

Paralegals typically work in an office environment. These locations are generally very active, with multiple meetings, projects, and activities occurring independent of one another. The environment can be fast-paced and often hectic. Paralegals also often perform research in law libraries, which are considerably quieter. Paralegals are rarely exposed to dangerous substances or situations, although confrontations between disputing parties can be contentious.

Transferable Skills and Abilities

Communication Skills
- Speaking effectively
- Writing concisely

Organization and Management Skills
- Organizing information or materials
- Paying attention to and handling details
- Performing duties which change frequently
- Performing routine work

Research and Planning Skills
- Analyzing information
- Gathering information
- Using logical reasoning

Human Environment

As part of a law office, government agency, or corporation, paralegals must work with many different professionals. They work most closely with attorneys, and often support several attorneys at once. They also interact with witnesses, clients, legal experts, interns, and administrative professionals.

Technological Environment

Paralegals are expected to have familiarity with basic office technology and computer systems in particular. They need to learn a number of software programs used for writing projects, spreadsheets, document storage (such as those used for scanning hard copies), and presentations.

EDUCATION, TRAINING, AND ADVANCEMENT

High School/Secondary

High school students who are interested in pursuing a career as a paralegal are encouraged to take courses that develop their writing skills, such as journalism. They will also need to study many fundamentals areas of law, such as political science, sociology, philosophy, economics, and history. They may also take business classes, which will help them apply their skills as a paralegal in a corporate environment.

Suggested High School Subjects
- Applied Communication
- Business English
- Business Law
- College Preparatory
- Composition
- Economics
- English
- Foreign Languages
- Government
- History
- Humanities
- Journalism
- Keyboarding
- Mathematics
- Philosophy
- Political Science
- Psychology
- Social Studies
- Sociology
- Speech

Related Career Pathways/Majors

Business, Management, and Administration Cluster
- Administrative and Information Support Pathway

Law, Public Safety, and Security Cluster
- Legal Services Pathway

Famous First

Philadelphia lawyer is a term to describe a lawyer who knows the most detailed and minute points of law or is an exceptionally competent lawyer. Its first known usage dates back to 1788. Philadelphia-based Colonial American lawyer Andrew Hamilton, a lawyer best known for his legal victory on behalf of printer and newspaper publisher John Peter Zenger, is believed to have inspired the term. This Zenger decision helped to establish that truth is a defense to an accusation of libel. His eloquent defense concluded with saying that the press has "a liberty both of exposing and opposing tyrannical power by speaking and writing truth." (Source: Wikipedia.org)

Postsecondary

The majority of paralegal professionals receive an associate's degree in paralegal studies. Those individuals who receive a degree through a four-year college can also obtain certificates in paralegal studies from a number of educational institutions. A large number of law schools, universities, and other schools offer formal training programs as well.

Related College Majors
- Paralegal/Legal Assistant Training

Adult Job Seekers

Adults who are interested in becoming paralegals may obtain jobs through career placement services and temporary employment companies. Some are able to learn about paralegal jobs while they attend a paralegal training or certification program. Still others first join a law firm as an intern and, based on their performance, may be hired as a full-time paralegal.

Professional Certification and Licensure

Paralegals are not necessarily required to receive certification as a professional paralegal. However, becoming certified can enhance a paralegal's qualifications. Certification demonstrates commitment to the field and underscores the individual's research, writing, and communications skills.

Several professional organizations offer certifications to experienced paralegals who complete an examination. Most certifications must be renewed through continuing education. The National Association of Legal Assistants, American Alliance of Paralegals, Inc., and National Federation of Paralegal Associations each have different requirements for certification. Consult credible professional associations within the field, such as the American Bar Association, and follow professional debate as to the relevancy and value of any certification program.

Additional Requirements

Paralegals are expected to have exceptional research skills, as they may be called upon to provide the full complement of facts, history, and other information relevant to the case or project assigned to them. They should have strong communications abilities and excellent organizational skills.

EARNINGS AND ADVANCEMENT

The median annual wage for paralegals and legal assistants was $50,940 in May 2018. The median wage is the wage at which half the workers in an occupation earned more than that amount and half earned less. The lowest 10 percent earned less than $31,400, and the highest 10 percent earned more than $82,050.

In May 2018, the median annual wages for paralegals and legal assistants in the top industries in which they worked were as follows:

Federal government	$67,340
Finance and insurance	$62,020
Local government, excluding education and hospitals	$50,400
Legal services	$48,880
State government, excluding education and hospitals	$46,970

Median annual wages, May 2018

Legal support workers: $51,410

Paralegals and legal assistants: $50,940

Total, all occupations: $38,640

Note: All Occupations includes all occupations in the U.S. Economy.
Source: U.S. Bureau of Labor Statistics, Employment Projections program

Earnings of paralegals depend on the type and geographic location of the employer and the employee's education, training and experience. Generally, those who work for large law firms or in large metropolitan areas earn more than those who work for smaller firms or in less populated regions. In addition to a salary, many paralegals receive bonuses.

EMPLOYMENT AND OUTLOOK

Paralegals and legal assistants held about 325,700 jobs in 2018. The largest employers of paralegals and legal assistants were as follows:

Legal services	73%
Local government, excluding education and hospitals	4%
Federal government	4%
State government, excluding education and hospitals	3%
Finance and insurance	3%

Employment of paralegals and legal assistants is projected to grow 12 percent from 2018 to 2028, much faster than the average for all occupations. As law firms try to increase the efficiency of legal services and reduce their costs, they are expected to hire more paralegals and legal assistants. In these cases, paralegals and legal assistants can take on a "hybrid" role within the firm, performing not only traditional paralegal duties but also some of the tasks previously assigned to legal secretaries or other legal support workers.

Law firms also are attempting to reduce billing costs as clients push for less expensive legal services. Due to their lower billing rates to clients, paralegals can be a less costly alternative to lawyers, performing a wide variety of tasks once done by entry-level lawyers. This should cause an increase in demand for paralegals and legal assistants.

Although law firms will continue to be the largest employers of paralegals, many large corporations are increasing their in-house legal departments to cut costs. For many companies, the high cost of outside counsel makes it more economical to have an in-house legal department. This will lead to an increase in the demand for legal workers in a variety of settings, such as finance and insurance firms, consulting firms, and healthcare providers.

Due to the rise of electronic discovery, formally trained paralegals with strong computer and database management skills should have the best job prospects.

Related Occupations
- Lawyer
- Research Assistant

Related Military Occupations
- Legal Specialist and Court Reporter

MORE INFORMATION

American Association for Paralegal Education (AAfPE)
222 S. Westmonte Drive, Suite 111
Altamonte Springs, FL 32714
407.774.7880
info@aafpe.org
www.aafpe.org

Lambda Epsilon Chi (LEX) Scholarship:
www.aafpe.org/m_lex/index.asp

American Bar Association Standing Committee on Paralegals
321 N. Clark Street
Chicago, IL 60654-7598
312.988.5522
www.americanbar.org/groups/paralegals

American Alliance of Paralegals, Inc.
4023 Kennett Pike, Suite 146
Wilmington, DE 19807
info@aapipara.org
www.aapipara.org

International Paralegal Management Association
P.O. Box 659
Avondale Estates, GA 30002-0659
404.292.4762
www.paralegalmanagement.org

National Association of Legal Assistants
7666 E. 61st Street, Suite 315
Tulsa, OK 74133
918.587.6828
nalanet@nala.org
www.nala.org

National Federation of Paralegal Associations, Inc.
3502 Woodview Trace, Ste. 300
Indianapolis, IN 46268
317.454.8312
info@paralegals.org
www.paralegals.org

NFPA/Thomson Reuters Scholarship:
www.paralegals.org/

Michael P. Auerbach/Editor

Postsecondary Teachers

Snapshot

Career Cluster(s): Education and Training

Interests: Teaching, research, writing, public speaking, helping others, communicating with others

Earnings (2018 Median): $78,470 yearly

Employment and Outlook: Much Faster Than Average Growth Expected

OVERVIEW

Sphere of Work

A postsecondary teacher (or college faculty member) is a professional instructor who teaches courses at a postsecondary institution. He or she has a master's or doctoral degree in a specific academic discipline and is considered qualified to teach within that discipline only. Faculty members design their own courses, plan discussion topics and reading and writing assignments, and plan and coordinate test and examination schedules. As they conduct their classes, faculty members lecture students,

grade papers and exams, and advise students on their major fields of study. A postsecondary teacher will typically research and write scholarly books and articles on their particular field of expertise and, occasionally, present their individual works at relevant conferences.

Work Environment

A member of a college faculty typically manages his or her classes individually (although at larger universities, many professors delegate grading papers and exams or running student discussion groups to graduate students). Outside of the classroom, however, they often collaborate with fellow professors in writing and editing scholarly books and articles. Furthermore, as part of the faculty, they will meet frequently with their department colleagues to discuss departmental policies and other school news. A college faculty member's workload is therefore diverse, although not physically strenuous.

The largest employers of postsecondary teachers were as follows:

Colleges, universities, and professional schools; private	40%
Colleges, universities, and professional schools; state	37%
Junior colleges; local	10%
Junior colleges; state	7%

Many postsecondary teachers find their jobs rewarding because they are surrounded by others who enjoy the subject they teach. The opportunity to share their expertise with others is appealing to many.

However, some postsecondary teachers must find a balance between teaching students and doing research and publishing their findings. This can be stressful, especially for beginning teachers seeking advancement in 4-year research universities. At the community college level, professors focus mainly on teaching students and administrative duties.

Classes are generally held during the day, although some are offered in the evenings and weekends to accommodate students who have jobs or family obligations.

Although some postsecondary teachers teach summer courses, many use that time to conduct research, involve themselves in professional development, or to travel.

Occupation Interest

Most people pursue careers in postsecondary institutions because they love to study a particular subject and share their insights with others. Aspiring college faculty members should also be interested in helping to shape young minds. College faculty members are, by nature, intellectuals willing to spend long hours researching, writing on, and teaching the many elements of their particular discipline.

College faculty members (often called professors) come from a wide range of backgrounds and demonstrate an equally broad range of perspectives, experience, and teaching styles. They are considered experts in their fields, having completed many years of study at the undergraduate and postgraduate levels.

A Day in the Life—Duties and Responsibilities

A member of a college faculty is primarily a teacher, using his or her past studies, research, and professional experience on a particular subject to help others learn more about it. He or she will select the required texts and articles for the course, design a course syllabus (an overview of the topics for discussion and required reading and homework for each scheduled class), prepare lectures and discussions for each class, lead effective class discussion, and issue and grade tests and student work. Depending on the nature and level of the course, the faculty member may simply lecture a class or provide a "seminar" approach in which students are expected to actively participate.

In addition to their responsibilities to the courses they teach, faculty members will also pursue their own projects, researching and writing scholarly works on topics within their discipline. Occasionally, when these works are published, professors will present these scholarly documents at regional, national, and international conferences. This individual research can help the faculty members continue to work at their respective colleges and even receive tenure (an agreement that the professor may stay on the faculty indefinitely).

College faculty members must also work with other members of their respective departments to shape departmental policies, activities, and courses. Periodically, these individuals may be selected to serve as department chairs, the senior-most position of a department's faculty.

Duties and Responsibilities

- Teach courses in their subject area
- Work with students who are taking classes to improve their knowledge or career skills
- Develop an instructional plan (known as a course outline or syllabus) for the course(s) they teach and ensure that it meets college and department standards
- Plan lessons and assignments
- Work with colleagues to develop or modify the curriculum for a degree or certificate program involving a series of courses
- Assess students' progress by grading assignments, papers, exams, and other work
- Advise students about which classes to take and how to achieve their goals
- Stay informed about changes and innovations in their field

WORK ENVIRONMENT

Immediate Physical Environment

A postsecondary teacher works at buildings that are situated on a university campus. Their immediate physical environment includes classrooms, lecture halls, laboratories, and seminar rooms. They will also perform some of their duties in their offices, such as advising students, meeting with peers, and grading and preparing for classes.

Faculty members who teach engineering, chemistry, and other scientific or vocational courses work in a lab environment and are required to follow certain safety procedures. Faculty may be exposed to some dangerous equipment or chemicals and are responsible for educating students as to their proper handling.

Human Environment

While professors at smaller colleges and universities tend to manage their classes alone, faculty members at larger institutions will often call upon graduate students to assist them in preparing syllabi, grading papers, and lecturing. Professors also meet frequently with one another on departmental matters and collaborate on research projects.

Postsecondary teachers, often referred to as professors or faculty, specialize in a variety of subjects and fields. At colleges and universities, professors are organized into departments that specialize in a degree field, such as history, science, business, or music. A professor may teach one or more courses within that department. For example, a mathematics professor may teach calculus, statistics, and a graduate seminar in a very specific area of mathematics.

Postsecondary teachers' duties vary with their positions in a university or college. In large colleges or universities, they may spend their time teaching, conducting research or experiments, publishing original research, applying for grants to fund their research, or supervising graduate teaching assistants who are teaching classes.

Postsecondary teachers who work in small colleges and universities or in community colleges often spend more time teaching classes and working with students. They may spend some time conducting research, but they do not have as much time to devote to it.

Full-time professors, particularly those who have tenure (a professor who cannot be fired without just cause), often are expected to spend more time on their research. They also may be expected to serve on more college and university committees.

Part-time professors, often known as *adjunct professors*, spend most of their time teaching students.

Professors may teach large classes of several hundred students (often with the help of graduate teaching assistants), smaller classes of about 40 to 50 students, seminars with just a few students, or laboratories where students practice the subject matter. They work with an increasingly varied student population as more part-time, older, and culturally diverse students are going to postsecondary schools.

Professors read scholarly articles, talk with colleagues, and participate in professional conferences to keep up with developments in their field. A tenured professor must do original research, document their analyses or critical reviews, and publish their findings.

Transferable Skills and Abilities

Communication Skills
- Expressing thoughts and ideas
- Persuading others
- Speaking effectively
- Writing concisely

Interpersonal/Social Skills
- Cooperating with others

Organization and Management Skills
- Coordinating tasks
- Making decisions
- Organizing information or materials

Research and Planning Skills
- Analyzing information
- Gathering information
- Using logical reasoning

Technological Environment

Faculty members typically use basic office technology and tools to aid them with lecturing, compiling research, organizing class materials, and in communicating with students. Professors working in scientific fields may use a number of other technologies that are relevant to their fields, such as particle accelerators, spectrometers, and engineering equipment. Some postsecondary teachers work for online universities or teach online classes. They use the Internet to present lessons and information, to assign and accept students' work, and to participate in course discussions. Online professors use email, phone, and video chat apps to communicate with students, and might never meet their students in person.

EDUCATION, TRAINING, AND ADVANCEMENT

High School/Secondary

In addition to taking courses in the intellectual discipline in which they are interested, high school students who wish to become college faculty members are encouraged to take classes and participate in clubs that help them develop their research and communications skills, such as debate teams, writing courses, and extracurricular clubs that focus on the field in which they are interested.

Suggested High School Subjects
- Algebra
- Arts
- Audio-Visual
- Biology
- Bookkeeping
- Business
- Business and Computer Technology
- Business Math
- Chemistry
- College Preparatory
- Composition
- Computer Science
- Earth Science
- Economics
- English
- Entrepreneurship
- Foreign Languages
- Geography
- History
- Humanities
- Literature
- Mathematics
- Merchandising
- Physics
- Science
- Social Studies

- Sociology
- Speech
- Statistics

Related Career Pathways/Majors
- Education and Training Cluster
- Teaching/Training Pathway

Famous First

Wilbur Lang Schramm (August 5, 1907–December 27, 1987) was a scholar and "authority on mass communications." He founded the Iowa Writers' Workshop in 1935 and served as its first director until 1941. Schramm helped establish departments of communication studies across U.S. universities. He was the first to identify himself as a communication scholar. Schramm's mass communication program in the Iowa School of Journalism was a pilot project for the doctoral program and for the Institute of Communications Research, which he founded in 1947 at the University of Illinois at Urbana–Champaign, now housed in the UIUC College of Media. (Source: Wikipedia.org)

Postsecondary

College faculty members develop their knowledge and experience over a period of many years at the undergraduate and postgraduate levels. Postsecondary students should continue to study all aspects of their chosen discipline at the undergraduate level. Many students choose to obtain an internship in their chosen field, studying this discipline outside of the college setting. Additionally, college professors are strongly encouraged to pursue master's and doctoral degrees in their chosen field, taking a wide range of courses at the graduate level and writing an extensive independent study known as a dissertation.

Related College Majors
- For this occupation, related college majors will vary, based on the area of faculty expertise.

Adult Job Seekers

College faculty positions are often difficult to obtain due to the large number of individuals with advanced degrees seeking jobs in higher education. Many adults who plan to become a full member of a faculty may start out as "adjunct" professors, teaching at an institution on a part-time basis. Many other people will attend conferences and similar events to meet and share their independent work with tenured professors and university officials to help secure a faculty position.

Professional Certification and Licensure

For most full-time postsecondary teachers, a master's and doctoral degree are required. Some institutions are willing to allow people to join without a doctorate, provided that those candidates have extensive experience and expertise in their fields.

Additional Requirements

College faculty members find satisfaction in researching, learning, and sharing knowledge with others. They must be self-motivated and able to motivate others as well. In addition, they should be willing to handle multiple tasks, such as managing multiple classes, working with students, and conducting their own individual research.

EARNINGS AND ADVANCEMENT

Earnings of postsecondary teachers depend largely on the academic qualifications, academic specialty, academic rank and experience of each individual, and the type of institution. Generally, professors of medicine, dentistry, engineering and law receive higher salaries than professors in other fields. Faculty in four-year schools earned higher salaries, on the average, than those in two-year schools.

The median annual wage for postsecondary teachers was $78,470 in May 2018. The median wage is the wage at which half the workers in an occupation earned more than that amount and half earned less. The lowest 10 percent earned less than $39,760, and the highest 10 percent earned more than $175,110.

Median annual wages for postsecondary teachers in May 2018 were as follows:

Law teachers, postsecondary	$111,140
Anthropology and archeology teachers, postsecondary	$83,940
Political science teachers, postsecondary	$83,370
History teachers, postsecondary	$74,590
Area, ethnic, and cultural studies teachers, postsecondary	$74,440
Sociology teachers, postsecondary	$74,140
Philosophy and religion teachers, postsecondary	$71,890
Social sciences teachers, postsecondary, all other	$71,600
Library science teachers, postsecondary	$71,560
Art, drama, and music teachers, postsecondary	$69,960
Communications teachers, postsecondary	$68,910
Social work teachers, postsecondary	$68,300
Foreign language and literature teachers, postsecondary	$67,640
English language and literature teachers, postsecondary	$66,590

In May 2018, the median annual wages for postsecondary teachers in the top industries in which they worked were as follows:

Junior colleges; local	$83,530
Colleges, universities, and professional schools; state	$81,120
Colleges, universities, and professional schools; private	$78,540
Junior colleges; state	$56,930

Wages can vary by institution type. Postsecondary teachers typically have higher wages in colleges, universities, and professional schools than they do in community colleges or other types of schools.

Many postsecondary teachers work part-time. They may work part-time at several colleges or universities, or have a full-time job in their field of expertise in addition to a part-time teaching position.

College faculty members may receive paid vacations, holidays, and sick days; life and health insurance; and retirement benefits. These are usually paid by the employer.

EMPLOYMENT AND OUTLOOK

There were approximately 1.4 million college and university faculty members employed nationally in 2018. Employment is expected to grow much faster than average for all occupations through the year 20280, which means employment is projected to increase 11 percent. Both part-time and full-time postsecondary teachers are included in this projection.

The number of people attending postsecondary institutions is expected to grow in the next decade. Students will continue to seek higher education to gain the additional education and skills necessary to meet their career goals. As more people enter colleges and universities, more postsecondary teachers will be needed to serve these additional students. Colleges and universities are likely to hire more part-time teachers to meet this demand. In all disciplines, there is expected to be a limited number of full-time nontenure and full-time tenure positions.

However, despite expected increases in enrollment, employment growth in public colleges and universities will depend on state and local government budgets. If budgets for higher education are reduced, employment growth may be limited.

Overall employment of postsecondary teachers is projected to increase, but it will vary by field. For example, employment of health specialties teachers is projected to grow 23 percent from 2018 to 2028, much faster than the average for all occupations. As an aging population increasingly demands healthcare services, additional postsecondary teachers are expected to be needed to help educate the workers who will provide these services.

There are expected to be more job opportunities for part-time postsecondary teachers since many institutions are filling vacancies with part-time rather than full-time teachers. There will be a limited number of full-time tenure-track positions and competition is expected to be high.

Related Occupations
- Anthropologist
- Education Administrator
- Historian
- Secondary and Middle School Teacher
- Social Scientist

Related Military Occupations
- Teacher and Instructor

Fast Fact

The most expensive book ever purchased? Codex Leicester, one of Leonardo Di Vinci's scientific journals. Buyer? Bill Gates. Cost? $30.8 million.

Source: englishbookgeorgia.com

Conversation With . . .
DAVID SCHUMAN

Director of Creative Writing and Senior Lecturer
Washington University
St. Louis, Missouri
Creative writing academia, 17 years

1. **What was your individual career path in terms of education/training, entry-level job, or other significant opportunity?**

As a kid, my real interest was visual art. I loved to draw and was one of those artsy kids all through middle and high school. Along the way, I also was a kid who was really drawn to literature and books. I started off reading a lot of sci fi and adventure novels, but by middle school was into John Steinbeck and later, short stories. I really got into Flannery O'Connor.

I majored in painting at University of the Arts in Philadelphia, then moved to New York City to try to make it as a painter. This was the early 90s, and the art world there was still a vicious place that required some lucky breaks and a lot of talent. I had some lucky breaks and some talent, but it didn't come together.

I worked a couple years as an editorial assistant at Viking-Penguin Books in the children's division and wrote copy for books, worked on catalogs, read the slush pile. During that time, I started to tinker with my own creative writing. I then started doing freelance illustration. At the same time, I took a night course in fiction writing at New York University and wrote some short stories. The teacher, a writer named Susie Mee, took me seriously and that was the first time I thought, "Oh. Maybe I'm good at writing. Maybe this is the real thing." She had a private workshop at her apartment in Chelsea and invited students she thought had promise. I started going in 1992 and continued for about eight years. During that time, I continued working as a commercial artist, met my wife, moved to New Jersey, and continued to read and discover new writers and figure out the kind of writing I wanted to do, which was literary short fiction.

Then, having published only one story in a literary magazine, I was accepted to an arts residency at the Blue Mountain Center in the Adirondacks. It was one month away to focus on my writing. I met new writers, who talked about Master of Fine Arts (MFA) writing programs. This was something I had never considered. I came home, talked to my wife, wound up applying, and got in at Washington University. I thought

I was going for two years and we'd come back to East Coast and I'd go back to art and design. I didn't think it would take me to the Midwest forever.

During graduate school, I started to publish stories in literary magazines. After two years, I won a fellowship for one more year to allow me to concentrate on working and teaching. I taught creative writing and really enjoyed that. After graduating, I taught as a part-time adjunct professor and was assistant director of the MFA program. After five or six years I became a fulltime lecturer, and I continue to teach fiction and nonfiction. I also was asked to direct the MFA program. In addition, I direct the Howard Nemerov Scholarship for undergraduate creative writing, which is competitive. I organize that community once they're here and teach a seminar for those students. We get together once a week to talk about writing and workshop stories.

In the summer, I find as much time as I can to get my own writing done. I'm writing a novel and have the interest of a literary agent who will hopefully take it and sell it. I've published a lot of fiction and was fortunate to win a Pushcart Prize. My story, "Stay," was listed as a distinguished story in *Best American Short Stories*. I've also started writing non-fiction and had success publishing essays. I recently had a small book of short stories—called a chapbook—accepted for publication.

I'm working to get my stuff out there.

Looking back, I can see that learning to draw taught me how to organize the world in a particular way, creating a shape in relationship to another shape. Writing is the same thing. You are organizing information.

2. What are the most important skills and/or qualities for someone in your profession?

Curiosity, a passion for literature, and being a reader. You can't be a writer without being a reader.

3. What do you wish you had known going into this profession?

An awareness of how long it would take to get into the position I want to be in, professionally and financially. This is a long process of educating yourself. Also, I love the work I do and feel lucky to teach courses I want and work with great students, which is unusual for a lecturer and not a tenured professor. But I do sometimes wonder what it would have been like if I had kept my design work and written on the side because academia puts a lot of pressure on you.

4. Are there many job opportunities in your profession? In what specific areas?

Being a writer in academia is not the only path. Creative writing can be used in advertising, publishing, journalism. Writers can work for businesses, who want creative people. If I have any advice, it would be, don't use another person's career trajectory as your trajectory. There is so much pressure on what's new and young but that is only one version of success. If you model on other people's success, you run the risk of being disenchanted. Chart your own course.

5. **How do you see your profession changing in the next five years? How will technology impact that change, and what skills will be required?**

I imagine that there will be a lot more online teaching. The way books are getting published is changing. There's been a rise of independent publishers and a rise of going back to the book as an art object, something to love. Hopefully that trend continues.

6. **What do you enjoy most about your job? What do you enjoy least about your job?**

Teaching-wise, I really love that I get to talk about the thing I'm most excited about with interested and engaged students. I get to learn from them and read their work.

The hard side is, it would be nice to have more money, and the pressures of getting job security can sort of weigh on a person. Universities are a wonderful place to work but can also be a difficult place to be. Currently, I'm worried about forces outside my career that may eventually impact my career, such as keeping tuition-paying international students away.

7. **Can you suggest a valuable "try this" for students considering a career in your profession?**

If you are in a city or town that has a literary scene, find a way to get involved in something outside your experience. Intern at a literary magazine. Find other people who like to write and visit a reading series at a local university or bookstore. Organize a reading series. This will help you understand that writers are actual people doing actual work. As a kid, I think I felt books fell out of the brains of brilliant people who existed above the rest of the world. Writers are people, and when you see that it will be easier to consider yourself a person who deserves to be there.

MORE INFORMATION

Academic Keys, LLC
P.O. Box 162
Storrs, CT 06268
860.429.0218
www.academickeys.com

American Association for Employment in Education
PO Box 510
Sycamore, IL 60178
614.485.1111
info@aaee.org
www.aaee.org

American Federation of Teachers
555 New Jersey Avenue, NW
Washington, DC 20001
202.879.4400
www.aft.org

Preparing Future Faculty
One Dupont Circle NW, Suite 230
Washington, DC 20036-1173
202.223.3791
www.preparing-faculty.org/

Michael P. Auerbach/Editor

Producers and Directors

Snapshot

Career Cluster(s): Arts, A/V Technology, and Communications, Information Technology
Interests: Theater, film, planning events, coordinating tasks
Earnings (2018 Median): $71,680 yearly; $34.46 hourly
Employment and Outlook: As Fast As Average Growth Expected

OVERVIEW

Sphere of Work

Directors and producers oversee all aspects of a film or theatrical production. Directors plan, coordinate, and manage the creative aspects of the production, including interpreting scripts, casting talent, approving artistic designs, and directing the work of actors, cinematographers, set designers, wardrobe designers, and other members of the cast and crew. Producers plan, coordinate, and manage the business side of a production, which includes raising money, approving and developing the

script, and performing any related administrative tasks. In most cases, directors and producers must both report to the executive producer (usually the person or entity who finances the project), who must approve all final decisions.

Work Environment

Like actors, directors and producers must be willing to work an irregular schedule with long hours and evening and weekend work, punctuated by frequent periods of unemployment. Productions may last from one day to several months, and during that time, directors and producers are expected to be on call and available to solve problems that arise before, during, and after a production has finished. They may also be away from home, or "on location," for extended periods. The irregular hours and intense competition in these occupations can result in stress, fatigue, and frustration. Most directors and producers must work day jobs or other employment unrelated to entertainment.

Profile

Interests: People, Things
Working Conditions: Work Inside, Work Both Inside and Outside
Physical Strength: Light Work
Education Needs: On-The-Job Training, Junior/Technical/Community College, Apprenticeship
Licensure/Certification: Usually Not Required
Physical Abilities Not Required: Not Climb, Not Kneel
Opportunities for Experience: Internship, Apprenticeship, Military Service, Volunteer Work, Part-time Work
Holland Interest Score: ESA, SEC, SEI

* See Appendix A

Occupation Interest

Prospective directors should be highly creative, confident, and possess a strong desire to tell stories. They must be extremely organized, be natural leaders, and understand all aspects of coordinating a theatrical or film production, including the role that each cast and crew member plays in the successful completion of a production. Prospective producers should be detail-oriented people who have a desire to take on both small and large tasks. Producers should enjoy planning, coordinating, and organizing an event from start to finish and should be willing to handle and resolve any issues that arise.

A Day in the Life—Duties and Responsibilities

There are many different styles of directing films and plays, just as there are many different styles of acting. Directors are ultimately responsible for the appearance, stylistic and emotional tone, and aesthetic organization of a dramatic production. A film studio or independent producer normally hires a director through the director's agent or manager. Before production begins, a director auditions and chooses actors, holds rehearsals, and prepares the cast for production. He or she also consults with set designers, choreographers, cinematographers, music supervisors, and other creative personnel to plan and develop a successful production. During production, a director guides and oversees the entire creative execution of a project, often with help from assistant directors and production assistants. Once production is finished, a director oversees any postproduction responsibilities, such as video and sound editing, graphic design, and music selection.

Producers are responsible for handling the business aspects of a production. They secure funds, set budget limitations, coordinate schedules, and ensure smooth management of the whole project. Producers also work with directors to approve their decisions regarding talent, locations, and other creative choices, as well as to ensure that deadlines are met and money is spent according to financier instructions. Larger productions usually require the services of associate or line producers to assist the producer with his or her duties.

Duties and Responsibilities

- Judging and motivating acting talent
- Making artistic interpretations of scripts
- Making optimum use of taping and production equipment
- Working with union representatives
- Managing contractual obligations
- Maintaining strict production time schedules

OCCUPATION SPECIALTIES

Producers make the business and financial decisions for a motion picture, TV show, commercial, or stage production. They raise money for the project and hire the director and crew. The crew may include set and costume designers, film and video editors, a musical director, a choreographer, and other workers. Some producers may assist in the selection of cast members. Producers set the budget and approve any major changes to the project. They make sure that the production is completed on time, and they are ultimately responsible for the final product.

Directors are responsible for the creative decisions of a production. They select cast members, conduct rehearsals, and direct the work of the cast and crew. During rehearsals, they work with the actors to help them portray their characters more accurately. For nonfiction video, such as documentaries or live broadcasts, directors choose topics or subjects to film. They investigate the topic and may interview relevant participants or experts on camera. Directors also work with cinematographers and other crew members to ensure that the final product matches the overall vision.

Directors work with set designers, costume designers, location scouts, and art directors to build a project's set. During a film's postproduction phase, they work closely with film editors and music supervisors to make sure that the final product comes out the way the producer and director envisioned. Stage directors, unlike television or film directors, who document their product with cameras, make sure that the cast and crew give a consistently strong live performance. For more information, see the profiles on actors, writers and authors, film and video editors and camera operators, dancers and choreographers, and multimedia artists and animators.

Large productions often have various producers who share responsibilities. For example, on a large movie set, an executive producer is in charge of the entire production and a line producer runs the day-to-day operations. A TV show may employ several assistant producers to whom the head or executive producer gives certain duties, such as supervising the costume and makeup teams.

Similarly, large productions usually employ several assistant directors, who help the director with smaller production tasks such as making set changes or notifying the performers when it is their time to go onstage. The specific responsibilities of assistant producers or directors vary with the size and type of production they work on.

Although directors are in charge of the creative aspects of a show, they ultimately answer to producers. Some directors also share producing duties for their own films.

Stage Directors

Stage Directors interpret scripts, direct technicians and conduct rehearsals to create stage presentations.

Motion Picture Directors

Motion Picture Directors read and interpret scripts, conduct rehearsals and direct the activities of cast and technical crews for motion picture films.

Television Directors

Television Directors interpret scripts, conduct rehearsals and direct television programs.

Radio Directors

Radio Directors direct radio rehearsals and broadcasts.

Casting Directors

Casting Directors audition and interview performers for specific parts.

Motion Picture Producers

Motion Picture Producers initiate and manage all the business needs of a motion picture production.

WORK ENVIRONMENT

Transferable Skills and Abilities

Communication Skills
- Describing feelings
- Expressing thoughts and ideas

Interpersonal/Social Skills
- Asserting oneself
- Being sensitive to others
- Cooperating with others
- Working as a member of a team

Organization and Management Skills
- Managing conflict
- Managing time
- Organizing information or materials
- Paying attention to and handling details
- Performing duties which change frequently

Research and Planning Skills
- Creating ideas

Immediate Physical Environment

Most directors and producers work on set during the production of a theatrical project. Set locations vary greatly and may be indoors or outdoors in any weather conditions. Some productions are held in different locations across the country or around the world. Before production begins (during "preproduction") and after a production finishes (during "postproduction"), directors and producers may work from an office or home studio.

Human Environment

Directors and producers constantly interact with other cast and crew members. Their coworkers typically include executive producers, actors, production staff, set designers, costume and makeup personnel, and assistants. Producers regularly work with external vendors, such as caterers, insurance representatives, and establishment owners.

Technological Environment

Directors and producers employ a wide variety of tools and equipment to assist them in the completion of their daily tasks. Directors use video cameras, lighting and sound equipment, two-way radios, cell phones, audiovisual editing equipment and software, and the Internet. Producers use schedules, budgets, contracts, e-mail and the Internet, laptops, cell phones, and other devices.

EDUCATION, TRAINING, AND ADVANCEMENT

High School/Secondary

High school students who wish to become directors or producers should have an inherent interest in the dramatic arts and should foster that interest by pursuing academic study in English literature, theater, public speaking, communications, and cinema. They should also learn as much as they can about management, business, and event planning. Involvement in school groups or extracurricular activities, such as drama clubs, plays, musical productions, dance performances, film clubs, and photography clubs, can provide a solid background in the arts. They should also enroll in a basic acting class to become familiar with the fundamentals of acting, dramatic literature, and theater production.

Suggested High School Subjects
- Accounting
- Arts
- Audio-Visual
- Business
- College Preparatory
- English
- Literature
- Mathematics
- Speech
- Theatre and Drama

Related Career Pathways/Majors

Arts, A/V Technology, and Communications Cluster
- Performing Arts Pathway

Information Technology Cluster
- Interactive Media Pathway

Famous First

Louis Aimé Augustin Le Prince was a French artist and the inventor of an early motion picture camera, and possibly the first person to shoot a moving picture sequence using a single lens camera and a strip of (paper) film. Le Prince's experiments culminated in 1888 in the city of Leeds, England, where he filmed moving-picture sequences of *Roundhay Garden, Leeds Bridge*. Le Prince was never able to perform a planned public demonstration in the U.S. because he mysteriously vanished; he was last known to be boarding a train on 16 September 1890. The reason for his disappearance remains unknown; the most likely explanation remains that he committed suicide, overcome by the shame of heavy debts and the failure of his experiments. (Source: Wikipedia.org)

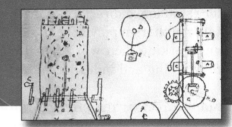

Postsecondary

Although an undergraduate degree is rarely required in order for one to become a director or producer, many people consider it helpful to have received some formal training at the postsecondary level. Many universities and colleges offer bachelor's degree programs in the dramatic arts. Some directors find it beneficial to have studied directing, filmmaking, writing, acting, designing, radio broadcasting, film history, or public speech at the college level. Producers can benefit by taking undergraduate business courses in marketing, public relations, management, and finance.

After obtaining a bachelor's degree, some directors and producers earn a master of fine arts degree (MFA) in directing, producing, acting, or screenwriting. Some conservatories, like the American Film Institute (AFI) in Los Angeles, offer MFA programs that teach students the practical skills needed to start a career in filmmaking. Often, students are required to complete a thesis film as part of their coursework, designed to simulate a large-scale production. Producers and directors must raise money, find talent, and promote their thesis films.

Related College Majors
- Acting and Directing
- Drama/Theater Arts, General

- Film-Video Making/Cinema and Production
- Film/Cinema Studies
- Playwriting and Screenwriting
- Radio and Television Broadcasting

Adult Job Seekers

Prospective directors and producers possess varying levels of experience. Those who attend conservatories often make valuable connections with faculty and other students, which eventually lead to production work. Others become apprentices, interns, or assistants for established directors or producers. Some job seekers begin by taking other employment positions in the entertainment industry and working their way up to director or producer positions through networking and industry contacts.

Many directors and producers are members of professional organizations, such as the Producers Guild of America and the Directors Guild of America, which protect the rights of the producers and provide networking opportunities.

Professional Certification and Licensure

Directors and producers are not required to receive any kind of professional certification or licensure in dramatic production. There is no official training for producers, but many directors train or take classes in directing and cinematography.

Additional Requirements

Directing and producing are highly competitive fields, and few people are able to achieve financial stability through these occupations. Candidates must be able to handle criticism well, demonstrate emotional and physical stamina, and remain incredibly driven to succeed. Being talented is not enough to make one successful in these fields—directors and producers must not give up easily, especially after experiencing rejection. They should be self-promoters who are passionate about their work and use every opportunity to meet potential investors, employers, and talent. Long hours and demanding or difficult employers or work conditions are common in these occupations.

EARNINGS AND ADVANCEMENT

The median annual wage for producers and directors was $71,680 in May 2018. The median wage is the wage at which half the workers in an occupation earned more than that amount and half earned less. The lowest 10 percent earned less than $34,450, and the highest 10 percent earned more than $163,540.

In May 2018, the median annual wages for producers and directors in the top industries in which they worked were as follows:

Advertising, public relations, and related services	$89,330
Motion picture and video industries	$84,770
Radio and television broadcasting	$63,620
Performing arts, spectator sports, and related industries	$59,080

Some producers and directors earn a percentage of ticket sales. A few of the most successful producers and directors have extraordinarily high earnings, but most do not.

Work hours for producers and directors can be long and irregular. Evening, weekend, and holiday work is common. Some work more than 40 hours per week. Many producers and directors do not work a standard workweek, because their schedules may change with each assignment or project.

Fast Fact

Fun film fact: the alien's face in *E.T.* was modeled after a combination of Albert Einstein, Carl Sandburg, and a pug.

Source: quora.com

EMPLOYMENT AND OUTLOOK

Percent change in employment, Projected 2018–28

Total, all occupations: 5%

Entertainers and performers, sports and related workers: 5%

Producers and directors: 5%

Note: All Occupations includes all occupations in the U.S. Economy.
Source: U.S. Bureau of Labor Statistics, Employment Projections program

The largest employers of producers and directors were as follows:

Motion picture and video industries	27%
Radio and television broadcasting	21%
Self-employed workers	19%
Performing arts, spectator sports, and related industries	8%
Advertising, public relations, and related services	5%

Employment of producers and directors is projected to grow 5 percent from 2018 to 2028, about as fast as the average for all occupations. Some job growth in the motion picture and video industry is expected to stem from strong demand from the public for movies and television shows, as well as an increased demand from foreign audiences for U.S.-produced films.

Consumer demand for reality shows on television is likely to increase, so more producers and directors will be needed to create and oversee editing of these programs. In addition, the volume of TV shows is expected to grow as the number of Internet-only platforms, such as streaming services, increases along with the number of shows produced for these platforms. This growth should lead to more work opportunities for producers and directors.

Theater producers and directors who work in small- and medium-sized theaters may see slower job growth because many of those theaters have difficulty finding funding as fewer tickets are sold. Large theaters in big cities, such as New York and Los Angeles, which usually have more stable sources of funding, should provide more opportunities.

Producers and directors face intense competition for jobs because there are more people who want to work in this field than there are jobs available. In film, directors who have experience on film sets should have the best job prospects. Producers who have good business skills will likely have the best prospects.

Related Occupations
- Actor
- Dancer/Choreographer

Related Military Occupations
- Audiovisual and Broadcast Director
- Audiovisual and Broadcast Technician

Conversation With . . . TODD WIDER

Wider Film Projects
New York City
Producer and Director, 18 years

1. What was your individual career path in terms of education/training, entry-level job or other significant opportunity?

I went to Princeton University in New Jersey as an undergraduate, where I took a class with Peter Adams Sitney, a historian of American avant-garde cinema. After college I decided to go to medical school and graduated from the Columbia School of Physicians and Surgeons in New York City. For many years, I was a very busy surgeon in New York City. I fell into film producing in a weird way.

My brother Jedd Wider is a lawyer who wanted my help raising money for an independent film about restorative justice, which repairs the harm caused by crime—often by meetings of victims, offenders and law enforcement.

We got very active in raising money for "Beyond Conviction" and ended up as producers. We eventually got involved in the creative process and decided we actually wanted to do our own films. The producer can help navigate the ship, but the director is the one steering it.

After years of producing, our first big directorial project was *God Knows Where I Am*, a documentary film about a woman named Linda Bishop who starved to death in an empty farmhouse in New Hampshire after being released from a mental health facility. She survived for four months of a harsh winter on apples and water while waiting for God to save her. She kept a diary of her days that showed her insight, intelligence and humor. The film raises some complex questions about the mental health system that ultimately failed Linda. It won numerous awards and was broadcast on PBS and Netflix in 2018.

My brother and I have produced many films and directed three: *God Knows Where I Am*, *To the Edge of the Sky*, and *The Winds of Downhill*.

2. **What are the most important skills and/or qualities for someone in your profession?**

Filmmaking is a team project, not a solo project. A producer needs to be focused, aware and respectful of the people you work for. A director needs to have a vision of what you're trying to do. The director is hired to bring vision to a written script. If you don't believe that actor's performance, it could be the director's fault.

The screenplay for a feature film is a 90 to 100-page document. When writing is used in documentary filmmaking, it generally involves things like writing a narration.

Usually, but not always, people are interviewed in making a documentary, and some of those interviews make it into the final film. The narration for Linda Bishop in *God Knows Where I Am* was based on her diary and interviews with relatives and people who knew her.

There is an art to telling a story in film. There are almost an unlimited number of ways of capturing images when you are shooting something. Choosing which path to pursue involves artistry.

3. **What do you wish you had known going into this profession?**

How important it is to spend time wisely. You need to organize your time and the time of others. You can't just shoot forever.

4. **Are there many job opportunities going into your profession? In what specific areas?**

There are a lot of producing and directing jobs out there. You can work for others and break out on your own, or start out with your own feature films. You could go to film school and learn from inside the business and work your way up.

5. **How do you see your profession changing in the next five years? How will technology impact that change and what skills will be required?**

I think society is turning more toward documentary filmmaking. Journalism schools often offer training in documentary filmmaking, which tends to be heavy on content and light on the art of filmmaking. It's content versus form.

Also, you're going to see the disappearance of actual film. It's being replaced by digital imagery you have immediate access to. It's more difficult to shoot in real film, as we did in *God Knows Where I Am*. You have to understand the interplay of light and dark with film.

6. What do you enjoy most about your job? What do you enjoy least?

It's very liberating creatively. I get to choose the subject of my films. Long before I made *God Knows Where I Am*, I was interested in the plight of homeless people with mental illness.

It's hard to choose what to throw away when you make a film. You become attached to the images. I hired professional and experienced editors to help me get through the decision-making process.

7. Can you suggest a valuable "try this" for students considering a career in your profession?

When you make a film, you need to see the world reduced to the rectangle of your frame, be it a cell phone or a 16-mm camera. Play with your phone and explore the way you see the world. In essence, that's what filmmaking is.

Enlist your friends or classmates to make a short film. You need a team. It is hard to do this alone. Write a five-minute scene and think of how to cast and shoot it. Get a tripod for your video camera or iPhone to keep it steady. You'll learn. You'll look at what you've made and say, "What can I do better?"

Take film history classes in high school or online. Watch lots of movies—and not just the blockbusters. Try watching twenty films that are considered culturally important.

MORE INFORMATION

Actors' Equity Association
165 West 46th Street
New York, NY 10036
212-869-8530
https://www.actorsequity.org/

American Film Institute
2021 North Western Avenue
Los Angeles, CA 90027-1657
323.856.7600
www.afi.com

Association of Independent Commercial Producers
3 West 18th Street, 5th Floor
New York, NY 10011
212.929.3000
www.aicp.com

Directors Guild of America
7920 Sunset Boulevard
Los Angeles, California 90046
310.289.2000
www.dga.org

National Association of Schools of Theatre
11250 Roger Bacon Drive, Suite 21
Reston, VA 20190-5248
703.437.0700
info@arts-accredit.org
nast.arts-accredit.org/index.jsp

Producers Guild of America
8530 Wilshire Boulevard, Suite 400
Beverly Hills, CA 90211
310.358.9020
www.producersguild.org

Briana Nadeau/Editor

Public Relations Specialists

Snapshot

Career Cluster(s): Business, Management, and Administration, Marketing, Sales and Service

Interests: Mass communications, media relations, public opinion, crisis management, marketing, writing

Earnings (2018 Median): $60,000 yearly; $28.85 hourly

Employment and Outlook: As Fast As Average Growth Expected

OVERVIEW

Sphere of Work

Public relations (PR) specialists are communication professionals who handle a wide range of functions to support clients in their efforts to build and maintain a positive public image, seek positive media exposure, and forge strong relationships with the public. Almost any organization or individual can be a client, such as businesses, industries, non-profit organizations, universities, hospitals, government, or celebrities. PR specialists are responsible for media

and community relations, consumer and industry relations, investor and employee relations, and interest-group representation, as well as political campaigns, fundraising, and conflict mediation.

As part of these functions, public relations specialists focus on maintaining contact with print and broadcast media, arranging media interviews, setting up speaker engagements, hosting events, writing speeches and press releases, and planning and conducting press conferences. Public relations specialists communicate key messages that have been strategically crafted. These messages must be approved by the client, be clear and understandable to the audience or market, and should align with short- and long-term client goals.

Profile

Interests: Data, People
Working Conditions: Work Inside
Physical Strength: Light Work
Education Needs: Bachelor's Degree
Licensure/Certification: Required
Physical Abilities Not Required: Not Climb, Not Kneel
Opportunities for Experience: Internship, Apprenticeship, Military Service, Volunteer Work, Part-time Work
Holland Interest Score: EAS

* See Appendix A

Occupation Interest

The public relations field attracts those who enjoy working with people from all industries and environments—who can easily communicate on many levels. Writing is an essential skill for public relations specialists, as is an ability to gauge public opinion, empathize with particular market segments, and assess the public perception of a given message.

Many colleges and universities offer a degree in public relations. Typical coursework includes core classes in English and writing, with specialty coursework in public relations, journalism, news and speech writing, media relations, communications, planning and analysis, crisis management, and public relations ethics.

A Day in the Life—Duties and Responsibilities

Public relations specialists are different from advertisers in that they get their stories covered by media instead of purchasing ad space in publications and on television. Like all communications experts, public relations specialists are consistently on alert for new and creative ways to achieve client goals and to protect, preserve, or enhance the client's image. In a typical day, public relations specialists will write and distribute news releases, prepare copy for annual reports, take and manage calls from journalists, plan press conferences or events, line up media interviews, provide executives with media training and debriefing after interviews, and attend strategy meetings with clients and public relations managers. Within a corporation, "clients" may be divisions or areas inside the company, with the public relations specialist preparing and disseminating various types of information for different departments, all under the banner of one key message.

Public relations specialists often face pressure from eager clients, and work frequently with outside reporters, producers, bloggers, and other social media specialists. In order to avoid the label of a "spin doctor"—a pejorative term often assigned to PR professionals in corporate or government communications—successful PR specialists do well to earn the trust of those in the media by maintaining a professional demeanor and a strict code of ethics. Successful PR specialists communicate a client's message by delivering it to the public in a truthful manner that provides positive exposure for the client and useful information to the customer.

Public relations specialists are employed in nearly every industry in some form or fashion, which makes this a flexible career option. Additionally, because of advances in technology, and through the use of email, videoconferencing, and online social media, public relations specialists can work from almost any location. Self-employment is common among PR specialists; however, most entry-level candidates do not yet have the experience required to branch out on their own.

Public relations specialists, also called *communications specialists* and *media specialists*, handle an organization's communication with the public, including consumers, investors, reporters, and other media specialists. In government, public relations specialists may be called press secretaries. In this setting, workers keep the public informed about the activities of government officials and agencies.

Public relations specialists contact people in the media who might print or broadcast their material. Many radio or television special reports, newspaper stories, and magazine articles start at the desks of public relations specialists. For example, a press release might describe a public issue, such as health, energy, or the environment, and what an organization does concerning that issue.

Press releases are increasingly being sent through the Internet and social media, in addition to publication through traditional media outlets. Public relations specialists are often in charge of monitoring and responding to social media questions and concerns.

Duties and Responsibilities

- Write press releases and prepare information for the media
- Respond to information requests from the media
- Help clients communicate effectively with the public
- Help maintain their organization's corporate image and identity
- Draft speeches and arrange interviews for an organization's top executives
- Evaluate advertising and promotion programs to determine whether they are compatible with their organization's public relations efforts
- Evaluate public opinion of clients through social media

OCCUPATION SPECIALTIES

Lobbyists

Lobbyists contact and confer with members of the legislature and other holders of public office to persuade them to support legislation favorable to their clients' interests.

Fundraising Directors

Fundraising Directors direct and coordinate the solicitation and disbursement of funds for community social-welfare organizations. They establish fund-raising goals according to the financial need of the agency and formulate policies for collecting and safeguarding the contributions.

Funds Development Directors

Funds Development Directors plan, organize and coordinate ongoing and special project funding programs for museums, zoos, public broadcasting stations and similar institutions. They prepare a statement of planned activities and enlist support from members of the institution staff and volunteer organizations.

Sales-Service Promoters

Sales-Service Promoters generate sales and create good will for a firm's products by preparing displays and touring the country. They call on merchants to advise them of ways to increase sales and demonstrate products.

WORK ENVIRONMENT

Immediate Physical Environment

Busy office settings predominate. In an agency environment, public relations specialists cater to the demands of more than one client and can expect a busy atmosphere with many phone calls and tight deadlines. In-office work includes writing and assistance in strategy sessions with clients and the agency itself. Public relations specialists can also work within a company's larger communication department, often as part of a marketing role. The ability to work as a team, providing a comprehensive communication strategy, is essential.

While most public relations specialists usually work in an office setting, it is not necessarily where they spend all their time. They are often on the road, with clients, meeting with journalists, hosting press conferences or events, and helping executives receive media training. Public relations specialists can be seen at trade shows and conventions, auditoriums, and broadcast or print offices, working with executives from all levels and all industries.

Transferable Skills and Abilities

Communication Skills
- Listening attentively
- Speaking effectively
- Writing concisely

Interpersonal/Social Skills
- Asserting oneself
- Cooperating with others
- Working as a member of a team

Organization and Management Skills
- Coordinating tasks
- Making decisions
- Managing people/groups
- Selling ideas or products

Research and Planning Skills
- Creating ideas
- Developing evaluation strategies
- Solving problems

Human Environment

Public relations specialists must have strong interpersonal skills because they are dealing with a wide variety of environments. They work with fast-paced news reporters and bloggers, broadcast producers, freelance writers, engineers, corporate executives, other business specialists, legal counsel, and the general public. At times, this can produce high stress levels and will require the ability to multitask and delegate. Public relations specialists often work in crisis management, and therefore need to maintain calm while thinking and acting quickly.

Technological Environment

Today, public relations specialists use a wide range of technology to achieve client goals. This technology includes everything from phone and email, to texting, tweeting, blogging, and monitoring online news organizations.

EDUCATION, TRAINING, AND ADVANCEMENT

High School/Secondary

It is best for public relations specialists to have a college degree with some experience, such as an internship. High school students can best prepare to be a public relations specialist through Advanced Placement (AP) English courses that include and encourage non-fiction or news editorial writing, creative writing, reading comprehension, public speaking, critical thinking, and decision making. Extracurricular activities, such as working with the school newspaper, can also help high school students gain admission to the universities they want to attend.

Suggested High School Subjects

- Business
- College Preparatory
- Composition
- English
- Graphic Communications
- Humanities
- Journalism
- Keyboarding
- Literature
- Political Science
- Psychology
- Social Studies
- Sociology
- Speech

Related Career Pathways/Majors

Business, Management, and Administration Cluster

- Management Pathway
- Marketing Pathway

Marketing, Sales and Service Cluster

- Marketing Communication and Promotion Pathway

Famous First

The Publicity Bureau, the first PR agency, was founded by former Boston journalists, including Ivy Lee, who is sometimes called the father of PR. In 1906, Lee published a *Declaration of Principles*, which said that PR work should be done in the open, should be accurate, and should cover topics of public interest. Ivy Lee is also credited with developing the modern press release and the "two-way-street" philosophy of both listening to and communicating with the public. In 1906, Lee helped facilitate the Pennsylvania Railroad's first positive media coverage after inviting press to the scene of a railroad accident, despite objections from executives.
(Source: Wikipedia.org)

Postsecondary

A bachelor's degree is highly recommended for success as a public relations specialist. Many universities offer communications programs, often specializing in journalism, which can include subspecialties within actual public relations majors.

Universities often provide internship opportunities, with the aim of the internship turning into an official entry-level job offer. College students are encouraged to make use of existing career centers, to question professors with well-thought out ideas, secure mentors, and seek input about studies and the jobs they can pursue.

Advanced degrees, such as a master's or PhD, are not necessary for public relations specialists; after earning a bachelor's degree, most of these professionals move through the job ranks through on-the-job experience and a successful portfolio.

Related College Majors
- Business and Personal Services Marketing Operations
- Business Administration and Management, General
- Mass Communications
- Public Relations and Organizational Communications

Adult Job Seekers

It is useful to maintain an up-to-date resume with other credentials, such as scholarships, internships, awards, and grants. Being prepared with a portfolio of accomplishments from previous jobs is a good way to demonstrate relevant skills.

Those who do well as public relations specialists are able to articulate the written and spoken word, have confidence, and relate easily to others. They are quick learners and thinkers, calm in the face of pressure, and are persuasive communicators.

Professional associations are often useful sources for those transitioning from another career to public relations, in that they track job openings and provide unique networking opportunities. The Public Relations Society of America (PRSA) and the International Association of Business Communicators (IABC) are two such professional associations.

Professional Certification and Licensure

Accreditations for public relations can be helpful but are not necessary. Employers have varying outlooks on certification. The PRSA has an accreditation program for members who have at least five years of professional experience. The IABC offers opportunities for professionals to be internationally recognized for their achievements through a variety of awards. Work portfolios that include accomplishments such as press clippings, published speeches, or bylined articles are helpful in receiving certification. Professional accreditation can indicate competence in the field which then can help people find jobs in the highly competitive environment of public relations. Consult credible professional associations within your field and follow professional debate as to the relevancy and value of any certification program.

Additional Requirements

Understanding clients' audiences and target markets is essential for aspiring public relations specialists. Public relations specialists must research client background and objectives, understand the business, and "sell" key messages to those people who will benefit from the specific product or service.

Fast Fact

A founding father of modern public relations, Edward Bernays, took Diaghilev's groundbreaking *Ballet Russes* across America in 1915. Among his tactics was pitching stories about costumes, fabric, and fashion design to newspapers' "women's pages."

Source: prmuseum.org.

EARNINGS AND ADVANCEMENT

The median annual wage for public relations specialists was $60,000 in May 2018. The median wage is the wage at which half the workers in an occupation earned more than that amount and half earned less. The lowest 10 percent earned less than $33,690, and the highest 10 percent earned more than $112,310.

Median annual wages, May 2018

Public relations specialistss: $60,000

Media and communication workers: $57,530

Total, all occupations: $38,640

Note: All Occupations includes all occupations in the U.S. Economy.
Source: U.S. Bureau of Labor Statistics, Employment Projections program

In May 2018, the median annual wages for public relations specialists in the top industries in which they worked were as follows:

Government	$64,530
Advertising, public relations, and related services	$63,490
Business, professional, labor, political, and similar organizations	$62,520
Educational services; state, local, and private	$55,790

Most public relations specialists work full-time during regular business hours. Long workdays are common, as is overtime. Public relations specialists may receive paid vacations, holidays, and sick days; life and health insurance; and retirement benefits. These are usually paid by the employer. Some employers may also provide an expense account.

EMPLOYMENT AND OUTLOOK

Public relations specialists held about 270,000 jobs in 2018. The largest employers of public relations specialists were as follows:

Advertising, public relations, and related services	13%
Educational services; state, local, and private	12%
Government	9%
Business, professional, labor, political, and similar organizations	8%

Employment of public relations specialists is projected to grow 6 percent from 2018 to 2028, about as fast as the average for all occupations.

Organizations will continue to emphasize community outreach and customer relations as a way to maintain and enhance their reputation and visibility. Public opinion can change quickly, particularly because both good and bad news spread rapidly through the Internet. Consequently, public relations specialists will be needed to respond to news developments and maintain their organization's reputation.

The use of social media also is expected to create opportunities for public relations specialists as they try to appeal to consumers and the general public in new ways. Public relations specialists will be needed to help their clients use these new types of social media effectively.

Because many college graduates apply for a limited amount of public relations positions each year, candidates can expect strong competition for jobs. Candidates can expect particularly strong competition at advertising firms, organizations with large media exposure, and prestigious public relations firms.

Related Occupations
- Advertising Account Executive
- Advertising Agent
- Copywriter

- Electronic Commerce Specialist
- General Manager and Top Executive
- Online Merchant

Related Military Occupations
- Public Information Officer

Conversation With . . .
ERIC FREEDMAN

Inside Tracker
Cambridge, Massachusetts
Vice President of Sales and Marketing
Marketing, 22 years

1. What was your individual career path in terms of education/training, entry-level job or other significant opportunity?

I majored in economics at Tufts University in Medford, Massachusetts. It was the closest I could get to business at a liberal arts university. I knew I wanted to do something in business, but I didn't want to go into banking or finance. I wanted to do something more creative. Someone said you should check out marketing—it seems like a good mix of left and right brain functions. After going to the college career advisory office, I found out about a reputable national advertising firm called Mullen and started making phone calls. I got an interview with a Tufts alumnus at Mullen and got an internship. I worked my butt off for three months and got a job as an account executive with Mullen after my internship ended. Account executives work with clients on their needs and plans and campaigns. The writing I did was business writing—presentations, proposals and estimates.

It wasn't long before I made the move from advertising to marketing, where I help businesses develop their brands. At Modernista!, I was head of interactive services and developed award-winning campaigns for Stop Handgun Violence, (RED), and Cadillac.

Next I oversaw programs for clients including Boston Beer, Houghton Mifflin, and Fast Company at Mechanica, a next generation branding agency, before becoming a senior vice president at Quantum Designs, a nutrition technology company founded by a Harvard professor. Now I'm vice president of sales and marketing at Inside Tracker, which uses blood tests to develop personalized nutrition plans for customers. Nutrition has been a passion of mine for a while.

I write presentations, proposals, contracts and strategic initiatives. We use copy writers and other writers to create advertising, blogs and social media posts. It's my job to inspire and guide them. It all starts with a good vision and strategic approach. What channel and format will we use to reach consumers? What kind of voice are we using—what kind of grammar? It's a very targeted approach.

2.	**What are the most important skills and/or qualities for people specializing in your profession?**

Resilience is really important. This is a tough business. Having a little bit of a tough shell helps. It's important to be passionate, bold and confident about your ideas, even if they don't work out. You have to be able to put yourself out there a little bit.

Insatiable curiosity is a plus. Let cultural trends help fuel your creativity. Empathy is also important. Get out of your own head and into the customer's shoes.

3.	**What do you wish you had known going into this profession?**

Don't pause and try to be perfect. The momentum is what really matters. Sometimes you've got to just get something to market and into the hands of customers.

4.	**Are there many job opportunities going into your profession? In what specific areas?**

The industry is going through monumental changes right now. It's very dynamic. Technology is changing the behavior of how people buy. Old guard full-service advertising and marketing agencies are being challenged by satellite agencies, freelancers, and in-house services.

Different types of companies and agencies are popping up. They are blossoming.

There's a lot of different channels out there—social media, info posts, podcasts—and they all need content writers. There's an increased need for creators—writers, film makers, and podcasters—in advertising and marketing.

5.	**How do you see your profession changing in the next five years? How will technology impact that change and what skills will be required?**

Technology is changing the behavior of how people buy. We're all drinking from the fountain of digital content these days. Digital and mobile first are everything. We need to be able to create shopping experiences that allow consumers to shop how they want to shop, across multiple screens.

Technology is getting smaller and smaller and more fundamentally integrated. But we're starting to see a pushback, with people getting off social media and going through digital detox. People are starting to get back to real genuine storytelling and content and are using digital media to do that.

6.	**What do you enjoy most about your job? What do you enjoy least?**

I like that it's never dull, ever. It is constantly moving and changing and dynamic and interesting. Right now I miss being closer to the creation. I'm a manager; I'm running a department.

7. Can you suggest a valuable "try this" for students considering a career in your profession?

Take an advertising or marketing course at your high school or online. Study what's going on in the world of advertising and marketing. Read the trade publications. Study the books.

And learn the fundamentals of writing—from grammar to syntax to voice. Writing is a muscle. Practice the craft.

MORE INFORMATION

4A's/American Association of Advertising Agencies
1065 Avenue of the Americas New York,
New York 10018
212.682.2500
OBD@aaaa.org
www.aaaa.org

Public Relations Society of America
20 Wall Street, 21st Fl.
New York, NY 10005-4024
212.460.1400
membership@prsa.org
www.prsa.org

Susan Williams/Editor

Radio and Television Broadcasters

Snapshot

Career Cluster(s): Arts, A/V Technology, and Communications

Interests: Broadcasting, mass communication, journalism, public speaking, writing and reporting

Earnings (2018 Median): $31,990 yearly; $15.38 hourly

Employment and Outlook: Little Or No Growth Expected

OVERVIEW

Sphere of Work

Announcers and newscasters deliver news and commentary on radio and television. Radio announcers and television newscasters are both also traditionally known as broadcasters. In addition to delivering news information to listeners and viewers, broadcasters conduct interviews, moderate discussions, and provide commentary for live sports competitions, musical selections, and developing news events. Several broadcasters also veer into journalism, researching and writing

about topics for discussion on their particular programs. As such, broadcasting has broadened into a multidisciplinary profession encompassing mass communication, journalism, and reportage.

Work Environment

Broadcasters operate primarily out of radio and television studios, where they work in concert with technical and production staff to prepare radio and television programs. It is not uncommon for broadcasters to travel to areas where important news events are unfolding, presenting their programs from a diverse array of locales from show to show. Broadcasters are also often called upon to visit interview subjects and develop stories from a variety of locations in and around their region, the country, or even the globe. In the past, most broadcasters worked nontraditional hours, including early mornings, late nights, weekends, and holidays, but newer technology has enabled more broadcasts to be prerecorded.

Profile

Interests: Data, People
Working Conditions: Work Inside
Physical Strength: Light Work
Education Needs: Bachelor's Degree
Licensure/Certification:
  Recommended
Physical Abilities Not Required: Not
  Climb, Not Handle, Not Kneel
Opportunities for Experience:
  Internship, Apprenticeship, Military
  Service, Volunteer Work, Part-time Work
Holland Interest Score: SEC

* See Appendix A

Occupation Interest

While radio announcers and television newscasters traditionally came from media communications backgrounds, the field is now populated by individuals who come from numerous academic and professional backgrounds, including journalism, politics, science, literature, music, and the arts.

Colleges and universities nationwide offer specific academic programs dedicated to both audio and visual broadcasting, which students often reinforce with course work dedicated to their other academic interests, notably English, politics, or sports management. Excellent time management, judgment, and organization are just as imperative as personality and conversational skills.

A Day in the Life—Duties and Responsibilities

Radio and television broadcasters spend their days planning future shows, filming or recording new broadcasts, and editing new recordings for public broadcast. On air, broadcasters generally introduce and close programs, present information, and lead discussions. Many of the specific occupational duties and responsibilities of radio and television broadcasters depend on the nature and frequency of the program for which they work.

Developing programs that air live on a daily basis predominantly involves preproduction tasks such as fact gathering, organizing specific questions, and preparing for guest interviews. Live television and radio production is often completed in a fast-paced environment under strict deadlines. As a result, radio and television broadcasters who work in live programming often must effectively adapt to evolving situations and on-air conversations.

Documentary-style radio and television programs conduct a large amount of investigative research and information gathering. Documentary programs tend to air on a less frequent basis, usually weekly or monthly; thus, much of the focus for developing such programs is placed on gathering video and audio copy, narrative construction, fact checking, and follow-up interviews with subjects. The protracted nature of documentary radio and television broadcasting necessitates a lot of editing work prior to presentation.

Duties and Responsibilities

- Introducing various types of radio or television programs
- Announcing news, commercials and public service messages
- Interviewing guests
- Describing sports and public events
- Writing scripts and news copy
- Selling commercial time
- Keeping records of programs and preparing program logs
- Reviewing and selecting recordings for air play

OCCUPATION SPECIALTIES

Commentators

Commentators analyze and write commentaries, based upon personal knowledge and experience with the subject matter, for broadcast. They interpret information on a topic and record their commentary or present it live during the broadcast.

Critics

Critics write critical reviews of literary, musical, or artistic works and performances for broadcast and publication. After attending art exhibitions, movie premieres, musical and dramatic performances, and reading books, they analyze and compare factors, such as theme, expression and technique. In the broadcast medium, they present these views in live or recorded form.

Disc Jockeys

Disc Jockeys announce radio programs of musical selections, and choose the selections to be made based upon knowledge of audience preference or requests. They also comment upon the music and other matters of interest to the audience, such as the weather, time, and traffic conditions.

WORK ENVIRONMENT

Immediate Physical Environment

Television and radio broadcasting studios are the broadcaster's primary work environment. These spaces are generally bright, soundproof, and temperature controlled. A considerable amount of fieldwork may also be required. Broadcasters may work in a variety of locations, including government buildings, sports arenas, and hospitals. They may also serve as station representatives at public events.

Transferable Skills and Abilities

Communication Skills
- Speaking effectively
- Writing concisely

Interpersonal/Social Skills
- Asserting oneself
- Being objective
- Cooperating with others
- Working as a member of a team

Organization and Management Skills
- Paying attention to and handling details
- Performing duties which change frequently

Research and Planning Skills
- Creating ideas

Human Environment

Radio and television broadcasters are often the public face of a larger team of technical and production staff with whom they are required to work closely with on a daily basis.

Technological Environment

Radio and television broadcasters use a wide range of communication and broadcasting technology, from microphones and teleprompters to sophisticated editing equipment.

EDUCATION, TRAINING, AND ADVANCEMENT

High School/Secondary

High school students can best prepare for a career in broadcasting with courses in public speaking, composition, the dramatic arts, and computer science. Many high schools have scholastic television and radio stations that instruct students on broadcasting basics. Exposure to local radio and television broadcasting stations through internships or volunteer work may also be highly beneficial. Writing and reporting on local events for a school or community newspaper will provide high school students with reportage and interviewing experience that can benefit a future career in broadcasting.

Suggested High School Subjects
- Applied Communication
- College Preparatory
- Composition
- English
- Foreign Languages
- Journalism
- Literature
- Speech
- Theatre and Drama

Related Career Pathways/Majors

Arts, A/V Technology, and Communications Cluster
- Journalism and Broadcasting Pathway

Famous First

Edward R. Murrow is widely regarded as the most important figure in the early days of U.S. television news. On his weekly news show See It Now on CBS, Murrow presented live reports from journalists on both the east and west coasts of the United States—the first program with live simultaneous transmission from coast to coast. See It Now focused on a number of controversial issues, but its most memorable moment was a 30-minute special on March 9, 1954, entitled "A Report on Senator Joseph McCarthy," which contributed to the eventual political downfall of the senator. (Source: Wikipedia.org)

Postsecondary

Hundreds of colleges and universities in the United States offer undergraduate- and graduate-level programs in broadcasting. The majority of entry-level radio and television broadcasting positions require a bachelor's degree in communication, broadcasting, or journalism.

Undergraduate programs in journalism outline the techniques and strategies that apply to television and radio reporters while honing students' reporting and storytelling skills. Journalism majors also learn the basic ethical standards that dictate news production across all types and levels of media. Undergraduate work in broadcasting exposes students to the vast array of media technologies and software used in the field and helps them learn the acoustics of speech, vocal delivery, and camera presence.

Graduate-level programs in broadcasting are usually completed in conjunction with an internship at a radio or television news studio. In addition to studying advanced topics such as media law, news production, and directing, graduate students also conduct research for a master's thesis dedicated to an area of their particular interest. Individuals with master's degrees often go on to professional careers as radio and television broadcasters, media researchers, or college-level academic instructors.

Related College Majors
- Acting and Directing
- Broadcast Journalism
- Creative Writing
- Drama/Theater Arts, General
- Film/Cinema Studies
- Journalism
- Music History and Literature
- Music, General
- Radio and Television Broadcasting

Adult Job Seekers

The educational and professional experience requirements of broadcasting can make it a difficult field for adult job seekers to enter. Due to the highly competitive job market and low turnover rate of established broadcasters, landing a professional role as a broadcaster can require several years of lower-level experience, during which one is expected to master the production, reporting, and editing aspects of the role. Advancement to higher-level, higher-paying positions often depends on proven ratings, contributions to the station's marketing efforts, and the station's size. Relocation is common.

Professional Certification and Licensure

Professional certification and licensure is not required of broadcast professionals, although membership and affiliation with national organizations and associations can boost credentials and improve networking opportunities.

Additional Requirements

Radio announcers and television newscasters are also often entertainers. Therefore, those interested in the field should be comfortable speaking and engaging with interviewees and audiences, have a sense of humor, work well under pressure, and adapt quickly to changing situations and circumstances.

EARNINGS AND ADVANCEMENT

The median annual wage for public address system and other announcers was $27,720 in May 2018. The median wage is the wage at which half the workers in an occupation earned more than that amount and half earned less. The lowest 10 percent earned less than $18,250, and the highest 10 percent earned more than $63,760.

Median annual wages, May 2018

Media and communication workers: $57,530

Total, all occupations: $38,640

Radio and television announcers: $33,220

Announcers: $31,990

Public address system and other announcers: $27,720

Note: All Occupations includes all occupations in the U.S. Economy.
Source: U.S. Bureau of Labor Statistics, Employment Projections program

The median annual wage for radio and television announcers was $33,220 in May 2018. The lowest 10 percent earned less than $19,120, and the highest 10 percent earned more than $94,450.

In May 2018, the median annual wages for public address system and other announcers in the top industries in which they worked were as follows:

Performing arts, spectator sports, and related industries	$33,700
Food services and drinking places	$24,540

In May 2018, the median annual wages for radio and television announcers in the top industries in which they worked were as follows:

Television broadcasting	$47,020
Educational services; state, local, and private	$43,890
Radio broadcasting	$31,050

In general, announcers working in larger markets earn more than those working in smaller markets.

Many radio and television stations are on air 24 hours a day. Some announcers present early morning shows, and others do late-night programs. Some announcers have to work weekends or on holidays.

The shifts, however, are not as varied today as in the past. More stations are recording shows during the day, eliminating the need to have an announcer work overnight hours.

EMPLOYMENT AND OUTLOOK

Public address system and other announcers held about 10,400 jobs in 2018. The largest employers of public address system and other announcers were as follows:

Performing arts, spectator sports, and related industries	29%
Self-employed workers	28%
Food services and drinking places	25%

Radio and television announcers held about 38,300 jobs in 2018. The largest employers of radio and television announcers were as follows:

Radio broadcasting	53%
Self-employed workers	27%
Television broadcasting	8%
Educational services; state, local, and private	3%

Overall employment of announcers is projected to decline 5 percent from 2018 to 2028. Employment of radio and television announcers is projected to decline 7 percent from 2018 to 2028. Employment of public address system and other announcers is projected to grow 3 percent from 2018 to 2028, slower than the average for all occupations.

Continuing consolidation of radio and television stations will limit the employment growth for radio and television announcers. Many stations have consolidated and centralized their programming functions, including on-air announcing positions. Consolidation among broadcasting companies also may contribute to increasing use of syndicated programming and programs originating outside a station's viewing or listening area. Radio stations can use voice tracking, also called "cyber jockeying," to prerecord their segments rather than air them live. A radio announcer, therefore, can record many segments for use at a later date or even on another radio station in another media market. This technique allows stations to use fewer employees, while still appearing to air live shows, and it can be more cost effective than airing live or local programming. However, it has eliminated most late-night shifts and allowed multiple stations to use material from the same announcer.

In addition, over-the-air radio broadcasts will continue to face competition from an increasing number of online and satellite radio stations. More listeners, particularly younger listeners, are tuning into these stations, which can be personalized and set to play nonstop music based on a listener's preferences. The growing popularity of these online stations may reduce the amount of time audiences spend listening to traditional radio broadcasts, in turn decreasing the demand for radio DJs. However, Internet radio and podcasts may positively influence employment growth. Startup costs for these mediums are relatively lower than the costs for land-based radio. These stations can be used to create niche programming or target a specific demographic or listening audience and provide new opportunities for announcers.

In addition, the growing number of national news and satellite stations may increase the demand for local radio and television programs. Listeners want local programs with news and information that are more relevant to their communities instead of nationalized content. Therefore, to distinguish themselves from other stations or other media formats, stations may add local elements to their broadcasts.

Public address system announcers will continue to be needed to present important information to customers or provide entertainment for special events.

Strong competition is expected for people seeking jobs as a radio or television announcer. Many of the openings will be due to people leaving jobs and the need to replace workers who move out of smaller markets or out of the radio or television fields entirely. Applicants need to be persistent and flexible because many entry-level positions will require moving to a smaller market city. Small radio and television stations are more inclined to hire beginners, but the pay is low.

Those with a formal education in journalism, broadcasting, or mass communications and with hands-on work experience at a radio or television network will have the best job prospects. In addition, because announcers may be responsible for gathering video or audio for their programs or for updating and maintaining the station's website, multimedia and computer skills are beneficial.

Related Occupations
- Actor
- Copywriter
- Journalist
- Professional Athlete
- Writer and Editor

Related Military Occupations
- Broadcast Journalism and Newswriter

Conversation With . . . ADAM POHL

Director of Broadcast and Corporate Partnerships,
Bowie BaySox
Voice of the Mount, Mount St. Mary's basketball
Radio broadcaster, 16 years

1. What was your individual career path in terms of education/training, entry-level job, or other significant opportunity?

I grew up in a musical family, played trumpet, went to the University of North Carolina-Chapel Hill on a scholarship, majored in music and loved it. But, I knew in the back of my mind that music wasn't what I wanted to do for the rest of my life. I had called games when I was a teenager, and that's what I wanted to do.

After junior year, I was a summer intern for the Asheboro Copperheads of the minor league Coastal Plain League. They allowed me to broadcast some of their games. The next year, I interned for UNC's Tarheels Sports Network, and that was a huge help. I did that for two years, which allowed me to get my first job, part-time, with Minor League Baseball's Burlington Royals. I got my first full-time job two seasons later, then went on to Maryland and got a job with the Frederick Keys, another MiLB team. I did PR, sales, and a lot of marketing before I was promoted to assistant general manager. But, the more I did with the Keys, the more I got away from what I wanted to do. I stayed with them seven seasons, then joined the Baysox, also in MiLB, to refocus my career and try to get to a higher level of broadcasting.

During my time in Frederick, I made connections at nearby Mount St. Mary's University. I started doing women's basketball games. Now, I'm the Voice of the Mount, and I do all men's and some women's basketball games. So, I broadcast basketball from mid-November to early March, and baseball from April to September. I'm also the Baysox's business development person, and handle those partnerships.

If you're sitting in your seat at a game, you're not hearing me. But if you're in your car or on the internet, you do. For a minor league baseball team, broadcasting games on the radio is not a big money maker, but it's great marketing.

2. What are the most important skills and/or qualities for someone in your profession?

You have to embrace the fact that you're going to work a lot of hours. This is a 9-to-5 job plus games at night. You must be engaging, able to tell a story, and bring the emotion of the game to those who are listening. It's important to connect with people.

3. What do you wish you had known going into this profession?

That nothing is promised to you. You have to value what you have. When you start, you don't make money. You have to really carve your way and battle for opportunities. I'd love to have that rare, dream job announcing for the Baltimore Orioles, but if, a decade from now, I'm 45 and don't see much forward movement, broadcasting may become a hobby.

4. Are there many job opportunities in your profession? In what specific areas?

You have to network. For all six positions I've had, a connection got my foot in the door. It's unusual to send your demo and get picked over 400 other people.

5. How do you see your profession changing in the next five years, what role will technology play in those changes, and what skills will be required?

Things are moving toward podcasting from AM radio. The ability to make money off what we do is moving from advertising-based to subscriber-based. There will be more content. I'm concerned that there will be fewer outlets to break into the industry but, if you are an established commodity, there will be money to be made.

6. What do you enjoy most about your job? What do you enjoy least about your job?

The thing I love most is the actual calling of the game. That's one fortunate thing about the shelf life of this job, as opposed to being an athlete. I'm going to be able to do this, and do it at a high level, for a long time. I also like working with people in the industry; my colleagues share the same passion and vigor for sports, so being around baseball – and sharing that together – is special.

Because I do baseball and basketball, I'm away from home all the time, including on the road for 120 to 130 games. Broadcasting keeps me away 200 to 220 nights of the year, and that's a lot.

7. Can you suggest a valuable "try this" for students considering a career in your profession?

Work in sports in whatever way you can as soon as you can. Try to create an inroad with a local news or radio station, because that's what it's all about. That doesn't mean getting on the air. Once you're able to get some experience, it's not about how much you get paid. It's all about getting on air. Nobody is good at broadcasting right away. Be your own worst critic. Prepare one or two things to say about a player. You can't be scrolling through looking for a note and leave three seconds of silence. Be ready; be seamless.

MORE INFORMATION

American Women in Radio and Television
8405 Greensboro Drive, Suite 800
McLean, VA 22102
703.506.3290
www.awrt.org

Association for Women in Communications
1717 E. Republic Rd. Ste A
Springfield, MO 65804
417.886.8606
www.womcom.org

Broadcast Education Association
1771 N Street, NW
Washington, DC 20036-2891
888.380.7222
beainfo@beaweb.org
www.beaweb.org

Federal Communications Commission
445 12th Street, NW
Washington, DC 20554
888.225.5322
fccinfo@fcc.gov
www.fcc.gov

National Association of Broadcasters
1771 N Street, NW
Washington, DC 20036
202.429.5300
nab@nab.org
www.nab.org

National Association of Digital Broadcasters
Washington, DC
www.thenadb.org

The Internet & Television Association
25 Massachusetts Avenue, NW, Suite 100
Washington, DC 20001
202.222.2300
webmaster@ncta.com
www.ncta.com

Screen Actors Guild
American Federation of Television & Radio Artists
5757 Wilshire Boulevard, 7th Floor
Los Angeles, CA 90036
955.724.2387
www.sagaftra.org

John Pritchard/Editor

Social Media Specialists

What They Do

Social media specialists communicate with the public through platforms that allow users to create and share content online. They run their employers' social media accounts, working to build a brand's reputation. These workers post content—such as images, text, or videos—to spark interest in a topic that relates to the brand as a whole. For example, they might share photos from a museum's exhibit of music history to make sure that all social platforms are telling stories that people can relate to.

In addition, social media specialists follow conversations

and interact with the public online. These workers sometimes collaborate with others to promote their employer's cause. For example, they might work on a team with marketing consultants to publicize an event.

To track the effectiveness of their communication strategies, social media specialists set goals and then measure success against those goals. For example, Lanae might aim for a social media campaign post to be shared 40 times and then use an online tool to analyze the results.

HOW TO BECOME ONE

To work as a social media specialist, you'll need certain skills, education, and other qualifications.

Skills

At a minimum, you must be familiar with social media platforms. You should also be comfortable using networking tools, such as ones designed to post across several social media accounts.

Equally important is the ability to understand your audience and its interests.If your audience is concerned about an issue that you don't address, for example, you're not being effective.

Creativity and communication skills are also key for presenting familiar content in interesting ways. And you should be able to make judgment calls quickly, particularly when handling sensitive topics.

Education

To become a social media specialist, you typically need a bachelor's degree. You should expect to study subjects such as public relations, communications, and business. A bachelor's degree in journalism and a master's degree in Internet marketing provides a solid foundation for both writing and marketing tasks.

While in school, you may consider pursuing an internship or activities that show your leadership, writing, or social media expertise. Touting those accomplishments may make you more attractive to future employers—especially for your first job after graduating.

Other Preparation

Employers often prefer to hire workers who have worked in social media, public affairs, or a related field. You might learn about social media use on your own, supplementing what you already know with what you read online. Taking classes or earning certifications may boost your credentials even more.

WHAT TO EXPECT

Managing an employer's social media accounts is often more challenging than managing personal accounts. But there's plenty to enjoy about the work.

Day to Day

As a social media specialist, you'll interact with the public in lots of different ways. One minute, you might be fielding criticism; the next, you'll respond to positive feedback. Throughout it all, you must maintain a professional tone and keep your employer's best interests in mind. Constantly monitoring the brand's reputation and keeping up with current events may be all-consuming. That can be both bad and good.

Jobs and Pay

The U.S. Bureau of Labor Statistics (BLS) groups social media specialists with other types of public relations specialists. These workers might go by a various job titles, including digital engagement specialist, social media strategist, and online community manager.

In May 2018, there were 270,000 public relations specialists' jobs working in wage and salary jobs, according to BLS. Their median annual wage was $60,000, higher than the $38,640 median for all workers. These data do not include employment and wages of self-employed workers.

Finding Work

Increased use of social media as a way for businesses to communicate with the public may mean that you'll find ample opportunities for work. But because of social media's popularity, you may encounter competition for those jobs.

Famous First

Born in Chicago, Justin Hall graduated Francis W. Parker High School in 1993. In 1994, while a student at Swarthmore College, Justin started his web-based diary, *Justin's Links from the Underground*, which offered one of the earliest guided tours of the web. Over time, the site came to focus on Hall's life in intimate detail. In December 2004, *New York Times Magazine* referred to him as "the founding father of personal blogging." (Source: Wikipedia.org)

Conversation With . . . LANAE SPRUCE

Social Media Specialist, Smithsonian Institution
Washington, D.C.

1. What do social media specialists do?

As a social media specialist for the Smithsonian Institution's new National Museum of African American History and Culture in Washington, D.C. I use social media to promote the museum's mission and vision. Like others in my field, I link the subject of my work with current events. There's always something going on in real time and we try to enhance the conversation through the perspective of our museum.

Social media specialists communicate with the public through platforms that allow users to create and share content online. They run their employers' social media accounts, working to build a brand's reputation. We post content—such as images, text, or videos—to spark interest in a topic that relates to the brand as a whole. For example, I might share photos from the museum's exhibit of music to make sure all of our social platforms are telling stories about our museum that people can relate to. In addition, social media specialists follow conversations and interact with the public online. You never know what to expect, especially when dealing with online content. A fun hashtag might pop up and, if appropriate, we find ways to respond and share our content.

We sometimes collaborate with others to promote their employer's cause. For example, we might work on a team with marketing consultants to publicize an event.

To track the effectiveness of their communication strategies, social media specialists set goals and then measure success against those goals. For example, I might aim for a social media campaign post to be shared 40 times and then use an online tool to analyze the results.

2. How do you become a social media specialist?

To work as a social media specialist, you'll need certain skills, education, and other qualifications. At a minimum, you must be familiar with social media platforms. You should also be comfortable using networking tools, such as ones designed to post across several social media accounts.

Equally important is the ability to understand your audience and its interests. It goes back to seeing what fans are talking about and knowing your audience and what it expects from you. If your audience is concerned about an issue that you don't address, for example, you're not being effective.

Creativity and communication skills are also key for presenting familiar content in interesting ways. We may have told the story a million times before, but we're always looking for a new angle, a new way to keep people engaged.

And you should be able to make judgment calls quickly, particularly when handling sensitive topics. You have to always be aware of what's going on. If there's a natural disaster, you don't want to be tweeting about what was on TV last night.

To become a social media specialist, you typically need a bachelor's degree. You should expect to study subjects such as public relations, communications, and business. I earned my bachelor's degree in journalism and my master's degree in Internet marketing, which gives me a solid foundation for both the writing and promoting I do in my job.

While in school, you may consider pursuing an internship or activities that show your leadership, writing, or social media expertise. Touting those accomplishments may make you more attractive to future employers—especially for your first job after graduating.

Employers often prefer to hire workers who have worked in social media, public affairs, or a related field. I gained experience after college by working for an online business, using social media to respond to customers.

You might learn about social media use on your own, supplementing what you already know with what you read online. Taking classes or earning certifications may boost your credentials even more.

3. What should you expect as a social media specialist?

Managing an employer's social media accounts is often more challenging than managing personal accounts. But there's plenty to enjoy about the work.

As a social media specialist, you'll interact with the public in lots of different ways. One minute, you might be fielding criticism; the next, you'll respond to positive feedback.

Throughout it all, you must maintain a professional tone and keep your employer's best interests in mind. You have to make sure that whatever you're posting reflects the brand's mission and goals, and you have to have a strategy.

Constantly monitoring the brand's reputation and keeping up with current events may be all-consuming. That can be both bad and good. It can be a challenge for your personal life. But the real-time piece that makes my job hard also makes it fun.

The U.S. Bureau of Labor Statistics (BLS) groups social media specialists with other types of public relations specialists. These workers might go by a various job titles, including digital engagement specialist, social media strategist, and online community manager.

Increased use of social media as a way for businesses to communicate with the public may mean that you'll find ample opportunities for work. But because of social media's popularity, you may encounter competition for those jobs.

I suggest staying up to date on social platforms and trends. Follow some of your favorite brands and watch what they do. As social media evolves and grows, you need to constantly look for ways to be better.

Elka Torpey/Editor

Software Developers

Snapshot

Career Cluster(s): Arts, A/V Technology, and Communications, Information Technology

Interests: Computer Software Technology, Math, Science, Information Technology

Earnings (2018 Median): $105,590; $50.77 hourly

Employment and Outlook: Much Faster Than Average Growth Expected

OVERVIEW

Sphere of Work

Software developers are the creative minds behind computer programs. Some develop the applications that allow people to do specific tasks on a computer or another device. Others develop the underlying systems that run the devices or that control networks. Software designers develop system, utility, and application software, as well as computer games. They also modify existing programs to improve functionality or to meet client needs.

On large-scale projects, software designers typically work with a team of professionals that includes software engineers, software architects, and computer programmers. In these cases, they might be primarily responsible for developing the functional or "front-end" user interface of the program to ensure that it is compatible with a particular platform and related components and that it works reliably and securely. On smaller jobs, software designers might also handle the programming, engineering, and architecture of the program.

Work Environment

Many software designers are self-employed and work at home or in small businesses. Others work for the military, government agencies, or industries such as telecommunications, health care, aerospace, e-commerce, video games, and education. Software designers working for corporations typically work forty-hour weeks, while those who are self-employed may set their own hours. In either case, strict deadlines or unexpected problems may require software designers to work additional hours as needed.

Profile

Interests: Data, People
Working Conditions: Work Inside
Physical Strength: Light Work
Education Needs: Bachelor's Degree
Licensure/Certification:
Recommended
Physical Abilities Not Required: Not Climb, Not Kneel, Not Hear and/or Talk
Opportunities for Experience:
Internship, Apprenticeship, Military Service, Part-time Work
Holland Interest Score: AES, IRE

* See Appendix A

Occupation Interest

People who are attracted to software design careers are analytical and mathematically inclined, with strong problem-solving skills and an aptitude for learning programming languages. They are detail oriented, yet also able to envision the overall design and application of products. Software designers need good communication skills to interact with team members and convey their ideas. Leadership and organizational skills are also important, as is the desire to be knowledgeable about new developments in the industry.

A Day in the Life—Duties and Responsibilities

Most computer programs are born out of a need. Software designers first evaluate that need, usually in consultation with a client, and then conceive of a program to solve the problem. They design computer games, applications for mobile phones, and other highly visible types of software. They also design behind-the-scenes programs known as utilities, which may help users download content from the Internet seamlessly, convert files to different formats, protect computers from malware or keylogging, or free up computer disk space when needed. Some software designers develop programs used in business, education, graphic arts, multimedia, web development, and many other fields, as well as programs intended just for other programmers.

Software developers are in charge of the entire development process for a software program. They may begin by asking how the customer plans to use the software. They must identify the core functionality that users need from software programs. Software developers must also determine user requirements that are unrelated to the functions of the software, such as the level of security and performance needs. They design the program and then write computer code and test it (although this function may be assigned to a computer programmer instead).

If the program does not work as expected or if testers find it too difficult to use, software developers go back to the design process to fix the problems or improve the program. After the program is released to the customer, a developer may perform upgrades and maintenance.

Developers who supervise a software project from the planning stages through implementation sometimes are called information technology (IT) project managers. These workers monitor the project's progress to ensure that it meets deadlines, standards, and cost targets. IT project managers who plan and direct an organization's IT department or IT policies are included in the profile on computer and information systems managers.

The following are examples of types of software developers:

Applications software developers design computer applications, such as word processors and games, for consumers. They may create custom software for a specific customer or commercial software to be sold to the general public. Some applications software developers create complex databases for organizations. They also create programs that people use over the Internet and within a company's intranet.

Systems software developers create the systems that keep computers functioning properly. These could be operating systems for computers that the general public buys or systems built specifically for an organization. Often, systems software developers also build the system's interface, which is what allows users to interact with the computer. Systems software developers create the operating systems that control most of the consumer electronics in use today, including those used by cell phones and cars. Software designers are often responsible for planning a project within budget and time constraints. They must consider compatibility issues, determining the type of platform or multi-platform on which the software will operate and the oldest version on which it will work reliably. They also consider issues such as the maintainability of the software (how often it will need to be updated).

Software designers then devise a schematic of the program that shows its structure, often displayed as a hierarchy consisting of modules. They develop algorithms, which are sets of instructions or steps needed to solve the problems identified by each module. Designers program the code line by line, or supervise other programmers. They test the modules, locate and correct any errors, and then test the program repeatedly until it is secure, user-friendly, and reliable. They might also add graphics and multimedia components or hand that job over to a graphic designer.

Duties and Responsibilities

- Analyze users' needs and then design, test, and develop software to meet those needs
- Recommend software upgrades for customers' existing programs and systems
- Design each piece of an application or system and plan how the pieces will work together
- Create a variety of models and diagrams (such as flowcharts) that show programmers the software code needed for an application
- Ensure that a program continues to function normally through software maintenance and testing
- Document every aspect of an application or system as a reference for future maintenance and upgrades
- Collaborate with other computer specialists to create optimum software

WORK ENVIRONMENT

Immediate Physical Environment

Software designers usually work in comfortable offices or from their homes, although some may also travel to meet with clients. They are at some risk for carpel tunnel syndrome, back problems, and eyestrain due to prolonged use of computers.

Transferable Skills and Abilities

Organization and Management Skills
- Paying attention to and handling details

Communication Skills
- Speaking effectively
- Writing concisely

Interpersonal/Social Skills
- Being able to work independently
- Working as a member of a team

Organization and Management Skills
- Organizing information or materials
- Performing routine work

Research and Planning Skills
- Creating ideas
- Identifying problems
- Solving problems
- Using logical reasoning

Human Environment

Software designers typically report to a project manager and are usually members of a development team, along with programmers, systems architects, quality assurance specialists, and others. The designer might also manage the team or oversee the work done by programmers. A high level of communication and cooperation is usually necessary for success. Many designers, however, work alone and are responsible only to their clients.

Technological Environment

Software designers use a variety of desktop computers, portable computer devices, video game consoles, and related hardware. They use and interface with various operating systems and database management programs. While software designers do not necessarily do programming, they should be familiar with various computer and markup languages, including C++, Java, ColdFusion, and HTML, as well as related compilers and interpreters.

EDUCATION, TRAINING, AND ADVANCEMENT

High School/Secondary

Students should take a strong college-preparatory program that includes English, chemistry, physics, and four years of mathematics, including trigonometry, calculus, and statistics. Computer science or technology, engineering, and electronics courses are also important. Students interested primarily in designing video games or visual-heavy programs should take computer graphics and drawing courses. Other potentially beneficial subjects include psychology, sociology, and business. Participation in technology clubs, science fairs, mathematics competitions, and other related extracurricular activities is encouraged, as is independent study and creation of programs.

Suggested High School Subjects
- Accounting
- Algebra
- Applied Communication
- Applied Math
- Bookkeeping
- Business and Computer Technology
- Business Data Processing
- Calculus
- College Preparatory
- Computer Programming
- Computer Science
- English
- Geometry
- Graphic Communications
- Keyboarding
- Mathematics
- Statistics
- Trigonometry

Related Career Pathways/Majors

Arts, A/V Technology, and Communications Cluster
- Visual Arts Pathway

Information Technology Cluster
- Interactive Media Pathway
- Programming and Software Development Pathway

Famous First

The very first time a stored-program computer held a piece of software in electronic memory and executed it successfully, was 11 a.m., June 21, 1948, at the University of Manchester, on the Manchester Baby computer. It was written by Tom Kilburn and calculated the highest factor of the integer 2^18 = 262,144. Starting with a large trial divisor, it performed division of 262,144 by repeated subtraction then checked if the remainder was zero. If not, it decremented the trial divisor by one and repeated the process. Google released a tribute to the Manchester Baby, celebrating it as the "birth of software." (Source: Wikipedia.org)

Postsecondary

Although some employers consider job applicants with an associate's degree, most prefer to hire workers with a bachelor's degree or higher in computer science, computer engineering, or a related technical field. Prospective software designers must be familiar with different types of computers and operating systems, systems organization and architecture, data structures and algorithms, computation theory, and other related topics. Internships and independent projects are recommended..

Related College Majors
- Computer Engineering
- Computer Engineering Technology
- Computer Maintenance Technology
- Computer Programming
- Computer Science

- Design and Visual Communications
- Educational/Instructional Media Design
- Graphic Design, Commercial Art, and Illustration
- Information Sciences and Systems
- Management Information Systems and Business Data Processing

Adult Job Seekers

Adults with a computer science or programming background who are returning to the field can update their skills and knowledge by taking continuing education courses offered by software vendors or colleges. Some courses are available online. Those with family obligations might want to consider self-employment, although regular full-time employment may offer more financial stability. Professional associations may provide networking opportunities, as well as job openings and connections to potential clients.

Advancement is partially dependent on the size of the company and the scale of projects. In large companies, software designers with leadership skills typically move into project management and higher-ranked positions as experience and education warrant. Experienced designers may also establish their own businesses, while designers with advanced degrees may move into college teaching.

Professional Certification and Licensure

There are no mandatory licenses or certifications needed for these positions, although voluntary certification from the Institute of Electrical and Electronics Engineers (IEEE), the Institute for Certification of Computing Professionals (ICCP), and other professional organizations can be especially advantageous for job hunting and networking. Software designers can be certified as Software Development Associates (CSDA) or Software Development Professionals (CSDP) through IEEE or as Computing Professionals (CCP) and Associate Computing Professionals (ACP) through ICCP. Software designers are encouraged to consult prospective employers and credible professional associations within the field as to the relevancy and value of any voluntary certification program.

Additional Requirements

Software designers must have excellent keyboarding skills. Some designers might need a driver's license to travel between job sites.

EARNINGS AND ADVANCEMENT

The median annual wage for software developers, applications was $103,620 in May 2018. The median wage is the wage at which half the workers in an occupation earned more than that amount and half earned less. The lowest 10 percent earned less than $61,660, and the highest 10 percent earned more than $161,290.

The median annual wage for software developers, systems software was $110,000 in May 2018. The lowest 10 percent earned less than $66,740, and the highest 10 percent earned more than $166,960. In May 2018, the median annual wages for software developers, applications in the top industries in which they worked were as follows:

Software publishers	$114,320
Manufacturing	$110,290
Finance and insurance	$107,960
Management of companies and enterprises	$104,420
Computer systems design and related services	$100,080

In May 2018, the median annual wages for software developers, systems software in the top industries in which they worked were as follows:

Manufacturing	$118,900
Engineering services	$113,250
Finance and insurance	$111,380
Software publishers	$110,920
Computer systems design and related services	$108,790

Software developers may receive paid vacations, holidays, and sick days; life and health insurance; and retirement benefits. These are usually paid by the employer.

EMPLOYMENT AND OUTLOOK

Software developers, applications held about 944,200 jobs in 2018. The largest employers of software developers, applications were as follows:

Computer systems design and related services	34%
Finance and insurance	10%
Software publishers	10%
Manufacturing	7%
Management of companies and enterprises	5%

Software developers, systems software held about 421,300 jobs in 2018. The largest employers of software developers, systems software were as follows:

Computer systems design and related services	31%
Manufacturing	19%
Finance and insurance	6%
Software publishers	5%
Engineering services	4%

Employment of software developers is projected to grow 21 percent from 2018 to 2028, much faster than the average for all occupations. Employment of applications developers is projected to grow 26 percent, and employment of systems developers is projected to grow 10 percent. The main reason for the growth in both applications developers and systems developers is a large increase in the demand for computer software.

Percent change in employment, Projected 2018–28

Software developers, applications: 26%

Software developers: 21%

Computer occupations: 12%

Software developers, systems software: 10%

Total, all occupations: 5%

Note: All Occupations includes all occupations in the U.S. Economy.
Source: U.S. Bureau of Labor Statistics, Employment Projections program

The need for new applications on smart phones and tablets will help increase the demand for applications software developers.

The health and medical insurance and reinsurance carriers industry will need innovative software to manage new healthcare policy enrollments and administer existing policies digitally. As the number of people who use this digital platform increases over time, demand for software developers will grow.

Systems developers are likely to see new opportunities because of an increase in the number of products that use software. For example, more computer systems are being built into consumer electronics and other products, such as cell phones and appliances.

Concerns over threats to computer security could result in more investment in security software to protect computer networks and electronic infrastructure. In addition, an increase in software offered over the Internet should lower costs and allow more customization for businesses, also increasing demand for software developers.

Job prospects will be best for applicants with knowledge of the most up-to-date programming tools and for those who are proficient in one or more programming languages.

Related Occupations
- Commercial Artist
- Computer and Information Systems Manager
- Computer Engineer
- Computer Operator
- Computer Programmer
- Computer Security Specialist
- Computer Support Specialist
- Computer Systems Analyst
- Computer-Control Tool Programmer
- Designer
- Graphic Designer
- Information Technology Project Manager
- Network and Computer Systems Administrator
- Network Systems and Data Communications Analyst
- Web Administrator
- Website Designer

Related Military Occupations
- Computer Programmer
- Computer Systems Specialist
- Graphic Designer and Illustrator

MORE INFORMATION

American Institute of Graphic Arts
222 Broadway
New York, NY 10038
212.807.1990
www.aiga.org

Association for Computing Machinery
1601 Broadway, 10th Floor
New York, NY 10019-7434
212.869.7440
acmhelp@acm.org
www.acm.org

ACM-W scholarships for female students to attend research conferences: http://women.acm.org/participate/scholarship/index.cfm

Graphic Artists Guild
31 West 34th Street, 8th Fl
New York, NY 10001
212.791.3400
pr@gag.org
www.gag.org

Institute for the Certification of Computer Professionals
244 S Randall Road #116
Elgin, IL 60123
800.843.8227
office@iccp.org
www.iccp.org

Institute of Electrical and Electronics Engineers (IEEE) Computer Society
2001 L Street, NW, Suite 700
Washington, DC 20036-4928
202.371.0101
help@computer.org
www.computer.org

A variety of IEEE scholarships, grants, and fellowships: www.computer.org/portal/web/studentactivities/home

Sally Driscoll/Editor

Technical Writers

Snapshot

Career Cluster(s): Arts, A/V Technology, and Communications, Information Technology

Interests: Computer Software Technology, Math, Science, Information Technology

Earnings (2018 Median): $71,850; $34.54 hourly

Employment and Outlook: Faster Than Average Growth Expected

OVERVIEW

What Technical Writers Do

Technical writers, also called technical communicators, prepare instruction manuals, how-to guides, journal articles, and other supporting documents to communicate complex and technical information more easily. They also develop, gather, and disseminate technical information through an organization's communications channels.

Technical writers create paper-based and digital operating instructions, how-to manuals, assembly instructions, and "frequently asked questions" pages to help technical support staff, consumers, and other users within a company or an industry. After a product is released, technical writers also may work with product liability specialists and customer-service managers to improve the end-user experience through product design changes.

Profile

Interests: Data, People, Things
Working Conditions: Work Inside
Physical Strength: Light Work
Education Needs: Bachelor's Degree
Licensure/Certification: Usually Not
  Required
Physical Abilities Not Required: Not
  Climb, Not Handle, Not Kneel
Opportunities for Experience:
  Internship, Apprenticeship

* See Appendix A

Technical writers often work with computer hardware engineers, computer support specialists, and software developers to manage the flow of information among project workgroups during development and testing. Therefore, technical writers must be able to understand and discuss complex information with people of diverse occupational backgrounds.

Technical writers may serve on teams that conduct usability studies to improve product design. Technical writers may research topics through visits to libraries and websites, discussions with technical specialists, and observation.
'

Technical writers are also responsible for managing the consistency of technical content and its use across departments including product development, manufacturing, marketing, and customer relations.

Some technical writers help write grant proposals for research scientists and institutions.

Increasingly, technical information is delivered online and through social media. Technical writers use the interactive technologies of the Web and social media to blend text, graphics, multidimensional images, sound, and video.

Duties and Responsibilities

Technical writers typically do the following:

- Determine the needs of users of technical documentation
- Study product samples and talk with product designers and developers
- Work with technical staff to make products and instructions easier to use
- Write or revise supporting content for products
- Edit material prepared by other writers or staff
- Incorporate animation, graphs, illustrations, or photographs to increase users' understanding of the material
- Select appropriate medium, such as manuals or videos, for message or audience
- Standardize content across platforms and media
- Collect user feedback to update and improve content

WORK ENVIRONMENT

Technical writers held about 55,700 jobs in 2018. The largest employers of technical writers were as follows:

Professional, scientific, and technical services	36%
Manufacturing	15%
Administrative and support services	9%
Publishing industries (except Internet)	8%

Most technical writers work full-time. They routinely work with engineers and other technology experts to manage the flow of information throughout an organization.

Although most technical writers are employed directly by the companies that use their services, some freelance and are paid per assignment. Freelancers are either self-employed or work for a technical consulting firm and are given short-term or recurring assignments, such as writing about a new product.

Technical writing jobs are usually concentrated in locations with a multitude of information technology or scientific and technical research companies, such as ones in California and Texas. Technical writers may be expected to work evenings and weekends to meet deadlines.

HOW TO BECOME A TECHNICAL WRITER

A college degree is usually required for a position as a technical writer. In addition, knowledge of or experience with a technical subject, such as science or engineering, is beneficial.

Education

Employers generally prefer candidates who have a bachelor's degree in English or another communications-related subject. Technical writing jobs may require candidates to have both a degree and knowledge of a technical field, such as engineering, computer science, or medicine.

Work Experience in a Related Occupation

Some technical writers begin their careers as specialists or research assistants in a technical field. They eventually develop technical communication skills and assume primary responsibilities for technical writing. In small firms, entry-level technical writers may work on projects right away; in large companies, beginning technical writers may shadow experienced writers and interact with specialists before being assigned projects.

Training

Many technical writers need short-term on-the-job training to adapt their narrative style to a descriptive style of writing.

Licenses, Certifications, and Registrations

Some associations, including the Society for Technical Communication, offer certification for technical writers. In addition, the American Medical Writers Association offers extensive continuing education programs and certificates in medical writing. These certificates are available to professionals in the medical and scientific communication fields.

Although not mandatory, these credentials demonstrate competence and professionalism, making candidates more attractive to employers. A professional credential also may increase a technical writer's opportunities for advancement.

Famous First

A Treatise on the Astrolabe by Geoffrey Chaucer is thought to be the "oldest work in English written upon an elaborate scientific instrument." The work is written in free flowing contemporary (1391) English, today commonly referred to as middle English. Chaucer explains this departure from use of Latin thus: "This treatis, ..., wol I shewe the ... in Englissh, for Latyn ne canst thou yit but small." Chaucer appeals to Royalty (his wife was a lady-in-waiting to Edward III's queen and sister to John of Gaunt's wife) in an early version of the phrase "the King's English": "And preie God save the King, that is lord of this language ..."
(Source: Wikipedia.org)

ADVANCEMENT

Prospects for advancement generally include working on projects that are more complex and leading or training junior staff.

Important Qualities

Critical-thinking skills. Technical writers must be able to simplify complex, technical information for colleagues and consumers who have nontechnical backgrounds.

Detail oriented. Technical writers create instructions for others to follow. As a result, they must be precise about every step.

Imagination. Technical writers must think about a procedure or product as if they are someone who does not have technical knowledge.

Teamwork. Technical writers must be able to work well with other writers, designers, editors, illustrators, and the technical workers whose procedure or product they are explaining.

Technical skills. Technical writers must be able to understand complex information. Technical writers may benefit from a background in fields such as engineering or science.

Writing skills. Technical communicators must have excellent writing skills to be able to explain technical information clearly.

PAY

The median annual wage for technical writers was $71,850 in May 2018. The median wage is the wage at which half the workers in an occupation earned more than that amount and half earned less. The lowest 10 percent earned less than $43,110, and the highest 10 percent earned more than $114,930.

Median annual wages, May 2018

Technical writers: $71,850

Media and communication workers: $57,530

Total, all occupations: $38,640

Note: All Occupations includes all occupations in the U.S. Economy.
Source: U.S. Bureau of Labor Statistics, Employment Projections program

In May 2018, the median annual wages for technical writers in the top industries in which they worked were as follows:

Manufacturing	$74,190
Publishing industries (except Internet)	$74,020
Professional, scientific, and technical services	$72,900
Administrative and support services	$71,570

Technical writers may be expected to work evenings and weekends to meet deadlines. Most work full-time.

JOB OUTLOOK

Technical writers held about 55,700 jobs in 2018. The largest employers of technical writers were as follows:

Professional, scientific, and technical services	36%
Manufacturing	15%
Administrative and support services	9%
Publishing industries (except Internet)	8%

Employment of technical writers is projected to grow 8 percent from 2018 to 2028, faster than the average for all occupations.

Percent change in employment, Projected 2018–28

Technical writers: 8%

Total, all occupations: 5%

Media and communication workers: 4%

Note: All Occupations includes all occupations in the U.S. Economy.
Source: U.S. Bureau of Labor Statistics, Employment Projections program

The continuing expansion of scientific and technical products and growth in Web-based product support will drive employment demand for technical writers. Growth and change in the high-technology and electronics industries will result in a greater need for those who can write instruction manuals and communicate information clearly to users.

Professional, scientific, and technical services firms are expected to continue to grow rapidly and should be a good source of new jobs even as the occupation finds acceptance in a broader range of industries.

Job opportunities, especially for applicants with technical skills, are expected to be good. The growing reliance on technology and the increasing demand for complex medical and scientific information will create job opportunities for technical writers. However, there will be competition among freelance technical writers.

Conversation With . . .
SHAYLA LOVE

Senior staff writer
VICE
Brooklyn, New York
Science writer, 4 years

1. What was your individual career path in terms of education/training, entry-level job, or other significant opportunity?

I first took a journalism class in high school, and then wrote for my high school newspaper. Our advisor treated us as though we were older than our years, meaning he trusted us to write important stories and put together an extremely sophisticated paper, though we were only 16 or 17. We all felt proud of this responsibility, and I learned to take joy and derive meaning from this work at an early age.

I went on to major in journalism at New York University as an undergraduate and interned at a local paper in the Bronx, the Gothamist website and *Harper's* Magazine.

My next move was to get a Master of Arts in science journalism from Columbia University so I could hone in on science and health. After grad school I swore I wouldn't do anymore internships—I was wrong. I interned at *The Washington Post*, then *Stat*—the health publication of Boston Globe Media. One more year of freelancing after that, I got my first staff job at *VICE*, where I work now.

This all sounds nice laid out after the fact—the truth is that between each internship or school degree I was fraught about what my next step would be. I applied to dozens of jobs or positions I never got and pitched many stories that got rejected. Between my junior and senior years at NYU I took a year off for mental health reasons and worked as a bartender until I got my staff position. I mention this as a reminder that everyone's journey is bumpy and nonlinear—even those with resumes that seem pristine on paper.

2. What are the most important skills and/or qualities for someone in your profession?

As a science writer, I think it's important to accept your own ignorance and be willing to be the dumbest person in the room. This requires a sacrifice of ego, but it's the best way I've found to actually learn new things, and tell stories about complex fields that you have no background experience in. Pairing a willingness to seem stupid with endless curiosity is the recipe for success. Being genuinely interested means that you'll never run out of things to write about as a science writer, and you'll always be able to earnestly engage with those you're interviewing.

3. What do you wish you had known going into this profession?

I constantly have to remind myself that relying only on outside affirmation to feel good about your work leads to heartbreak. The same applies to choosing your topics: Are you writing about something because you think a lot of people will click on that story? You can't reliably predict what your readers will latch onto and what they'll ignore, so the best response is to follow your own authentic interests and feelings, and let your audience be drawn to that authenticity.

4. Are there many job opportunities in your profession? In what specific areas?

I think it's always helpful to specialize. I'm a science writer, and I'm not sure if there are more opportunities for me as a result, but they're easier to find since what I do is so specific. I would say that no matter what your interests are, dive deep into them and become a connoisseur. There's a place in the world for generalists too, but it can be so refreshing to put your trust in the hands of someone who really knows what they're talking about—be that kind of guide.

5. How do you see your profession changing in the next five years? How will technology impact that change, and what skills will be required?

Storytelling is moving beyond just long articles made of words. People get their information in all sorts of ways, from data visualizations to Twitter to TikTok. It's important to be open to how your work can be repurposed or told in other formats. How can your feature article be retold in a series of charts? Or through an Instagram story?

As far as learning new skills, I don't think there's a need to become an expert at every medium. Pick something you can be authentically passionate about—video, podcasts, Twitter—and get help from others to make something new.

6. What do you enjoy most about your job? What do you enjoy least?

I love the reporting process. I love long calls with scientists where we talk about why they do what they do, their burning questions about life, biology, the mind, and how they hope to answer those questions. I love to hear a source say something especially lyrical or profound, get chills, and know what a good quote it will make.

The part of my job I like the least is also probably the most rewarding: the writing. I'm a perfectionist and incredibly hard on myself, so producing a first draft is difficult for me.

7. **Can you suggest a valuable "try this" for students considering a career in your profession?**

Read a neuroscience or other scientific paper and explain to a friend why the findings were so cool. Or a paper about birds, or bacteria, or slime molds— whatever! Published research can be written in complex and dense language, but a big part of our jobs as science writers is to extract the "so what" and make others care. If you can drum up emotions from another person about a scientist's findings, you've done the job correctly!

MORE INFORMATION

American Medical Writers Association
30 West Gude Drive, Suite 525
Rockvill4, MD 20850-4347
240.238.0940
https://www.amwa.org/

National Association of Science Writers
P.O. Box 7905
Berkeley, CA 94707
510.647.9500
webmaster@nasw.org.

Society for Technical Communication
3251 Old Lee Highway, Suite 406
Fairfax, VA 22030
703.522.4114
www.stc.org

Kylie Grimshaw Hughes/Editor

Writers and Editors

Snapshot

Career Cluster(s): Arts, A/V Technology, and Communications, Business, Management, and Administration, Information Technology, Science, Technology, Engineering and Mathematics
Interests: Language and grammar, proofreading, publishing, communication, journalism
Earnings (2018 Median): $62,170 yearly; $29.89 hourly
Employment and Outlook: Little or No Change In Growth Expected

OVERVIEW

Sphere of Work

Writers and editors are employed in all realms of business and industry. In addition to journalism, publishing, and media, employment for writers can be found in government, marketing, law, entertainment, and sales. Writers employed by local, state, or federal governments may craft legislation or produce speeches and press releases for elected representatives. Every industrial sector, be it the automobile industry, healthcare, education, retail, agriculture, or mining, utilizes

writers to communicate with colleagues and clients and develop messaging regarding their productivity and business plan. Freelance writing and editing, or writing and editing under temporary contract, is common. Many freelancers work for online publishers, producing content for clients that adheres to specific guidelines.

Work Environment

Most writers and editors work in an office environment. Writers and editors in the media often work in the field, gathering data and interviewing people for news reports. Many freelance writers and editors work from a home office. Some freelance writers work at rented office spaces.

Profile

Interests: Data, People, Things
Working Conditions: Work Inside
Physical Strength: Light Work
Education Needs: Bachelor's Degree
Licensure/Certification: Usually Not Required
Physical Abilities Not Required: Not Climb, Not Handle, Not Kneel
Opportunities for Experience: Internship, Apprenticeship, Military Service, Volunteer Work, Part-time Work
Holland Interest Score: AES, SEA,

* See Appendix A

Occupation Interest

Writers and editors enjoy working with language and ideas. They enjoy the challenge of communicating complex ideas in a way that is readily digestible to a specific audience. Writers and editors have a penchant for grammar and the intricacies of publishing formats and editorial guidelines. Those who are employed by a specific industry or business sector should have a passion for that area of communication and commerce. For examples, sports writers need to be knowledgeable about a particular sport's rules and regulations, teams, and players. Individuals interested in writing public policy or producing content for the news media should be interested in government, politics, and current events.

A Day in the Life—Duties and Responsibilities

The daily life of a writer is highly dependent upon the field in which they are employed. For example, writers and editors employed in a marketing department may research a particular product line before beginning to write about it for a particular client or consumer market. Speechwriters and those working in the legal or political field will research archival material and conduct interviews with voters and policy makers. Other writing and editing work is more routine. Writers and editors working for publishing companies traditionally follow a product development schedule. Technical writers produce product manuals, assembly instructions, or troubleshooting guidelines. The work of a freelance writer and editor will vary day-to-day depending on the project.

Writers must establish their credibility with editors and readers through clean prose, strong research, and the use of sources and citations. Writers and authors select the material they want to use and then convey the information to readers. With help from editors, they may revise or rewrite sections, searching for the clearest language and phrasing.

Some writers and authors are self-employed or freelancers. They sell their written content to book and magazine publishers; news organizations; advertising agencies; and movie, theater, and television producers. They may be hired to complete specific short-term or recurring assignments, such as writing a newspaper column, contributing to a series of articles in a magazine, or producing an organization's newsletter.

A number of writers produce material that is published only online, such as for digital news organizations or blogs.

The following are examples of types of writers and authors:

Biographers write a thorough account of a person's life. They gather information from interviews and research about the person to accurately describe important life events.

Bloggers write posts to a Web log (blog) that may pertain to any topic or a specific field, such as fashion, news, or sports.

Content writers write about any topic of interest, unlike writers who usually specialize in a given field.

Copywriters prepare advertisements to promote the sale of a good or service. They often work with a client to produce written content, such as an advertising slogan.

Novelists write books of fiction, creating characters and plots that may be imaginary or based on real events.

Playwrights write scripts for theatrical productions. They come up with a concept, write lines for actors to say, produce stage direction for actors to follow, and suggest ideas for theatrical set design.

Screenwriters create scripts for movies and television. They may produce original stories, characters, and dialogue, or adapt a book into a movie or television script.

Speechwriters compose orations for business leaders, politicians, and others who must speak in front of an audience. Because speeches are often delivered live, speechwriters must think about audience reaction and rhetorical effect.

Duties and Responsibilities

- Choose subjects that interests readers
- Write fiction or nonfiction scripts, biographies, and other formats
- Conduct research to get factual information and authentic detail
- Write advertising copy for newspapers, magazines, broadcasts, and the Internet
- Present drafts to editors and clients for feedback
- Work with editors and clients to shape material for publishing

OCCUPATION SPECIALTIES

Critics

Critics write critical reviews of literary, musical, or artistic works or performances for broadcast or publication.

Fiction and Nonfiction Prose Writers

Fiction and Nonfiction Prose Writers write original prose material for publication.

Screen Writers

Screen Writers write scripts for motion pictures or television.

News Writers

News Writers write news items for newspapers, magazine or news broadcasts.

Technical Publications Writers

Technical Publications Writers write about scientific and technical information in clear language.

Publications Editors

Publications Editors plan the contents and budget of publications and supervise their preparation.

Assignment Editors

Assignment Editors work under an executive editor and assign writers to particular subjects.

Newspaper Editors

Newspaper Editors formulate editorial policies and direct the operation of a newspaper.

News Editors

News Editors receive the news copy, photos, and advertising copy, and direct the layout of the newspaper.

Magazine Editors

Magazine Editors work with executives, department heads, and editorial staff to formulate policies, coordinate department activities, establish production schedules, solve publication problems, and make organizational changes.

Greeting Card Editors

Greeting Card Editors select and edit original sentiments that appear in greeting cards.

WORK ENVIRONMENT

Immediate Physical Environment

Freelance or contract writers and editors work primarily from home offices or in designated sections of their homes. Freelance work has no set hours or specified work schedule, and freelancers often work atypical hours and on weekends. Some long-term contracts require that writers or editors work at the company who is hiring them, which would require the writer or editor to work in an office setting during regular business hours for the length of the project they have been hired to complete.

Writers or editors who are hired as full-time employees for a company or organization work in office settings and during standard business hours and days.

Human Environment

Writers and editors interact frequently with clients and colleagues and good communication skills are essential to their work. While many writers and editors work alone, nearly all communicate regularly with colleagues and clients about project-specific guidelines and goals.

Transferable Skills and Abilities

Communication Skills
- Expressing thoughts and ideas
- Speaking effectively
- Writing concisely

Interpersonal/Social Skills
- Being able to work independently
- Cooperating with others
- Working as a member of a team

Organization and Management Skills
- Managing time
- Meeting goals and deadlines
- Paying attention to and handling details

Research and Planning Skills
- Analyzing information

Technical Skills
- Using technology to process information
- Working with data or numbers
- Working with machines, tools or other objects

Technological Environment

Writers and editors utilize a wide range of computer software to produce content. This includes writing and editing platforms such as Microsoft Word. Many publishing companies and media organizations utilize proprietary computer software that is specific to their workflow. The work of a writer and editor requires excellent research skills; both web-based research skills and traditional library-based research skills are important. Many writers and editors also use digital recording equipment for conducting interviews or taking notes.

EDUCATION, TRAINING, AND ADVANCEMENT

High School/Secondary

High school students can best prepare for a career as a writer or editor by completing coursework in English, history, and computer science. Advanced coursework in a field of particular interest can prepare students for writing knowledgably and coherently about that field. Participation in extracurricular activities such as debate clubs, school papers, or school television and radio programs can also help students develop the skills needed for a career in writing and editing.

Suggested High School Subjects
- Applied Communication
- College Preparatory
- Composition
- Computer Science
- English
- Journalism
- Keyboarding
- Literature
- Speech

Related Career Pathways/Majors

Arts, A/V Technology, and Communications Cluster
- Journalism and Broadcasting Pathway
- Performing Arts Pathway

Business, Management, and Administration Cluster
- Marketing Pathway

Information Technology Cluster
- Information Support and Services Pathway
- Interactive Media Pathway

Science, Technology, Engineering and Mathematics Cluster
- Engineering and Technology Pathway
- Science and Mathematics Pathway

Famous First

Amelia Simmons's American Cookery (1796), was the first cookbook of American authorship printed in the United States. The book's full title is *American Cookery, or the art of dressing viands, fish, poultry, and vegetables, and the best modes of making pastes, puffs, pies, tarts, puddings, custards, and preserves, and all kinds of cakes, from the imperial plum to plain cake: Adapted to this country, and all grades of life.* Numerous recipes adapting traditional dishes by substituting native American ingredients, such as corn, squash, and pumpkin, are printed here for the first time. Simmons's "Pumpkin Pudding," baked in a crust, is the basis for the classic American pumpkin pie.
(Source: Wikipedia.org)

Postsecondary

Postsecondary education is often a requirement for vacancies in the writing and editing field. Postsecondary coursework that can contribute to the numerous skills and vast frame of reference required of writers and editors includes education, literature, history, government, international business, economics, politics, and government.

Related College Majors
- Advertising
- Broadcast Journalism
- Business Communications
- Communications, General
- Creative Writing
- Journalism
- Playwriting and Screenwriting

Adult Job Seekers

There are numerous opportunities for adult job seekers interested in writing and editing. Working knowledge or experience in a particular field, such as education, marking, or retail, represent skills that can be transferable to writing and editing work.

Professional Certification and Licensure

Certification or licensure is not required to be employed as an editor or writer. The majority of hiring companies and organizations require that applicants have at least an undergraduate degree with a concentration in either English or another field that pertains to the position needing to be filled.

Additional Requirements

Writers and editors must possess a love of the language and a commitment to quality writing. Writers and editors often work alone or from their homes, so individuals who want to explore this line of work should be comfortable in solitary settings.

EARNINGS AND ADVANCEMENT

The median annual wage for writers and authors was $62,170 in May 2018. The median wage is the wage at which half the workers in an occupation earned more than that amount and half earned less. The lowest 10 percent earned less than $31,700, and the highest 10 percent earned more than $121,670.

In May 2018, the median annual wages for writers and authors in the top industries in which they worked were as follows:

Performing arts, spectator sports, and related industries	$69,430
Religious, grantmaking, civic, professional, and similar organizations	$68,430
Professional, scientific, and technical services	$62,330
Information	$59,580

Some writers and authors work part-time. Most keep regular office hours, either to stay in contact with sources and editors or to set up a writing routine, but many set their own hours. Others may need to work evenings and weekends to produce something acceptable for an editor or client. Self-employed or freelance writers and authors may face the pressures of juggling multiple projects or continually looking for new work.

EMPLOYMENT AND OUTLOOK

Writers and authors held about 123,200 jobs in 2018. The largest employers of writers and authors were as follows::

Self-employed workers	61%
Professional, scientific, and technical services	11%
Information	11%
Performing arts, spectator sports, and related industries	3%
Religious, grantmaking, civic, professional, and similar organizations	3%

Employment of writers and authors is projected to show little or no change from 2018 to 2028.

Percent change in employment, Projected 2018–28

Total, all occupations: 5%

Media and communication workers: 4%

Writers and authors: 0%

Note: All Occupations includes all occupations in the U.S. Economy.
Source: U.S. Bureau of Labor Statistics, Employment Projections program

Online publications and services are growing in number and sophistication, spurring demand for writers and authors with Web and multimedia experience. However, employment of writers and authors in the newspaper and book and periodical publication industries is projected to decline.

Some experienced writers should find work in the public relations departments of corporations and nonprofit organizations. Self-employed or freelance writers and authors may find work with newspaper, magazine, or journal publishers, and some will write books.

Strong competition is expected for most job openings, given that many people are attracted to this occupation. Competition for jobs with newspapers and magazines will be particularly strong because employment in the publishing industry is projected to decline.

Writers and authors who have adapted to online and social media, and who are comfortable writing for and working with a variety of electronic and digital tools, should have an advantage in finding work. The declining costs of self-publishing and the popularity of electronic books will allow many freelance writers to have their work published.

Related Occupations
- Actor
- Copywriter
- Electronic Commerce Specialist
- Journalist
- Online Merchant
- Radio/TV Announcer and Newscaster
- Technical Writer

Related Military Occupations
- Public Information Officer

Conversation With . . .
JON FRANKLIN

Professor Emeritus

University of Maryland

Writer and Writing Professor, 70 years

1. What was your individual career path in terms of education/training, entry-level job, or other significant opportunity?

I moved around from little town to little town in the middle of the country in the 50s, moving from school to school with no continuity at all. I got into literature. If you're a young kid, you can put your world into some kind of order through literature. The ability to write is one of the most powerful abilities in the world. I started writing at probably age 7. My father wrote. So did my mother, and she painted. We didn't have many books. Science also was central to me; I paid attention to science. It's exciting and you don't have to endanger yourself.

I dropped out of high school at 16, got married at 17, and joined the U.S. Navy, where I spent eight years. I very quickly decided I wanted to do journalism and went on to become a staff writer for *All Hands* magazine, the Navy's premiere publication. I also got a GED.

I had always wanted to go to college and did so on the Cold War GI Bill. I worked for a local newspaper while going to the University of Maryland's journalism school. It was the middle of the war. I was a vet. I had a friend from the Navy who was working for the *Baltimore Evening Sun* and got a call one day. Riots had broken out on campus over the invasion of Cambodia, and protestors crashed the administration building. I was able to get into the building and walk through and report on what was going on. I wrote my first story for them, which was a front-page story. Any artist has to do something to get noticed.

After that story and a couple more, the editor called and basically asked me if I'd go to work for him. I went on to write features, because it was the closest thing to literature. Making a choice about my specialty and being in Baltimore where Johns Hopkins University and Hospital are located, I got into brain science and wrote about people with brain surgery. I was in on the ground floor and chased that story for 12 to 15 years. I had an incredible amount of fun. Both of my stories that won Pulitzer Prizes were part of a series on the brain. The first was the first-ever Pulitzer for feature writing and the second was the first-ever for explanatory journalism.

My second Pulitzer came six years after the first, about what might happen—and, as it turns out, now has happened—creating a revolution in psychiatry. I had been applying to teach at the University of Maryland and when I got the second Pulitzer; it was apparently equal to a PhD. They hired me.

I would have loved to have gotten a PhD but I couldn't have afforded it and my life was going 180 miles per hour. I have two honorary doctorates. I taught courses on science writing and writing complex stories at Maryland for three years, left, and went to direct the Creative Writing Program at the University of Oregon for three years. I then moved on to the *Raleigh News & Observer*, where I was writing coach and narrative writer, and returned to Maryland in 2001 as its first Merrill Chair of Journalism. I retired nine years later.

I've published six books. I write poetry in secret. I'm working on a fiction book, and I'm working on another writing book to follow *Writing for Story*, which I published in 1986. It was a radical departure from what had come before it for 30 years. Journalists had forgotten how to tell stories, and my book is about telling stories.

2. **What are the most important skills and/or qualities for someone in your profession?**

Number one is my ability to understand the material I'm working with and number two is being able to write that material in a way that is understanding and appealing. Number three is to make a living.

You need a really strong desire to know what's going on. Persistence is necessary, very necessary. Moral courage. Knowledge of the language in the beginning is sort of necessary. Write something original. I wrote about ecology when no one else did.

3. **What do you wish you had known going into this profession?**

I didn't know history, and it caused me no end of trouble.

4. **Are there many job opportunities in your profession? In what areas?**

To be perfectly honest, I'm not sure how to answer that question. There are a zillion jobs. There are very few jobs that are worth having, though, and they're very hard to get. That's where literature is right now. The thing to expect is change. How many jobs there are varies dramatically every, say, five years. This is true for all media.

There are a lot of things you can do in the media and there is a lot of need for writers. The danger is how competitive it is. It's a long march. Poets do well in their teens, 20s, and early 30s. Not so for writers, and that's because the language is so complicated, and what you expect it to do is understand a society that doesn't understand itself and doesn't necessarily appreciate that. Knowing how to do the writing and understanding the "politics" of doing so is like being in a small boat trying to go upstream in a whitewater situation.

5. **How do you see your profession changing in the next five years? How will technology impact that change, and what skills will be required?**

   Things are moving fast. It's difficult to predict what will happen but based on what I have seen, things are going to get better. Because of Amazon, I no longer need to have a publisher who takes a large percent of the money. That's going to revolutionize everything. Short stories are going to come back; they died because they were unfriendly to the printing industry.

6. **hat do you enjoy most about your job? What do you enjoy least about your job?**

   I most enjoy getting in places other people can't go. For instance, I was on Mount St. Helen's in 1980, about ten days before it went off. It was really something to see. I least enjoy the paperwork.

7. **Can you suggest a valuable "try this" for students considering a career in your profession?**

   If you're trying to decide, volunteer at a local newspaper. It could be a weekly. And if I could say one thing to young people it would be: pick your teachers, not your subjects.

MORE INFORMATION

Accrediting Council on Education in Journalism and Mass Communications (ACEJMC)
201 Bishop Hall, P.O. Box 1848
University, MS 38677-1848
662.915.5550
pthomps1@olemiss.edu
https://www.acejmc.org/

American Society of Journalists and Authors
355 Lexington Avenue, 15th Floor
New York, NY 10017-6603
212.997.0947
www.asja.org

American Society of Magazine Editors
28-07 Jackson Ave.
New York, NY 11101
212.872.3737
asme@magazine.org
www.magazine.org/editorial/asme

Association for Women in Communications
1717 E. Republic Rd. Ste A
Springfield, MO 65804
703.370.7436
www.womcom.org

Dow Jones Newspaper Fund, Inc.
P.O. Box 300
Princeton, NJ 08543-0300
609.452.2820
djnf@dowjones.com
www.newsfund.org

Editorial Freelancers Association
266 West 37th Street, 20th Floor
New York, NY 10018
212.920.4816
www.the-efa.org

International Association of Business Communicators
649 Mission Street 5th Floor
San Francisco, CA 94105
415.544.4700
service_centre@iabc.com
www.iabc.com

National Association of Science Writers
P.O. Box 7905
Berkeley, CA 94707
510.647.9500
webmaster@nasw.org.

National Newspaper Association
101 S. Palafox, Unit 13323
Pensacola, FL 32591
850.542.7087
www.nnaweb.org

News Media Alliance
4401 N. Fairfax Dr., Suite 300
Arlington, VA 22203-1867
571.366.1000
info@newsmediaalliance.org
https://www.newsmediaalliance.org/

Newspaper Guild-CWA
501 Third Street NW, 6th Floor
Washington, DC 20001-2797
202.434.7177
guild@cwa-union.org
www.newsguild.org

**Society for Technical
Communication**
3251 Old Lee Highway, Suite 406
Fairfax, VA 22030
703.522.4114
www.stc.org

**Society of Professional Journalists
Eugene S. Pulliam National
Journalism Center**
3909 N. Meridian Street
Indianapolis, IN 46208
317.927.8000
www.spj.org

Price Grisham/Editor

What Are Your Career Interests?

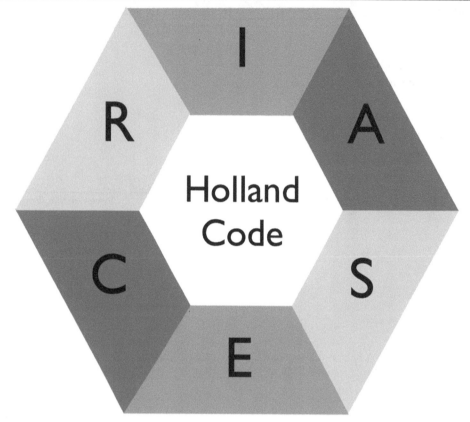

This is based on Dr. John Holland's theory that people and work environments can be loosely classified into six different groups. Each of the letters above corresponds to one of the six groups described in the following pages.

Different people's personalities may find different environments more to their liking. While you may have some interests in and similarities to several of the six groups, you may be attracted primarily to two or three of the areas. These two or three letters are your "Holland Code." For example, with a code of "RES" you would most resemble the Realistic type, somewhat less resemble the Enterprising type, and resemble the Social type even less. The types that are not in your code are the types you resemble least of all.

Most people, and most jobs, are best represented by some combination of two or three of the Holland interest areas. In addition, most people are most satisfied if there is some degree of fit between their personality and their work environment.

The rest of the pages in this booklet further explain each type and provide some examples of career possibilities, areas of study at MU, and co-curricular activities for each code. To take a more in-depth look at your Holland Code, take a self-assessment such as the SDS, Discover, or a card sort at the MU Career Center with a Career Specialist.

Realistic *(Doers)*

People who have athletic ability, prefer to work with objects, machines, tools, plants or animals, or to be outdoors.

Are you?		**Can you?**	**Like to?**
practical	independent	fix electrical things	tinker with machines/vehicles
straightforward/frank	ambitious	solve electrical problems	work outdoors
mechanically inclined	systematic	pitch a tent	be physically active
stable		play a sport	use your hands
concrete		read a blueprint	build things
reserved		plant a garden	tend/train animals
self-controlled		operate tools and machine	work on electronic equipment

Career Possibilities
(Holland Code):

Air Traffic Controller (SER)	Dental Technician (REI)	Laboratory Technician (RIE)	Property Manager (ESR)
Archaeologist (IRE)	Farm Manager (ESR)	Landscape Architect (AIR)	Recreation Manager (SER)
Athletic Trainer (SRE)	Fish and Game Warden (RES)	Mechanical Engineer (RIS)	Service Manager (ERS)
Cartographer (IRE)	Floral Designer (RAE)	Optician (REI)	Software Technician (RCI)
Commercial Airline Pilot (RIE)	Forester (RIS)	Petroleum Geologist (RIE)	Ultrasound Technologist (RSI)
Commercial Drafter (IRE)	Geodetic Surveyor (IRE)	Police Officer (SER)	Vocational Rehabilitation
Corrections Officer (SER)	Industrial Arts Teacher (IER)	Practical Nurse (SER)	Consultant (ESR)

Investigative *(Thinkers)*

People who like to observe, learn, investigate, analyze, evaluate, or solve problems.

Are you?		**Can you?**	**Like to?**
inquisitive	intellectually self-confident	think abstractly	explore a variety of ideas
analytical	Independent	solve math problems	work independently
scientific	logical	understand scientific theories	perform lab experiments
observant/precise	complex	do complex calculations	deal with abstractions
scholarly	Curious	use a microscope or computer	do research
cautious		interpret formulas	be challenged

Career Possibilities
(Holland Code):

Actuary (ISE)	Chemical Engineer (IRE)	Geologist (IRE)	Physician, General Practice (ISE)
Agronomist (IRS)	Chemist (IRE)	Horticulturist (IRS)	Psychologist (IES)
Anesthesiologist (IRS)	Computer Systems Analyst (IER)	Mathematician (IER)	Research Analyst (IRC)
Anthropologist (IRE)	Dentist (ISR)	Medical Technologist (ISA)	Statistician (IRE)
Archaeologist (IRE)	Ecologist (IRE)	Meteorologist (IRS)	Surgeon (IRA)
Biochemist (IRS)	Economist (IAS)	Nurse Practitioner (ISA)	Technical Writer (IRS)
Biologist (ISR)	Electrical Engineer (IRE)	Pharmacist (IES)	Veterinarian (IRS)

Artistic *(Creators)*

People who have artistic, innovating, or intuitional abilities and like to work in unstructured situations using their imagination and creativity.

Are you?
creative
imaginative
innovative
unconventional
emotional
independent
Expressive

original
introspective
impulsive
sensitive
courageous
complicated
idealistic
nonconforming

Can you?
sketch, draw, paint
play a musical instrument
write stories, poetry, music
sing, act, dance
design fashions or interiors

Like to?
attend concerts, theatre, art
   exhibits
read fiction, plays, and poetry
work on crafts
take photography
express yourself creatively
deal with ambiguous ideas

**Career Possibilities
(Holland Code):**

Actor (AES)
Advertising Art Director (AES)
Advertising Manager (ASE)
Architect (AIR)
Art Teacher (ASE)
Artist (ASI)

Copy Writer (ASI)
Dance Instructor (AER)
Drama Coach (ASE)
English Teacher (ASE)
Entertainer/Performer (AES)
Fashion Illustrator (ASR)

Interior Designer (AES)
Intelligence Research Specialist
   (AEI)
Journalist/Reporter (ASE)
Landscape Architect (AIR)
Librarian (SAI)

Medical Illustrator (AIE)
Museum Curator (AES)
Music Teacher (ASI)
Photographer (AES)
Writer (ASI)
Graphic Designer (AES)

Social *(Helpers)*

People who like to work with people to enlighten, inform, help, train, or cure them, or are skilled with words.

Are you?
friendly
helpful
idealistic
insightful
outgoing
understanding

cooperative
generous
responsible
forgiving
patient
kind

Can you?
teach/train others
express yourself clearly
lead a group discussion
mediate disputes
plan and supervise an activity
cooperate well with others

Like to?
work in groups
help people with problems
do volunteer work
work with young people
serve others

**Career Possibilities
(Holland Code):**

City Manager (SEC)
Clinical Dietitian (SIE)
College/University Faculty (SEI)
Community Org. Director
   (SEA)
Consumer Affairs Director
   (SER)Counselor/Therapist
   (SAE)

Historian (SEI)
Hospital Administrator (SER)
Psychologist (SEI)
Insurance Claims Examiner
   (SIE)
Librarian (SAI)
Medical Assistant (SCR)
Minister/Priest/Rabbi (SAI)
Paralegal (SCE)

Park Naturalist (SEI)
Physical Therapist (SIE)
Police Officer (SER)
Probation and Parole Officer
   (SEC)
Real Estate Appraiser (SCE)
Recreation Director (SER)
Registered Nurse (SIA)

Teacher (SAE)
Social Worker (SEA)
Speech Pathologist (SAI)
Vocational-Rehab. Counselor
   (SEC)
Volunteer Services Director
   (SEC)

<u>E</u>nterprising *(Persuaders)*

People who like to work with people, influencing, persuading, leading or managing for organizational goals or economic gain.

Are you?
self-confident
assertive
persuasive
energetic
adventurous
popular

ambitious
agreeable
talkative
extroverted
spontaneous
optimistic

Can you?
initiate projects
convince people to do things
  your way
sell things
give talks or speeches
organize activities
lead a group
persuade others

Like to?
make decisions
be elected to office
start your own business
campaign politically
meet important people
have power or status

Career Possibilities
(Holland Code):

Advertising Executive (ESA)
Advertising Sales Rep (ESR)
Banker/Financial Planner (ESR)
Branch Manager (ESA)
Business Manager (ESC)
Buyer (ESA)
Chamber of Commerce Exec
  (ESA)

Credit Analyst (EAS)
Customer Service Manager
  (ESA)
Education & Training Manager
  (EIS)
Emergency Medical Technician
  (ESI)
Entrepreneur (ESA)

Foreign Service Officer (ESA)
Funeral Director (ESR)
Insurance Manager (ESC)
Interpreter (ESA)
Lawyer/Attorney (ESA)
Lobbyist (ESA)
Office Manager (ESR)
Personnel Recruiter (ESR)

Politician (ESA)
Public Relations Rep (EAS)
Retail Store Manager (ESR)
Sales Manager (ESA)
Sales Representative (ERS)
Social Service Director (ESA)
Stockbroker (ESI)
Tax Accountant (ECS)

<u>C</u>onventional *(Organizers)*

People who like to work with data, have clerical or numerical ability, carry out tasks in detail, or follow through on others' instructions.

Are you?
well-organized
accurate
numerically inclined
methodical
conscientious
efficient
conforming

practical
thrifty
systematic
structured
polite
ambitious
obedient
persistent

Can you?
work well within a system
do a lot of paper work in a short
  time
keep accurate records
use a computer terminal
write effective business letters

Like to?
follow clearly defined
  procedures
use data processing equipment
work with numbers
type or take shorthand
be responsible for details
collect or organize things

Career Possibilities
(Holland Code):

Abstractor (CSI)
Accountant (CSE)
Administrative Assistant (ESC)
Budget Analyst (CER)
Business Manager (ESC)
Business Programmer (CRI)
Business Teacher (CSE)
Catalog Librarian (CSE)

Claims Adjuster (SEC)
Computer Operator (CSR)
Congressional-District Aide (CES)
Cost Accountant (CES)
Court Reporter (CSE)
Credit Manager (ESC)
Customs Inspector (CEI)
Editorial Assistant (CSI)

Elementary School Teacher
  (SEC)
Financial Analyst (CSI)
Insurance Manager (ESC)
Insurance Underwriter (CSE)
Internal Auditor (ICR)
Kindergarten Teacher (ESC)

Medical Records Technician
  (CSE)
Museum Registrar (CSE)
Paralegal (SCE)
Safety Inspector (RCS)
Tax Accountant (ECS)
Tax Consultant (CES)
Travel Agent (ECS)

GENERAL BIBLIOGRAPHY

Alexander, Edward P, Mary Alexander, and Juilee Decker. *Museums in Motion: An Introduction to the History and Functions of Museums*. Rowman & Littlefield, 2017. Print.

American Library Directory, 2016-2017. Medford, NJ: Information Today, 2016. Print.

Anderson, Wayne, and Marilyn Headrick. *The Legal Profession: Is It for You?* Cincinnati: Thomson Executive Press, 1996.

Appleton, Dina, and Daniel Yankelevits. *Hollywood Dealmaking: Negotiating Talent Agreements for Film, TV, and New Media*. New York: Allworth Press, 2010.

Aspray, William, and Paul E. Ceruzzi, eds. *The Internet and American Business*. Cambridge, Mass.: MIT Press, 2008.

Balio, Tino. *Grand Design: Hollywood as a Modern Business Enterprise, 1930-1939*. Berkeley: University of California Press, 2007.

Battles, Matthew. *Library: An Unquiet History*. New York: W. W. Norton, 2004.

Bay, Jason W. *Start Your Video Game Career: Proven Advice on Jobs, Education, Interviews, and More for Starting and Succeeding in the Video Game Industry*. , 2017. Print.

Beeching, Angela M. *Beyond Talent: Creating a Successful Career in Music*. New York: Oxford University Press, 2020.

Belson, Ken. "Universities Cutting Teams as They Trim Their Budgets." *The New York Times*, May 3, 2009.

Bielby, Denise D., and C. Lee Harrington. *Global TV: Exporting Television and Culture in the World Market*. New York: New York University Press, 2008.

Bogart, Dave, ed. *Library and Book Trade Almanac, 2015*. 60th ed. Medford, N.J.: Information Today, 2015.

Borg, Bobby. *The Musician's Handbook: A Practical Guide to Understanding the Music Business*. New York: Watson-Guptill Publications, 2008.

Boris, Elizabeth T., et al. *What Drives Foundation Expenses and Compensation: Results of a Three-Year Study*. New York: Urban Institute, Foundation Center, and Philanthropic Research, 2008.

Bountouri, Lina. *Archives in the Digital Age: Standards, Policies and Tools*. Oxford: Chandos Publishing, 2017. Print.

Bridges, David, et al., eds. *Higher Education and National Development: Universities and Societies in Transition*. New York: Routledge, 2012.

Buller, Jeffrey. *The Essential College Professor: A Practical Guide to an Academic Career*. New York: John Wiley & Sons, 2010.

Burdick, Jan E. *Creative Careers in Museums*. New York: Allworth Press, 2008.

Burns, Alfred. *The Power of the Written Word: The Role of Literacy in the History of Western Civilization*. New York: Lang, 1989.

Camenson, Blythe. *Opportunities in Museum Careers*. New York: McGraw-Hill, 2007.

Campbell-Kelly, Martin, and William Aspray. *Computer: A History of the Information Machine*. 2d ed. Boulder, Colo.: Westview Press, 2004.

Cappo, Joe. *The Future of Advertising: New Media, New Clients, New Consumers in the Post-television Age*. New York: Crain Communications, 2005.

Carson, Nancy. *Raising a Star: The Parent's Guide to Helping Kids Break into Theater, Film, Television, or Music*. New York: St. Martin's Press, 2005.

Center for the Future of Museums. *Museums and Society, 2034: Trends and Potential Futures*. Washington, D.C.: American Association of Museums, 2008.

Chaplin, Heather, and Aaron Ruby. *Smartbomb: The Quest for Art, Entertainment, and Big Bucks in the Videogame Revolution*. Chapel Hill, N.C.: Algonquin Books of Chapel Hill, 2005.

Chen, Sheying, ed. *Academic Administration: A Quest for Better Management and Leadership in Higher Education*. Hauppauge, N.Y.: Nova Science, 2009.

Cohen, Arthur M., and Carrie B. Kisker. *The Shaping of American Higher Education: Emergence and Growth of the Contemporary System*. 2d ed. New York: John Wiley & Sons, 2010.

"Computer and Video Game Designers." *Encyclopedia of Careers and Vocational Guidance*. 17th ed. Vol. 2. New York: Ferguson, 2008.

Computer History Museum. "Internet History." http://www.computerhistory.org/internet_history.

Cosper, Alex. "History of Record Labels and the Music Industry." Playlist Research, 2009. http://www.playlistresearch.com/recordindustry.htm.

Cox, Richard J. *Archives and Archivists in the Information Age*. New York: Neal-Schuman, 2005.

Dewitz, Peter, and Michael F. Graves. *Teaching Reading in the 21st Century: Motivating All Learners*. Hoboken, NH: Pearson, 2020. Print.

Duesterhaus, Alan P. "College Board of Trustees and University-Structure and Composition, Governance, Authority, Responsibilities, Board Committees." Education Encyclopedia-StateUniversity.com.

Eberhart, George M. *The Whole Library Handbook 4*. Chicago: American Library Association, 2009.

Echaore-McDavid, Susan. *Career Opportunities in Law and the Legal Industry*. New York: Checkmark Books, 2007.

Edery, David, and Ethan Mollick. *Changing the Game: How Video Games Are Transforming the Future of Business*. Upper Saddle River, N.J.: FT Press, 2009.

Feuer, Alan. "A Study in How Major Law Firms Are Shrinking." *The New York Times*, June 5, 2009.

Finney, Angus. *The International Film Business: A Market Guide Beyond Hollywood*. New York: Routledge, 2015.

Furi-Perry, Ursula. *Fifty Unique Legal Paths: How to Find the Right Job*. Chicago: American Bar Association, 2008.

Gaquin, Deirdre. *Artists in the Workforce: 1990-2005*. Washington, D.C.: National Endowment for the Arts, 2008.

Gassler, Robert Scott. *The Economics of Nonprofit Enterprise: A Study in Applied Economic Theory*. Lanham, Md.: University Press of America, 1986.

Glenn, Lawrence M., and F. Martin Nikirk. "How Career and Technical Education Can Jumpstart a New Industry." *Techniques*, October, 2009, 26-29.

Goldin, Claudia, and Katz, Lawrence F. *The Shaping of Higher Education: The Formative Years in the United States, 1890 to 1940*. Working Paper No. W6537. Cambridge, Mass.: National Bureau of Economic Research, 1988.

Gordon, Steve. *The Future of the Music Business*. 4th ed. Milwaukee: Hal Leonard Books, 2015.

Grady, Jenifer, and Denise M. Davis. *ALA-APA Salary Survey—Librarian—Public and Academic: A Survey of Library Positions Requiring an ALA-Accredited Master's Degree*. Chicago: American Library Association, 2015.

Hazard, Geoffrey C., and Angelo Dondi. *Legal Ethics: A Comparative Study*. Stanford, Calif.: Stanford University Press, 2004.

Institute for Career Research. *Careers in Museums: Director, Curator, Conservator, Exhibit Designer, Archivist*. Chicago: Author, 2007.

International Television Expert Group. "TV Market Data/Global TV Funding, 2008-2013." http://www.international-television.org/tv_market_data/pay-tv-and-tv-funding-worldwide_2008-2013.html.

Johnson, James Allen, et al. *Foundations of American Education: Perspectives on Education in a Changing World*. 15th ed. Boston: Pearson/Allyn & Bacon, 2011.

Keating, Barry, and Maryann O. Keating. *Microeconomics for Public Managers*. Chichester, U.K: Wiley-Blackwell, 2009. Print.

Koszarski, Richard. *Hollywood on the Hudson: Film and Television in New York from Griffith to Sarnoff*. New Brunswick, N.J.: Rutgers University Press, 2008.

Krasilovsky, M. William, and Sydney Shemel. *This Business of Music: The Definitive Guide to the Music Industry*. 10th ed. New York: Billboard Books, 2007.

Lacy, Sarah. *Once You're Lucky, Twice You're Good: The Rebirth of Silicon Valley and the Rise of Web 2.0*. New York: Gotham Books, 2008.

Langford, Barry. *Post-Classical Hollywood: Film Industry, Style, and Ideology Since 1945*. Edinburgh: Edinburgh University Press, 2010.

Lankford, Ronald D. *What Is the Future of the Music Industry?* Farmington Hills, MI: Greenhaven Press 2013.

Lears, Jackson. *Fables of Abundance: A Cultural History of Advertising in America*. New York: Basic Books, 2009.

Lee, Valerie E., et al. "Inside Large and Small High Schools: Curriculum and Social Relations." *Educational Evaluation and Policy Analysis* 22, no. 2 (Summer, 2000): 147-171.

Lowell, Stephanie. *Careers in the Nonprofit Sector*. Cambridge, Mass.: Harvard Business School, 2000.

Luft, Oliver. "Advertising Boss: Print Will Struggle to Recover After Recession." *The Guardian*, May 5, 2009.

Lynch, Mary Jo. "Reaching Sixty-Five: Lots of Librarians Will Be There Soon." *American Libraries* 33, no. 2 (March, 2002).

Mackay, Adrian, ed. *The Practice of Advertising*. 5th ed. Oxford, England: Elsevier Butterworth-Heinemann, 2005.

Madigan, C. *The Collapse of the Great American Newspaper*. Chicago: Ivan R. Dee, 2007.

Martin, S., and D. Copeland. *The Function of Newspapers in Society: A Global Perspective*. Westport, Conn.: Greenwood Press, 2003.

McAllister, Ken. *Game Work: Language, Power, and Computer Game Culture*. Tuscaloosa: University of Alabama Press, 2005.

McCarthy, Kevin, et al. *The Performing Arts in a New Era*. Santa Monica, Calif.: Rand, 2001.

Mehta, Rini Bhattacharya, and Rajeshwari Pandharipande. *Bollywood and Globalization: Indian Popular Cinema, Nation, and Diaspora*. New York: Anthem Press, 2010.

Meyer, P. *The Vanishing Newspaper*. Columbia: University of Missouri Press, 2004.

Moorehouse, A. C. *The Triumph of the Alphabet: A History of Writing*. New York: Henry Schuman, 1953.

Motion Picture Association of America. *The Economic Impact of the Motion Picture and Television Industry on the United States*. Washington, D.C.: Author, 2009.

Munneke, Gary. *Careers in Law*. 3d ed. New York: McGraw-Hill, 2003.

Musselin, Christine. *The Market for Academics*. New York: Routledge, 2012.

Musser, Charles. *The Emergence of Cinema: The American Screen to 1907*. New York: Maxwell Macmillan International, 1990.

Negus, Keith. *Music Genres and Corporate Cultures*. New York: Routledge, 1999.

Norris, James D. *Advertising and the Transformation of American Society, 1865-1920*. Westport, Conn.: Greenwood Press, 1990.

Novak, Jeannie. *Game Development Essentials: An Introduction*. Clifton Park, N.Y.: Thomson/Learning, 2012.

O'Neil, Brian. *Acting as a Business: Strategies for Success*. New York: Vintage Books, 2014.

Olasky, Marvin. *The Tragedy of American Compassion*. Preface by Charles Murray. Washington, D.C.: Regnery, 2008.

Organization for Economic Cooperation and Development. *The Non-profit Sector in a Changing Economy*. Paris: Author, 2003.

Parkay, Forrest W., and Beverly Hardcastle Stanford. *Becoming a Teacher*. 11th ed. Boston: Pearson, 2020.

Peddie, R. A. *Printing: A Short History of the Art*. London: Grafton, 1927.

Pulliam, John D., and James J. Van Patten. *The History of Education in America*. 9th ed. Upper Saddle River, N.J.: Merrill, 2007.

Rapaport, Diane. *A Music Business Primer*. Upper Saddle River, N.J.: Prentice Hall, 2003.

Raymond, Susan U. *The Future of Philanthropy: Economics, Ethics, and Management*. Hoboken, N.J.: John Wiley & Sons, 2004.

Rentzhog, Sten. *Open Air Museums: The History and Future of a Visionary Idea*. Stockholm: Carlsson, 2007.

Rutter, Jason, and Jo Bryce. *Understanding Digital Games*. Thousand Oaks, Calif.: Sage, 2006.

Schlatter, N. Elizabeth. *Museum Careers: A Practical Guide for Novices and Students*. Walnut Creek, Calif.: Left Coast Press, 2008.

Scott, David Meerman. *The New Rules of Marketing and PR: How to Use Social Media, Blogs, News Releases, Online Video, and Viral Marketing to Reach Buyers Directly*. 6th ed. Hoboken, N.J.: John Wiley & Sons, 2017.

Siebert, Eric. *Careers in Marketing: The Comprehensive Guide to Traditional and Digital Marketing Careers*. Charleston: CreateSpace, 2016.

Simkin, Joyce P. *American Salary and Wages Survey*. 14th ed. Farmington Hills, Mich.: Gale Cengage, 2017.

Society of American Archivists. "So You Want to Be an Archivist: An Overview of the Archival Profession." http://www2.archivists.org/profession.

Sorid, Daniel. "Writing the Web's Future in Numerous Languages." *The New York Times*, December 30, 2009.

Spear, Martha J. "The Top Ten Reasons to Be a Librarian." *American Libraries* 33, no. 9 (October, 2002).

Stein, Tobie, and Jessica Bathurst. *Performing Arts Management: A Handbook of Professional Practices*. New York: Allworth Press, 2008.

Stibel, Jeffrey M. *Wired for Thought: How the Brain Is Shaping the Future of the Internet*. Boston: Harvard Business Press, 2009.

Taylor, T. Allan, and James Robert Parrish. *Careers in the Internet, Video Games, and Multimedia*. New York: Ferguson, 2007.

Tempel, Eugene R, Timothy L. Seiler, and Dwight Burlingame. *Achieving Excellence in Fundraising*. , 2016. Print.

Thall, Peter W. *What They'll Never Tell You About the Music Business: The Myths, the Secrets, the Lies (and a Few Truths)*. New York: Billboard Books, 2006.

Twitchell, James B. *Adcult USA: The Triumph of Advertising in American Culture*. New York: Columbia University Press, 1996.

Vogel, Harold L. *Entertainment Industry Economics: A Guide for Financial Analysis*. New York: Cambridge University Press, 2007.

Webb, Duncan. *Running Theaters: Best Practices for Leaders and Managers*. New York: Allworth Press, 2020.

Wilmshurst, John, and Adrian Mackay. *The Fundamentals of Advertising*. 2d ed. Oxford, England: Elsevier Butterworth-Heinemann, 1999.

Wing, Kennard T., Katie L. Roediger, and Thomas H. Pollak. *The Nonprofit Sector in Brief: Public Charities, Giving, and Volunteering, 2009*. Washington, D.C.: Urban Institute, 2010. http://www.urban.org/uploadedpdf/412085-nonprofit-sector-brief.pdf.

Wolch, Jennifer L. *The Shadow State: Government and Voluntary Sector in Transition*. New York: Foundation Center, 1990.

WEB RESOURCES

Advertising and Marketing Industry

American Advertising Federation
1101 Vermont Ave. NW, Suite 500
Washington, DC 20005
Tel: (800) 999-2231
Fax: (202) 898-0159
http://www.aaf.org

American Association of Advertising
Agencies
405 Lexington Ave., 18th Floor
New York, NY 10174
Tel: (212) 682-2500
http://www.aaaa.org

Asian American Advertising Federation
P.O. Box 69851
West Hollywood, CA 90069
Tel: (310) 289-5500
Fax: (310) 289-5501
http://www.3af.org

Association of Hispanic Advertising
Agencies
8400 Westpark Dr., 2d Floor
McLean, VA 22102
Tel: (703) 610-9014
Fax: (703) 610-0227
http://www.ahaa.org

International Advertising Association
275 Madison Ave., Suite 2102
New York, NY 10016
Tel: (212) 557-1133
Fax: (212) 983-0455
http://www.iaaglobal.org

World Advertising Research Center
1 Ivory Square
Plantation Wharf
London SW11 3UE
United Kingdom
Tel: 44-20-7326-8600
Fax: 44-20-7326-8601
http://www.warc.com

Legal Services and Law Firms

American Association for Justice
777 6th St. NW
Washington, DC 20001
Tel: (800) 424-2725
http://www.justice.org

American Bar Association
321 N Clark St.
Chicago, IL 60654-7598
Tel: (800) 285-2221
http://www.abanet.org

American Civil Liberties Union
125 Broad St.
New York, NY 10004
Tel: (212) 507-3300
http://www.aclu.org

Amnesty International USA
5 Penn Plaza
New York, NY 10001
Tel: (212) 807-8400
http://www.amnestyusa.org

Legal Aid Society
199 Water St.
New York, NY 10038
Tel: (212) 577-3300
http://www.legal-aid.org

National Association for Law Placement
1025 Connecticut Ave. NW, Suite 1110
Washington, DC 20036-5413
Tel: (202) 835-1001
http://www.nalp.org

National Association of Criminal Defense
Lawyers
1660 L St. NW, 12th Floor
Washington, DC 20036
Tel: (202) 872-8600
http://www.criminaljustice.org

National Legal Aid and Defender
Organization
1140 Connecticut Ave. NW, Suite 900
Washington, DC 20036
Tel: (202) 452-0620
http://www.nlada.org

Libraries and Archives Industry

American Archivist
527 S Wells St., 5th Floor
Chicago, IL 60607
Tel: (312) 922-0140
Fax: (312) 347-1452
http://www.archivists.org

American Association of School
Librarians
50 E Huron St.
Chicago, IL 60611-2729
Tel: (800) 545-2433, ext. 4382
Fax: (312) 280-5276
http://www.ala.org/aasl

American Library Association
50 E Huron St.
Chicago, IL 60611-2729
Tel: (800) 545-2433
Fax: (312) 440-9374
http://www.ala.org

Society of American Archivists
17 N State St., Suite 1425
Chicago, IL 60602-3315
Tel: (312) 606-0722
Fax: (312) 606-0728
http://www.archivists.org

Motion Picture and Television Industry

Academy of Motion Picture Arts and
Sciences
8949 Wilshire Blvd.
Beverly Hills, CA 90211
Tel: (310) 247-3000
Fax: (310) 859-9619
http://www.oscars.org

Academy of Television Arts and Sciences
5220 Lankershim Blvd.
North Hollywood, CA 91601
Tel: (818) 754-2800
http://www.emmys.org
Motion Picture Association of America
1600 Eye St. NW
Washington, DC 20006
Tel: (202) 293-1966
Fax: (202) 296-7410
http://www.mpaa.org

Museums and Cultural Institutions Industry

American Association for State and Local
History
1717 Church St.
Nashville, TN 37203-2991
Tel: (615) 320-3203
Fax: (615) 327-9013
http://www.aaslh.org

American Association of Museums
1575 Eye St. NW, Suite 400
Washington, DC 20005
Tel: (202) 289-1818
Fax: (202) 289-6578
http://www.aam-us.org

Association for Living History, Farms,
and Agricultural Museums
8774 Rte. 45 NW
North Bloomfield, OH 44450
Tel: (440) 685-4410
http://www.alhfam.org

Association of Children's Museums
1300 L St. NW, Suite 975
Washington, DC 20005
Tel: (202) 898-1080
Fax: (202) 898-1086
http://www.childrensmuseums.org

Association of College and University
Museums and Galleries
40 Arts Circle Dr.
Evanston, IL 60208-2410
Tel: (847) 491-5893
Fax: (847) 467-4609
http://www.acumg.org

Museum Studies and Reference Library
National Museum of Natural History
Smithsonian Institution
10th and Constitution Ave. NW
Washington, DC 20560
Tel: (202) 633-1700
http://www.sil.si.edu

Society of American Archivists
17 N State St., Suite 1425
Chicago, IL 60602-3315
Tel: (312) 606-0722
Fax: (312) 606-0728
http://www.archivists.org

Music Industry

American Society of Composers, Authors, and Publishers
1 Lincoln Plaza
New York, NY 10023
Tel: (212) 621-6000
http://www.ascap.com

American Symphony Orchestra League
33 W 60th St.
New York, NY 10023
Tel: (212) 262-5161
http://www.symphony.org

Billboard
BPI Communications
1515 Broadway
New York, NY 10036
Tel: (800) 745-8922
http://www.billboard-online.com

Pollstar
4697 W Jacquelyn Ave.
Fresno, CA 93722
Tel: (559) 271-7900
http://www.pollstar.com

Recording Industry Association of America
1025 F St. NW, 10th Floor
Washington, DC 20004
Tel: (202) 775-0101
http://www.riaa.com

Philanthropic, Charitable, Religious, Civic, and Grant-Making Industry

Alliance for Nonprofit Management
1899 L St. NW, 7th Floor
Washington, DC 20036
Tel: (202) 955-8406
Fax: (202) 822-0669
http://www.allianceonline.org

Council on Foundations
2121 Crystal Dr., Suite 700
Arlington, VA 22202
Tel: (800) 673-9036
http://www.cof.org

Foundations Center
79 5th Ave.
New York, NY 10003-3076
Tel: (212) 620-4230
http://foundationcenter.org

National Council of Churches
475 Riverside Dr., Suite 800
New York, NY 10115
Tel: (212) 870-2228
Fax: (212) 870-2030
http://www.nccsusa.org

Publishing and Information Industry

American Society of Newspaper Editors
11690-B Sunrise Valley Dr.
Reston, VA 20191
Tel: (703) 453-1122
http://www.asne.org

Association of American Publishers
50 F St. NW, 4th Floor
Washington, DC 20001
Tel: (202) 347-3375
Fax: (202) 347-3690
http://www.publishers.org

International Publishers Association
3 Ave. de Miremont
1206 Geneva
Switzerland
Tel: 41-22-704-1820
Fax: 41-22-704-1821
http://www.internationalpublishers.org

Magazine Publishers of America
810 7th Ave., 24th Floor
New York, NY 10019
Tel: (212) 872-3700
http://www.magazine.org

Newspaper Association of America
4401 Wilson Blvd., Suite 900
Arlington, VA 22203
Tel: (517) 336-1000
Fax: (571) 366-1195
http://www.naa.org

Small Publishers Association of North
America
1618 W Colorado Ave.
Colorado Springs, CO 80904
Tel: (719) 475-1726
Fax: (719) 471-2182
http://www.spannet.org

Theater and Performing Arts Industry

Actors' Equity Association
165 W 46th St.
New York, NY 10036
Tel: (212) 869-8530
Fax: (212) 719-9815
http://www.actorsequity.org

American Federation of Musicians
1501 Broadway, Suite 600
New York, NY 10036
Tel: (212) 869-1330
Fax: (212) 764-6134
http://www.afm.org

Americans for the Arts
1 E 53rd St., 2d Floor
New York, NY 10022
Tel: (212) 223-2787
Fax: (212) 980-4857
http://www.artsusa.org

National Dance Education Association
8609 2d Ave., Suite 203-B
Silver Springs, MD 20910
Tel: (301) 585-2880
Fax: (301) 585-2888
http://www.ndeo.org

National Endowment for the Arts
1100 Pennsylvania Ave. NW
Washington, DC 20506-0001
Tel: (202) 682-5400
Fax: (202) 682-5496
http://www.nea.gov

Video, Computer, and Virtual Reality Games Industry

Entertainment and Leisure Software
Association
111/113 High St.
Evesham, Worcestershire WR11 4XP
United Kingdom
Tel: 44-20-7534-0580
http://www.elspa.com

Entertainment Software Association
575 7th St. NW, Suite 300
Washington, DC 20004
Tel: (202) 223-2400
Fax: (202) 223-2401
http://www.theesa.com

International Game Developers
Association
19 Mantua Rd.
Mt. Royal, NJ 08061
Tel: (856) 423-2990
Fax: (856) 423-3420
http://www.igda.org

Major League Gaming
420 Lexington Ave., #2820
New York, NY 10170
Tel: (213) 370-1444
http://www.mlgpro.com

Software and Information Industry
Association
1090 Vermont Ave. NW, 6th Floor
Washington, DC 20005-4095
Tel: (202) 289-7442
Fax: (202) 289-7097
http://www.siia.net

INDEX

R